Takeru
Opera Susanoh
Sword of the Devil™

SUSANOH～魔性の剣（劇団☆新感線）より

HAMBURG // LONDON // LOS ANGELES // TOKYO

CONTENTS

Chapter 1: Day of Meeting..5

Chapter 2: The Battle of Yomogahara..................................55

Chapter 3: The Queens of Jagara..................................89

Chapter 4: The Three Trials..................................129

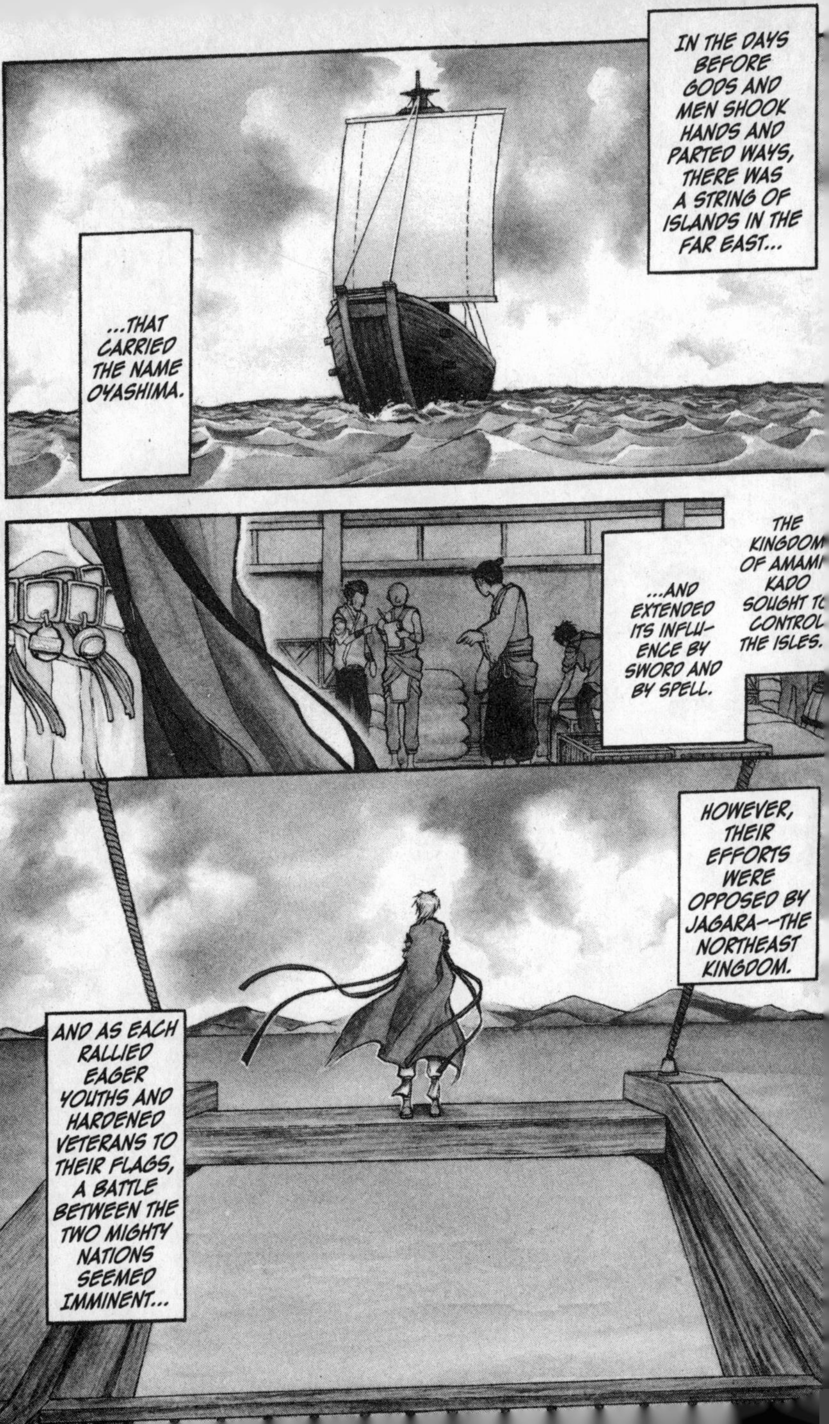
IN THE DAYS BEFORE GODS AND MEN SHOOK HANDS AND PARTED WAYS, THERE WAS A STRING OF ISLANDS IN THE FAR EAST...
...THAT CARRIED THE NAME OYASHIMA.
THE KINGDOM OF AMAMI KADO SOUGHT TO CONTROL THE ISLES.
...AND EXTENDED ITS INFLUENCE BY SWORD AND BY SPELL.
HOWEVER, THEIR EFFORTS WERE OPPOSED BY JAGARA--THE NORTHEAST KINGDOM.
AND AS EACH RALLIED EAGER YOUTHS AND HARDENED VETERANS TO THEIR FLAGS, A BATTLE BETWEEN THE TWO MIGHTY NATIONS SEEMED IMMINENT...

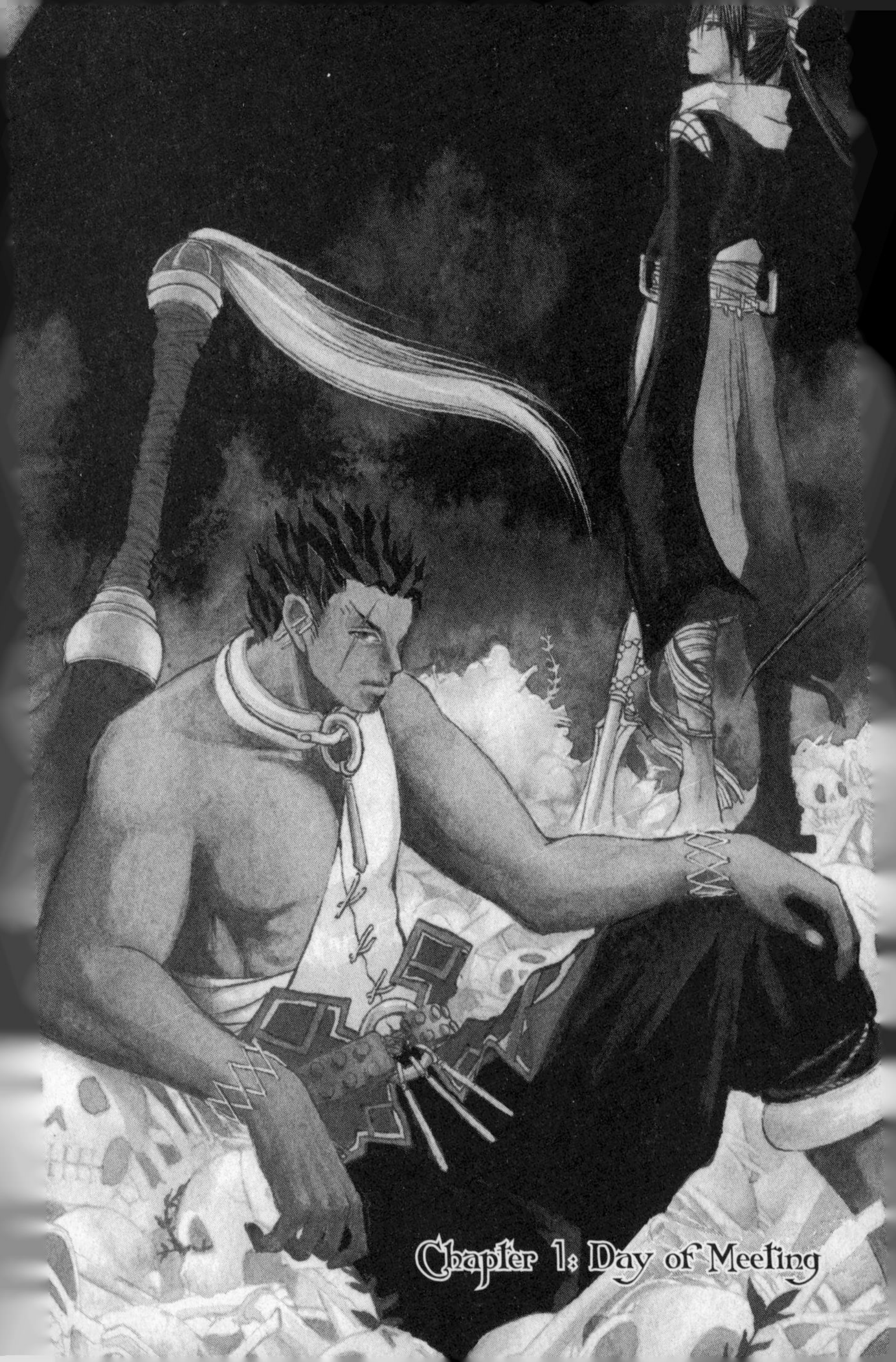

Chapter 1: Day of Meeting

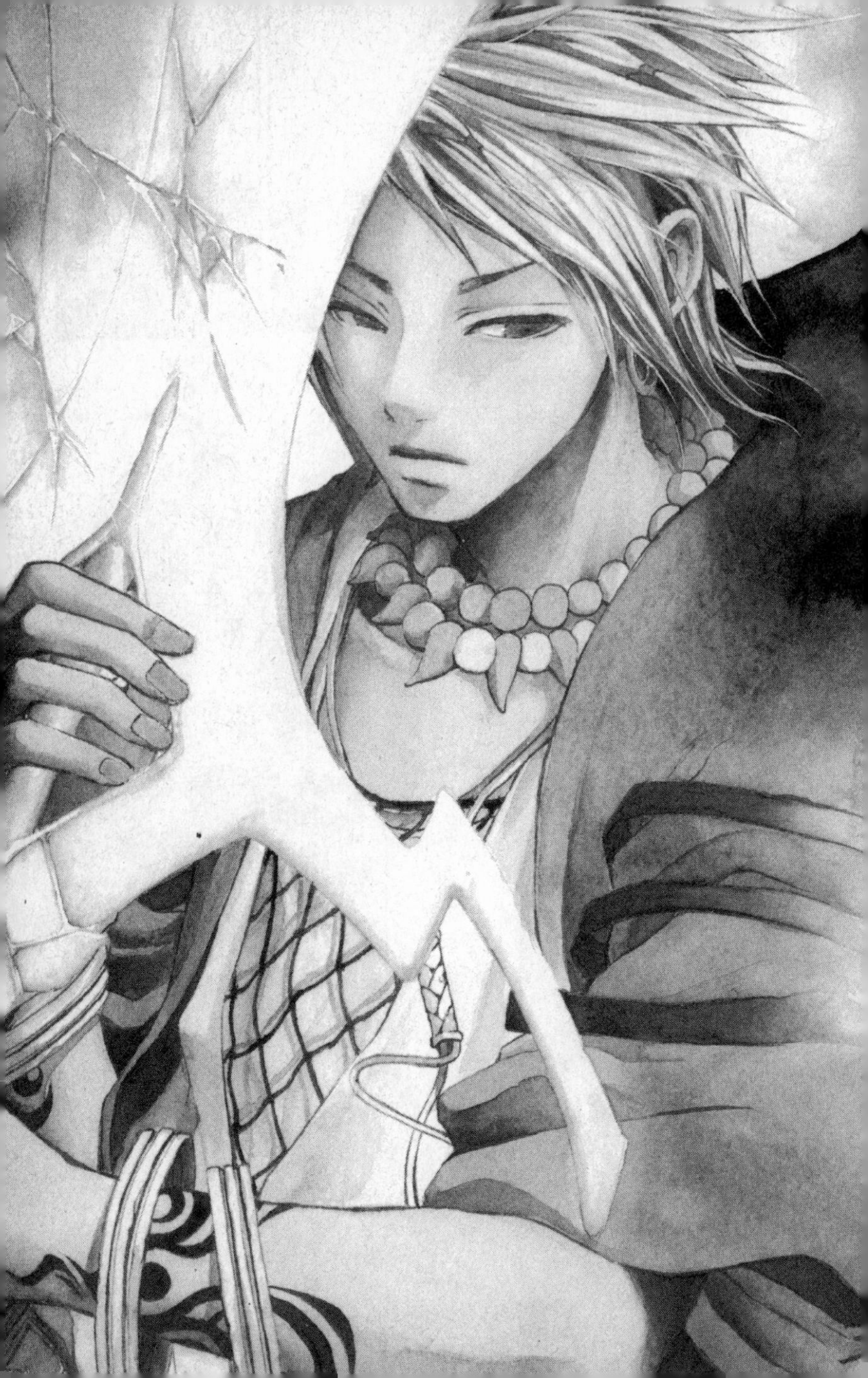

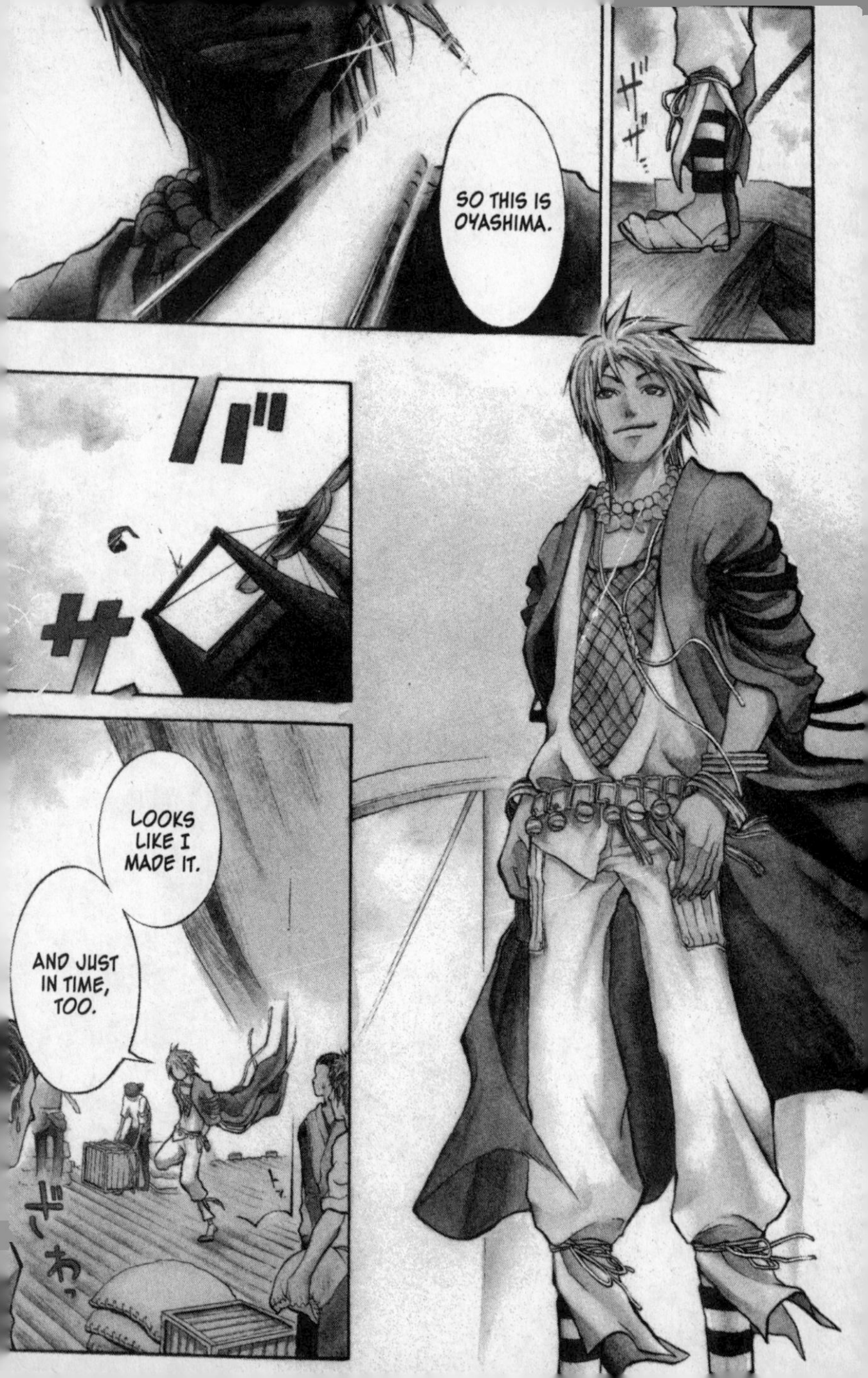
ザザ…
SO THIS IS OYASHIMA.
バサ
LOOKS LIKE I MADE IT.
AND JUST IN TIME, TOO.
ざわっ

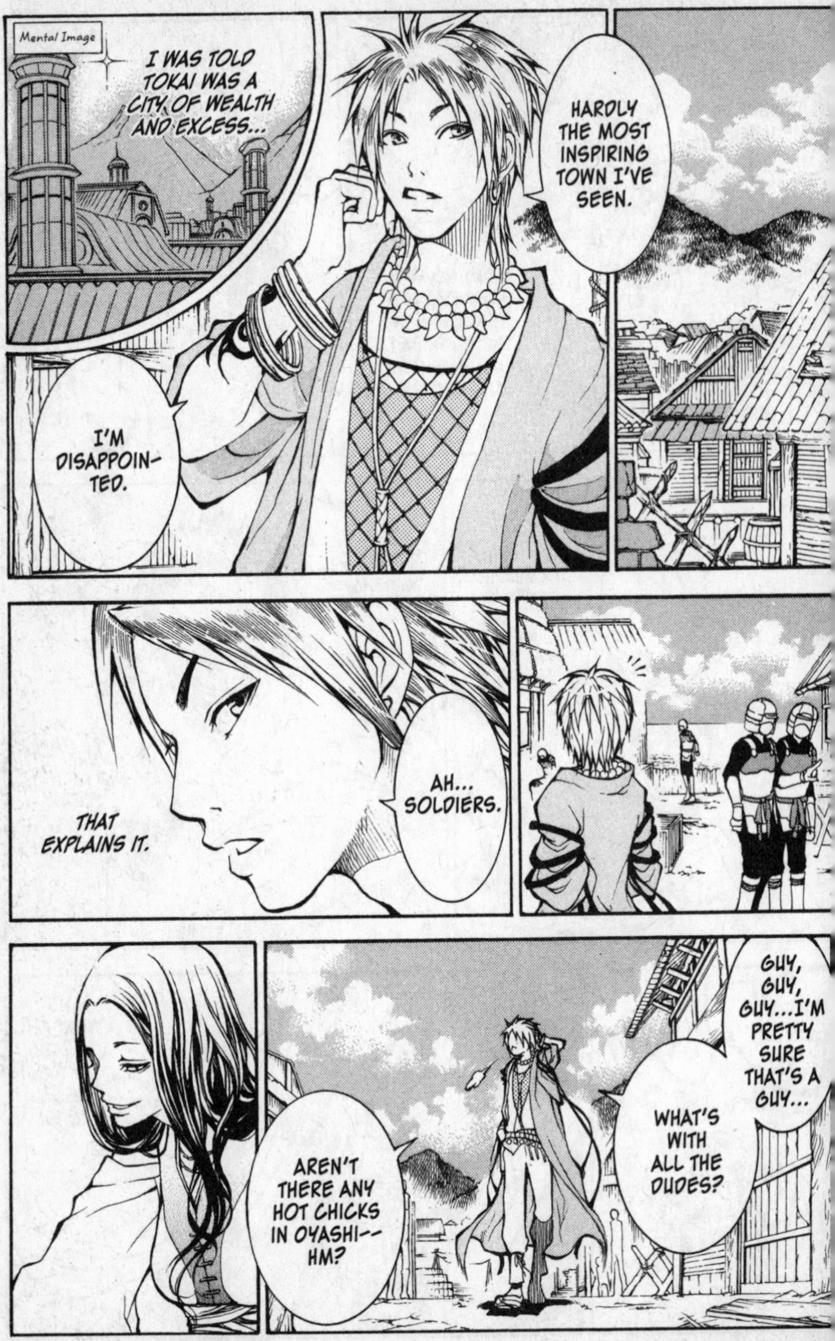
HARDLY THE MOST INSPIRING TOWN I'VE SEEN.
Mental Image
I WAS TOLD TOKAI WAS A CITY OF WEALTH AND EXCESS...
I'M DISAPPOIN-TED.
AH... SOLDIERS.
THAT EXPLAINS IT.
GUY, GUY, GUY...I'M PRETTY SURE THAT'S A GUY...
WHAT'S WITH ALL THE DUDES?
AREN'T THERE ANY HOT CHICKS IN OYASHI--HM?

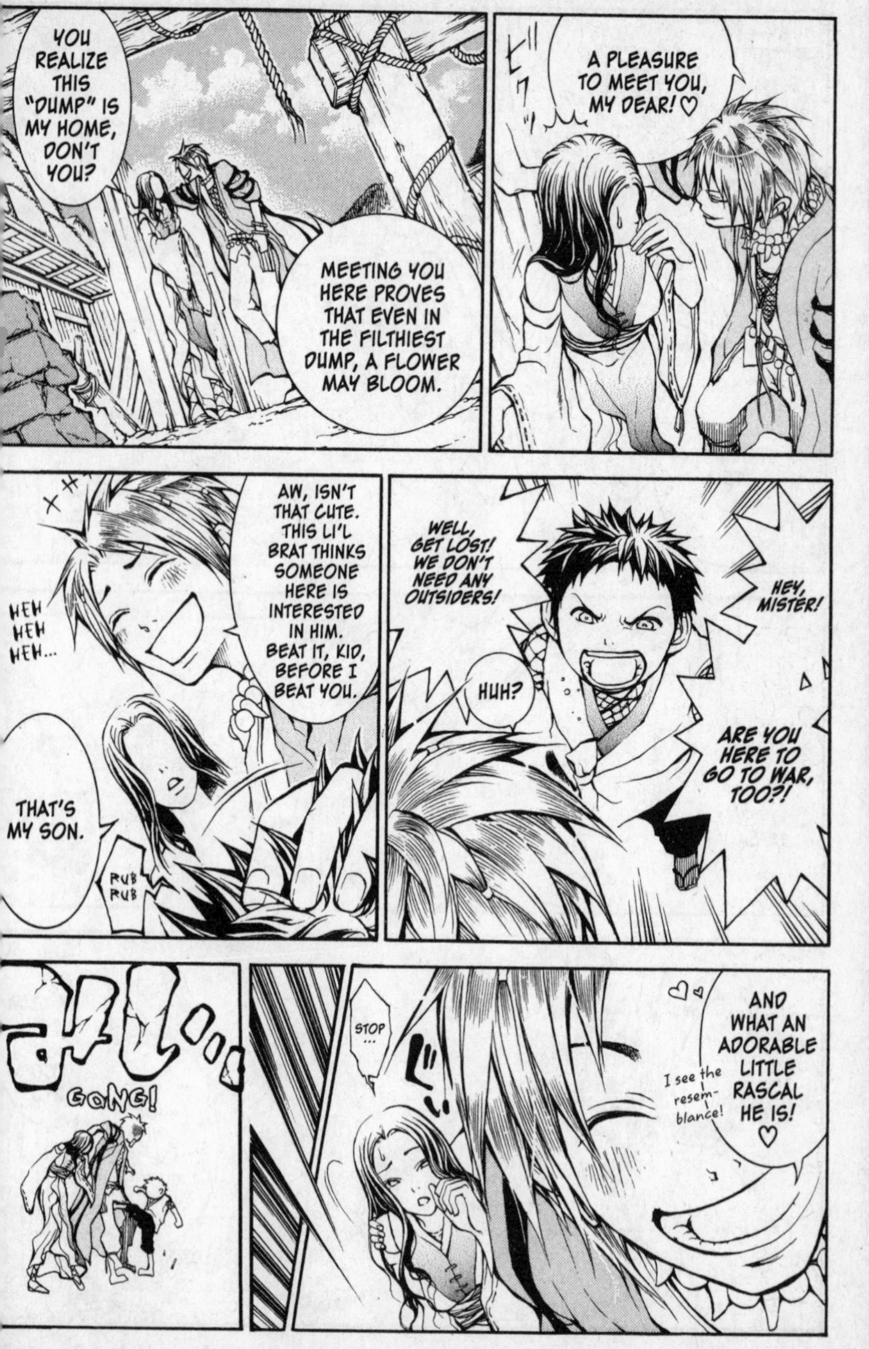
A PLEASURE TO MEET YOU, MY DEAR! ♡
MEETING YOU HERE PROVES THAT EVEN IN THE FILTHIEST DUMP, A FLOWER MAY BLOOM.
YOU REALIZE THIS "DUMP" IS MY HOME, DON'T YOU?
HEY, MISTER!
ARE YOU HERE TO GO TO WAR, TOO?!
WELL, GET LOST! WE DON'T NEED ANY OUTSIDERS!
HUH?
AW, ISN'T THAT CUTE. THIS LI'L BRAT THINKS SOMEONE HERE IS INTERESTED IN HIM. BEAT IT, KID, BEFORE I BEAT YOU.
HEH HEH HEH...
THAT'S MY SON.
RUB RUB
AND WHAT AN ADORABLE LITTLE RASCAL HE IS! ♡
I see the resem-blance!
STOP...
GONG!

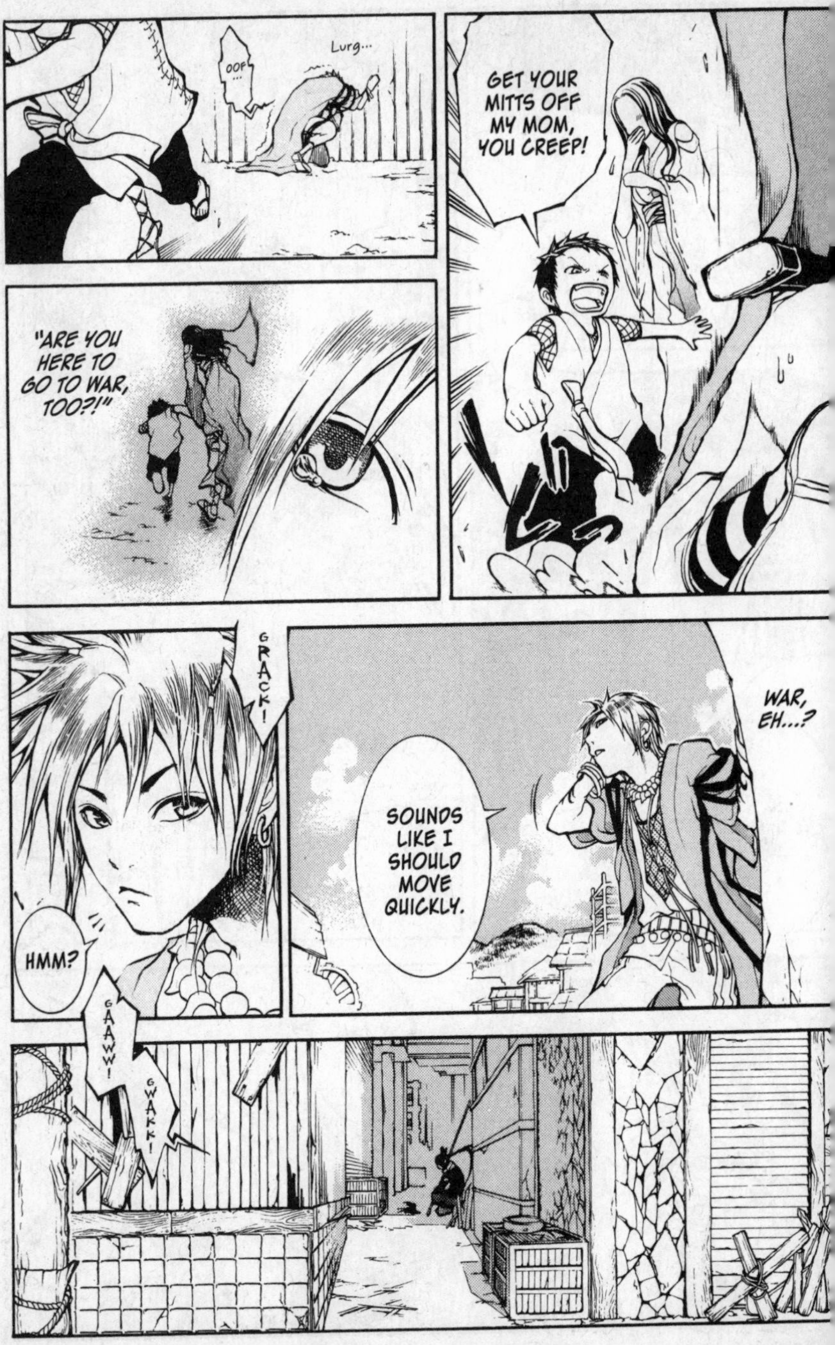
GET YOUR MITTS OFF MY MOM, YOU CREEP!
OOF...
Lurg...
"ARE YOU HERE TO GO TO WAR, TOO?!"
WAR, EH...?
SOUNDS LIKE I SHOULD MOVE QUICKLY.
GRACK!
HMM?
GAAWW!
GWAKK!

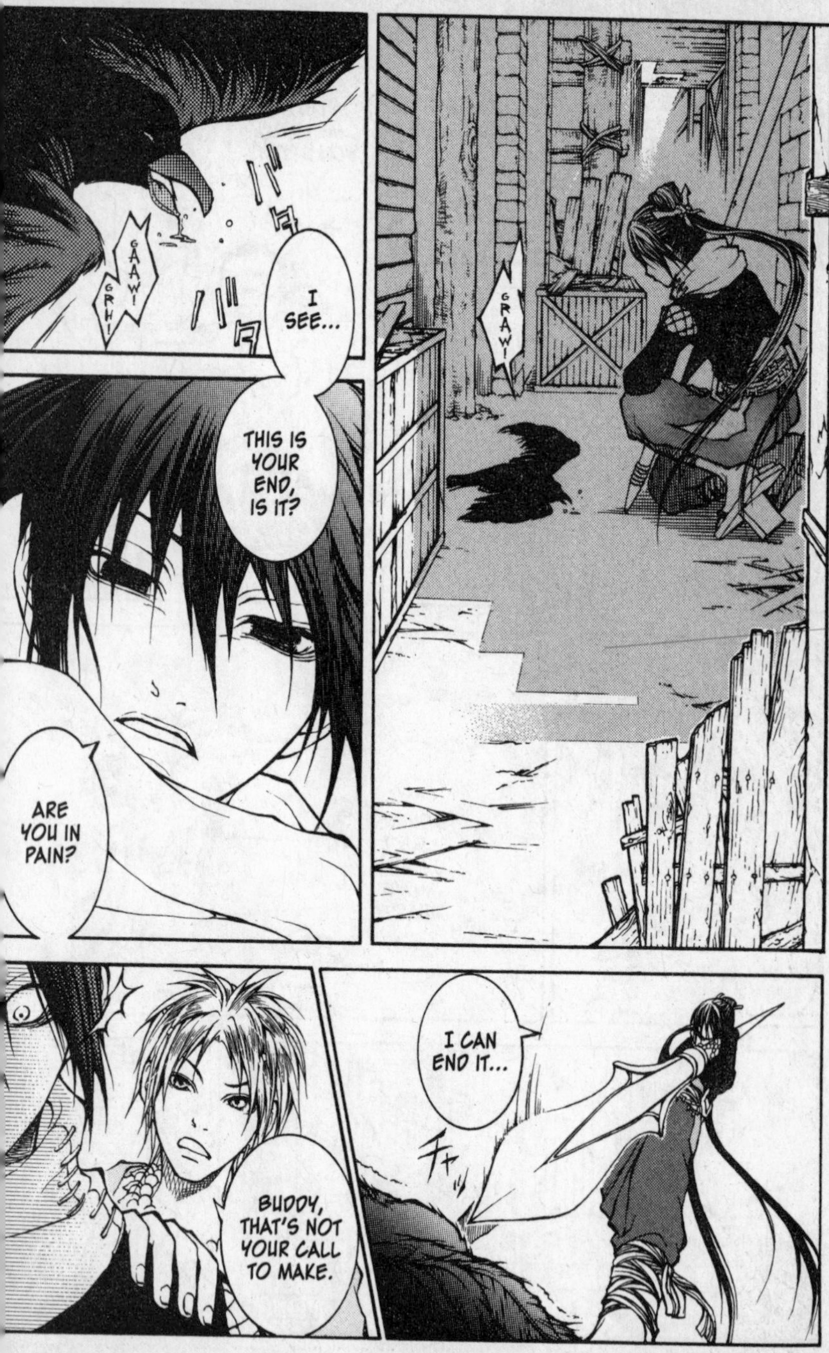
GRAW!
GAAW!
GRH!
I SEE...
THIS IS YOUR END, IS IT?
ARE YOU IN PAIN?
I CAN END IT...
BUDDY, THAT'S NOT YOUR CALL TO MAKE.

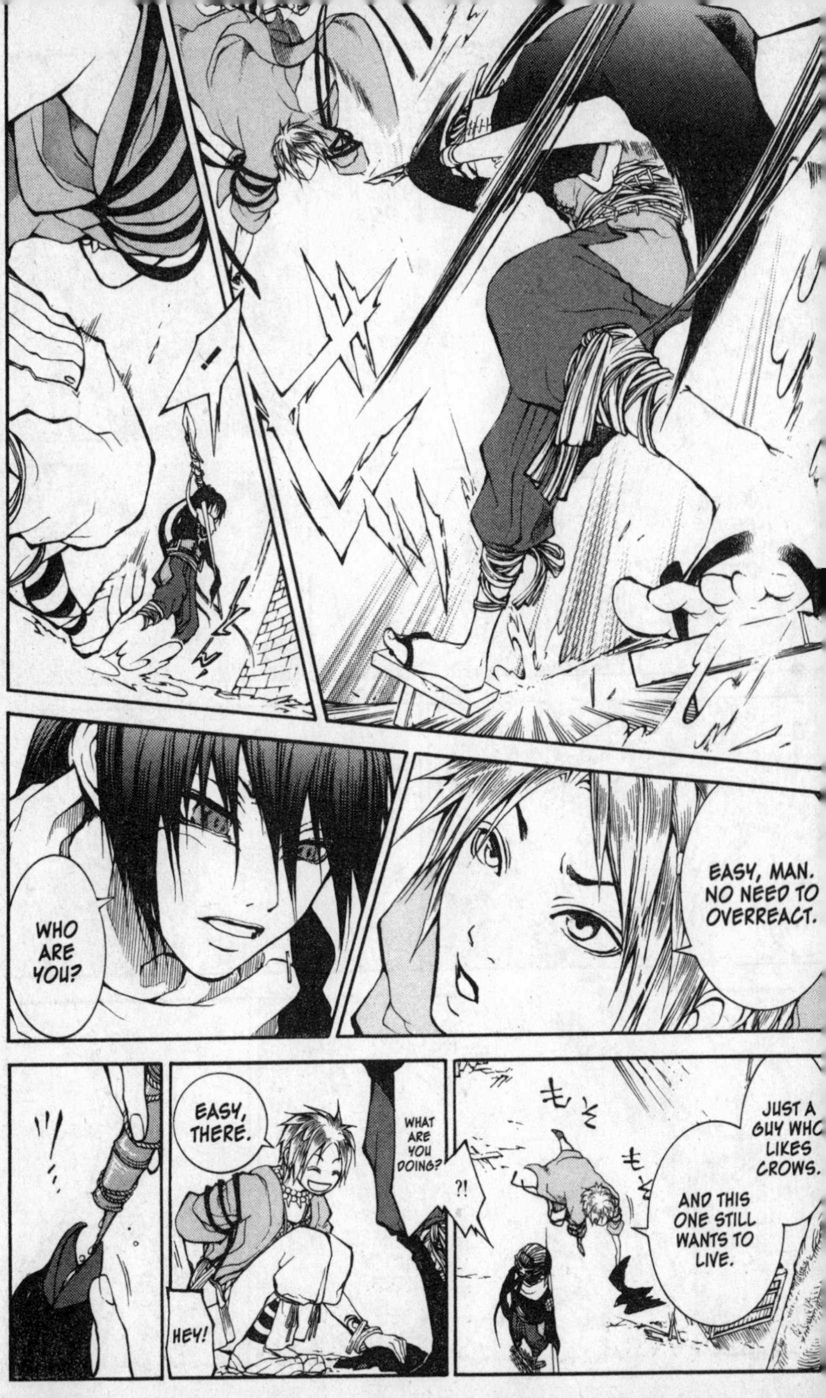
EASY, MAN. NO NEED TO OVERREACT.
WHO ARE YOU?
もそ
もそ
JUST A GUY WHO LIKES CROWS.
AND THIS ONE STILL WANTS TO LIVE.
?!
WHAT ARE YOU DOING?
EASY, THERE.
HEY!

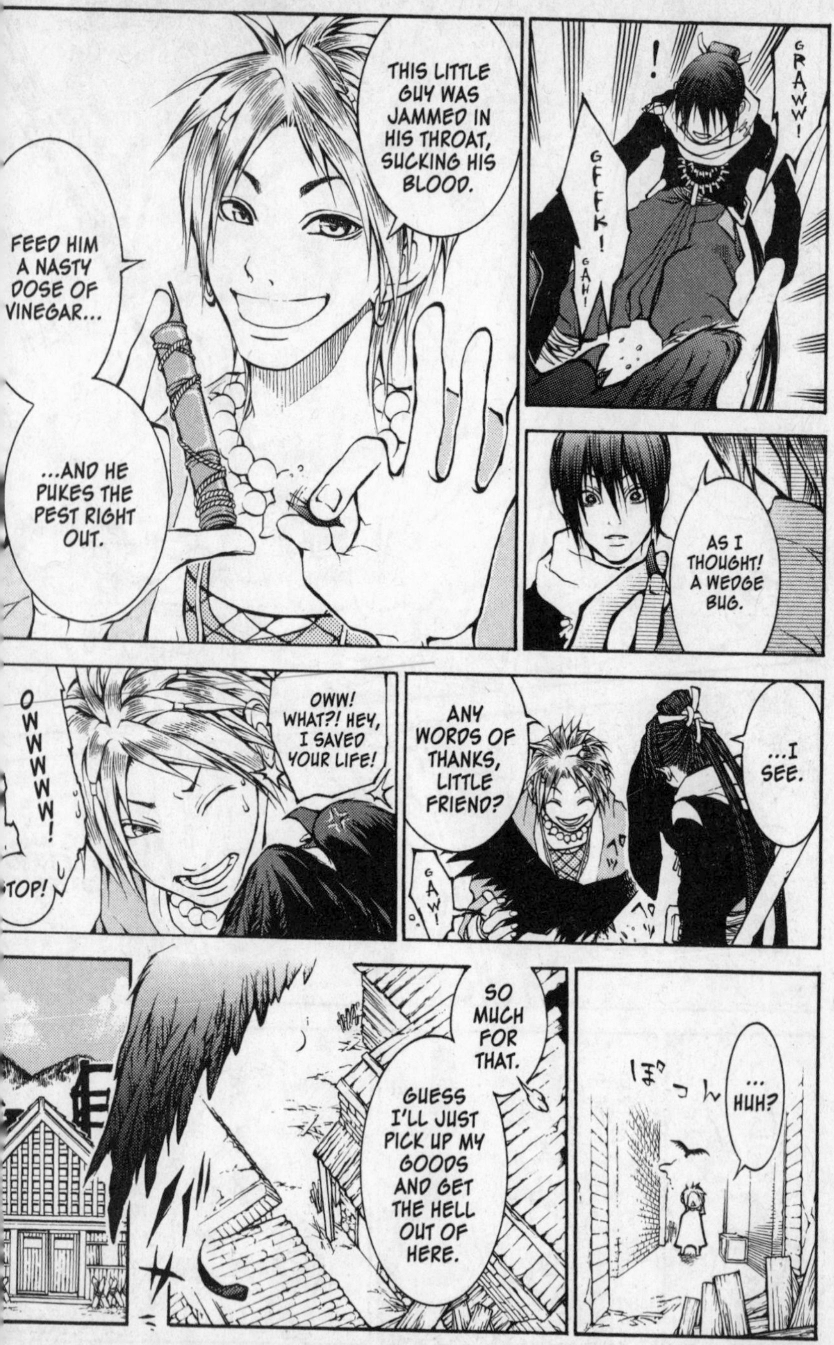
GRAWW!
!
GFFK!
GAH!
AS I THOUGHT! A WEDGE BUG.
THIS LITTLE GUY WAS JAMMED IN HIS THROAT, SUCKING HIS BLOOD.
FEED HIM A NASTY DOSE OF VINEGAR...
...AND HE PUKES THE PEST RIGHT OUT.
...I SEE.
ANY WORDS OF THANKS, LITTLE FRIEND?
GAW!
OWW! WHAT?! HEY, I SAVED YOUR LIFE!
OWWWWWW!
TOP!
ぽつん
...HUH?
SO MUCH FOR THAT.
GUESS I'LL JUST PICK UP MY GOODS AND GET THE HELL OUT OF HERE.

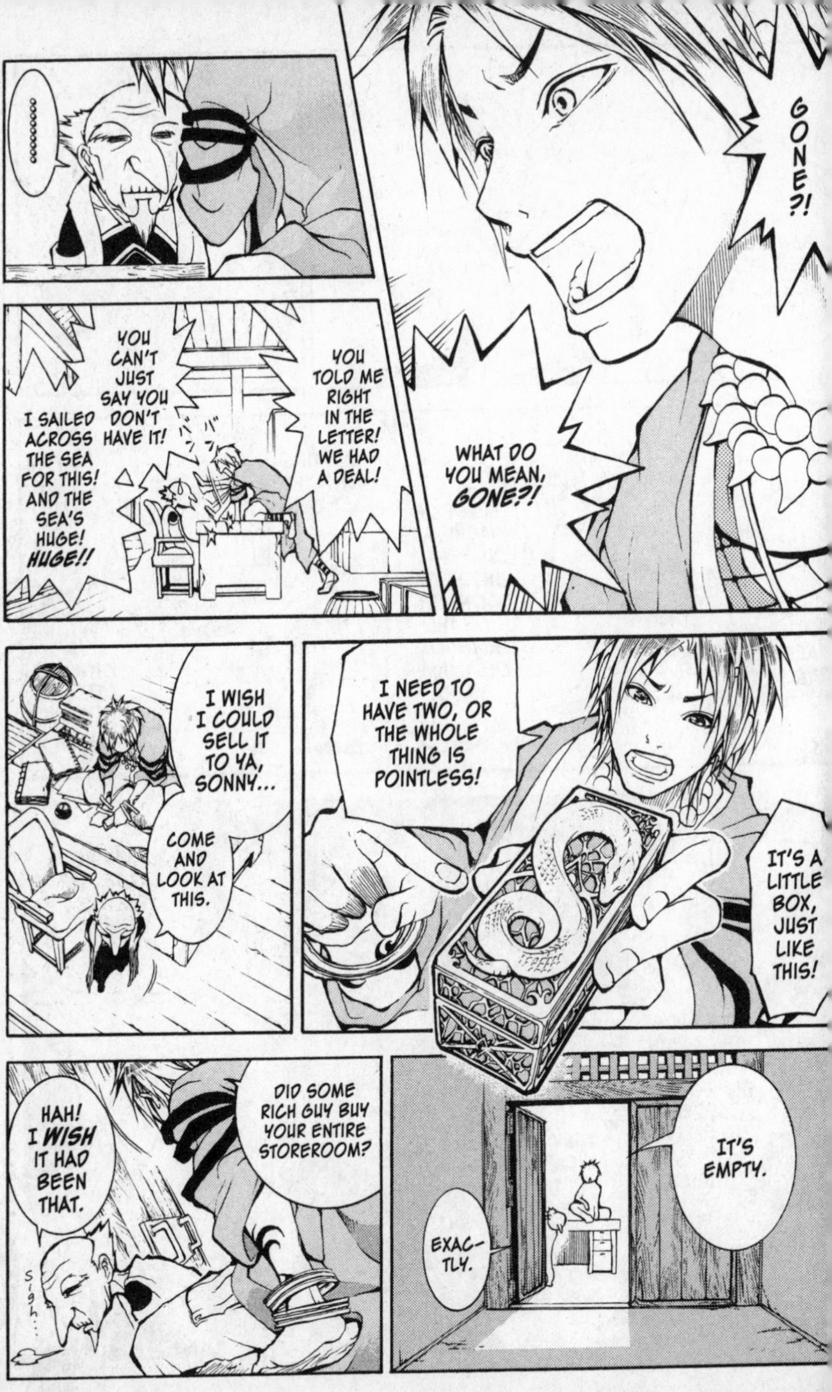
GONE?!
WHAT DO YOU MEAN, ***GONE?!***
....
YOU TOLD ME RIGHT IN THE LETTER! WE HAD A DEAL!
YOU CAN'T JUST SAY YOU DON'T HAVE IT!
I SAILED ACROSS THE SEA FOR THIS! AND THE SEA'S HUGE! ***HUGE!!***
I NEED TO HAVE TWO, OR THE WHOLE THING IS POINTLESS!
IT'S A LITTLE BOX, JUST LIKE THIS!
I WISH I COULD SELL IT TO YA, SONNY...
COME AND LOOK AT THIS.
IT'S EMPTY.
EXAC-TLY.
DID SOME RICH GUY BUY YOUR ENTIRE STOREROOM?
HAH! I ***WISH*** IT HAD BEEN THAT.
Sigh...

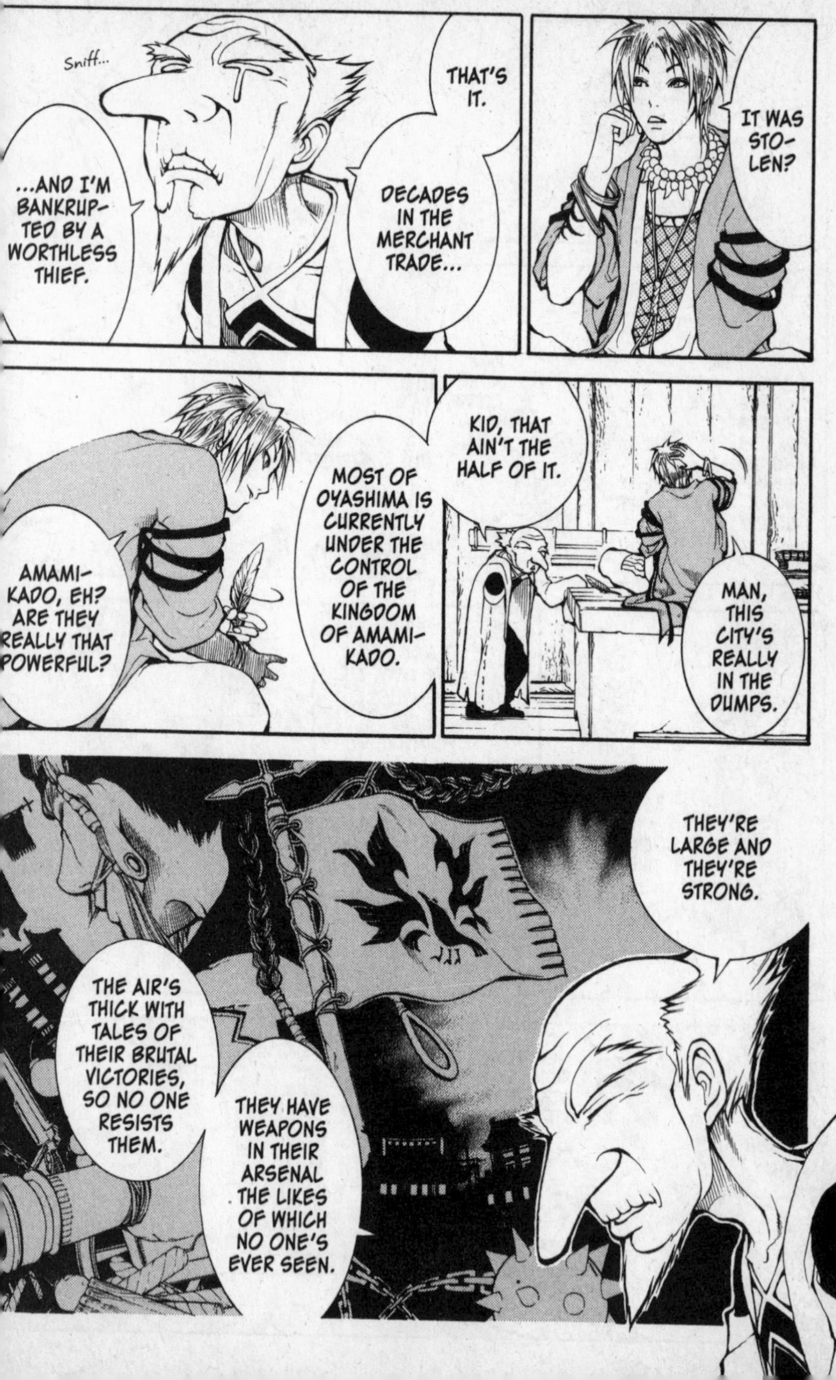
IT WAS STO-LEN?
THAT'S IT.
Sniff...
DECADES IN THE MERCHANT TRADE...
...AND I'M BANKRUP-TED BY A WORTHLESS THIEF.
MAN, THIS CITY'S REALLY IN THE DUMPS.
KID, THAT AIN'T THE HALF OF IT.
MOST OF OYASHIMA IS CURRENTLY UNDER THE CONTROL OF THE KINGDOM OF AMAMI-KADO.
AMAMI-KADO, EH? ARE THEY REALLY THAT POWERFUL?
THEY'RE LARGE AND THEY'RE STRONG.
THEY HAVE WEAPONS IN THEIR ARSENAL THE LIKES OF WHICH NO ONE'S EVER SEEN.
THE AIR'S THICK WITH TALES OF THEIR BRUTAL VICTORIES, SO NO ONE RESISTS THEM.

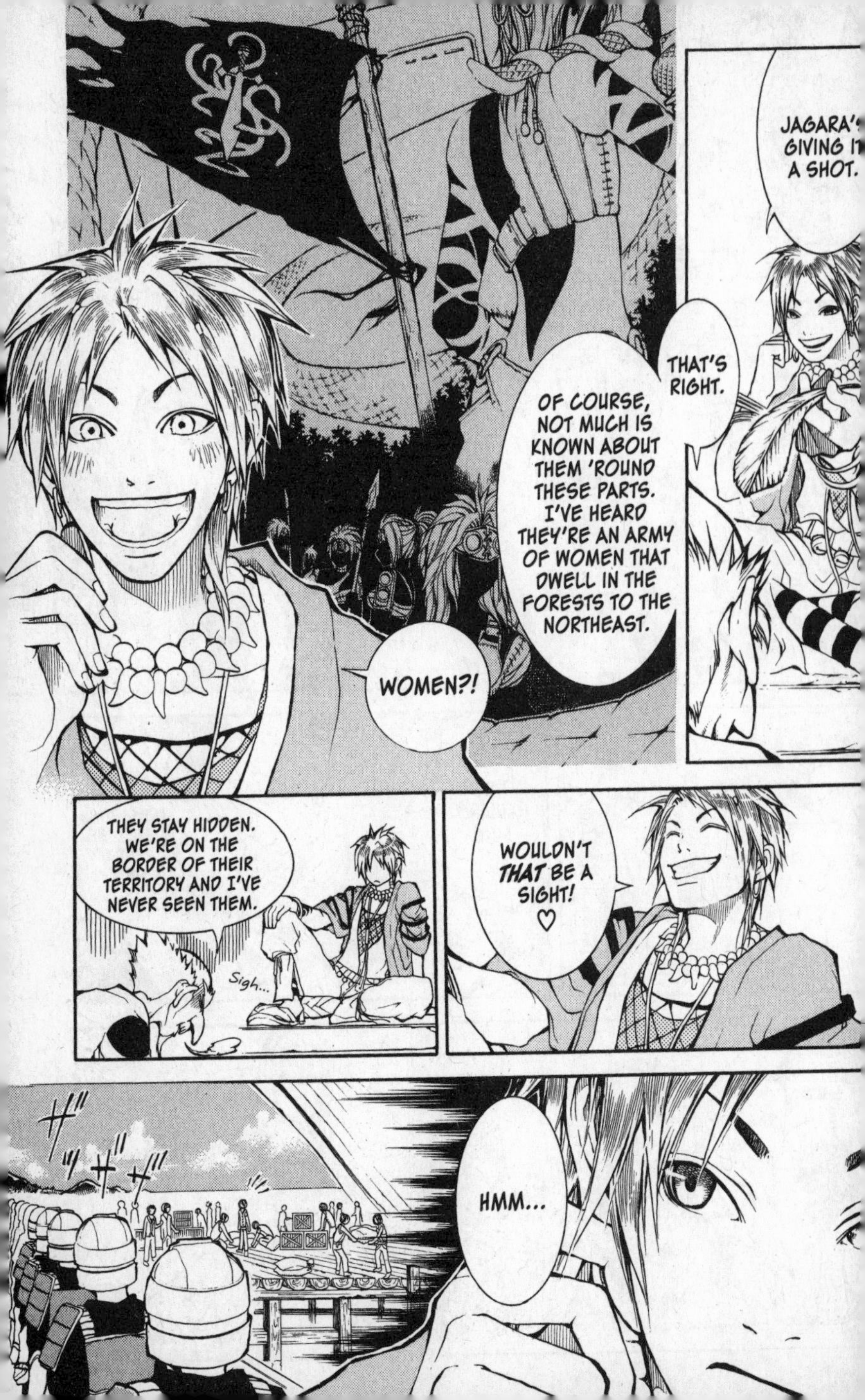
JAGARA'S GIVING IT A SHOT.
THAT'S RIGHT.
OF COURSE, NOT MUCH IS KNOWN ABOUT THEM 'ROUND THESE PARTS. I'VE HEARD THEY'RE AN ARMY OF WOMEN THAT DWELL IN THE FORESTS TO THE NORTHEAST.
WOMEN?!
WOULDN'T THAT BE A SIGHT! ♡
THEY STAY HIDDEN. WE'RE ON THE BORDER OF THEIR TERRITORY AND I'VE NEVER SEEN THEM.
Sigh...
HMM...

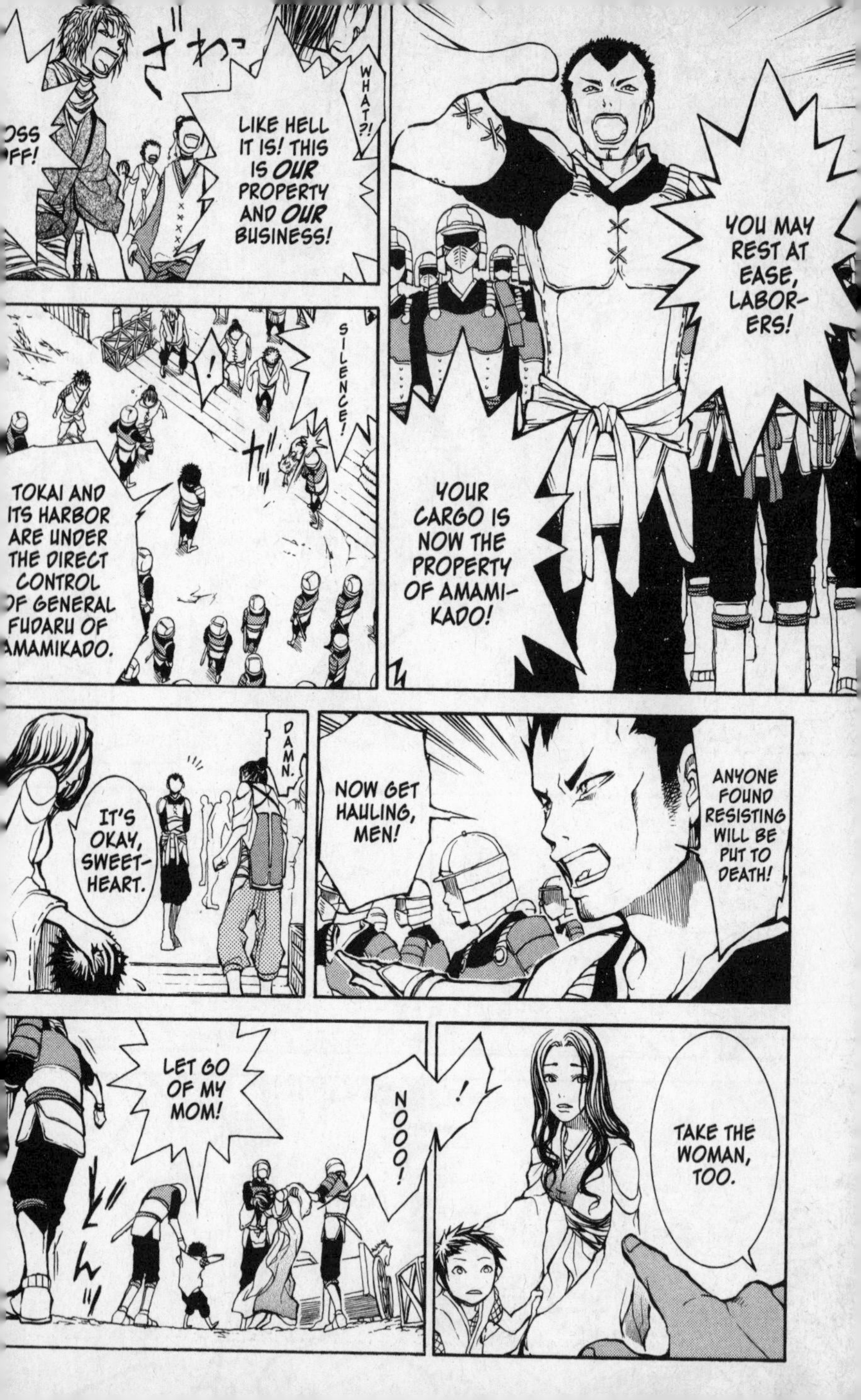
YOU MAY REST AT EASE, LABOR-ERS!
YOUR CARGO IS NOW THE PROPERTY OF AMAMI-KADO!
WHAT?!
LIKE HELL IT IS! THIS IS *OUR* PROPERTY AND *OUR* BUSINESS!
ざわっ
OSS
FF!
SILENCE!
!
TOKAI AND ITS HARBOR ARE UNDER THE DIRECT CONTROL OF GENERAL FUDARU OF AMAMIKADO.
ANYONE FOUND RESISTING WILL BE PUT TO DEATH!
NOW GET HAULING, MEN!
DAMN.
IT'S OKAY, SWEET-HEART.
TAKE THE WOMAN, TOO.
!
NOOO!
LET GO OF MY MOM!

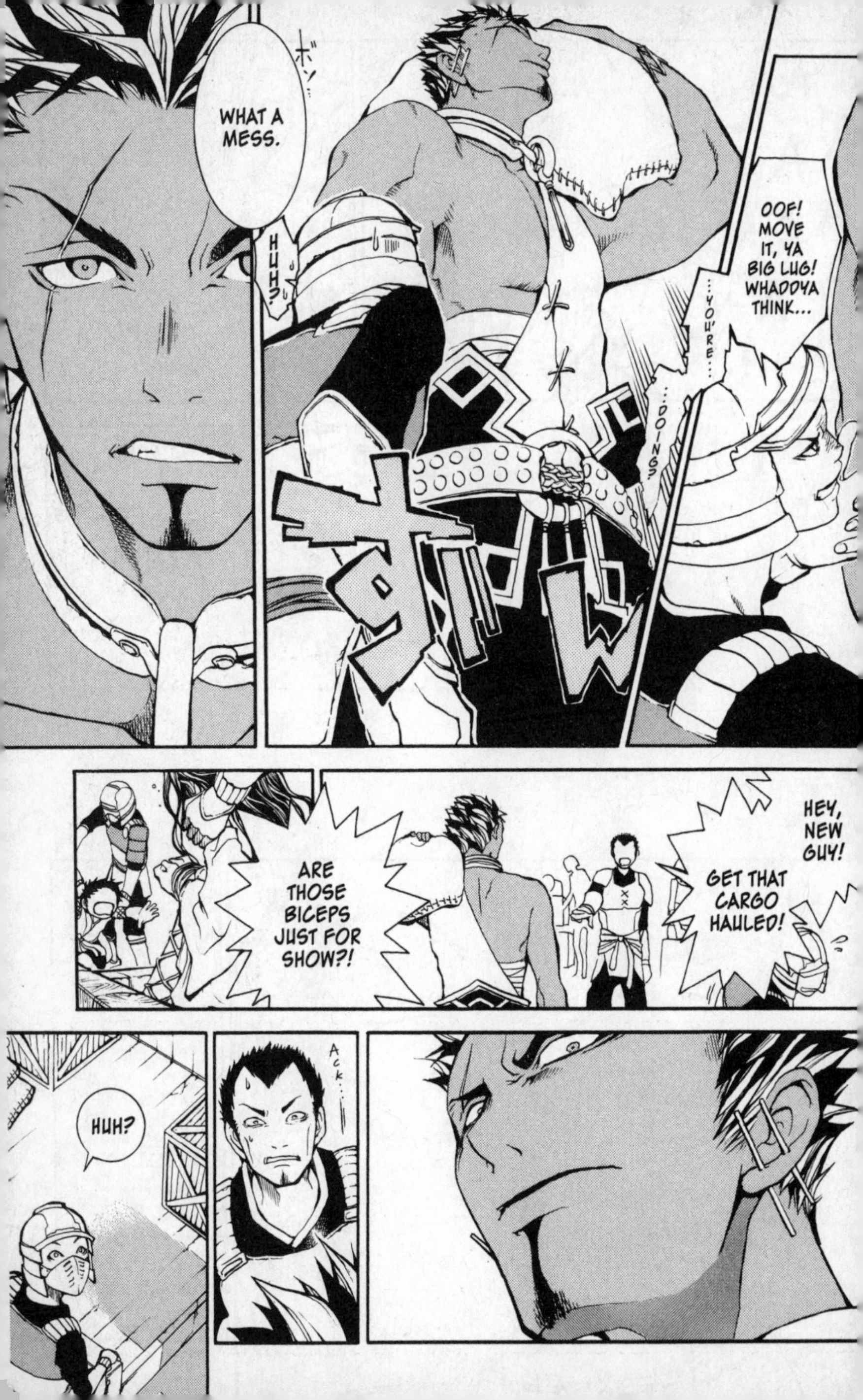
OOF! MOVE IT, YA BIG LUG! WHADDYA THINK...
...YOU'RE...
...DOING?
HUH?
WHAT A MESS.
HEY, NEW GUY!
GET THAT CARGO HAULED!
ARE THOSE BICEPS JUST FOR SHOW?!
Ack...
HUH?

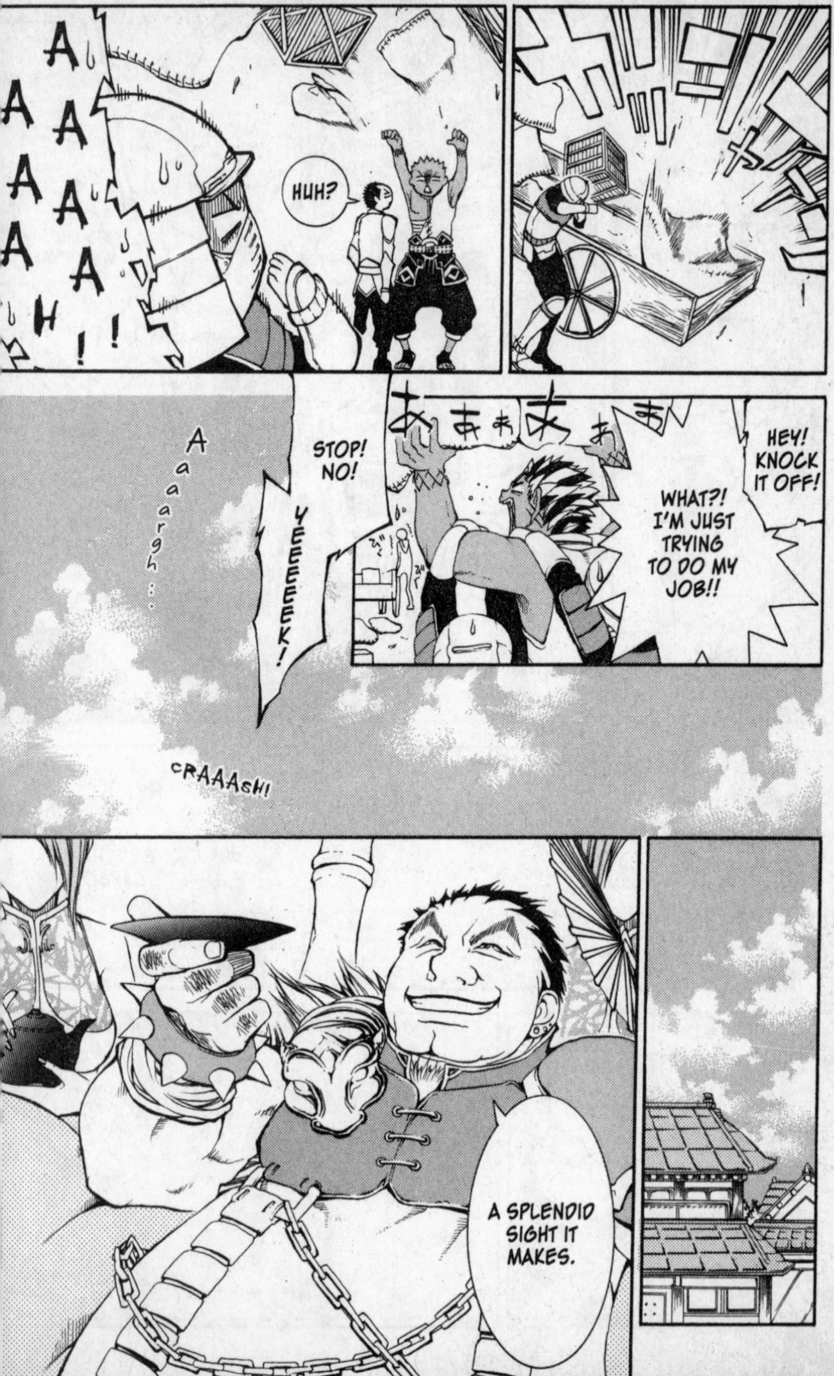
HUH?
AAAAAAAAH!!
HEY! KNOCK IT OFF!
WHAT?! I'M JUST TRYING TO DO MY JOB!!
STOP! NO!
YEEEEEEEK!
Aaaargh..
CRAAASH!
A SPLENDID SIGHT IT MAKES.

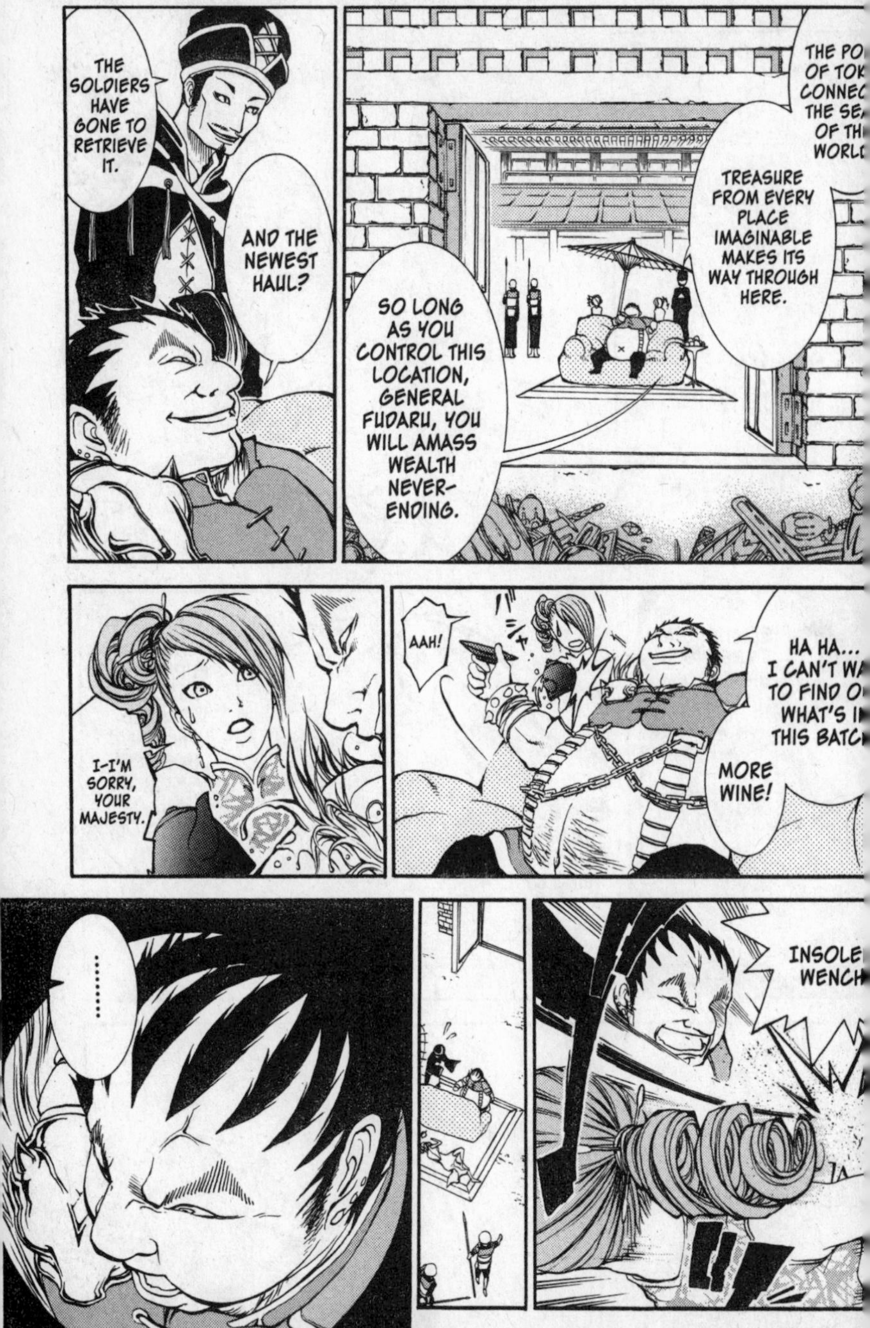
THE PO OF TOK CONNEC THE SE OF TH WORLD
TREASURE FROM EVERY PLACE IMAGINABLE MAKES ITS WAY THROUGH HERE.
SO LONG AS YOU CONTROL THIS LOCATION, GENERAL FUDARU, YOU WILL AMASS WEALTH NEVER-ENDING.
AND THE NEWEST HAUL?
THE SOLDIERS HAVE GONE TO RETRIEVE IT.
HA HA... I CAN'T WA TO FIND O WHAT'S I THIS BATC
MORE WINE!
AAH!
I-I'M SORRY, YOUR MAJESTY.
INSOLE WENCH
....

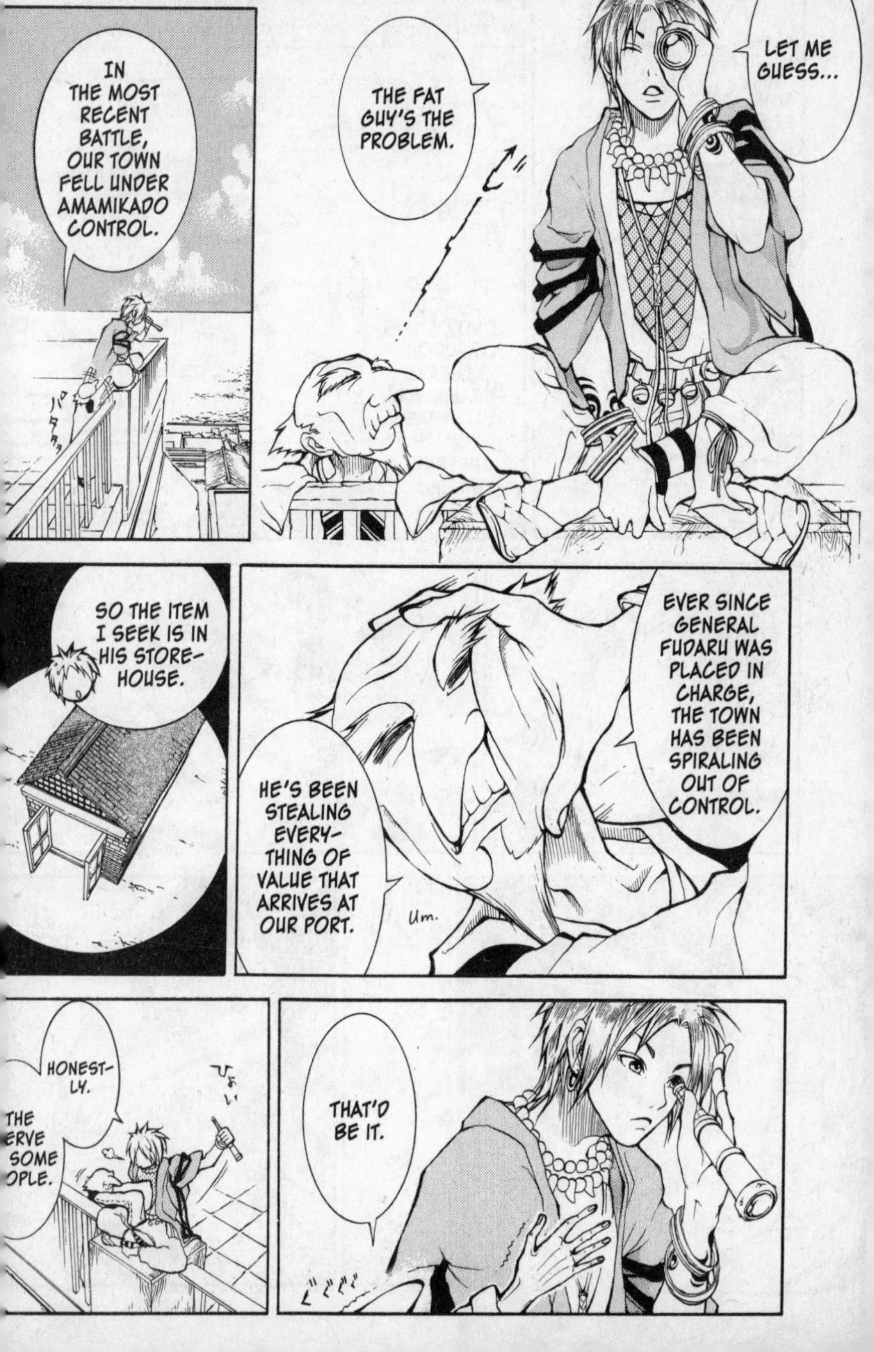
LET ME GUESS...
THE FAT GUY'S THE PROBLEM.
IN THE MOST RECENT BATTLE, OUR TOWN FELL UNDER AMAMIKADO CONTROL.
EVER SINCE GENERAL FUDARU WAS PLACED IN CHARGE, THE TOWN HAS BEEN SPIRALING OUT OF CONTROL.
HE'S BEEN STEALING EVERY-THING OF VALUE THAT ARRIVES AT OUR PORT.
Um.
SO THE ITEM I SEEK IS IN HIS STORE-HOUSE.
THAT'D BE IT.
HONEST-LY.
THE ERVE SOME OPLE.

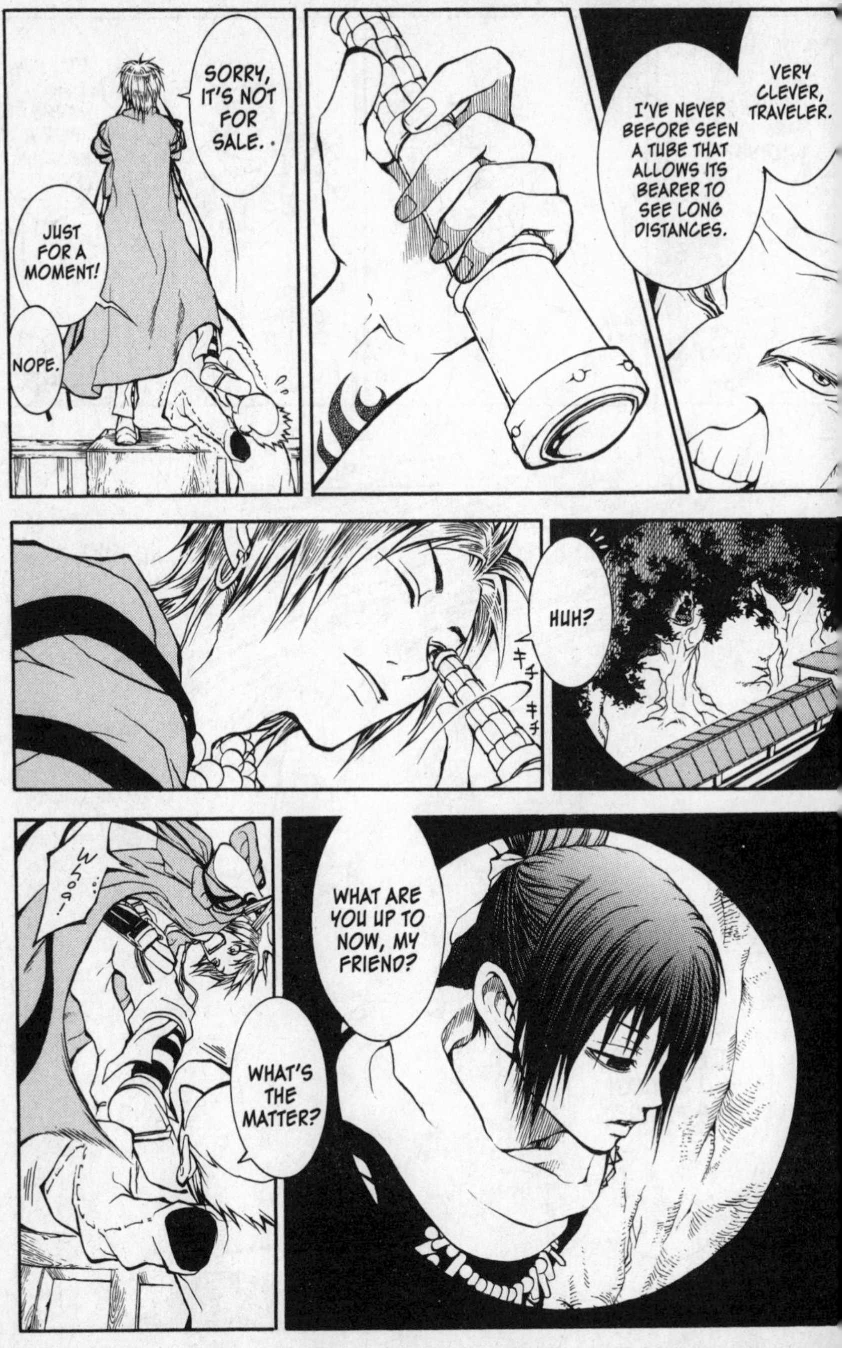
VERY CLEVER, TRAVELER.
I'VE NEVER BEFORE SEEN A TUBE THAT ALLOWS ITS BEARER TO SEE LONG DISTANCES.
SORRY, IT'S NOT FOR SALE..
JUST FOR A MOMENT!
NOPE.
HUH?
キチ
キチ
WHAT ARE YOU UP TO NOW, MY FRIEND?
whoa!
WHAT'S THE MATTER?

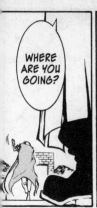

I'LL BUY THAT TUBE FOR A HEALTHY PRICE.
Ha ha!
NOT GONNA SELL IT.
GO ON, NAME YOUR PRICE.
GIVE IT A REST!
WHERE ARE YOU GOING?
HE STOLE THAT WHICH I SOUGHT AWAY FROM ME.
I FIGURED I'D RETURN THE FAVOR.

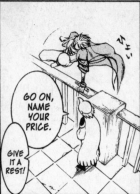

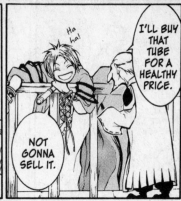

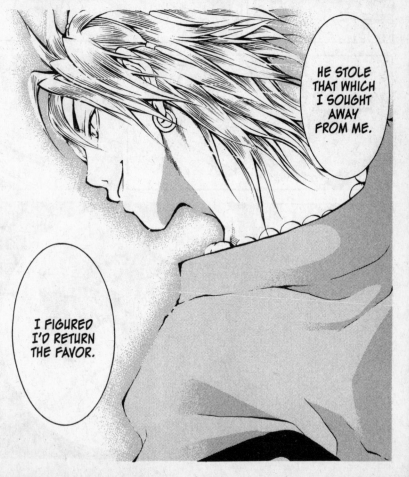

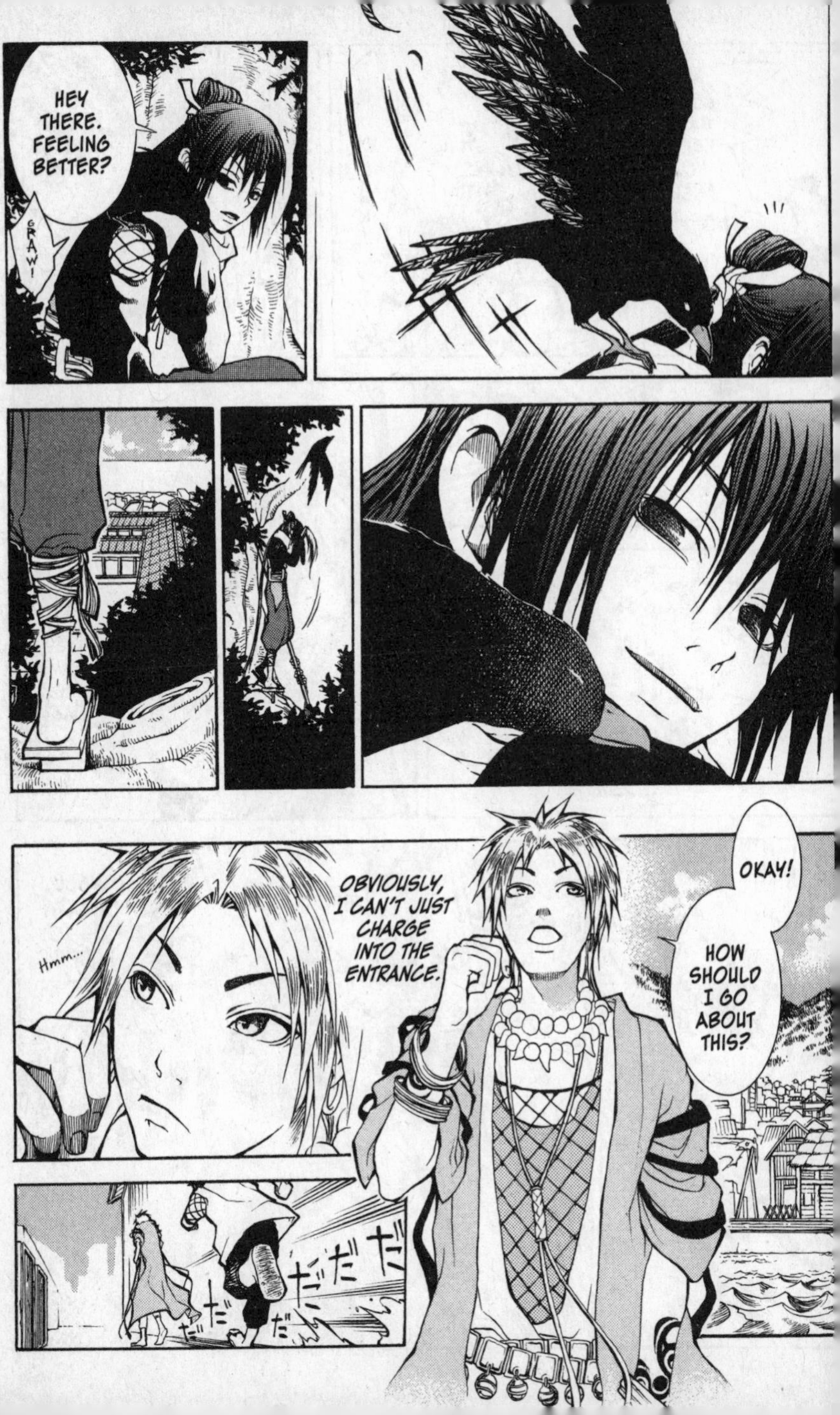
HEY THERE. FEELING BETTER?
GRAW!
OKAY!
HOW SHOULD I GO ABOUT THIS?
OBVIOUSLY, I CAN'T JUST CHARGE INTO THE ENTRANCE.
Hmm...
だだだ
だだだ

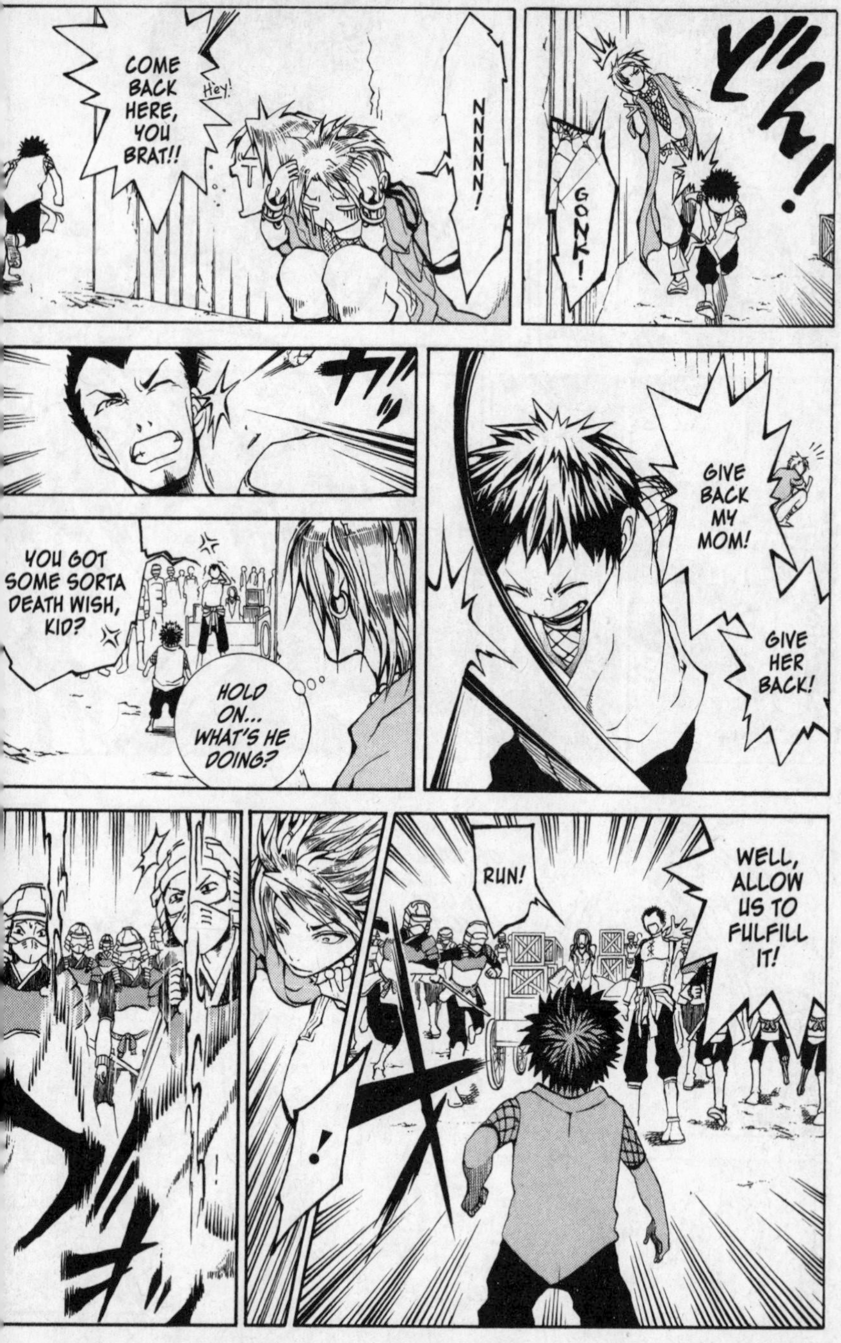
GONK!
NNNNN!
Hey!
COME BACK HERE, YOU BRAT!!
GIVE BACK MY MOM!
GIVE HER BACK!
YOU GOT SOME SORTA DEATH WISH, KID?
HOLD ON... WHAT'S HE DOING?
WELL, ALLOW US TO FULFILL IT!
RUN!

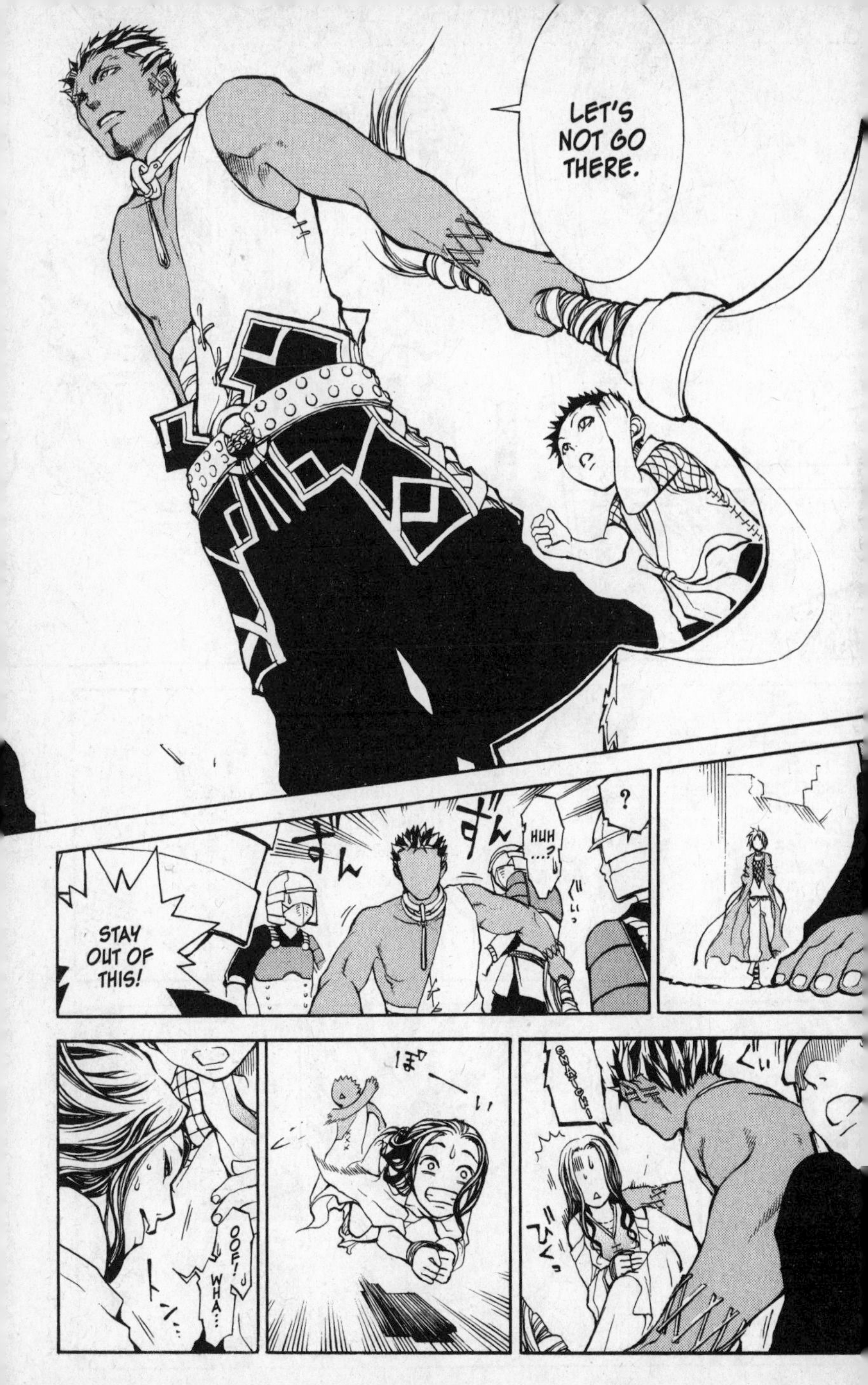
LET'S NOT GO THERE.
ずん
ずん
?
HUH ...?
STAY OUT OF THIS!
SNATCH!
ぐい
びくっ
ぽーい
OOF!
WHA...

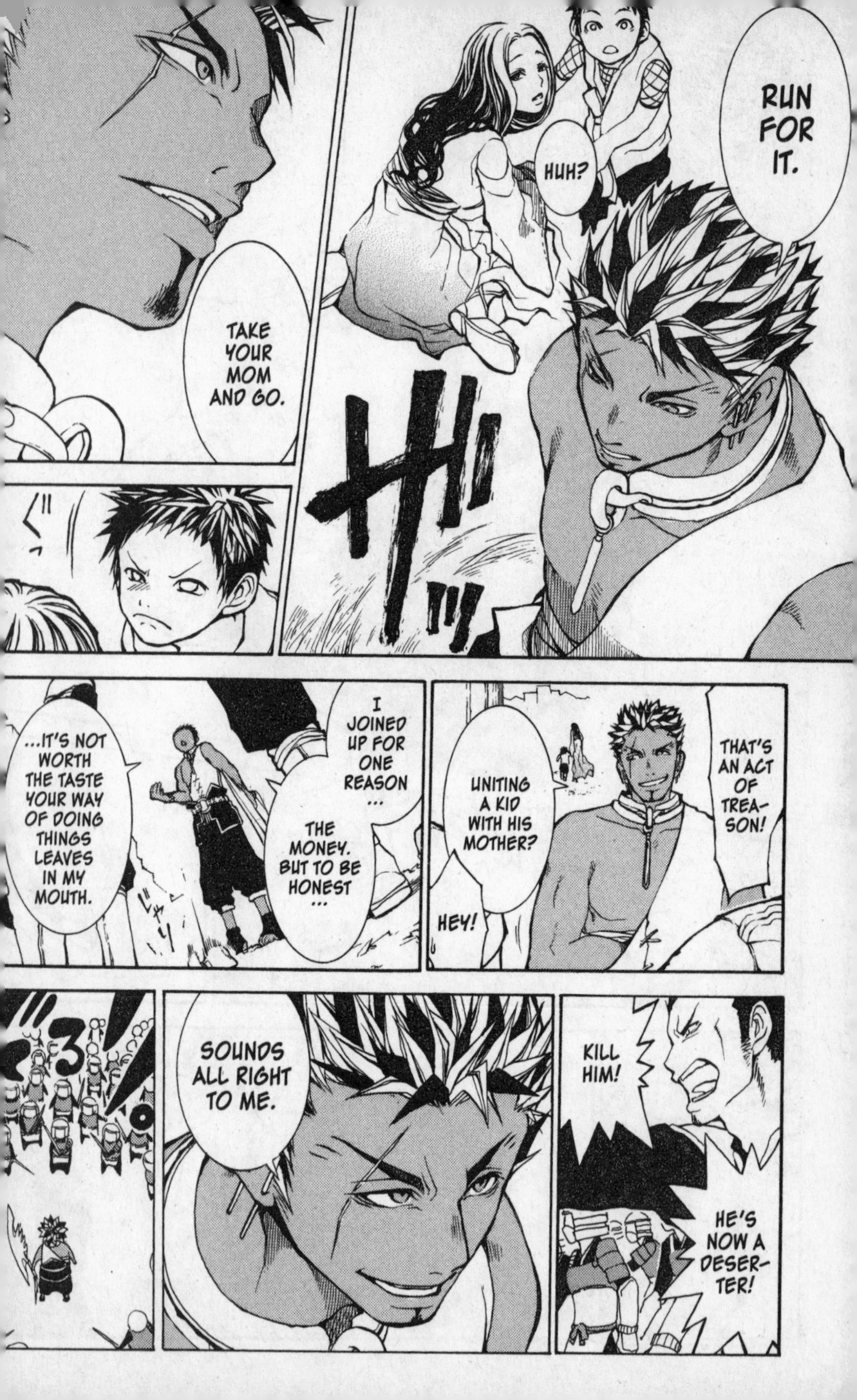
RUN FOR IT.
HUH?
TAKE YOUR MOM AND GO.
THAT'S AN ACT OF TREA-SON!
UNITING A KID WITH HIS MOTHER?
HEY!
I JOINED UP FOR ONE REASON...
THE MONEY. BUT TO BE HONEST...
...IT'S NOT WORTH THE TASTE YOUR WAY OF DOING THINGS LEAVES IN MY MOUTH.
KILL HIM!
HE'S NOW A DESER-TER!
SOUNDS ALL RIGHT TO ME.

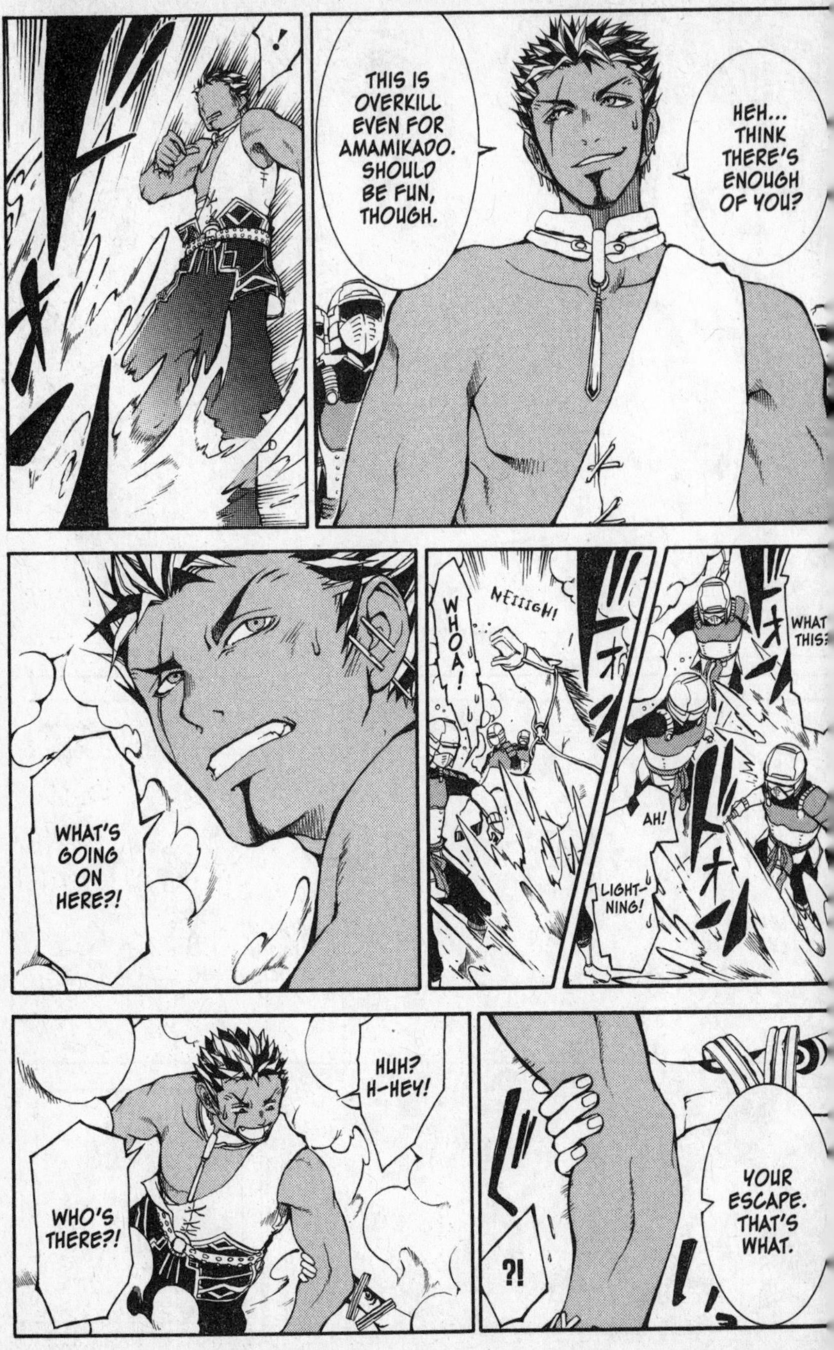
HEH... THINK THERE'S ENOUGH OF YOU?
THIS IS OVERKILL EVEN FOR AMAMIKADO. SHOULD BE FUN, THOUGH.
!
WHAT THIS?
AH!
LIGHT-NING!
NEIIIGH!
WHOA!
WHAT'S GOING ON HERE?!
YOUR ESCAPE. THAT'S WHAT.
?!
HUH? H-HEY!
WHO'S THERE?!

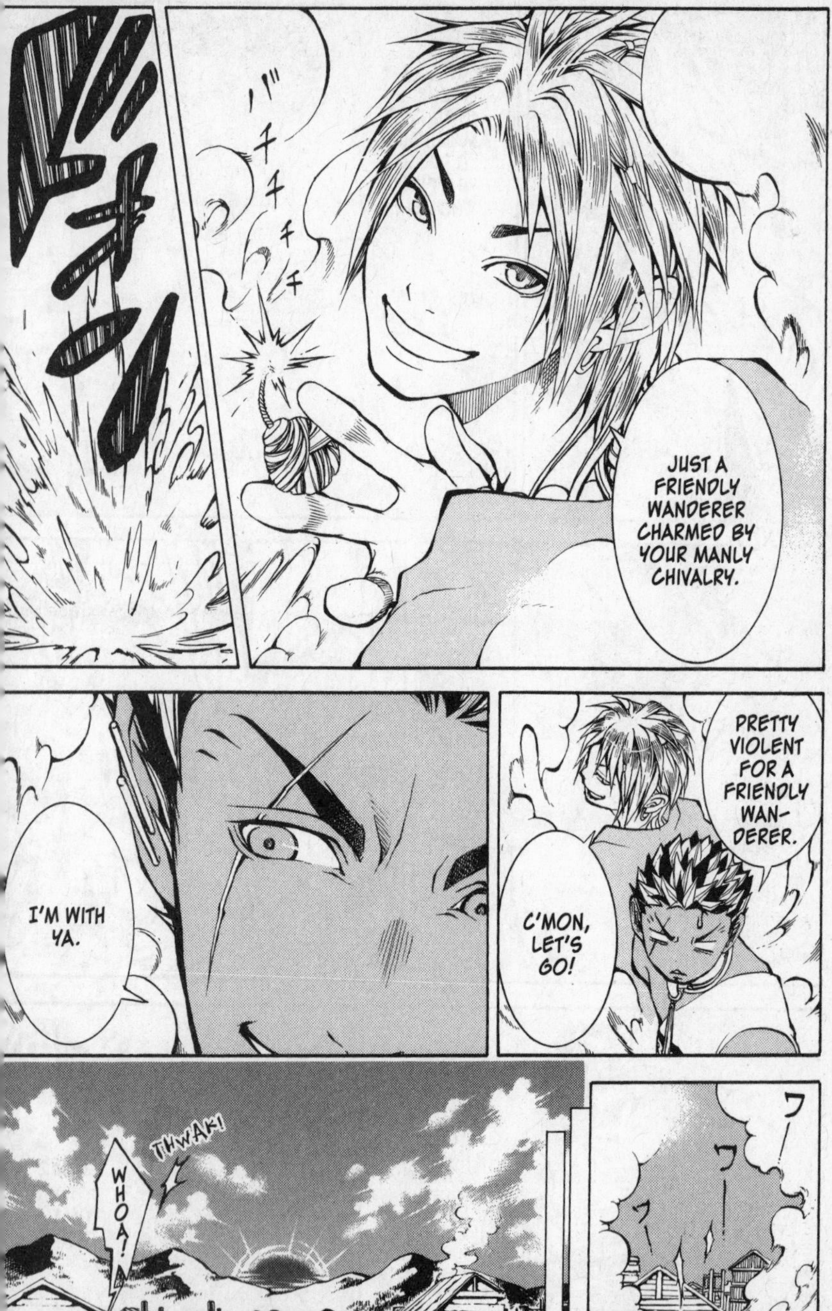
バチチチチ
JUST A FRIENDLY WANDERER CHARMED BY YOUR MANLY CHIVALRY.
PRETTY VIOLENT FOR A FRIENDLY WAN-DERER.
C'MON, LET'S GO!
I'M WITH YA.
ワーワーワー
THWAK!
WHOA!

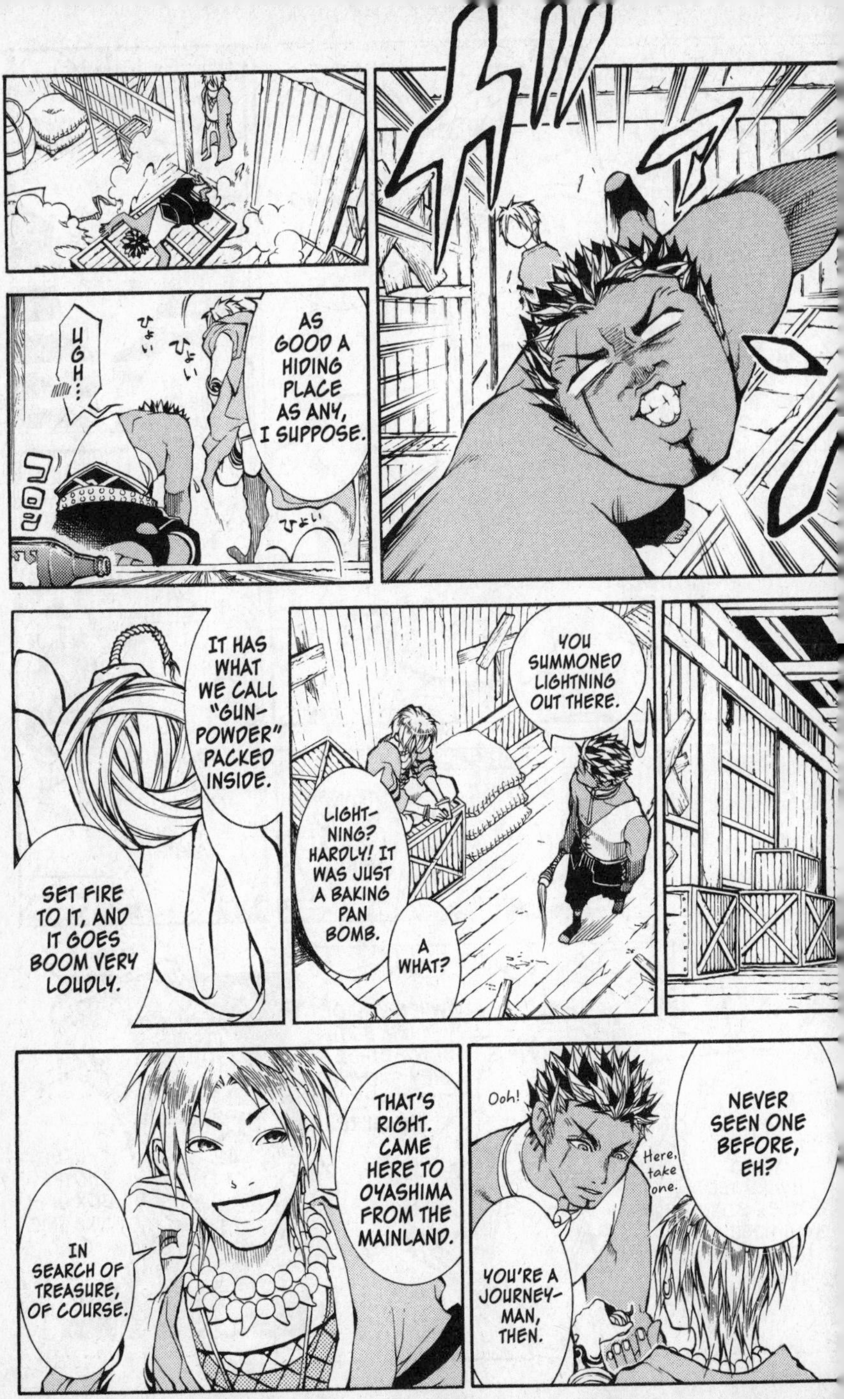
UGH...
AS GOOD A HIDING PLACE AS ANY, I SUPPOSE.
ひょい
ひょい
ひょい
YOU SUMMONED LIGHTNING OUT THERE.
LIGHTNING? HARDLY! IT WAS JUST A BAKING PAN BOMB.
A WHAT?
IT HAS WHAT WE CALL "GUN-POWDER" PACKED INSIDE.
SET FIRE TO IT, AND IT GOES BOOM VERY LOUDLY.
NEVER SEEN ONE BEFORE, EH?
Ooh!
Here, take one.
YOU'RE A JOURNEYMAN, THEN.
THAT'S RIGHT. CAME HERE TO OYASHIMA FROM THE MAINLAND.
IN SEARCH OF TREASURE, OF COURSE.

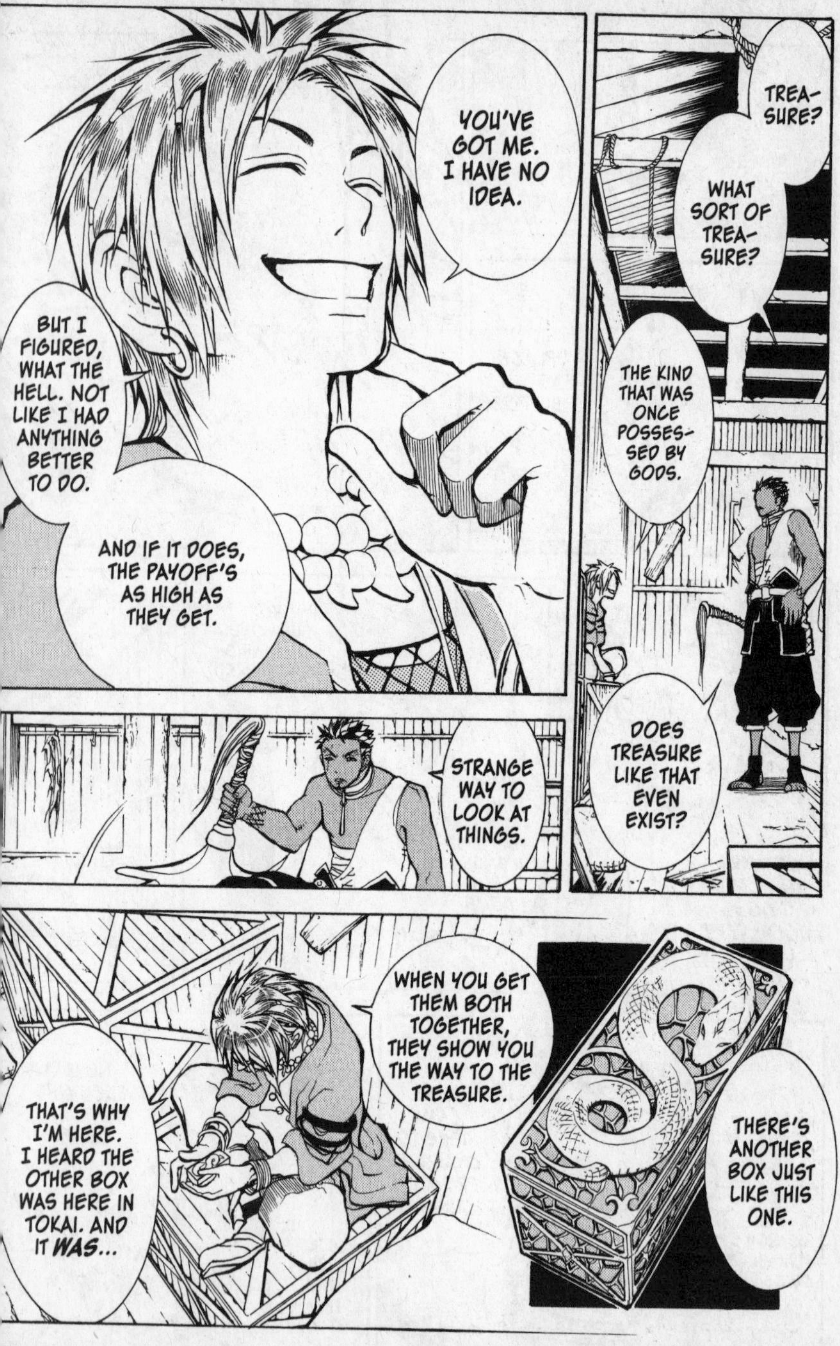
TREA-SURE?
WHAT SORT OF TREA-SURE?
THE KIND THAT WAS ONCE POSSES-SED BY GODS.
DOES TREASURE LIKE THAT EVEN EXIST?
YOU'VE GOT ME. I HAVE NO IDEA.
BUT I FIGURED, WHAT THE HELL. NOT LIKE I HAD ANYTHING BETTER TO DO.
AND IF IT DOES, THE PAYOFF'S AS HIGH AS THEY GET.
STRANGE WAY TO LOOK AT THINGS.
THERE'S ANOTHER BOX JUST LIKE THIS ONE.
WHEN YOU GET THEM BOTH TOGETHER, THEY SHOW YOU THE WAY TO THE TREASURE.
THAT'S WHY I'M HERE. I HEARD THE OTHER BOX WAS HERE IN TOKAI. AND IT *WAS*...

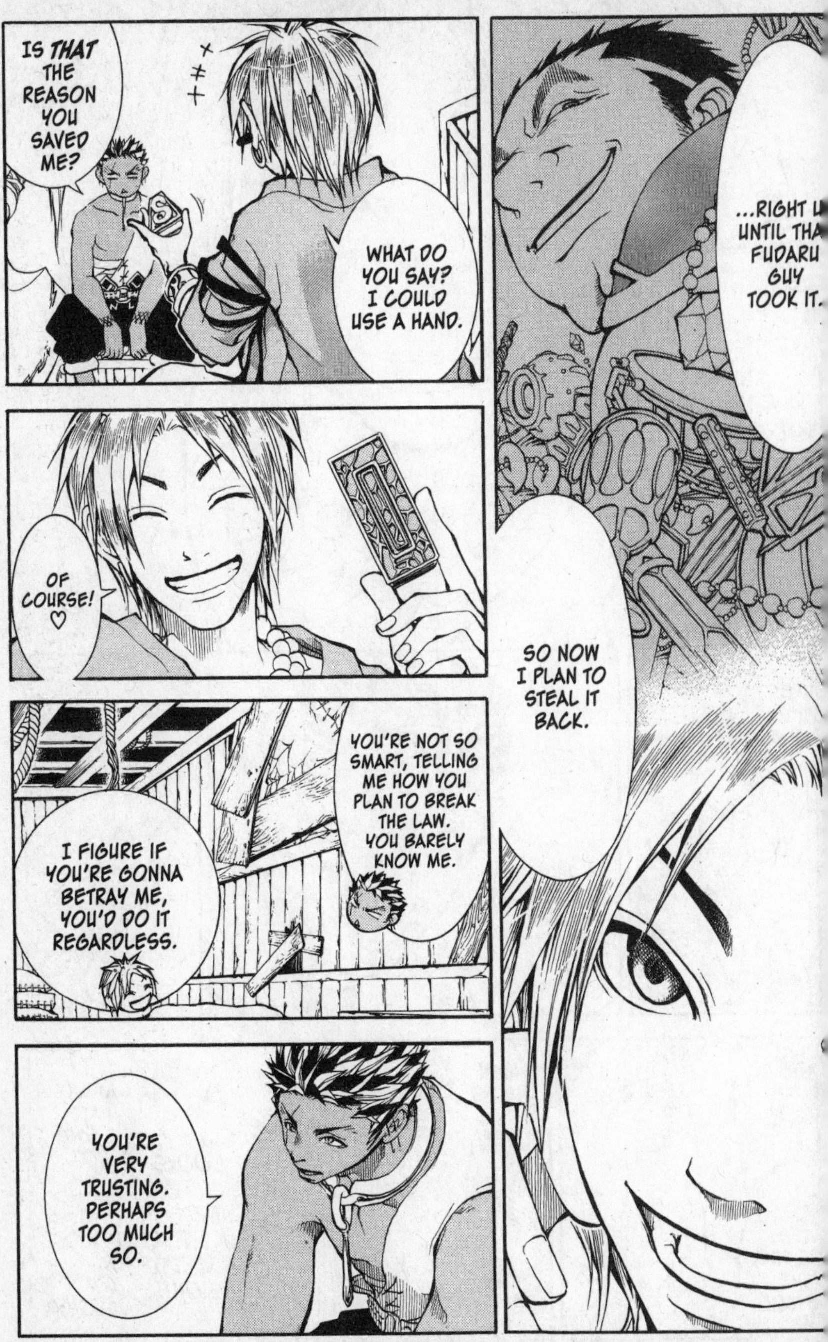
...RIGHT U UNTIL THA FUDARU GUY TOOK IT.
SO NOW I PLAN TO STEAL IT BACK.
IS *THAT* THE REASON YOU SAVED ME?
WHAT DO YOU SAY? I COULD USE A HAND.
OF COURSE! ♡
YOU'RE NOT SO SMART, TELLING ME HOW YOU PLAN TO BREAK THE LAW. YOU BARELY KNOW ME.
I FIGURE IF YOU'RE GONNA BETRAY ME, YOU'D DO IT REGARDLESS.
YOU'RE VERY TRUSTING. PERHAPS TOO MUCH SO.

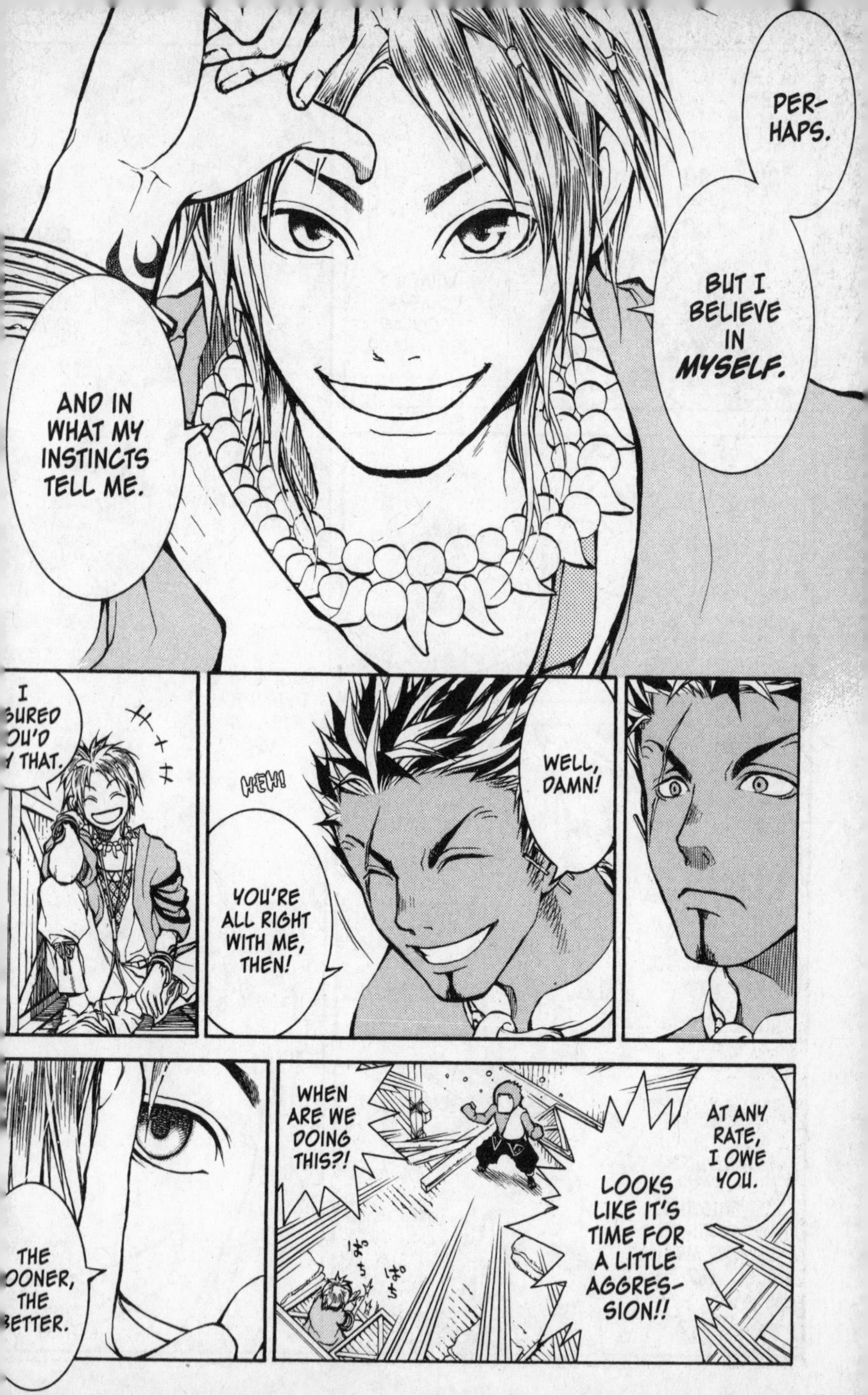
PER-HAPS.
BUT I BELIEVE IN MYSELF.
AND IN WHAT MY INSTINCTS TELL ME.
WELL, DAMN!
HEH!
YOU'RE ALL RIGHT WITH ME, THEN!
I SURED OU'D Y THAT.
AT ANY RATE, I OWE YOU.
LOOKS LIKE IT'S TIME FOR A LITTLE AGGRES-SION!!
WHEN ARE WE DOING THIS?!
ぱち ぱち
THE OONER, THE ETTER.

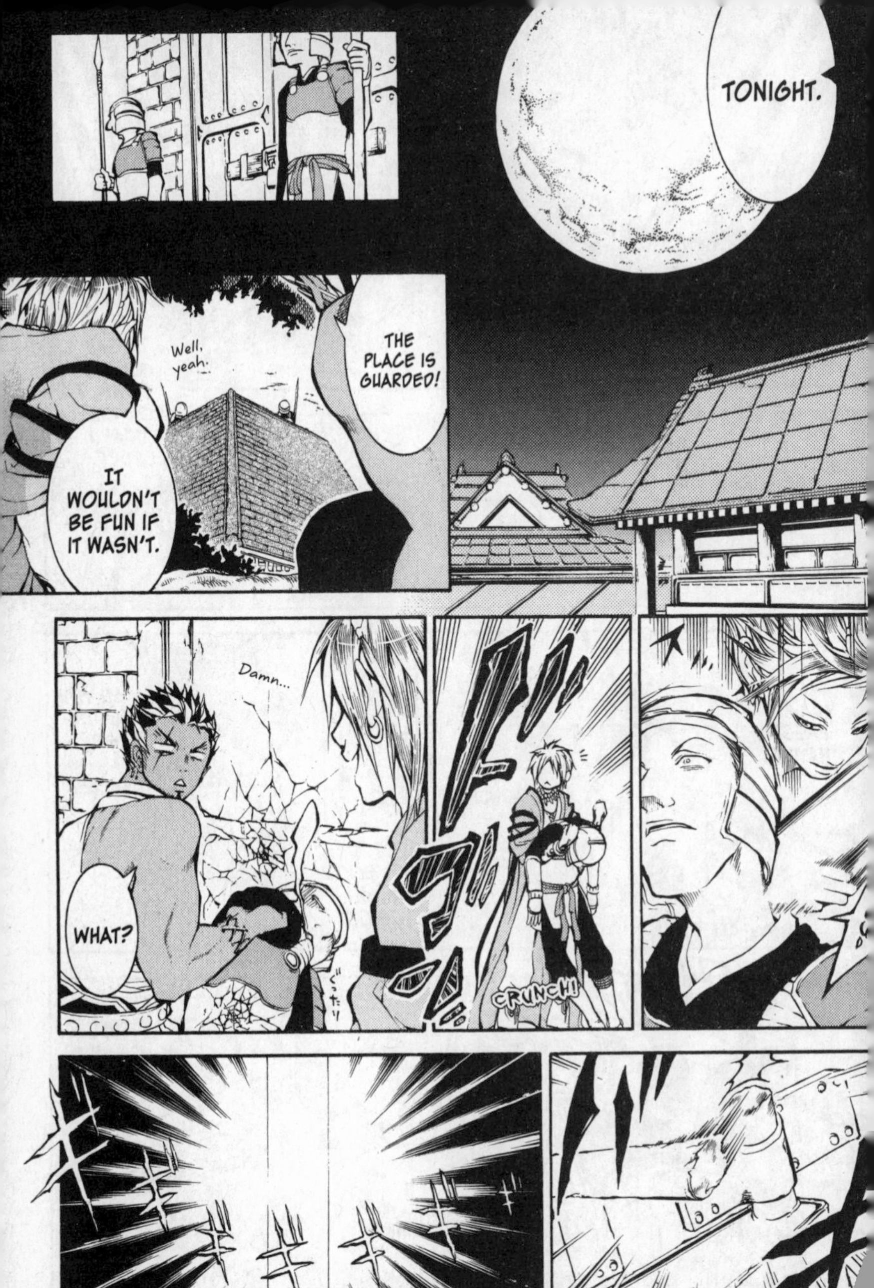
TONIGHT.
THE PLACE IS GUARDED!
Well, yeah.
IT WOULDN'T BE FUN IF IT WASN'T.
CRUNCH!
Damn...
WHAT?

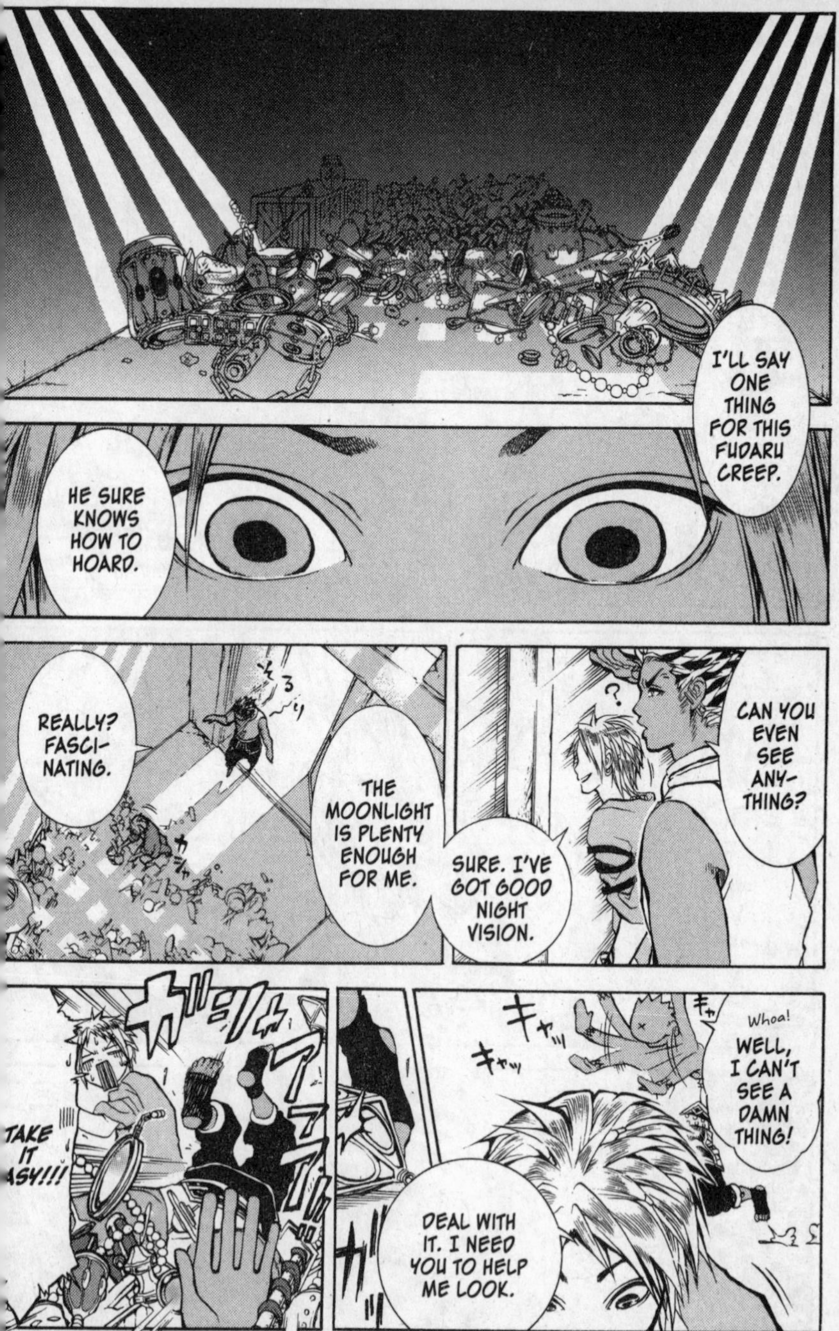
I'LL SAY ONE THING FOR THIS FUDARU CREEP.
HE SURE KNOWS HOW TO HOARD.
CAN YOU EVEN SEE ANYTHING?
SURE. I'VE GOT GOOD NIGHT VISION.
THE MOONLIGHT IS PLENTY ENOUGH FOR ME.
REALLY? FASCINATING.
Whoa!
WELL, I CAN'T SEE A DAMN THING!
DEAL WITH IT. I NEED YOU TO HELP ME LOOK.
TAKE IT ASY!!!

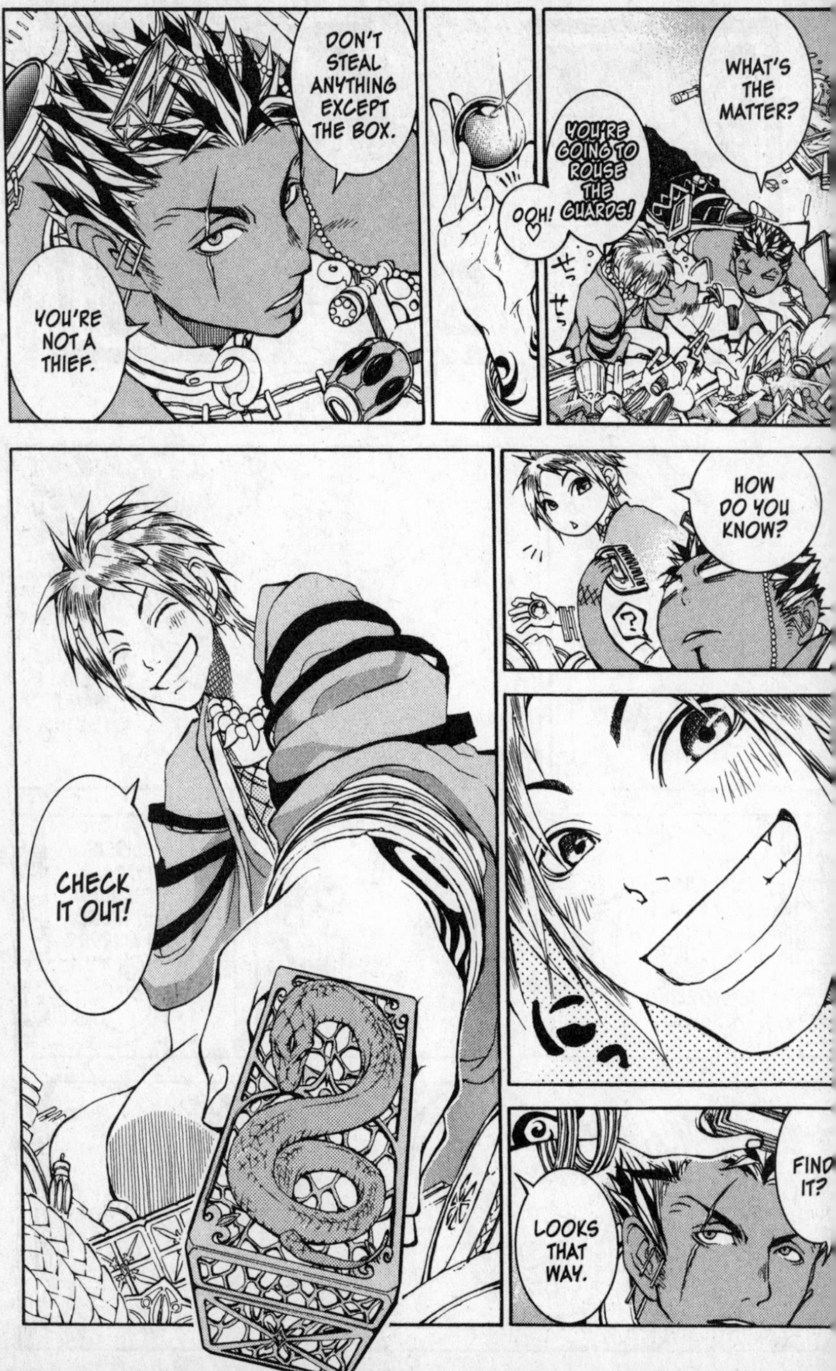
WHAT'S THE MATTER?
YOU'RE GOING TO ROUSE THE GUARDS!
OOH! ♡
DON'T STEAL ANYTHING EXCEPT THE BOX.
YOU'RE NOT A THIEF.
HOW DO YOU KNOW?
FIND IT?
LOOKS THAT WAY.
CHECK IT OUT!

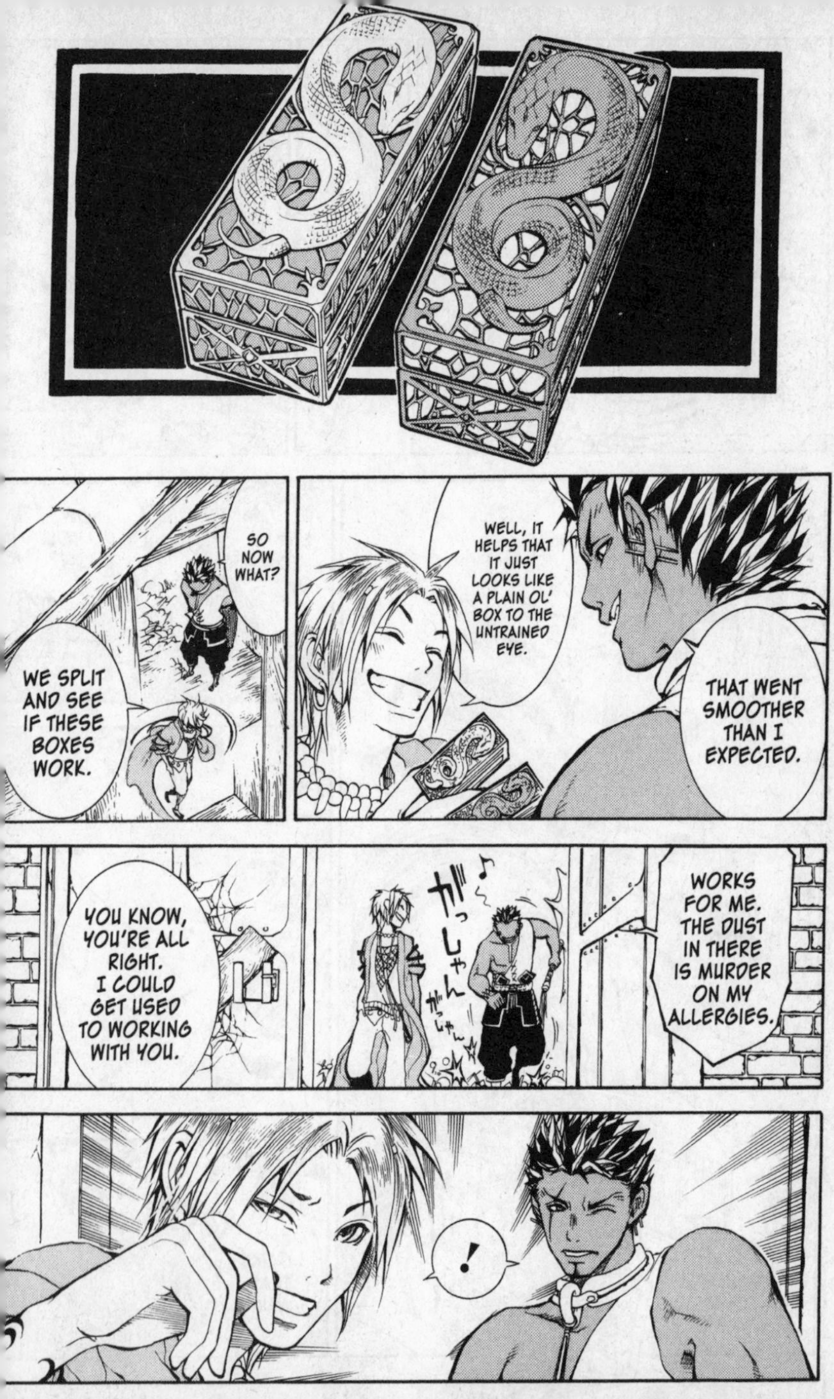
THAT WENT SMOOTHER THAN I EXPECTED.
WELL, IT HELPS THAT IT JUST LOOKS LIKE A PLAIN OL' BOX TO THE UNTRAINED EYE.
SO NOW WHAT?
WE SPLIT AND SEE IF THESE BOXES WORK.
WORKS FOR ME. THE DUST IN THERE IS MURDER ON MY ALLERGIES.
がっしゃん ♪
がっしゃん
YOU KNOW, YOU'RE ALL RIGHT. I COULD GET USED TO WORKING WITH YOU.
!

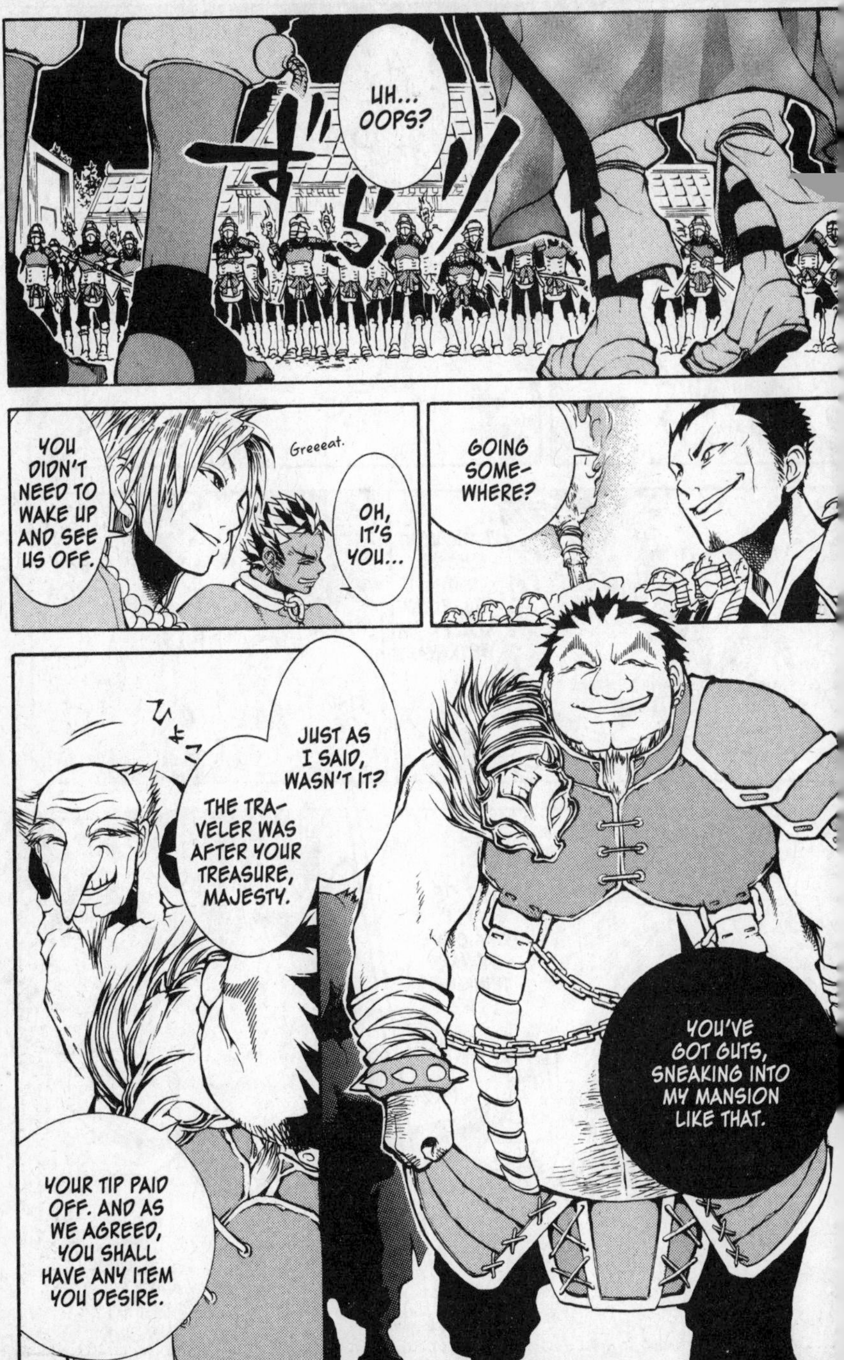
UH... OOPS?
GOING SOME-WHERE?
Greeeat.
OH, IT'S YOU...
YOU DIDN'T NEED TO WAKE UP AND SEE US OFF.
JUST AS I SAID, WASN'T IT?
THE TRA-VELER WAS AFTER YOUR TREASURE, MAJESTY.
YOU'VE GOT GUTS, SNEAKING INTO MY MANSION LIKE THAT.
YOUR TIP PAID OFF. AND AS WE AGREED, YOU SHALL HAVE ANY ITEM YOU DESIRE.

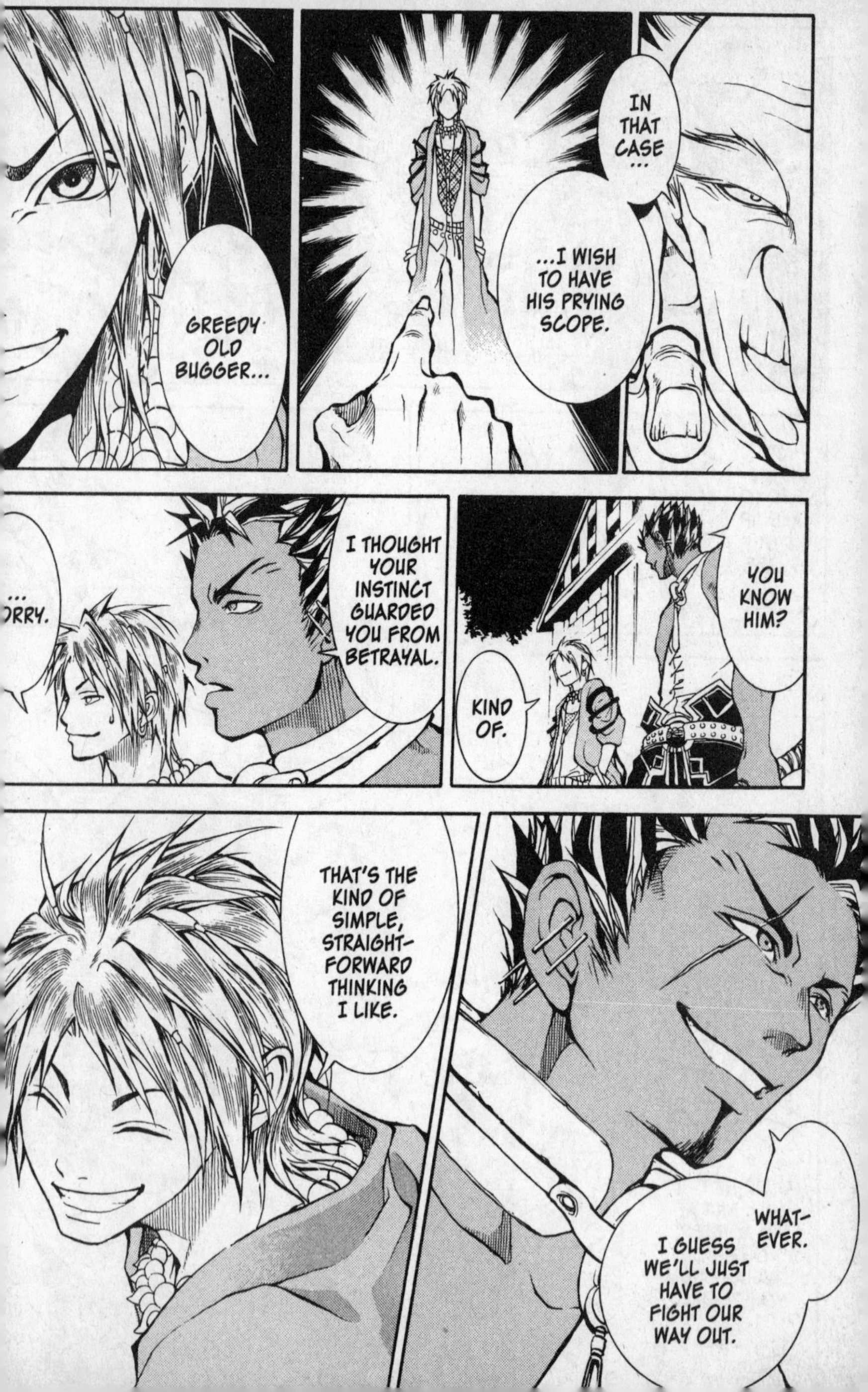
IN THAT CASE...
...I WISH TO HAVE HIS PRYING SCOPE.
GREEDY OLD BUGGER...
YOU KNOW HIM?
KIND OF.
I THOUGHT YOUR INSTINCT GUARDED YOU FROM BETRAYAL.
...ORRY.
WHAT-EVER.
I GUESS WE'LL JUST HAVE TO FIGHT OUR WAY OUT.
THAT'S THE KIND OF SIMPLE, STRAIGHT-FORWARD THINKING I LIKE.

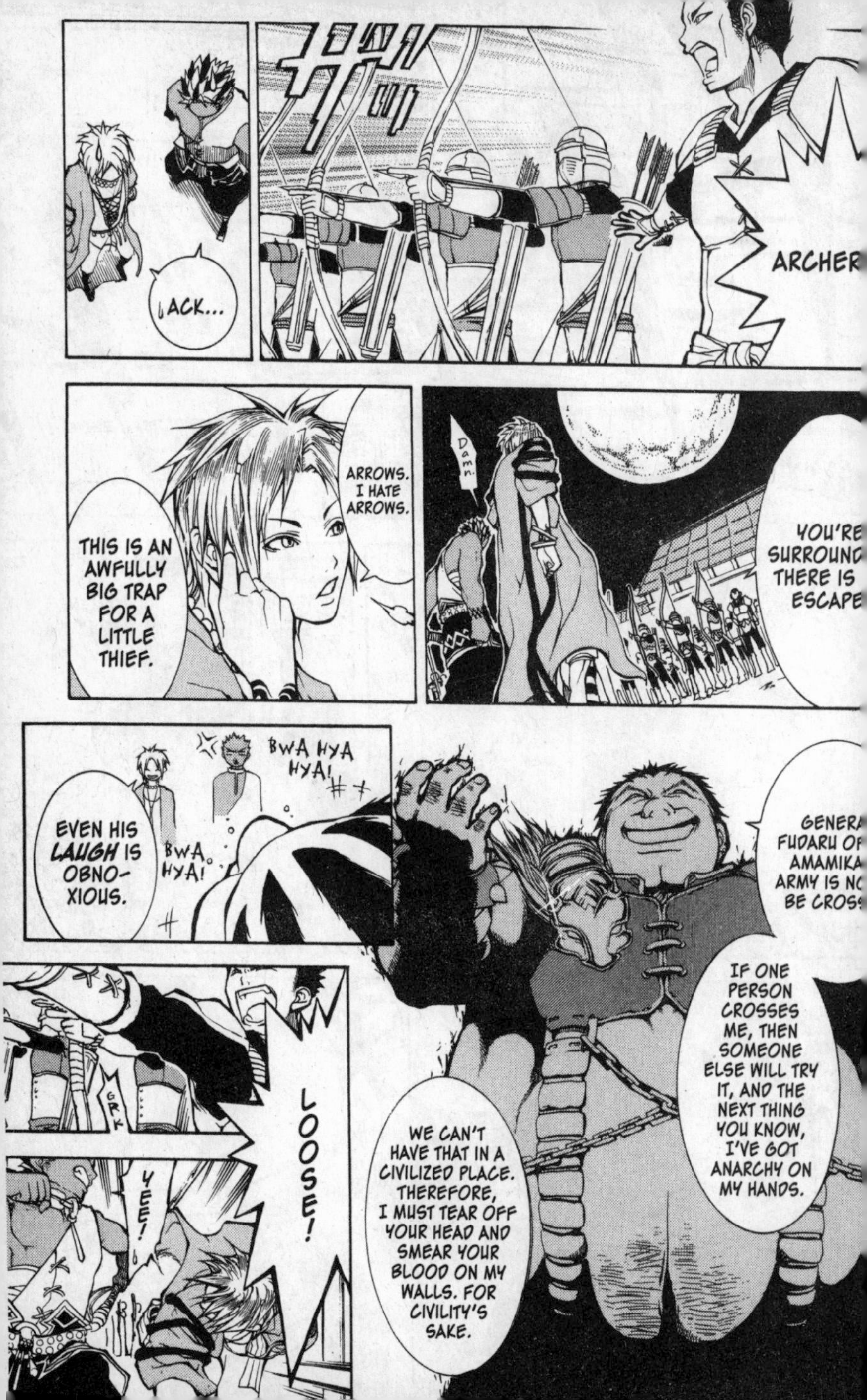
ARCHER
ACK...
YOU'RE SURROUND THERE IS ESCAPE
Damn.
ARROWS. I HATE ARROWS.
THIS IS AN AWFULLY BIG TRAP FOR A LITTLE THIEF.
GENERA FUDARU OF AMAMIKA ARMY IS NO BE CROSS
IF ONE PERSON CROSSES ME, THEN SOMEONE ELSE WILL TRY IT, AND THE NEXT THING YOU KNOW, I'VE GOT ANARCHY ON MY HANDS.
WE CAN'T HAVE THAT IN A CIVILIZED PLACE. THEREFORE, I MUST TEAR OFF YOUR HEAD AND SMEAR YOUR BLOOD ON MY WALLS. FOR CIVILITY'S SAKE.
BWA HYA HYA!
BWA HYA!
EVEN HIS *LAUGH* IS OBNO-XIOUS.
LOOSE!
GRK
YEE!

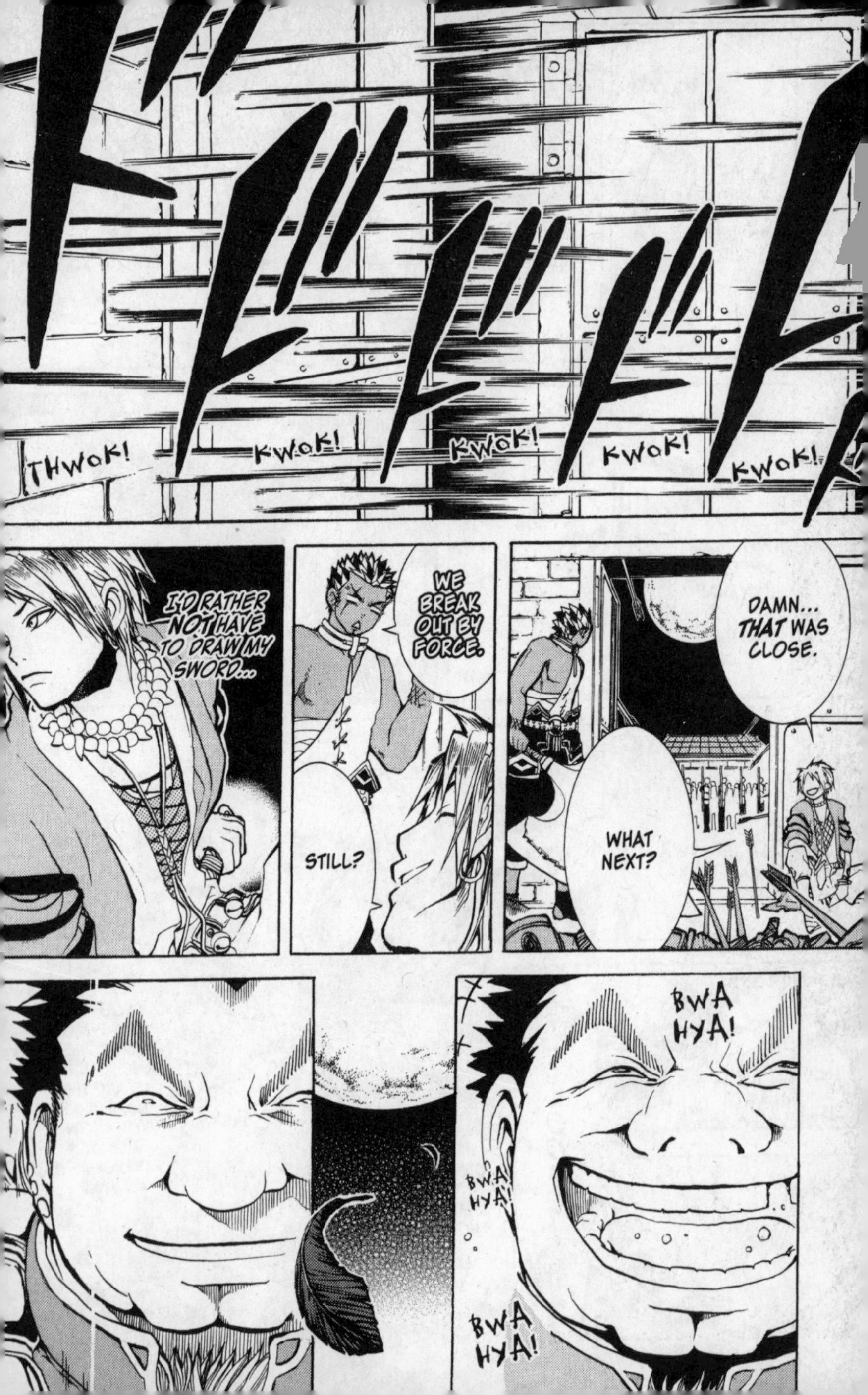
KWOK!
KWOK!
KWOK!
KWOK!
THWOK!
DAMN... *THAT* WAS CLOSE.
WHAT NEXT?
WE BREAK OUT BY FORCE.
STILL?
I'D RATHER *NOT* HAVE TO DRAW MY SWORD...
BWA HYA!
BWA HYA!
BWA HYA!

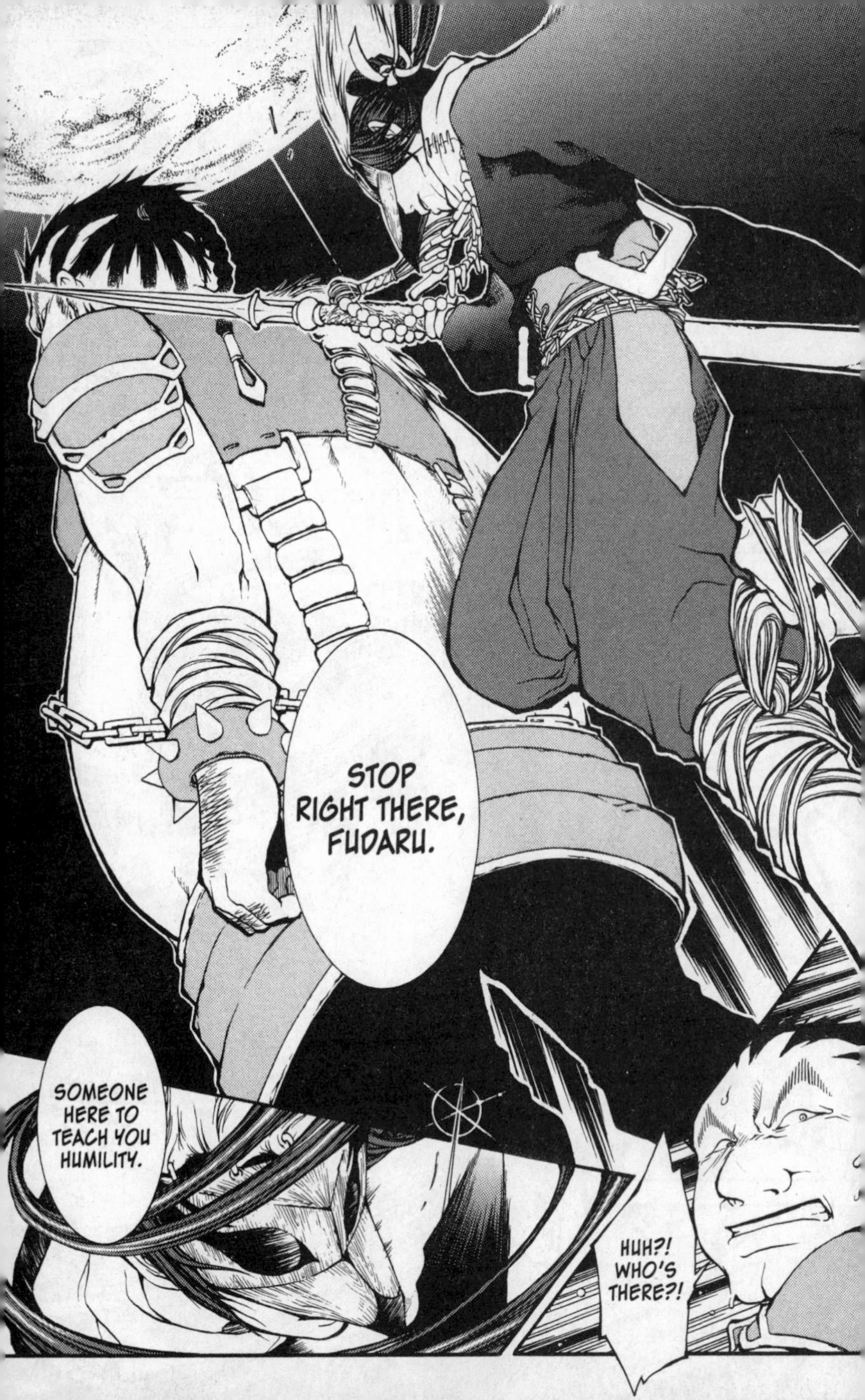
STOP RIGHT THERE, FUDARU.
HUH?! WHO'S THERE?!
SOMEONE HERE TO TEACH YOU HUMILITY.

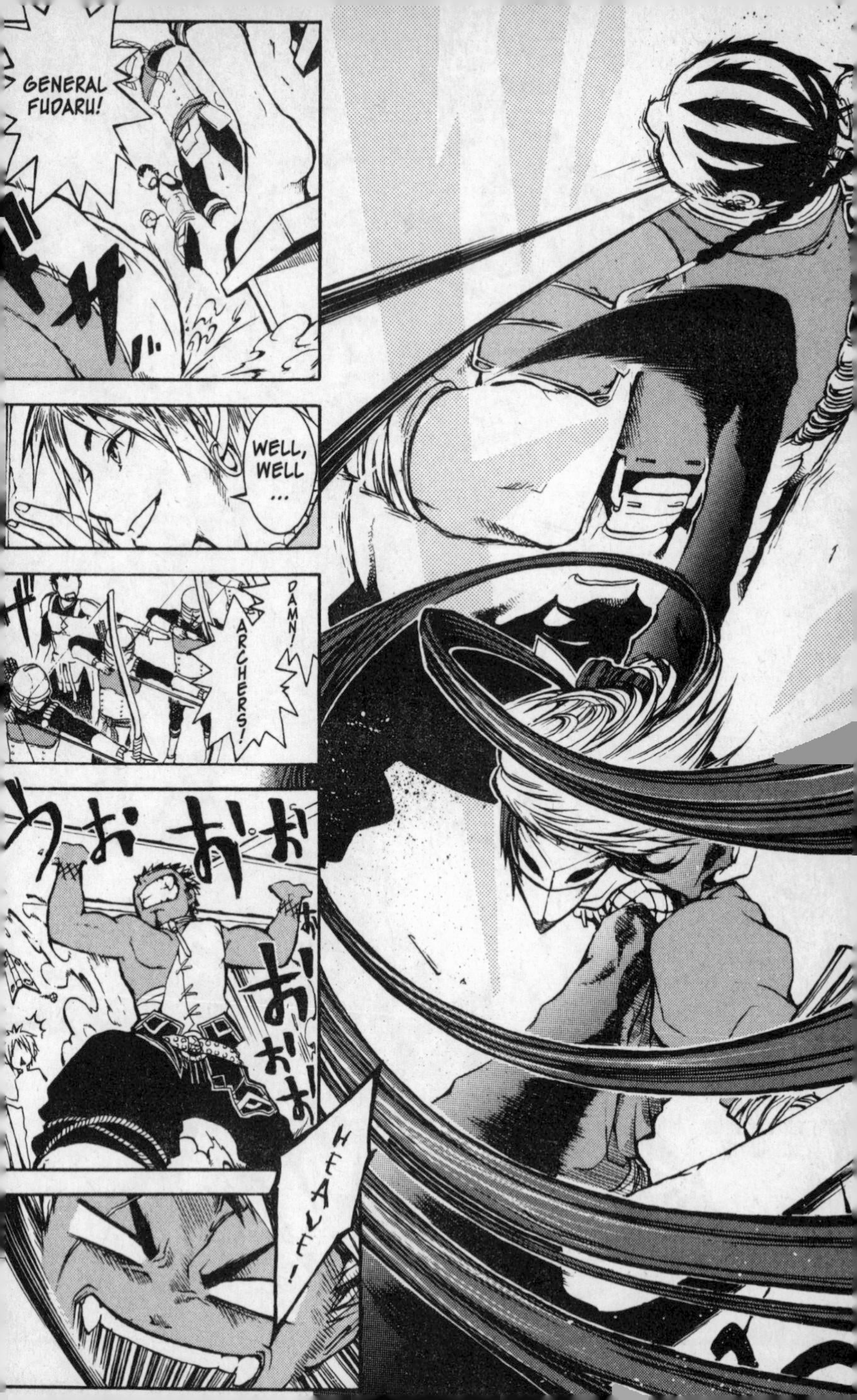
GENERAL FUDARU!
WELL, WELL ...
DAMN!
ARCHERS!
わおお!お
おお!お!お
HEAVE!

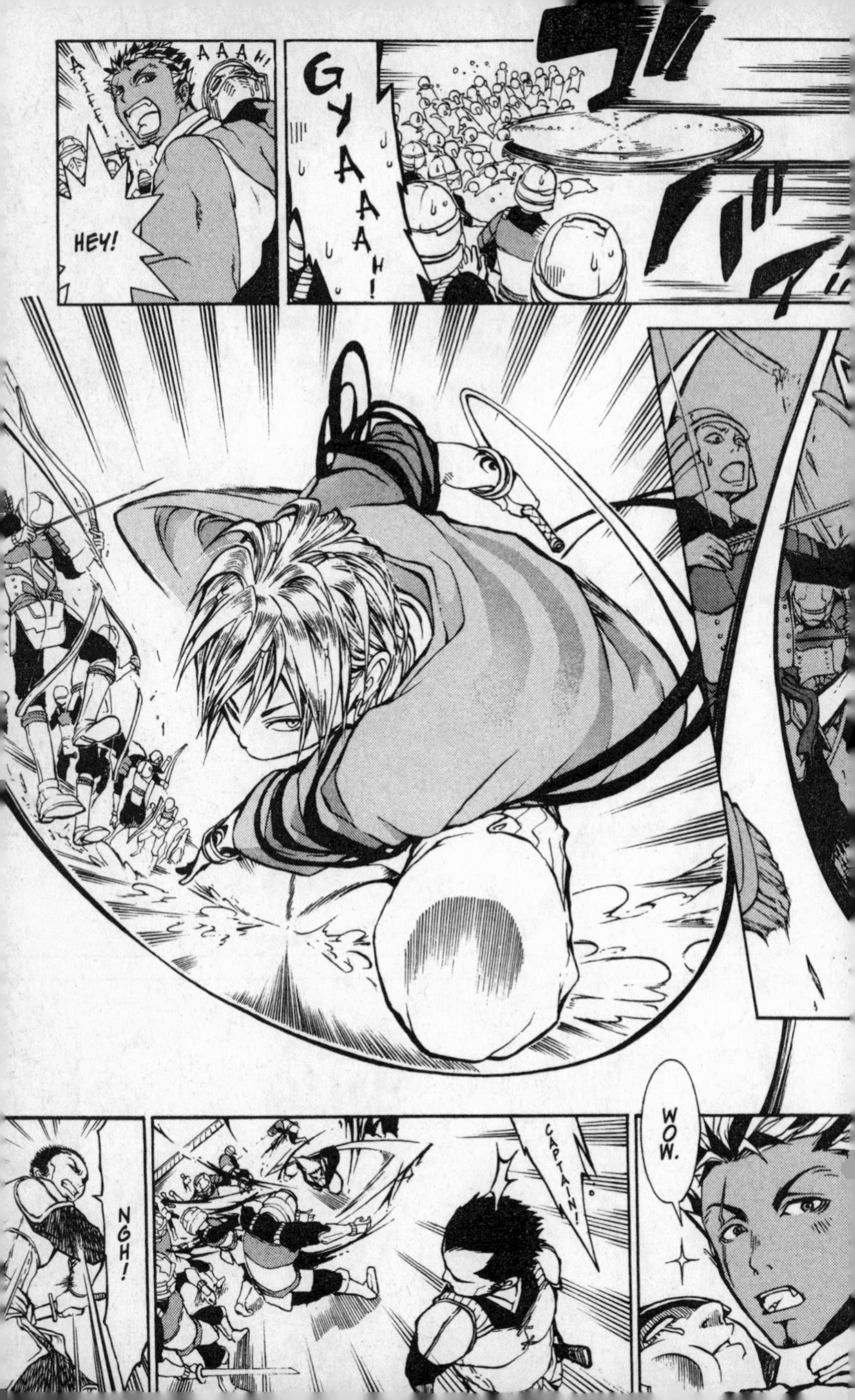
GYAAAAH!
AIIEE!
AAAAH!
HEY!
WOW.
CAPTAIN!
NGH!

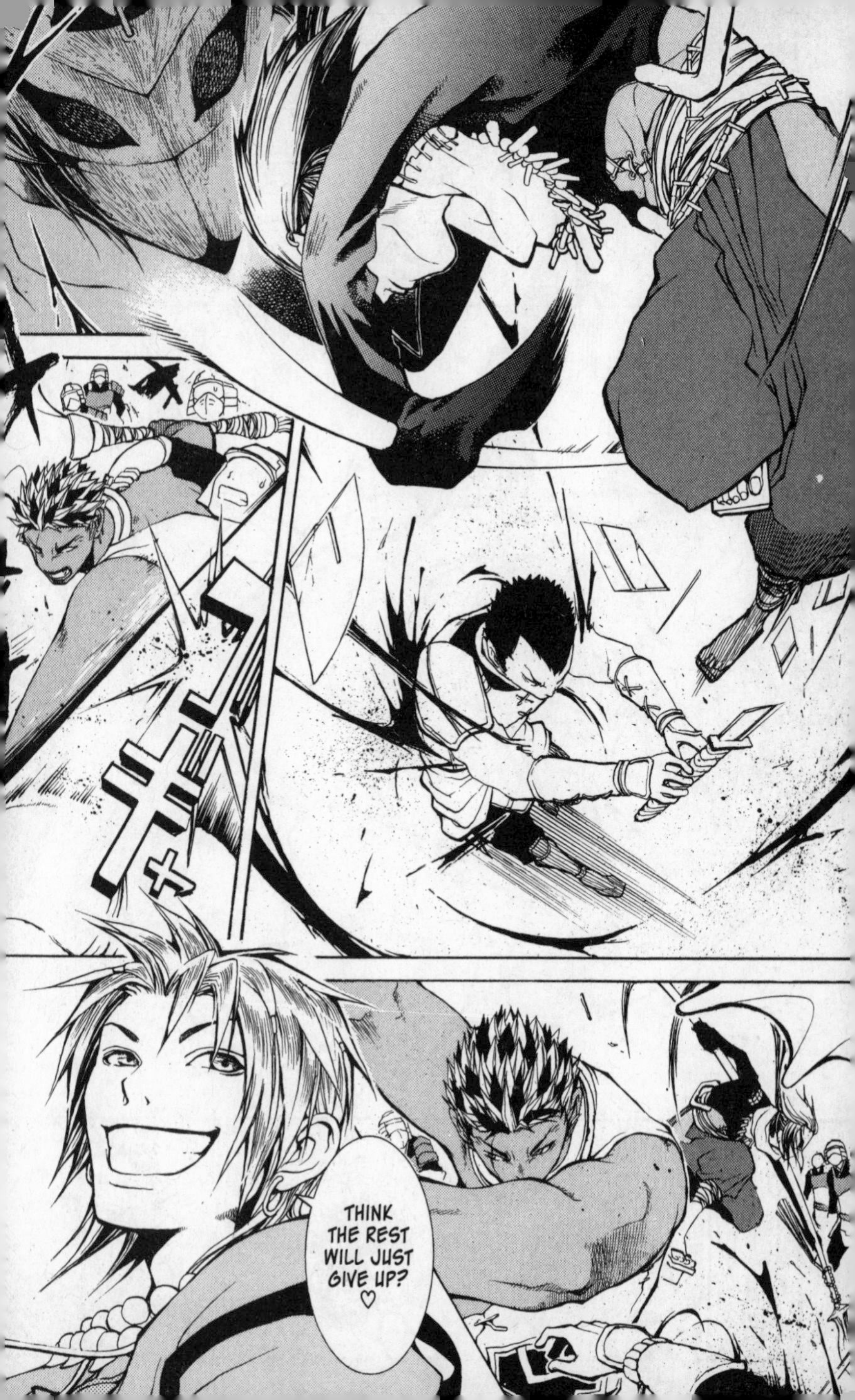
THINK THE REST WILL JUST GIVE UP? ♡

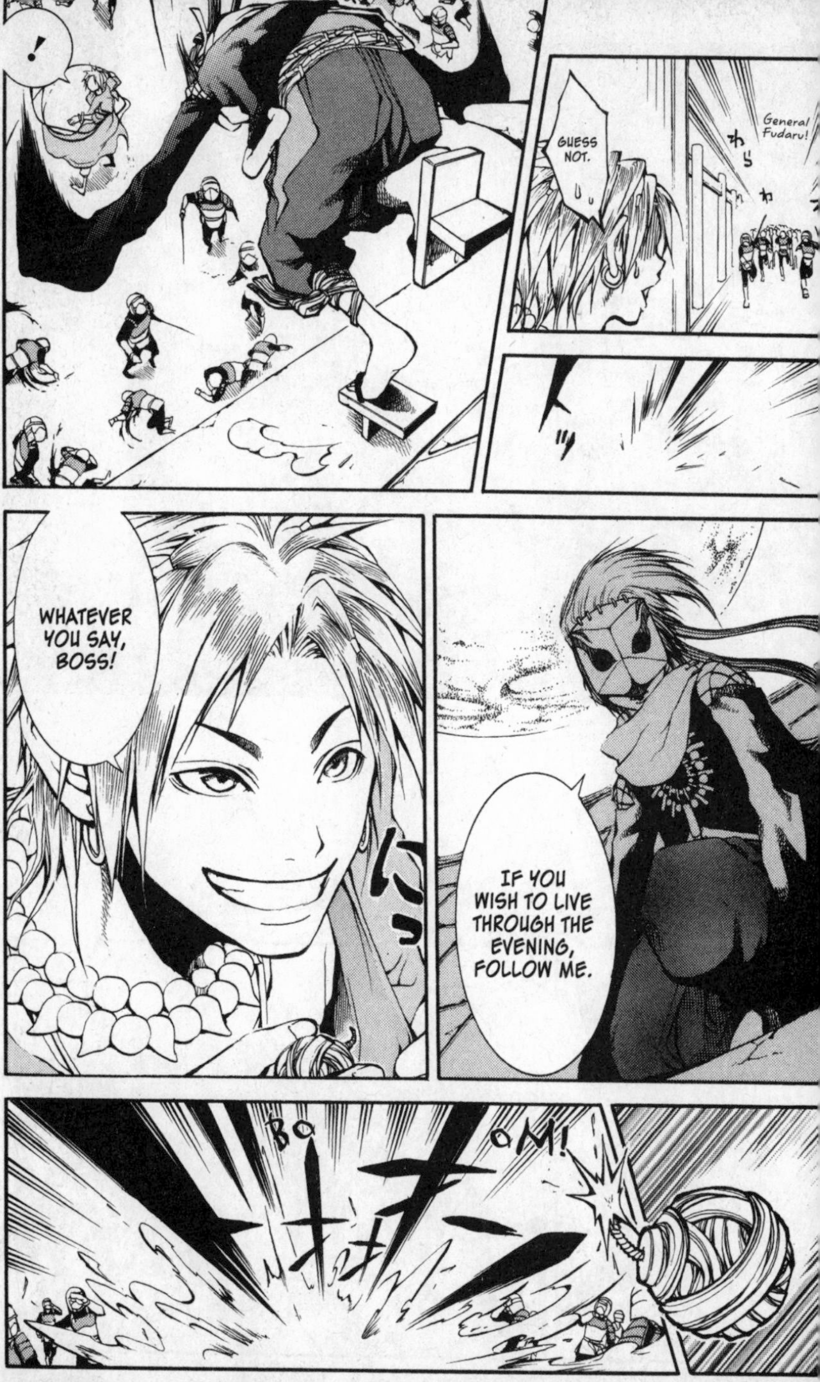
General Fudaru!
GUESS NOT.
!
IF YOU WISH TO LIVE THROUGH THE EVENING, FOLLOW ME.
WHATEVER YOU SAY, BOSS!
BOOM!

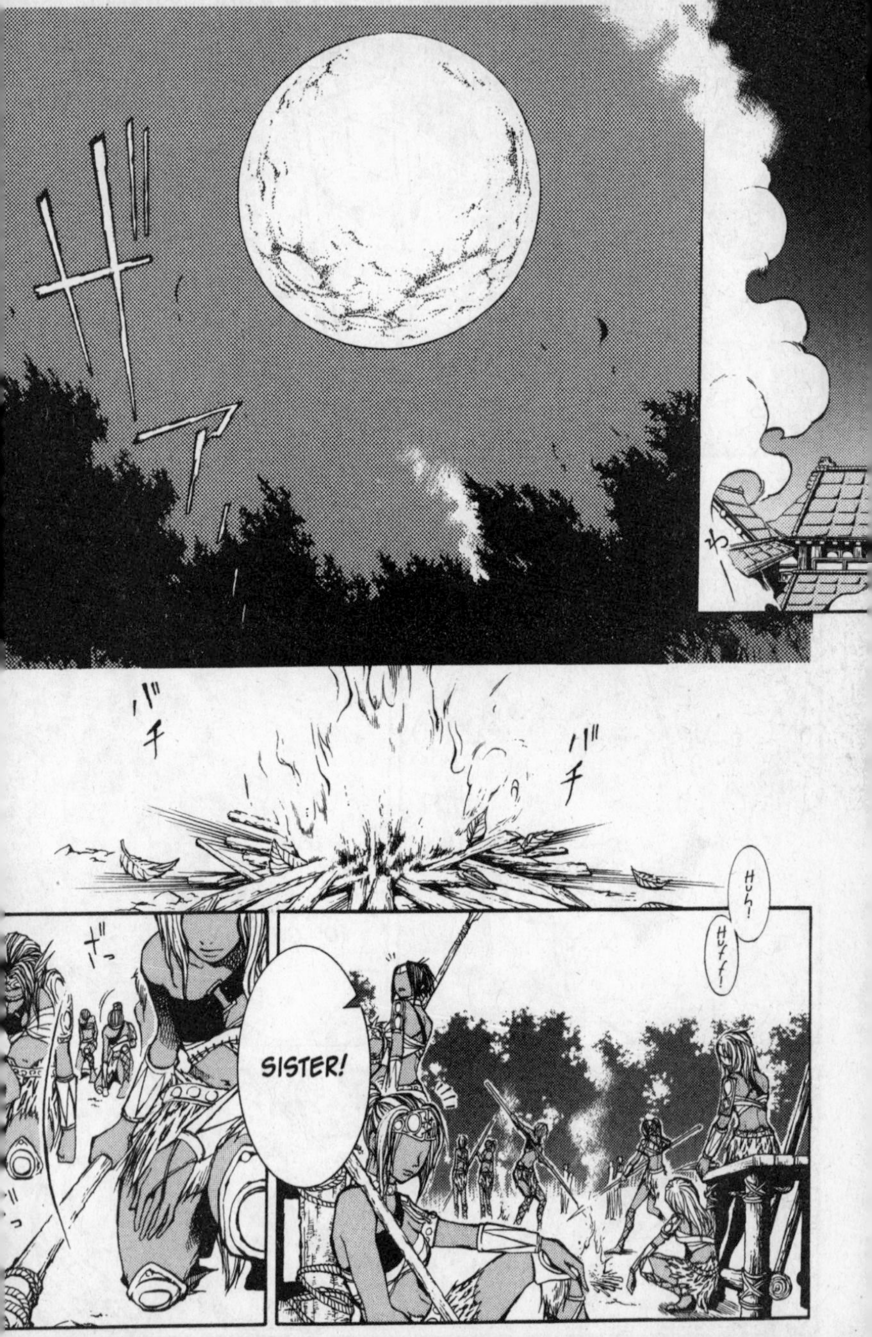
ザァ
バチ
バチ
Huh! Huff!
SISTER!
ざっ

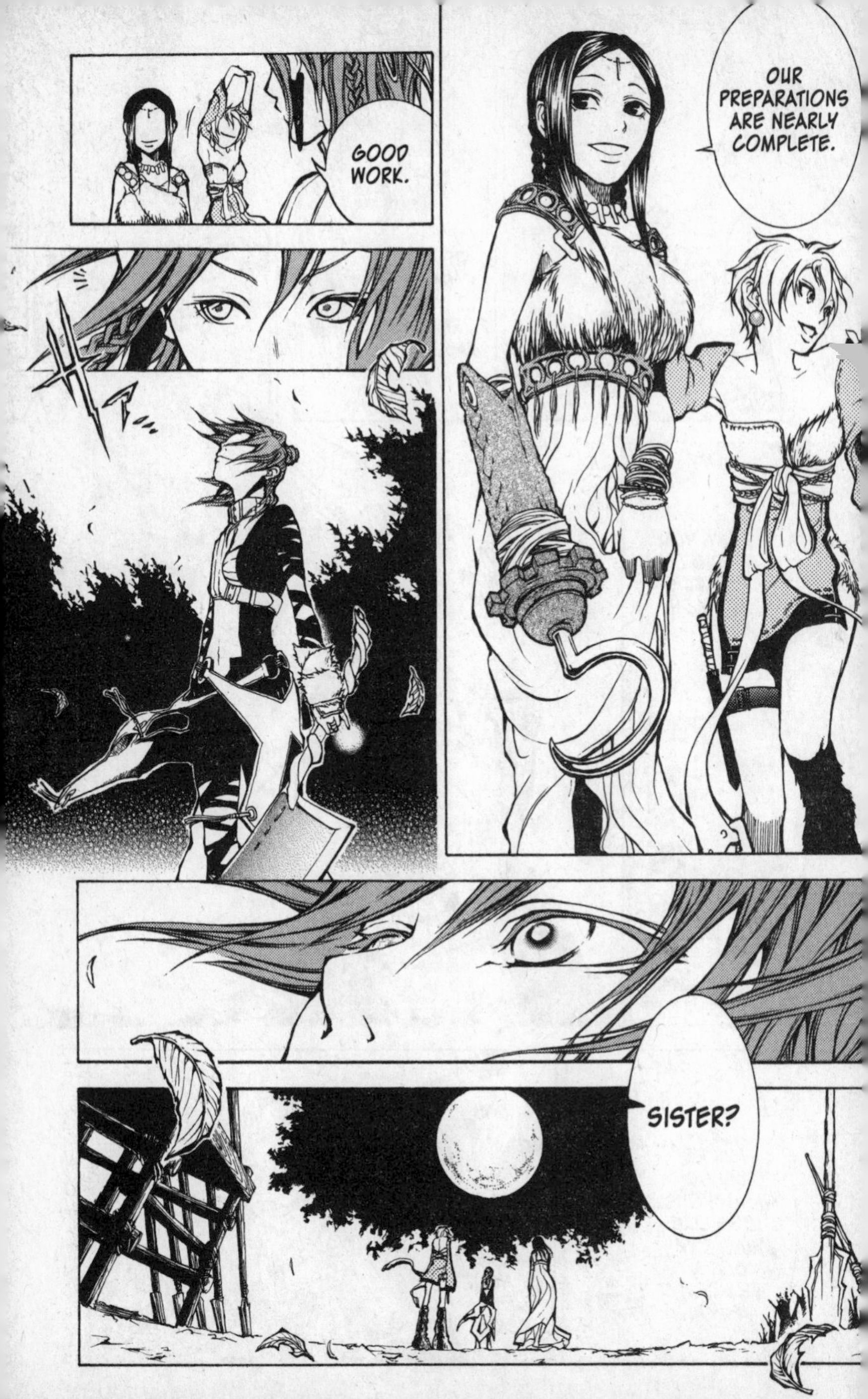
OUR PREPARATIONS ARE NEARLY COMPLETE.
GOOD WORK.
SISTER?

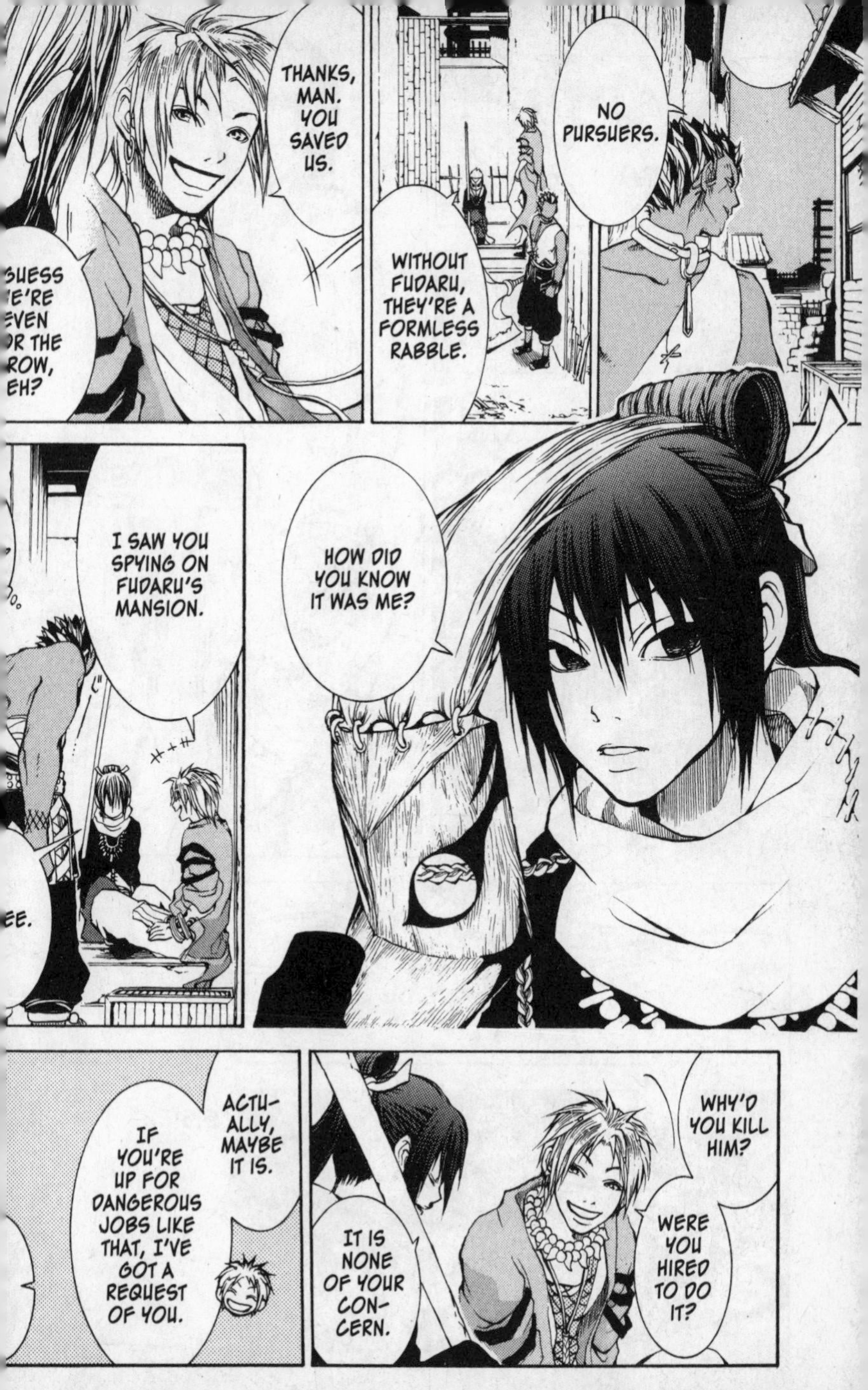
NO PURSUERS.
WITHOUT FUDARU, THEY'RE A FORMLESS RABBLE.
THANKS, MAN. YOU SAVED US.
GUESS 'E'RE EVEN OR THE ROW, EH?
HOW DID YOU KNOW IT WAS ME?
I SAW YOU SPYING ON FUDARU'S MANSION.
EE.
WHY'D YOU KILL HIM?
WERE YOU HIRED TO DO IT?
IT IS NONE OF YOUR CON-CERN.
ACTU-ALLY, MAYBE IT IS.
IF YOU'RE UP FOR DANGEROUS JOBS LIKE THAT, I'VE GOT A REQUEST OF YOU.

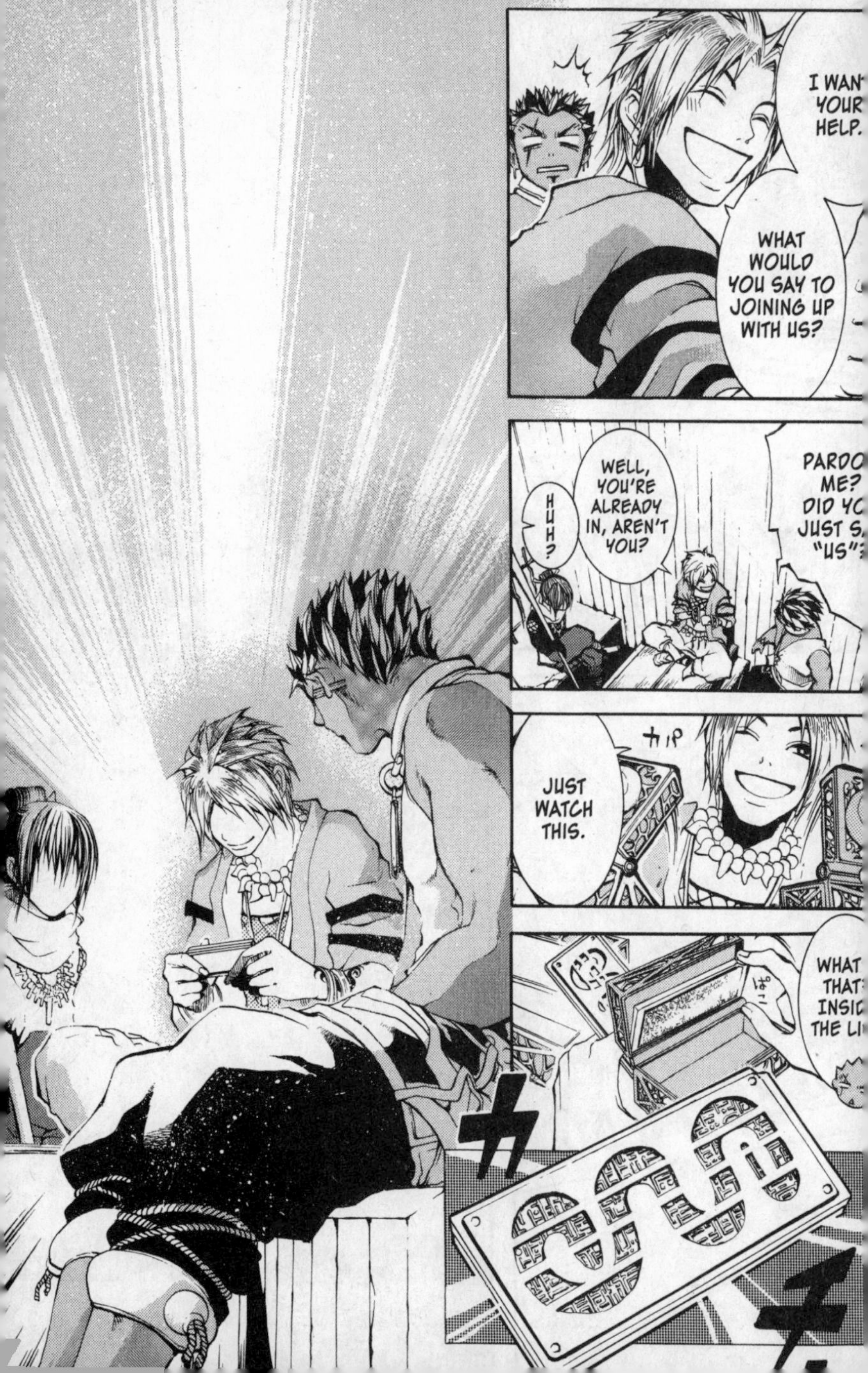
I WAN
YOUR
HELP.
WHAT WOULD YOU SAY TO JOINING UP WITH US?
PARDO
ME?
DID YO
JUST S
"US"
WELL, YOU'RE ALREADY IN, AREN'T YOU?
HUH?
カチ
JUST WATCH THIS.
WHAT
THAT
INSID
THE LI
カ
チ

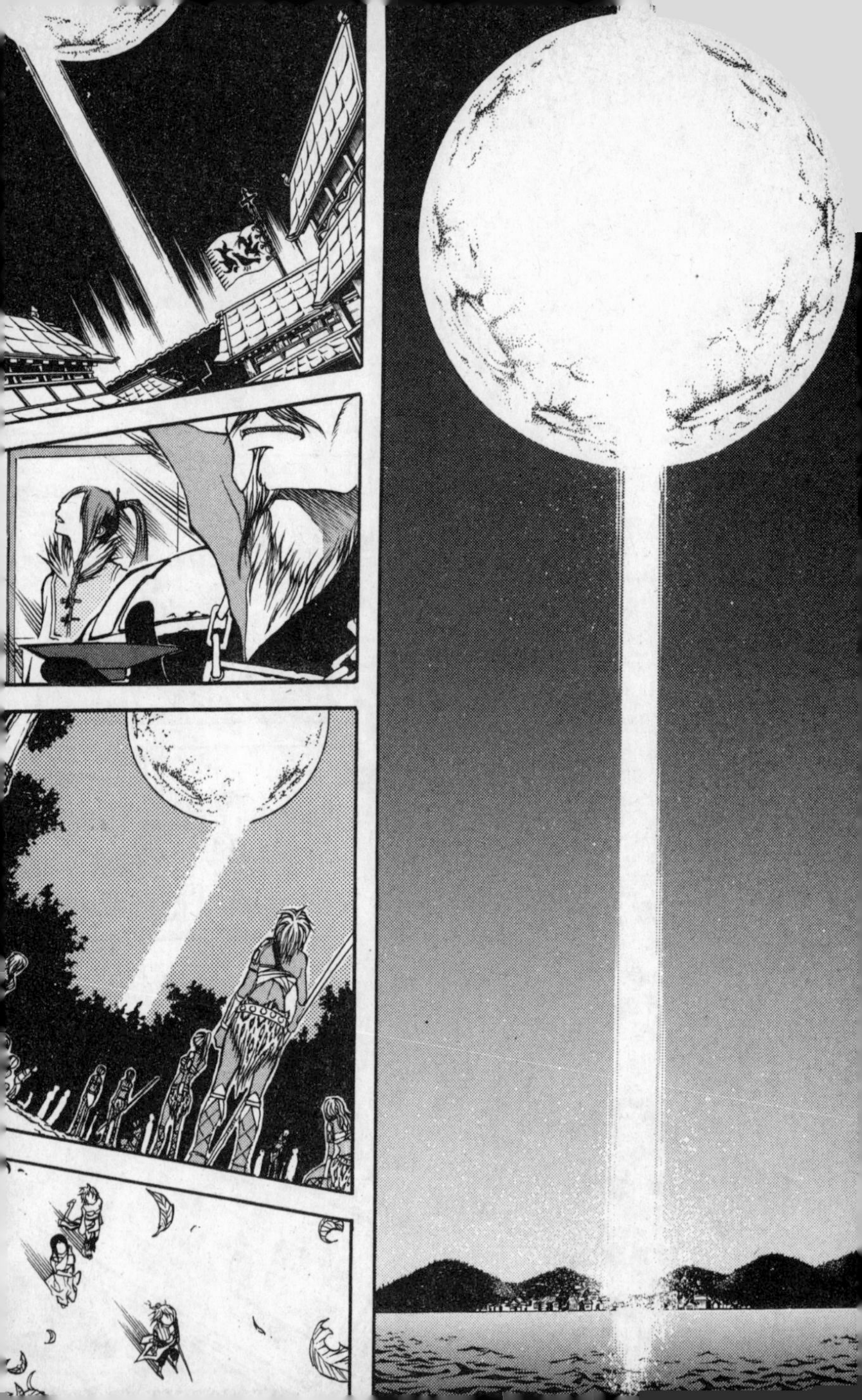

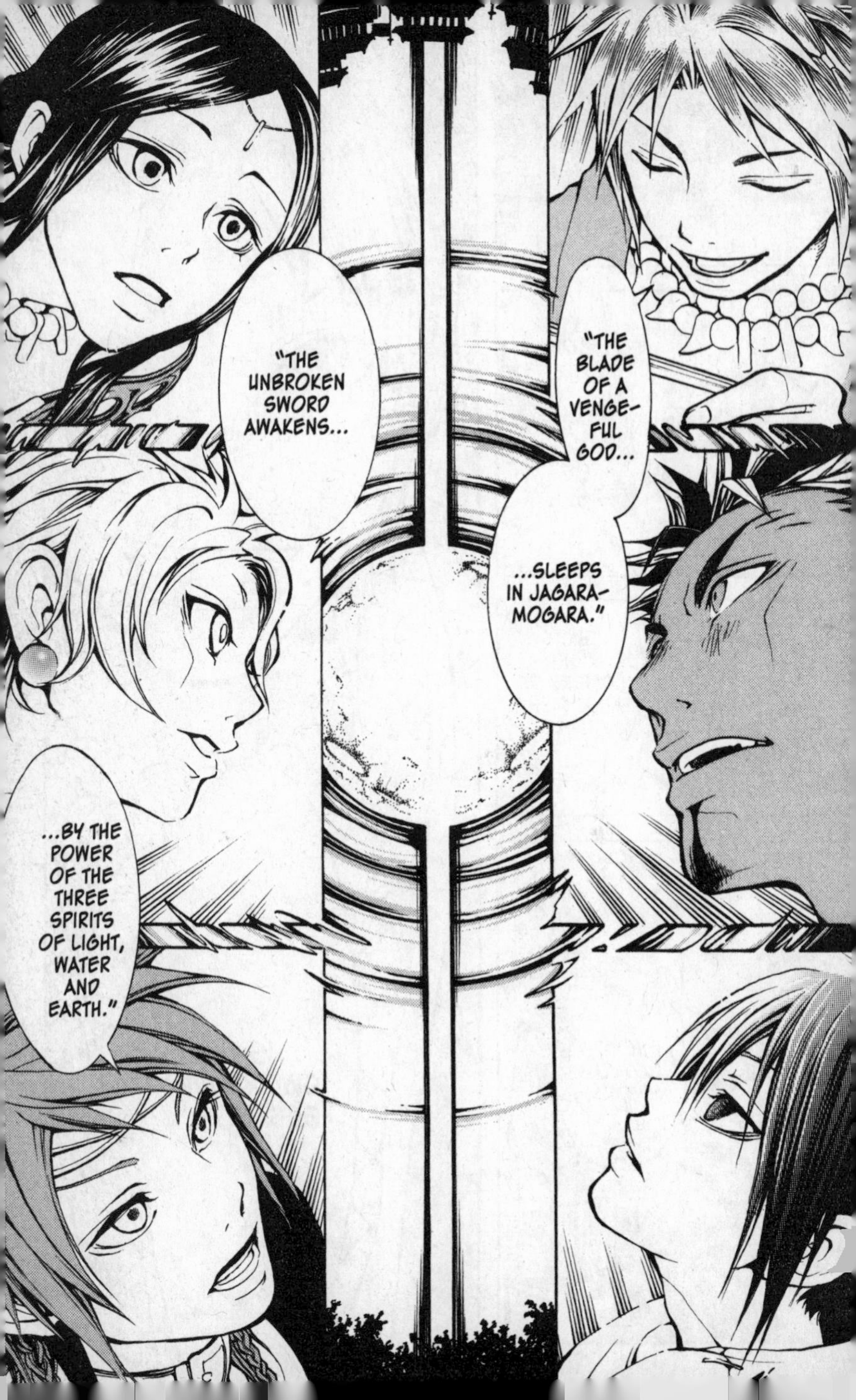
"THE BLADE OF A VENGE-FUL GOD...
...SLEEPS IN JAGARA-MOGARA."
"THE UNBROKEN SWORD AWAKENS...
...BY THE POWER OF THE THREE SPIRITS OF LIGHT, WATER AND EARTH."

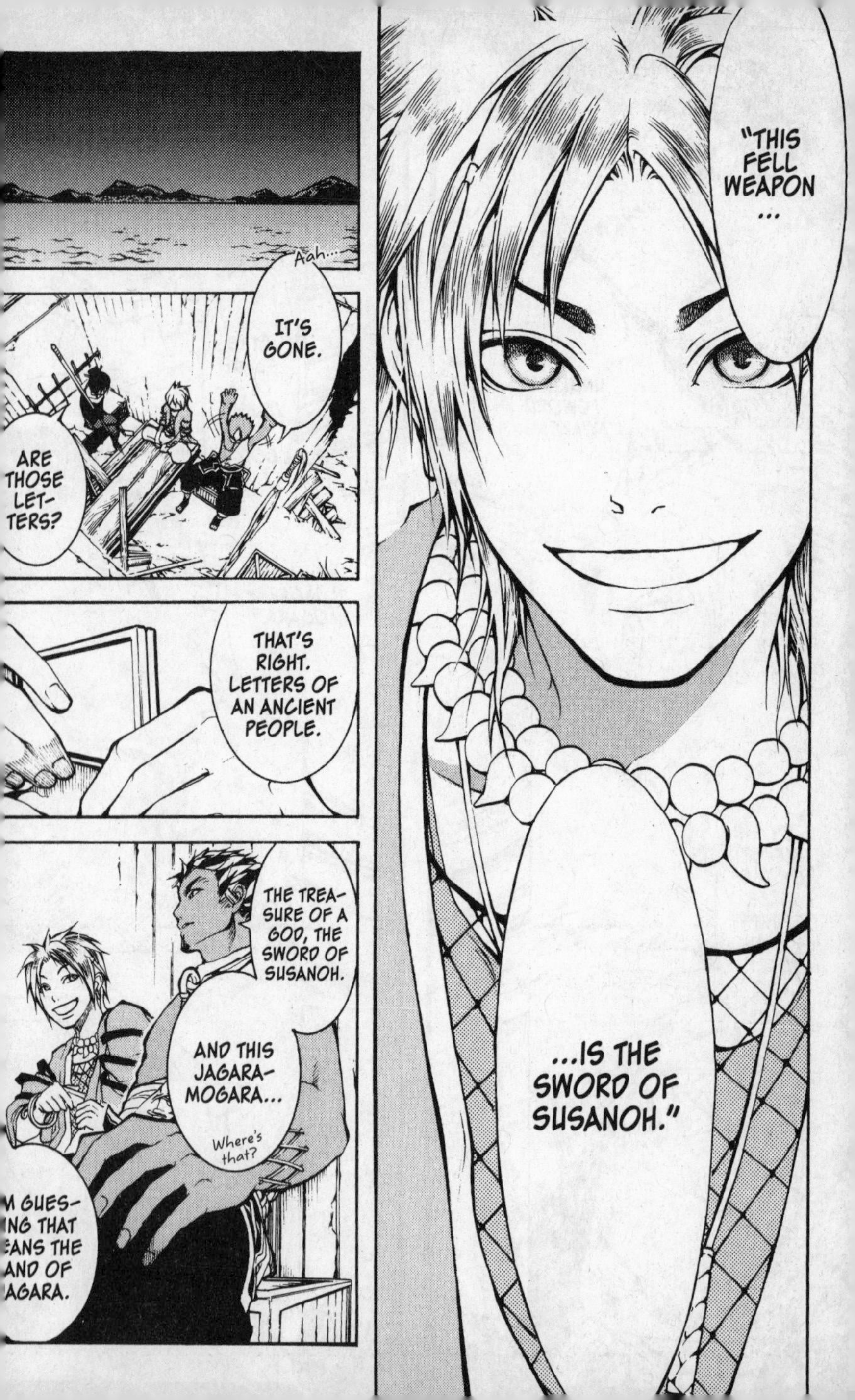
"THIS FELL WEAPON ...
...IS THE SWORD OF SUSANOH."
Aah...
IT'S GONE.
ARE THOSE LETTERS?
THAT'S RIGHT. LETTERS OF AN ANCIENT PEOPLE.
THE TREASURE OF A GOD, THE SWORD OF SUSANOH.
AND THIS JAGARAMOGARA...
Where's that?
M GUESSING THAT EANS THE AND OF AGARA.

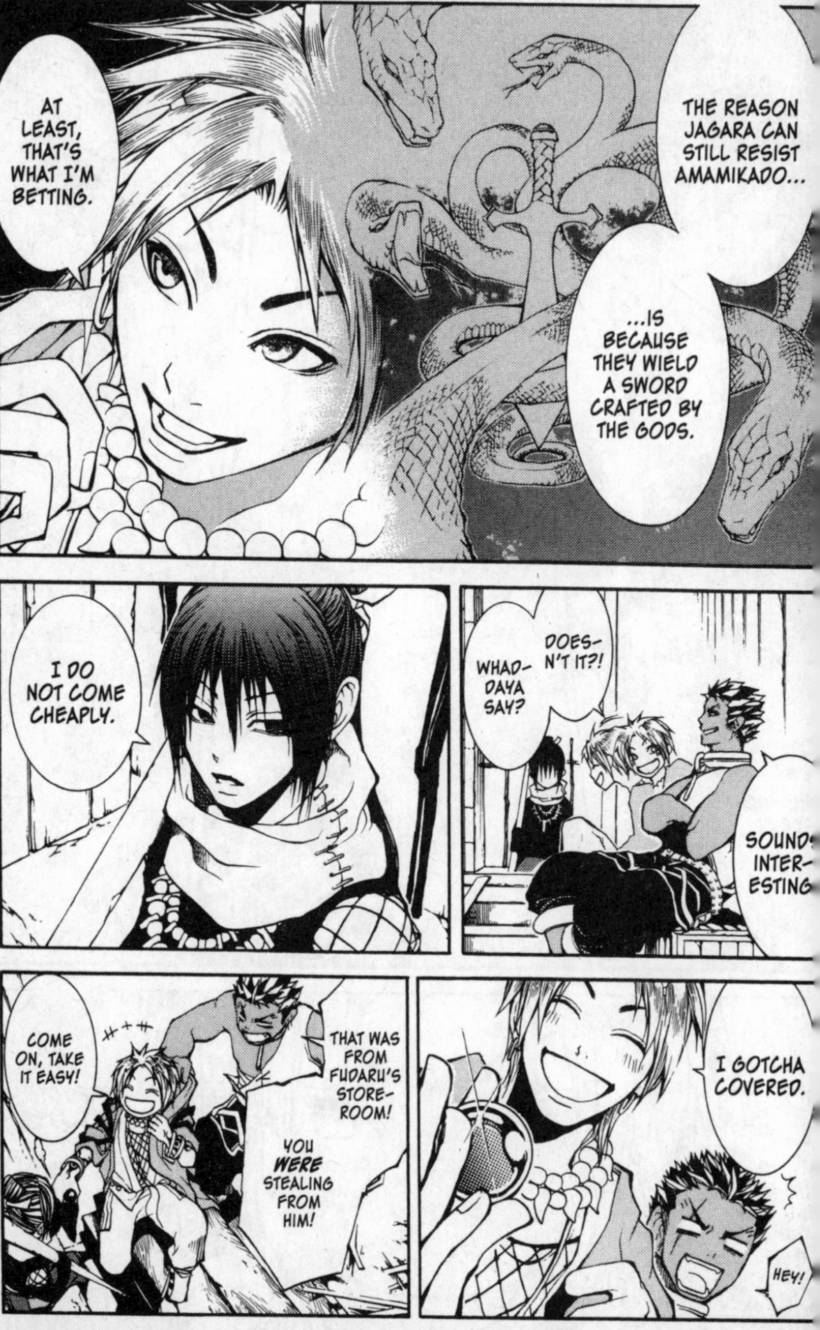
THE REASON JAGARA CAN STILL RESIST AMAMIKADO...
...IS BECAUSE THEY WIELD A SWORD CRAFTED BY THE GODS.
AT LEAST, THAT'S WHAT I'M BETTING.
SOUND INTER-ESTING
DOES-N'T IT?!
WHAD-DAYA SAY?
I DO NOT COME CHEAPLY.
I GOTCHA COVERED.
HEY!
THAT WAS FROM FUDARU'S STORE-ROOM!
YOU *WERE* STEALING FROM HIM!
COME ON, TAKE IT EASY!

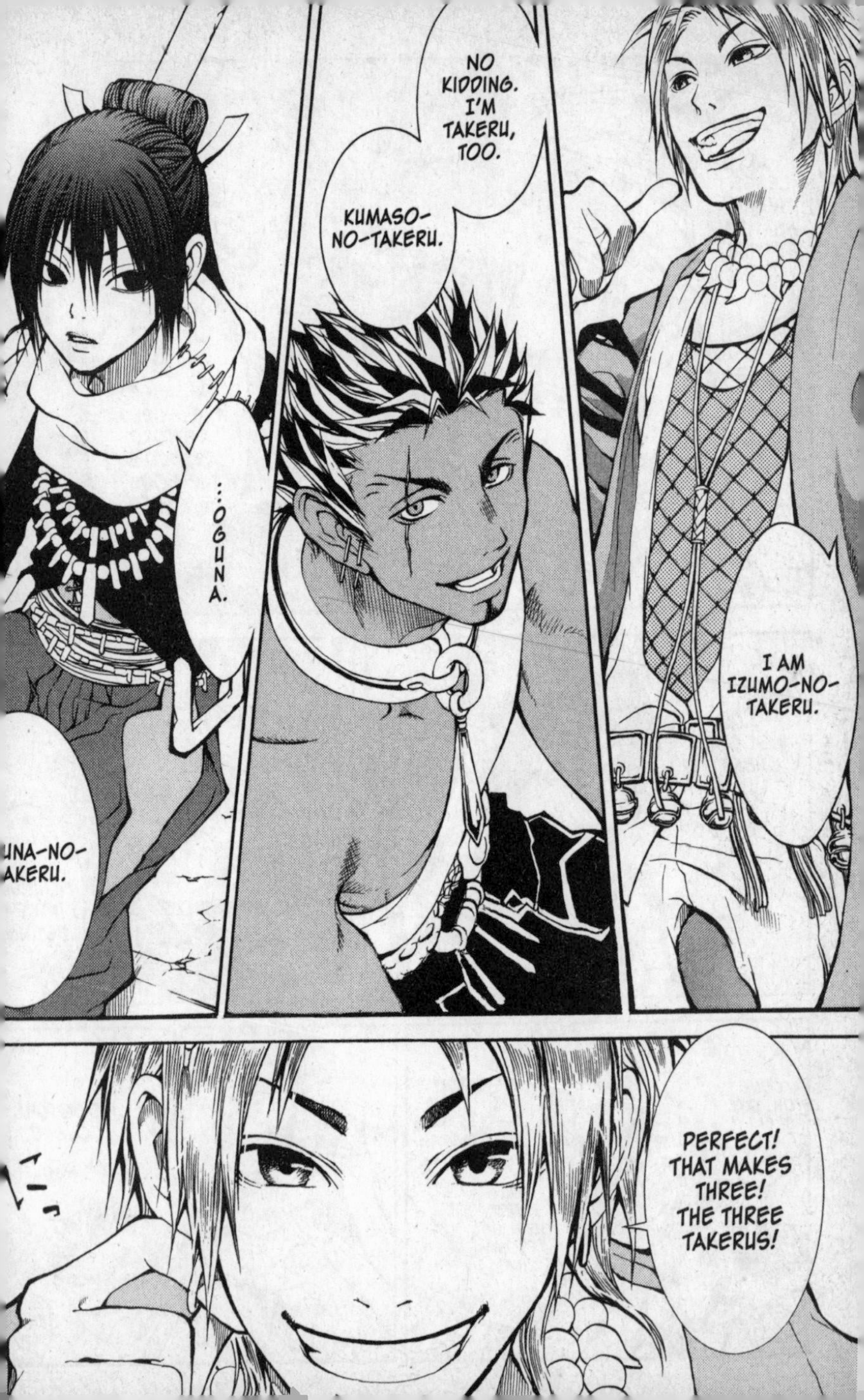
I AM IZUMO-NO-TAKERU.
NO KIDDING. I'M TAKERU, TOO.
KUMASO-NO-TAKERU.
...OGUNA.
UNA-NO-AKERU.
PERFECT! THAT MAKES THREE! THE THREE TAKERUS!

AND ON A DAY AS BLACK AS THE MINERAL THEY RALLIED BEHIND...

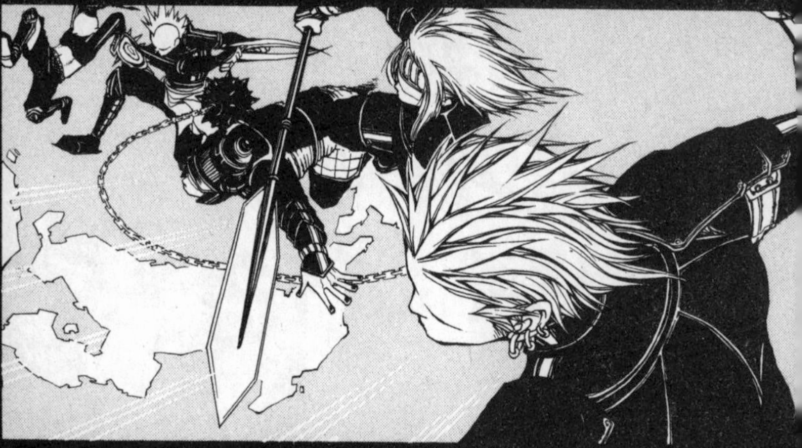

...THE PEOPLE OF IRON INVADED THE JUNGLE KINGDOM OF THE CROUCHING DRAGONS, SLICING THEIR WAY THROUGH TREE AND WARRIOR ALIKE. AND AS THE FORESTS AROUND THEM SMOLDERED...

...THE SWORD OF SUSANOH AWOKE.

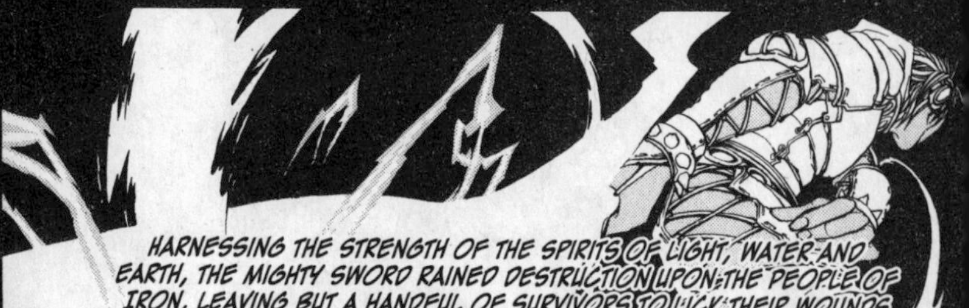
HARNESSING THE STRENGTH OF THE SPIRITS OF LIGHT, WATER AND EARTH, THE MIGHTY SWORD RAINED DESTRUCTION UPON THE PEOPLE OF IRON, LEAVING BUT A HANDFUL OF SURVIVORS TO LICK THEIR WOUNDS AND WHISPER TALES OF A WEAPON THAT KNOWS NO WEAKNESS.

THE CROUCHING DRAGONS BECAME GUARDIANS OF THE BLADE--AN ARTIFACT THEY BOTH EXALTED AND FEARED. THEY CALLED IT THE SWORD OF THE FOREST GOD.

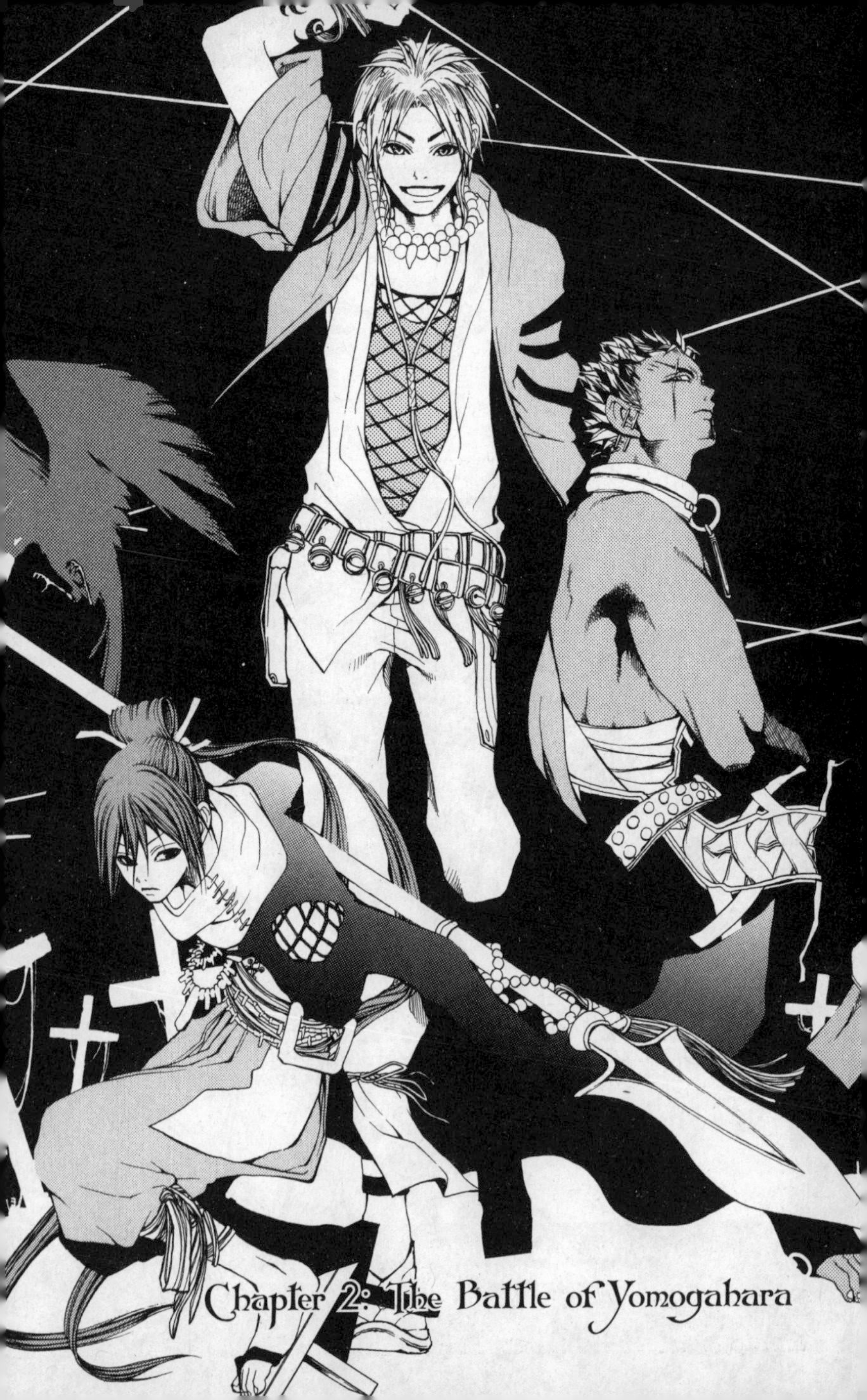

Chapter 2: The Battle of Yomogahara

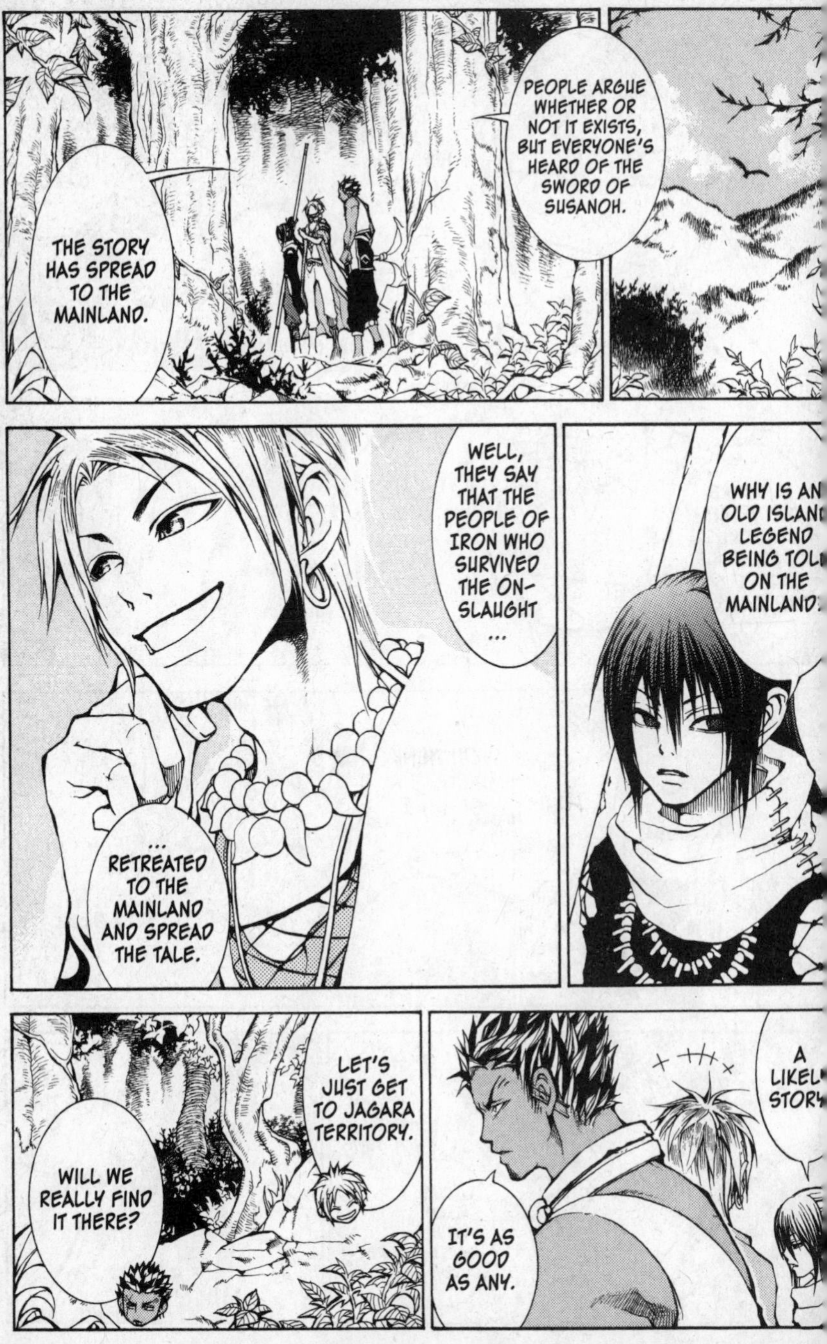
PEOPLE ARGUE WHETHER OR NOT IT EXISTS, BUT EVERYONE'S HEARD OF THE SWORD OF SUSANOH.
THE STORY HAS SPREAD TO THE MAINLAND.
WHY IS AN OLD ISLAN LEGEND BEING TOL ON THE MAINLAND
WELL, THEY SAY THAT THE PEOPLE OF IRON WHO SURVIVED THE ON-SLAUGHT ...
... RETREATED TO THE MAINLAND AND SPREAD THE TALE.
A LIKEL STORY
IT'S AS GOOD AS ANY.
LET'S JUST GET TO JAGARA TERRITORY.
WILL WE REALLY FIND IT THERE?

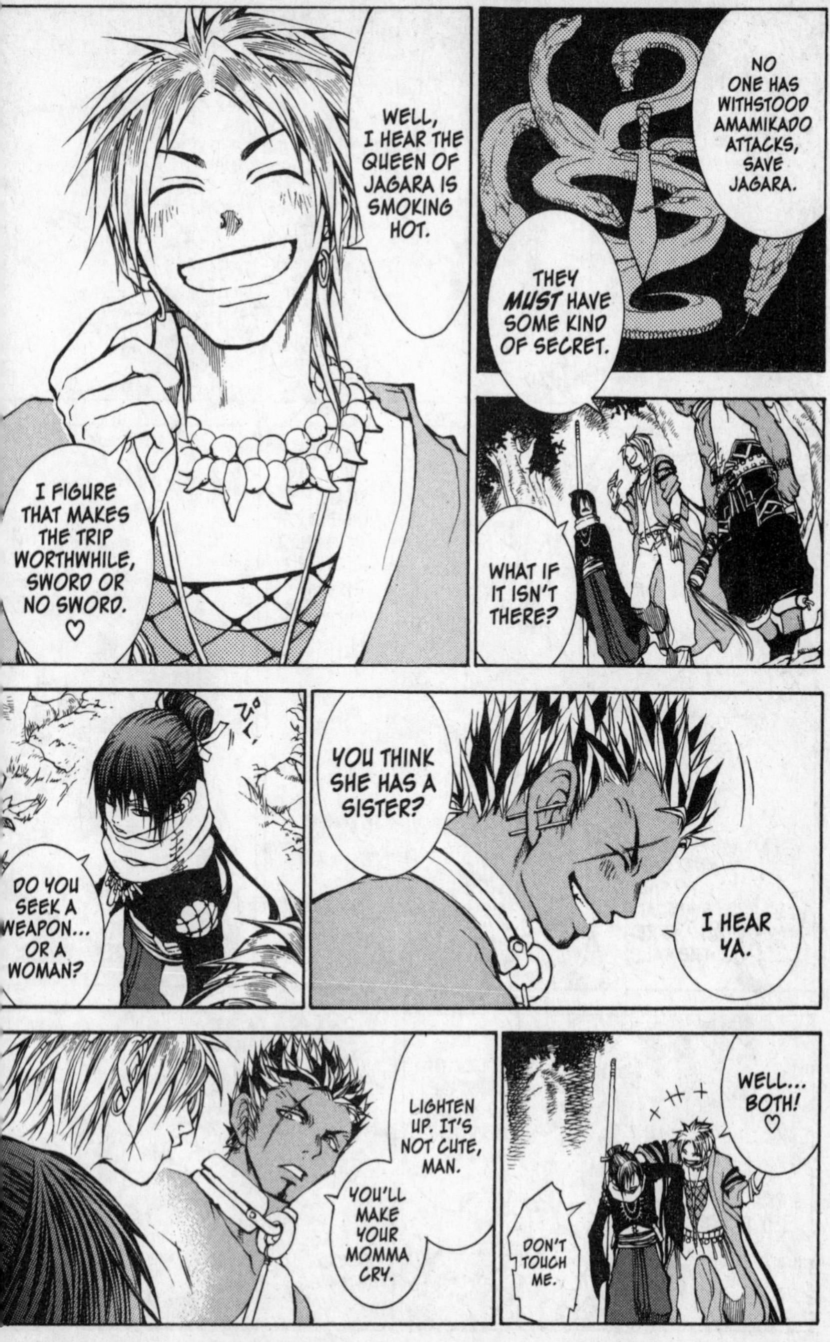
NO ONE HAS WITHSTOOD AMAMIKADO ATTACKS, SAVE JAGARA.
THEY *MUST* HAVE SOME KIND OF SECRET.
WHAT IF IT ISN'T THERE?
WELL, I HEAR THE QUEEN OF JAGARA IS SMOKING HOT.
I FIGURE THAT MAKES THE TRIP WORTHWHILE, SWORD OR NO SWORD. ♡
YOU THINK SHE HAS A SISTER?
I HEAR YA.
DO YOU SEEK A WEAPON... OR A WOMAN?
WELL... BOTH! ♡
DON'T TOUCH ME.
LIGHTEN UP. IT'S NOT CUTE, MAN.
YOU'LL MAKE YOUR MOMMA CRY.

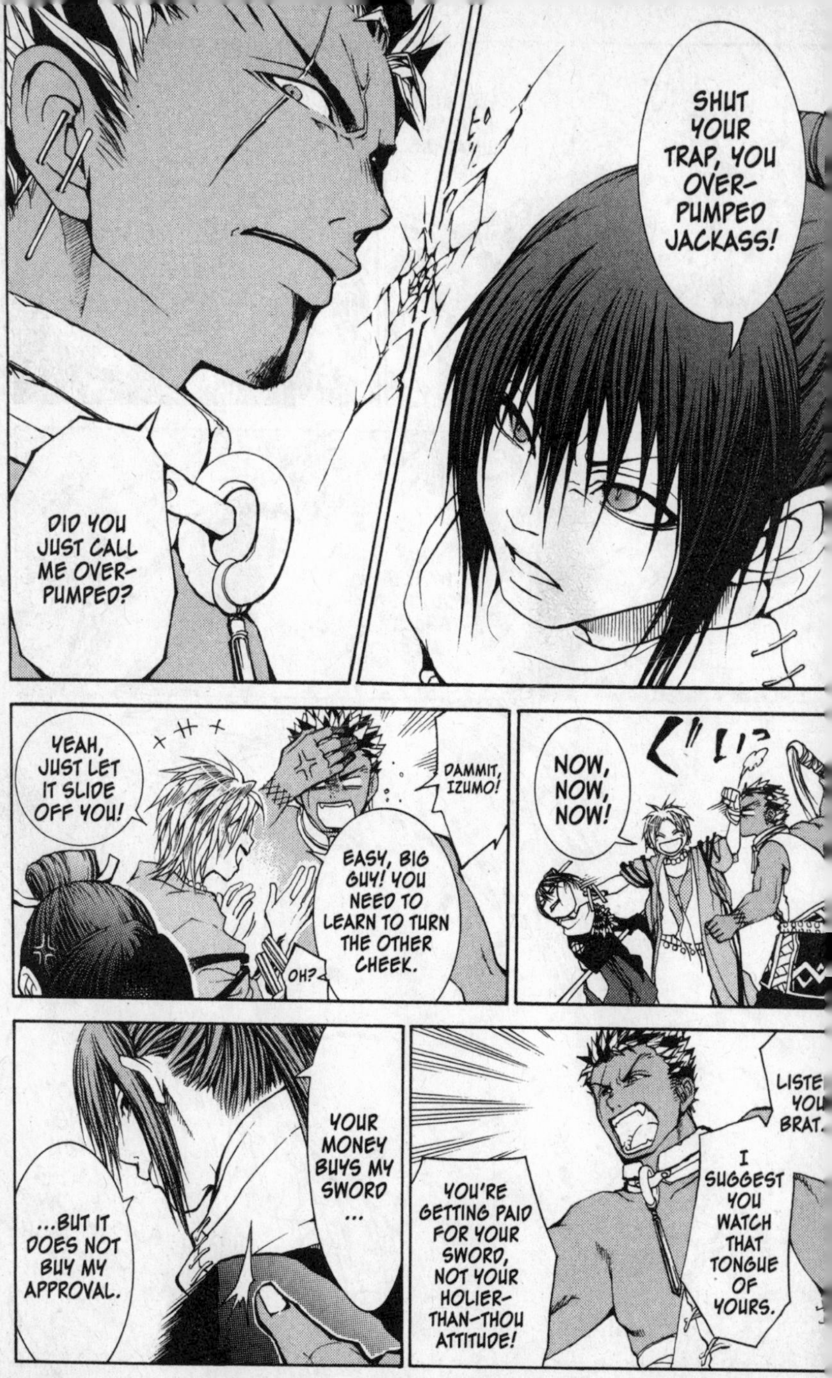
SHUT YOUR TRAP, YOU OVER-PUMPED JACKASS!
DID YOU JUST CALL ME OVER-PUMPED?
NOW, NOW, NOW!
DAMMIT, IZUMO!
YEAH, JUST LET IT SLIDE OFF YOU!
EASY, BIG GUY! YOU NEED TO LEARN TO TURN THE OTHER CHEEK.
OH?
LISTE YOU BRAT.
I SUGGEST YOU WATCH THAT TONGUE OF YOURS.
YOU'RE GETTING PAID FOR YOUR SWORD, NOT YOUR HOLIER-THAN-THOU ATTITUDE!
YOUR MONEY BUYS MY SWORD ...
...BUT IT DOES NOT BUY MY APPROVAL.

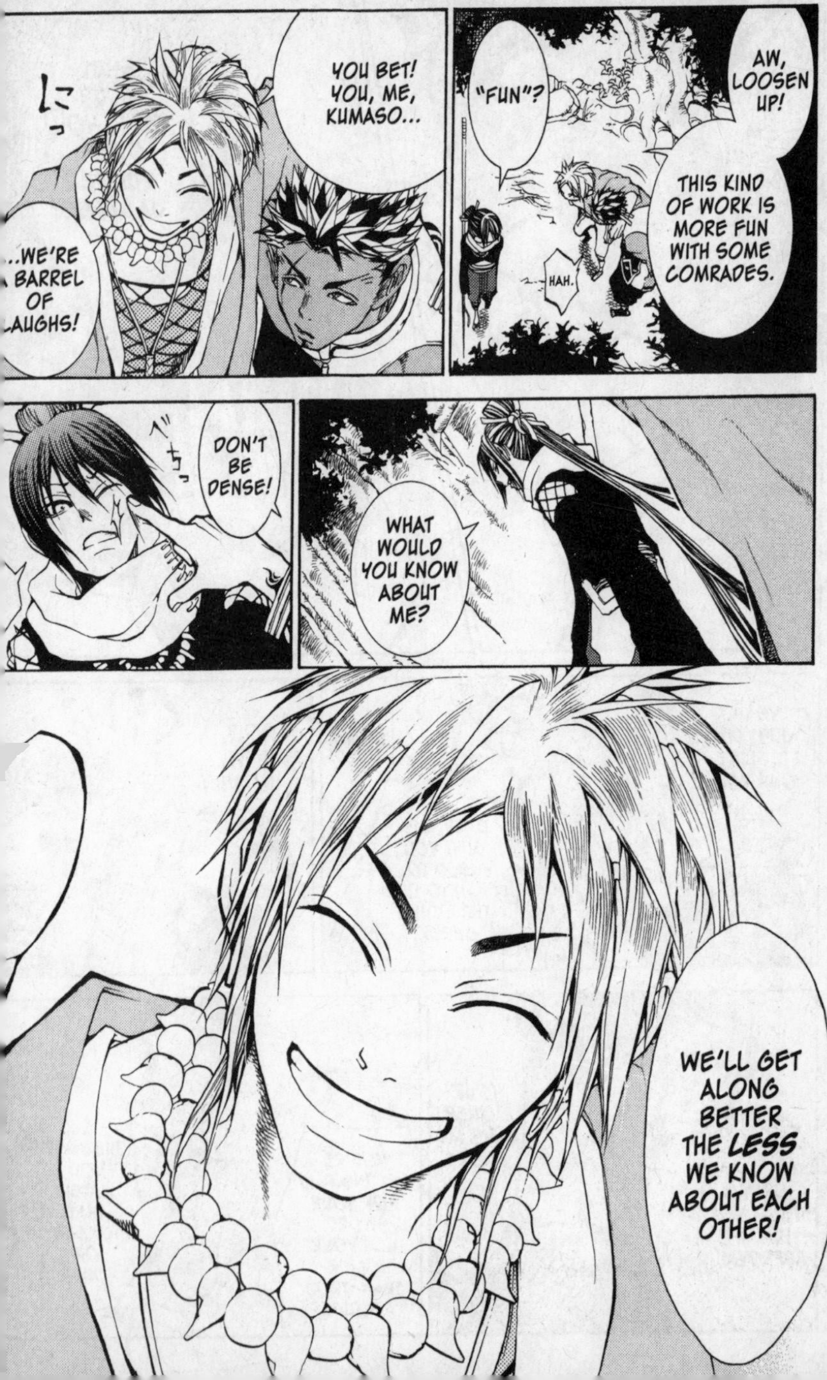
AW, LOOSEN UP!
THIS KIND OF WORK IS MORE FUN WITH SOME COMRADES.
HAH.
"FUN"?
にっ
YOU BET! YOU, ME, KUMASO...
..WE'RE BARREL OF AUGHS!
WHAT WOULD YOU KNOW ABOUT ME?
DON'T BE DENSE!
べちっ
WE'LL GET ALONG BETTER THE *LESS* WE KNOW ABOUT EACH OTHER!

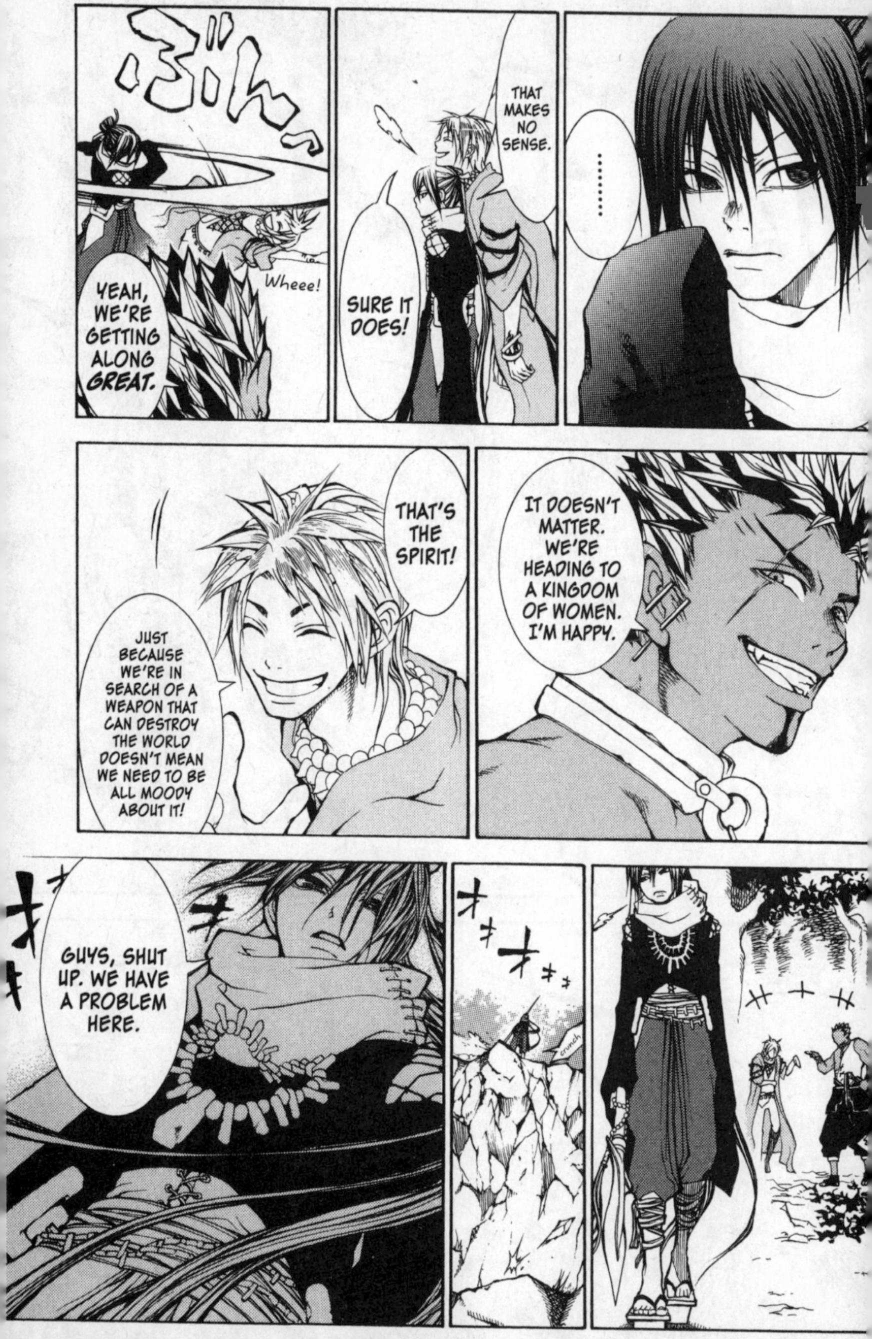
......
THAT MAKES NO SENSE.
SURE IT DOES!
ぶん
Wheee!
YEAH, WE'RE GETTING ALONG **GREAT.**
IT DOESN'T MATTER. WE'RE HEADING TO A KINGDOM OF WOMEN. I'M HAPPY.
THAT'S THE SPIRIT!
JUST BECAUSE WE'RE IN SEARCH OF A WEAPON THAT CAN DESTROY THE WORLD DOESN'T MEAN WE NEED TO BE ALL MOODY ABOUT IT!
crunch
GUYS, SHUT UP. WE HAVE A PROBLEM HERE.

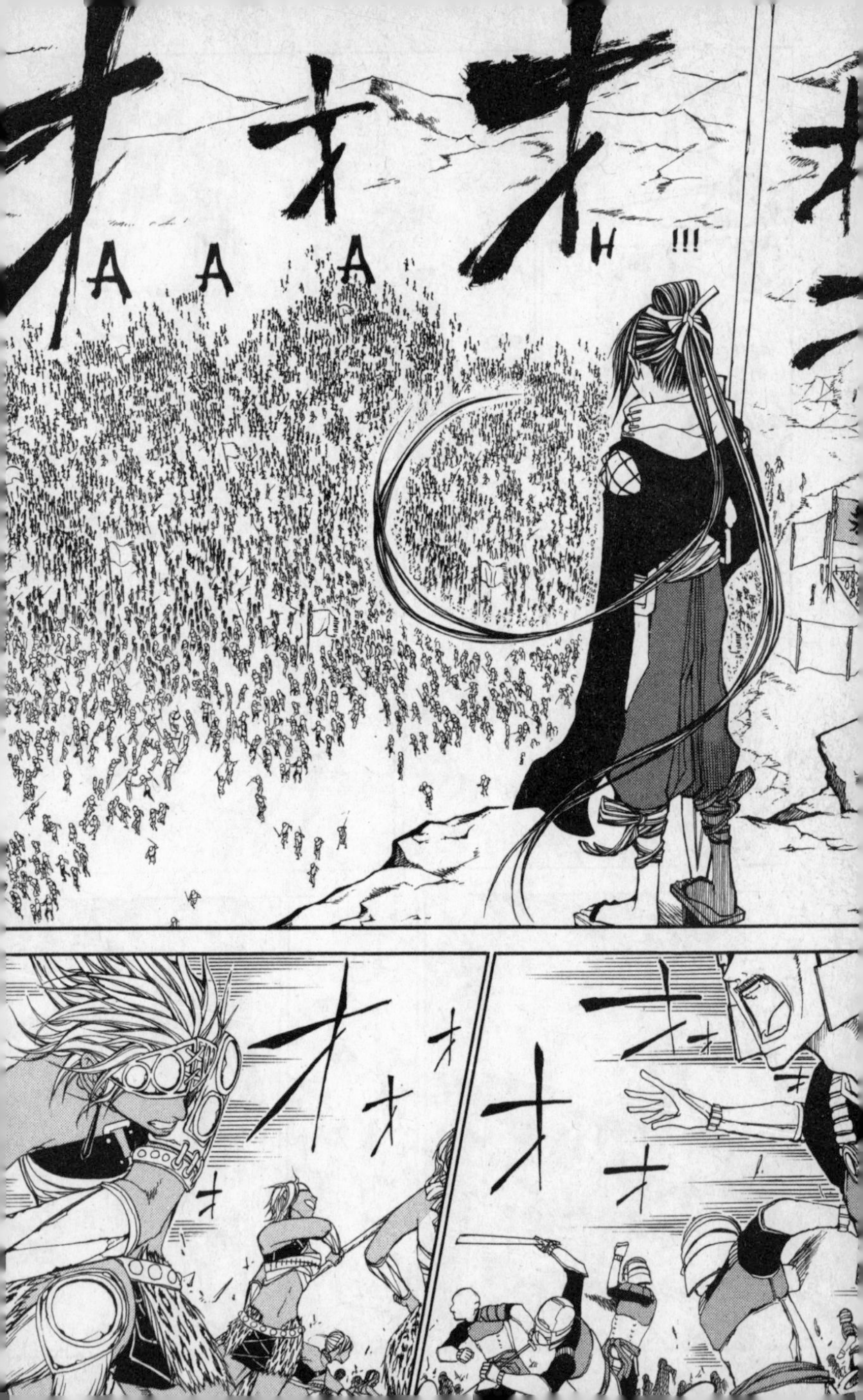

オオオオ
AAAH!!!
オオオオ
オオオオ

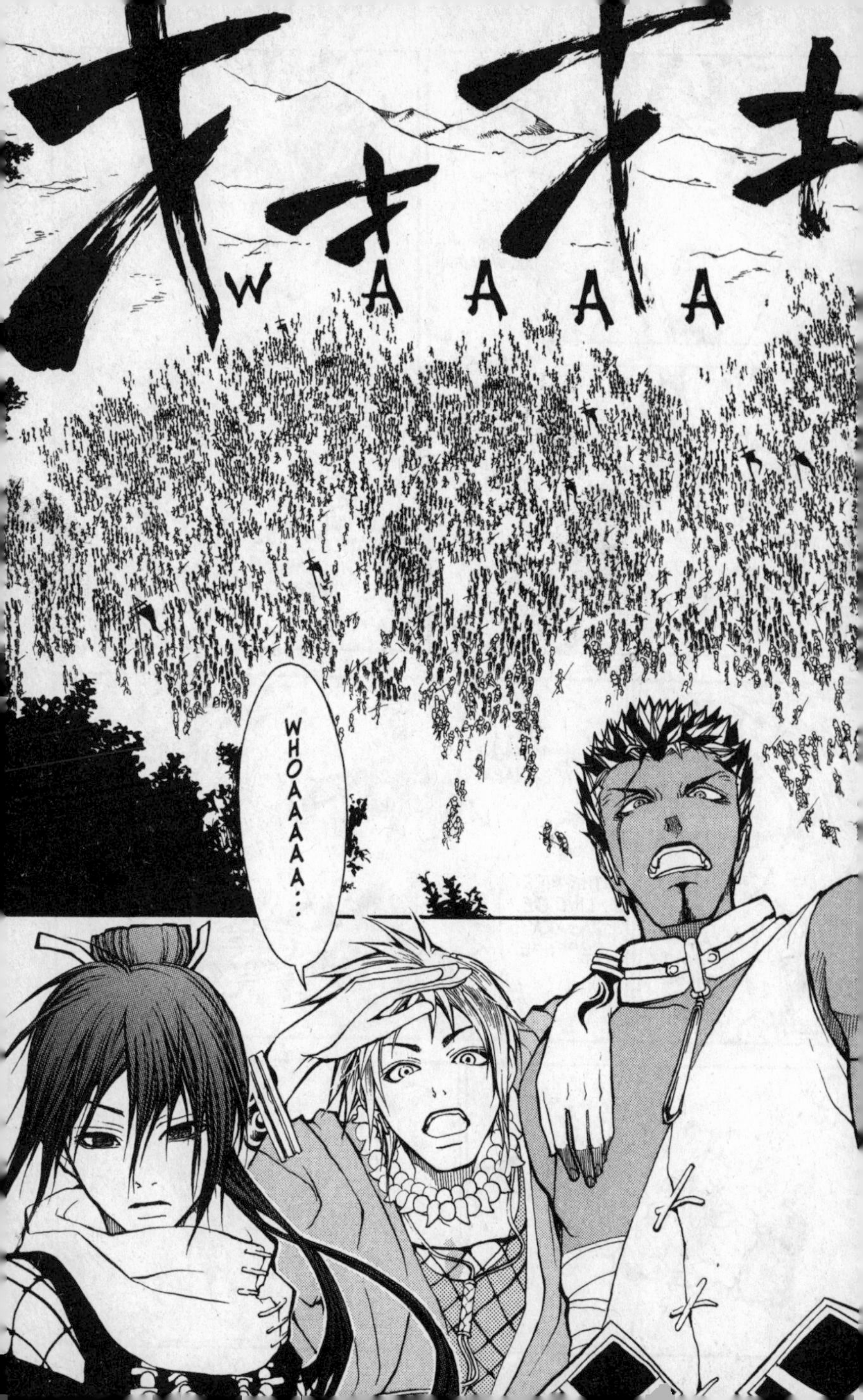
オォオォ
WAAAAA
WHOAAAAAA...

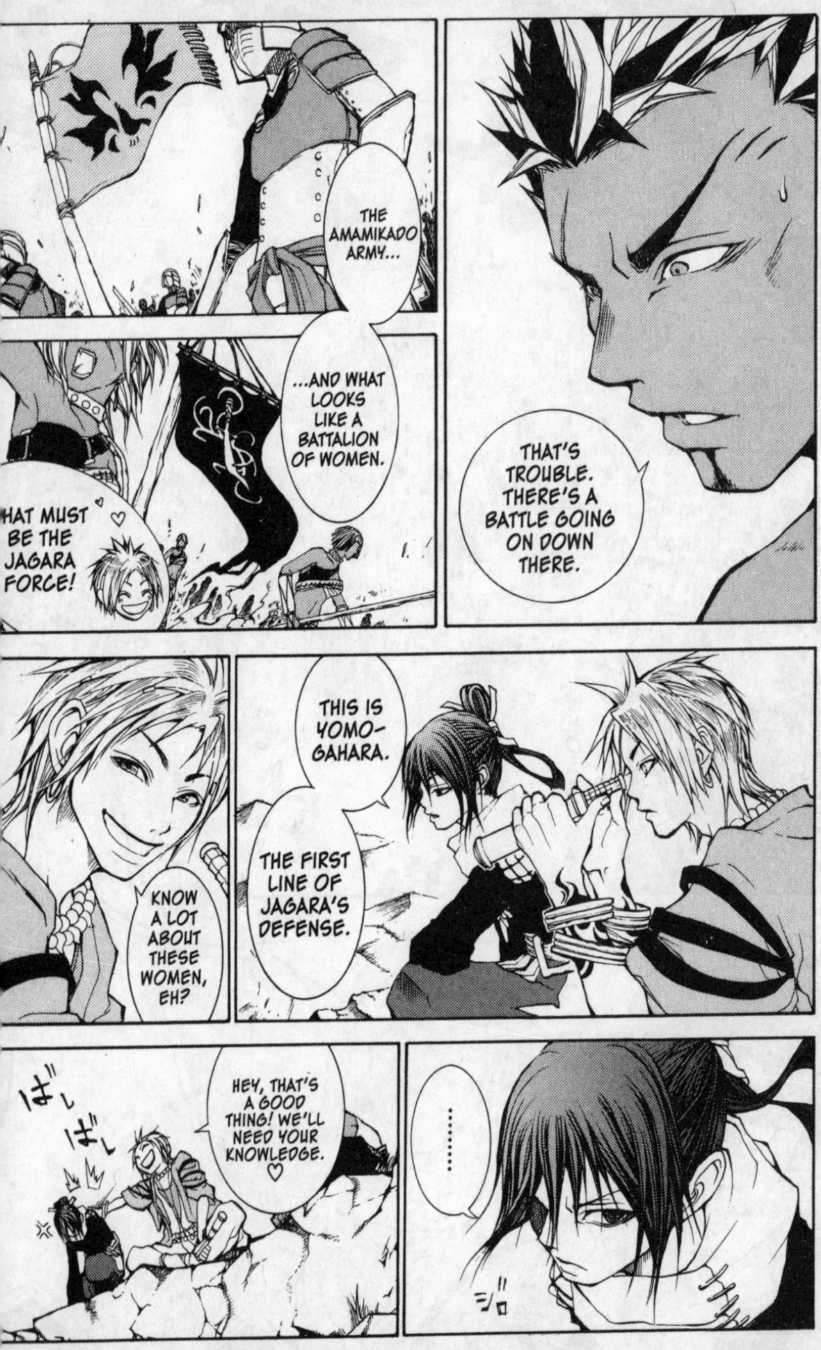
THAT'S TROUBLE. THERE'S A BATTLE GOING ON DOWN THERE.
THE AMAMIKADO ARMY...
...AND WHAT LOOKS LIKE A BATTALION OF WOMEN.
HAT MUST BE THE JAGARA FORCE! ♡
THIS IS YOMO-GAHARA.
THE FIRST LINE OF JAGARA'S DEFENSE.
KNOW A LOT ABOUT THESE WOMEN, EH?
......
ジロ
HEY, THAT'S A GOOD THING! WE'LL NEED YOUR KNOWLEDGE. ♡
ばし ばし

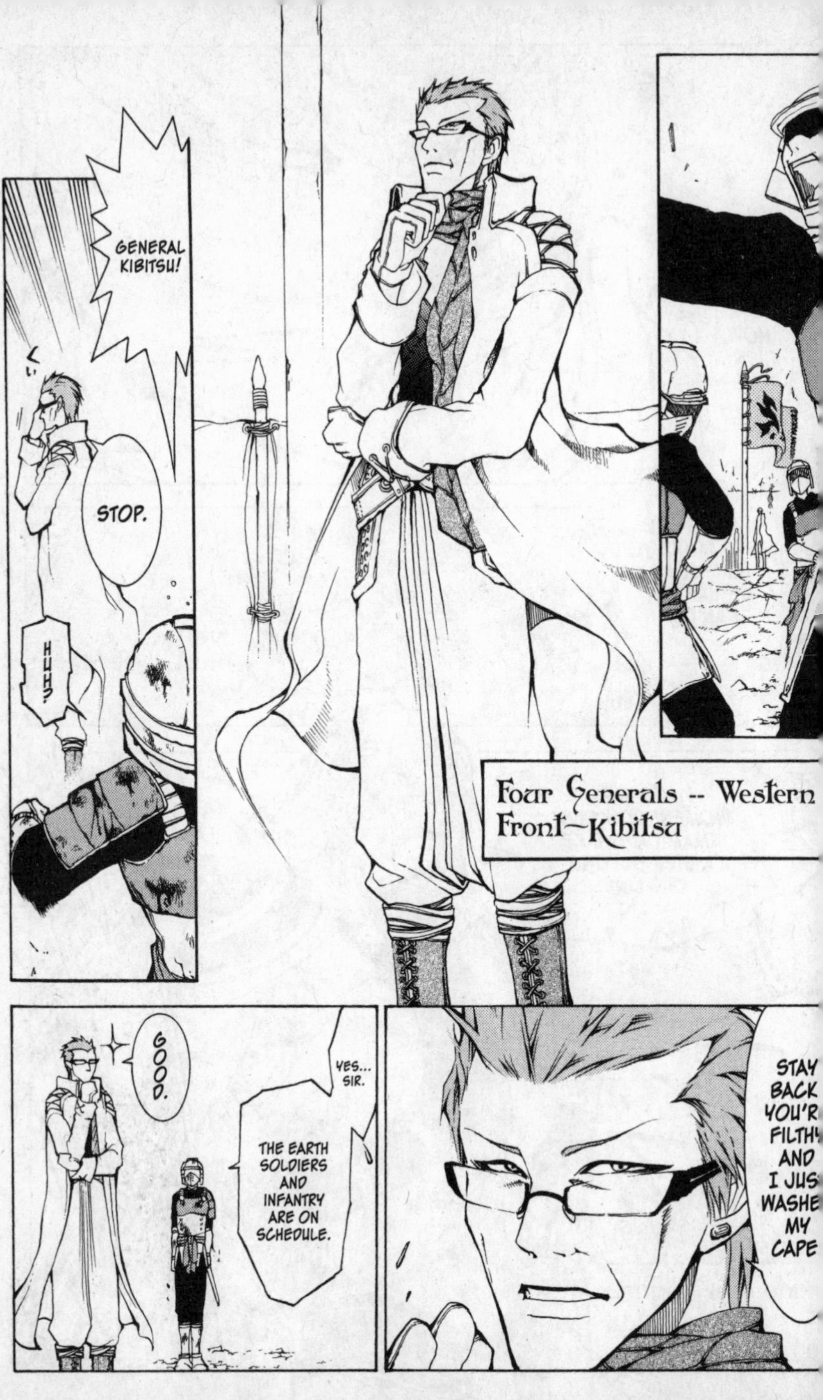
Four Generals -- Western Front~Kibitsu
GENERAL KIBITSU!
STOP.
HUH?
STAY BACK YOU'R FILTHY AND I JUS WASHE MY CAPE
YES... SIR.
THE EARTH SOLDIERS AND INFANTRY ARE ON SCHEDULE.
GOOD.

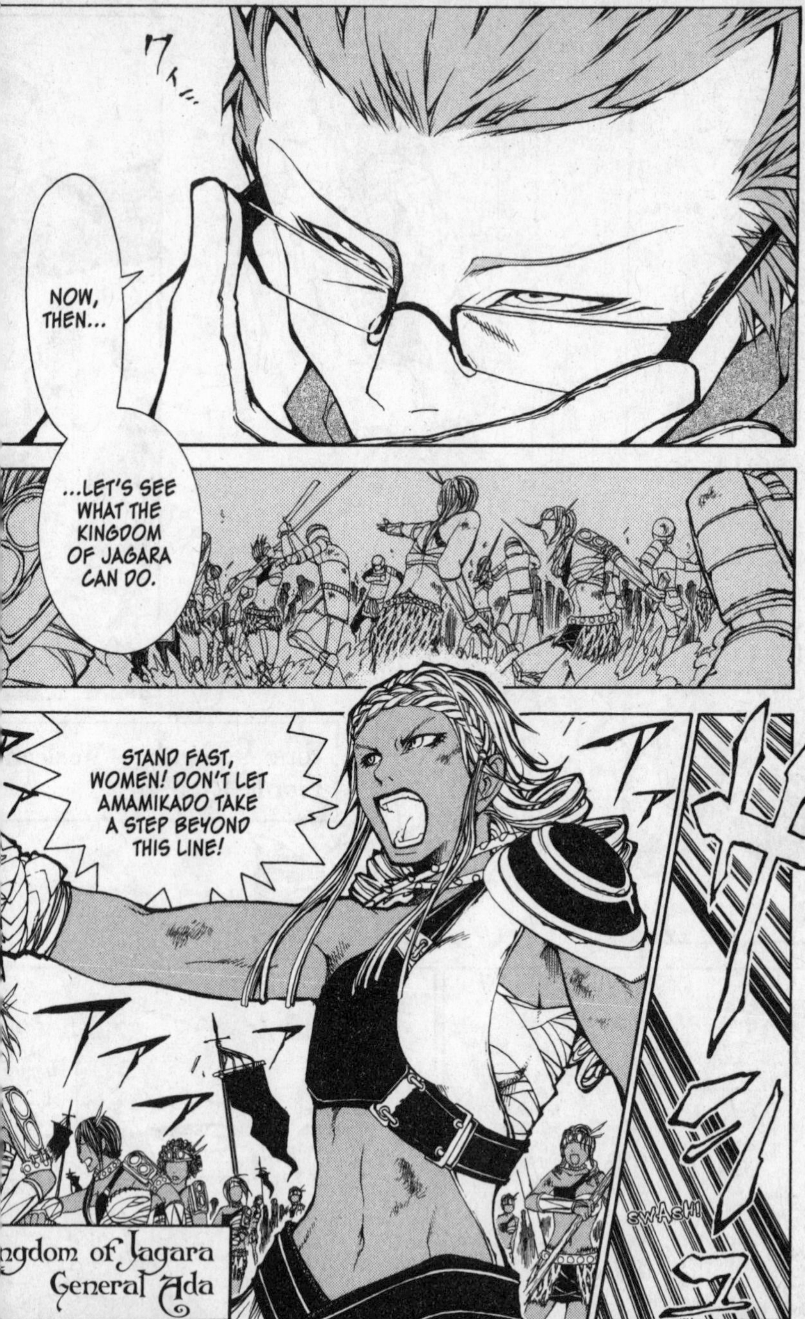
NOW, THEN...
...LET'S SEE WHAT THE KINGDOM OF JAGARA CAN DO.
STAND FAST, WOMEN! DON'T LET AMAMIKADO TAKE A STEP BEYOND THIS LINE!
SWASH!
ngdom of Jagara General Ada

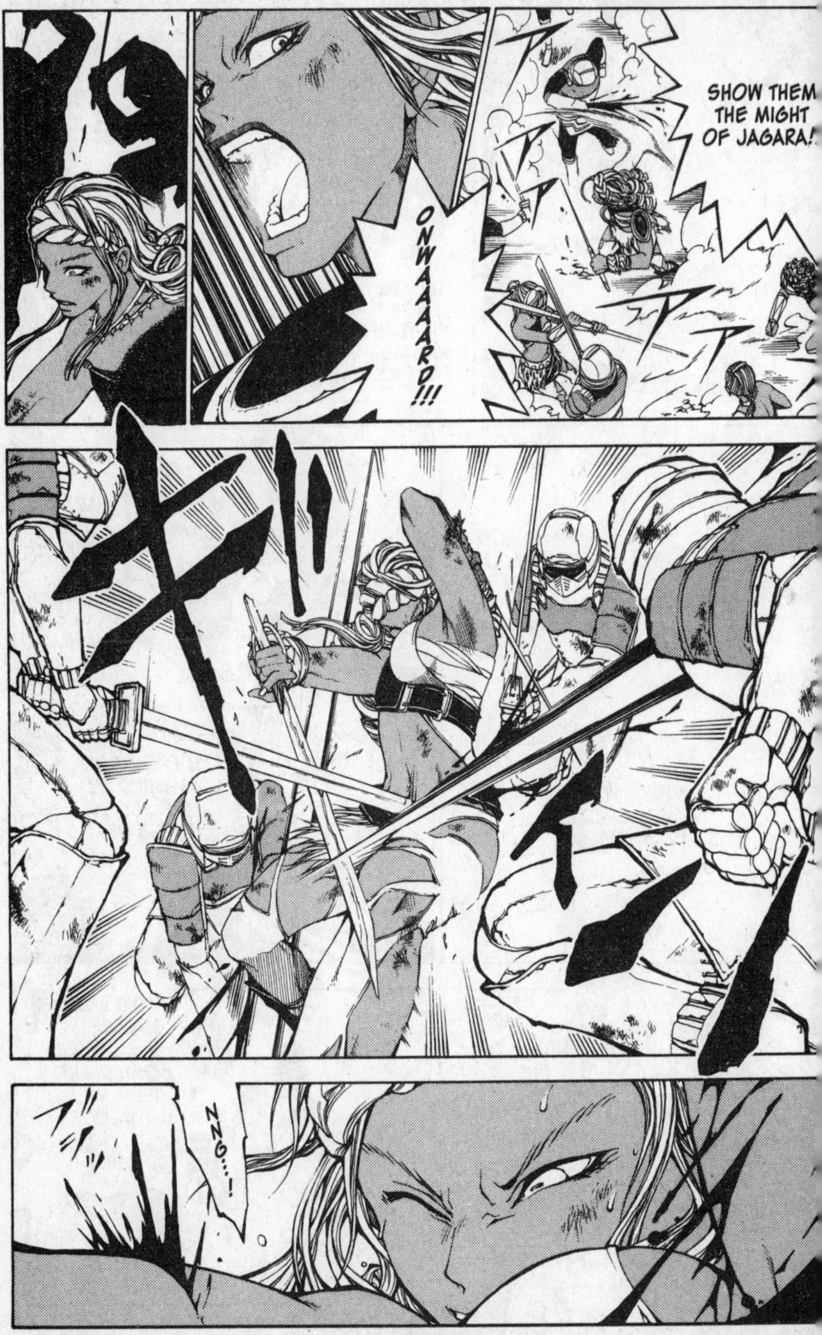
SHOW THEM THE MIGHT OF JAGARA!!
ONWAAAAARD!!!
NNG...!

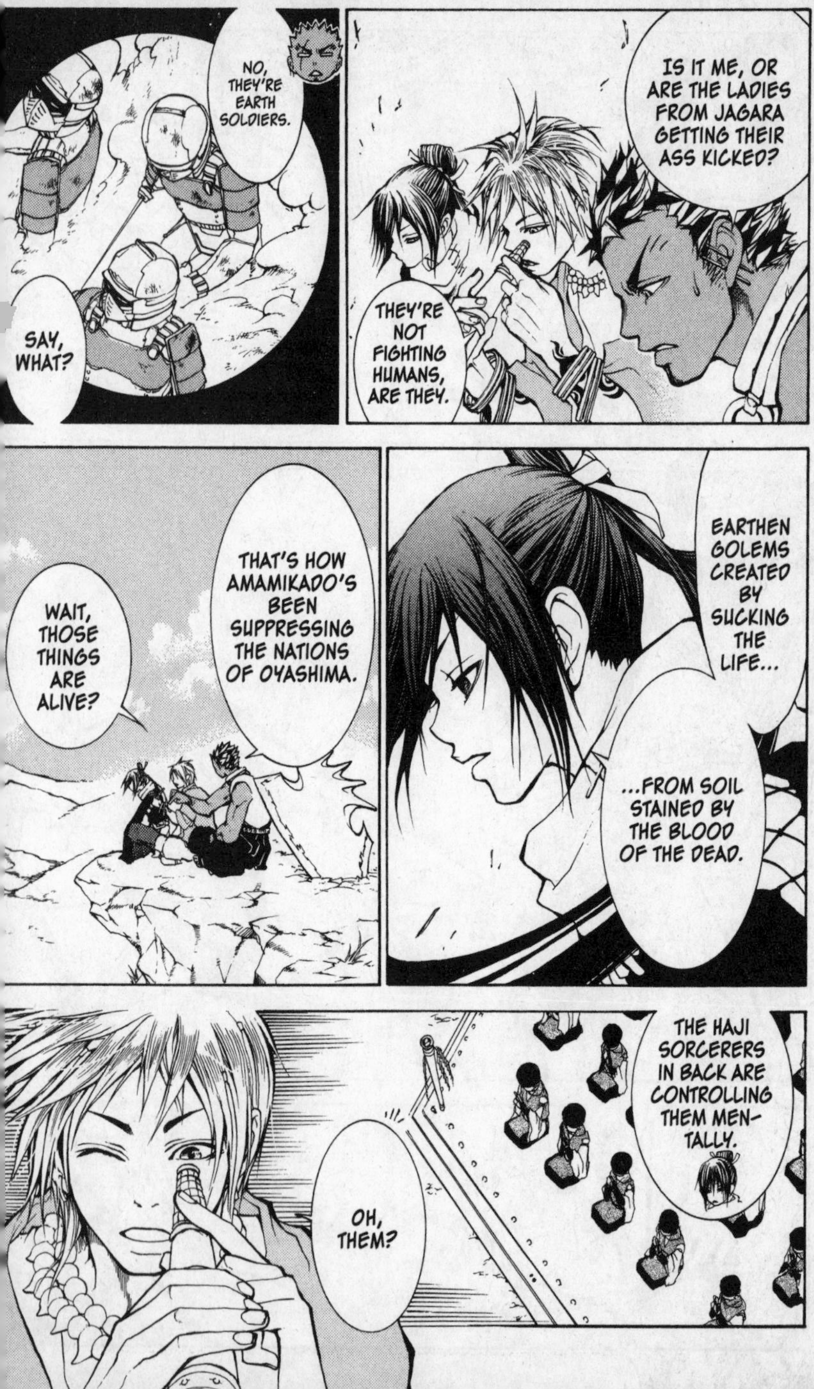
IS IT ME, OR ARE THE LADIES FROM JAGARA GETTING THEIR ASS KICKED?
THEY'RE NOT FIGHTING HUMANS, ARE THEY.
NO, THEY'RE EARTH SOLDIERS.
SAY, WHAT?
EARTHEN GOLEMS CREATED BY SUCKING THE LIFE...
...FROM SOIL STAINED BY THE BLOOD OF THE DEAD.
THAT'S HOW AMAMIKADO'S BEEN SUPPRESSING THE NATIONS OF OYASHIMA.
WAIT, THOSE THINGS ARE ALIVE?
THE HAJI SORCERERS IN BACK ARE CONTROLLING THEM MEN-TALLY.
OH, THEM?

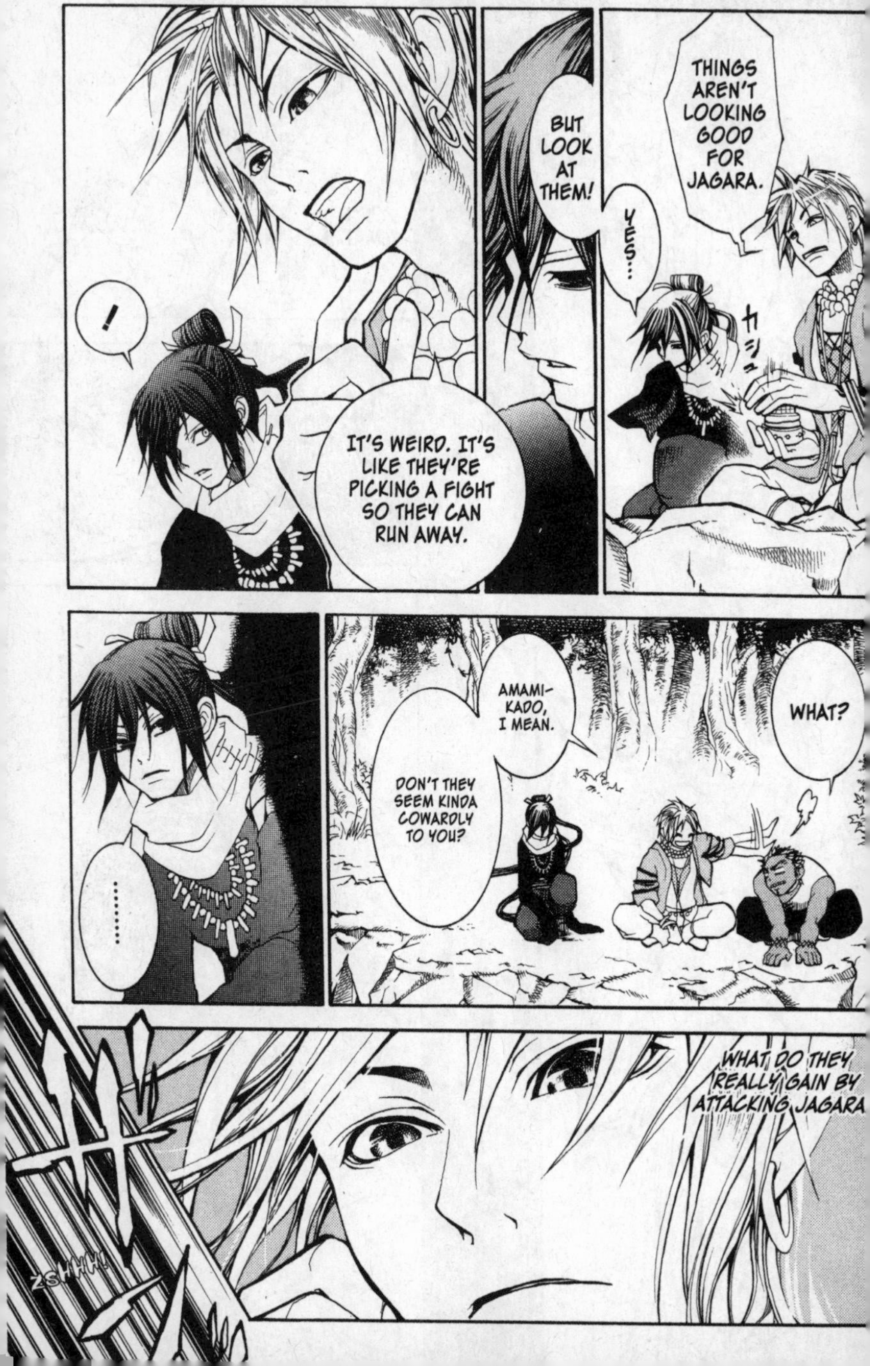
THINGS AREN'T LOOKING GOOD FOR JAGARA.
YES...
カシュ
BUT LOOK AT THEM!
!
IT'S WEIRD. IT'S LIKE THEY'RE PICKING A FIGHT SO THEY CAN RUN AWAY.
WHAT?
AMAMI-KADO, I MEAN.
DON'T THEY SEEM KINDA COWARDLY TO YOU?
......
WHAT DO THEY REALLY GAIN BY ATTACKING JAGARA
ZSHHH!

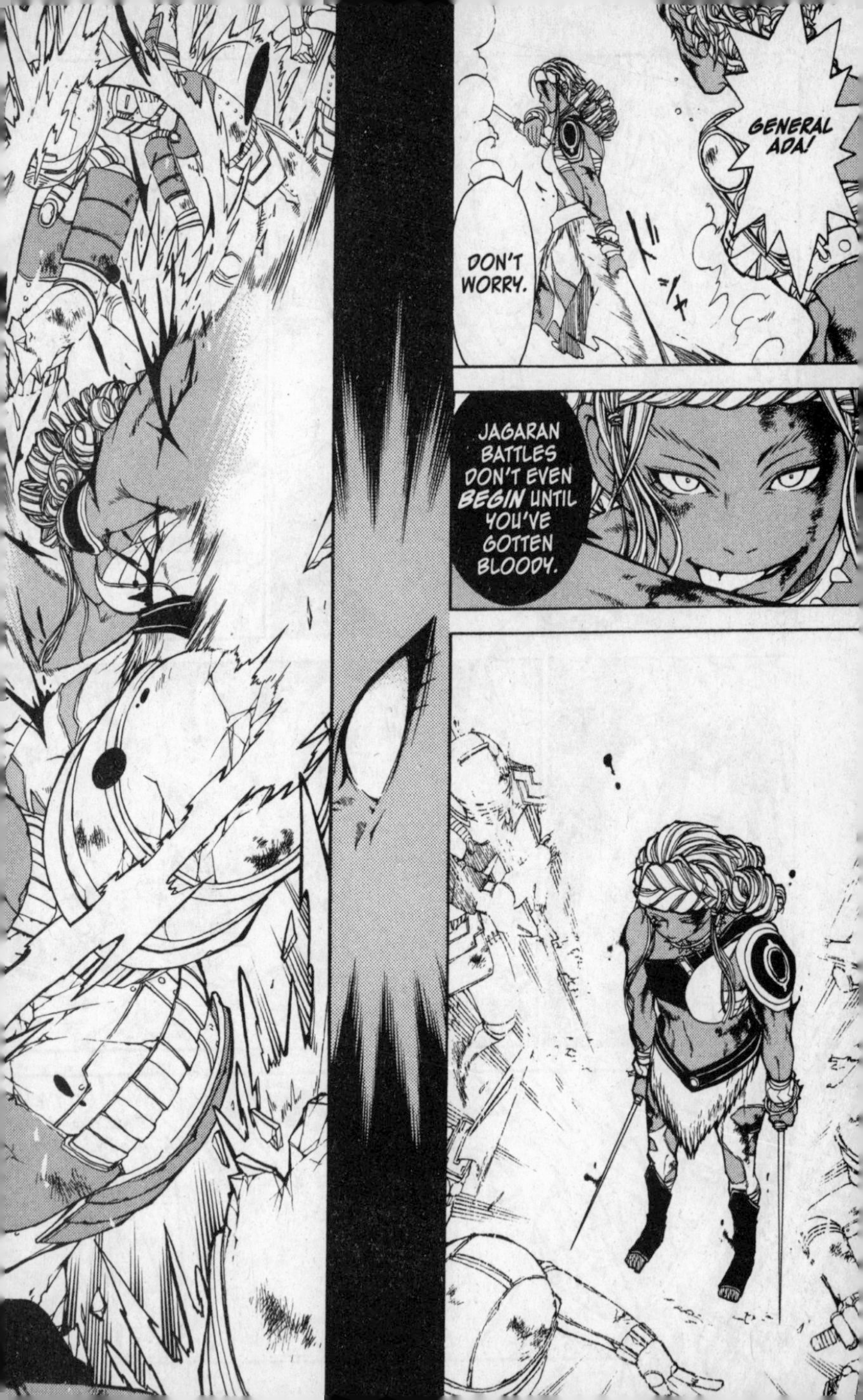
GENERAL ADA!
DON'T WORRY.
JAGARAN BATTLES DON'T EVEN BEGIN UNTIL YOU'VE GOTTEN BLOODY.

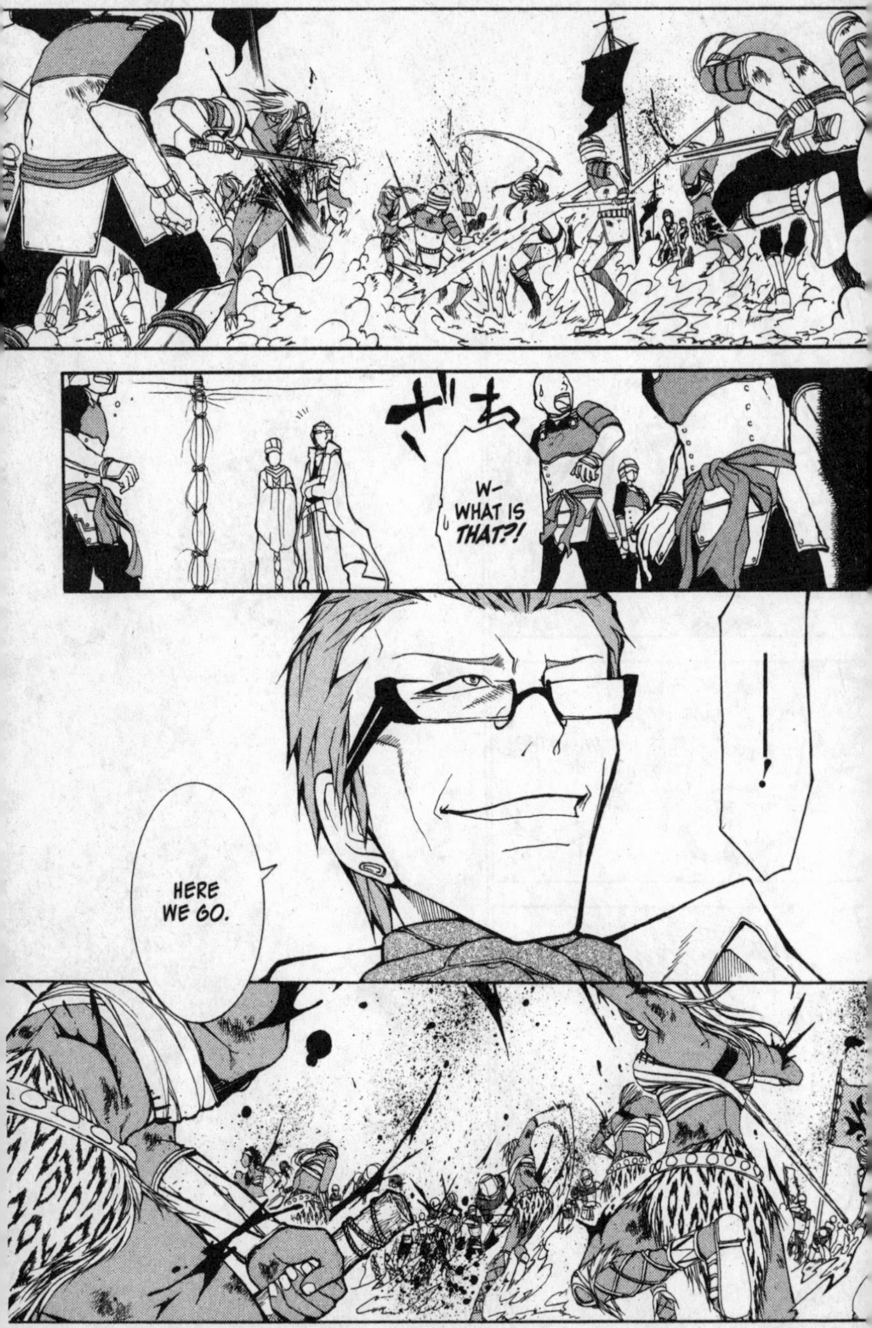

ざわ
W- WHAT IS THAT?!
!
HERE WE GO.

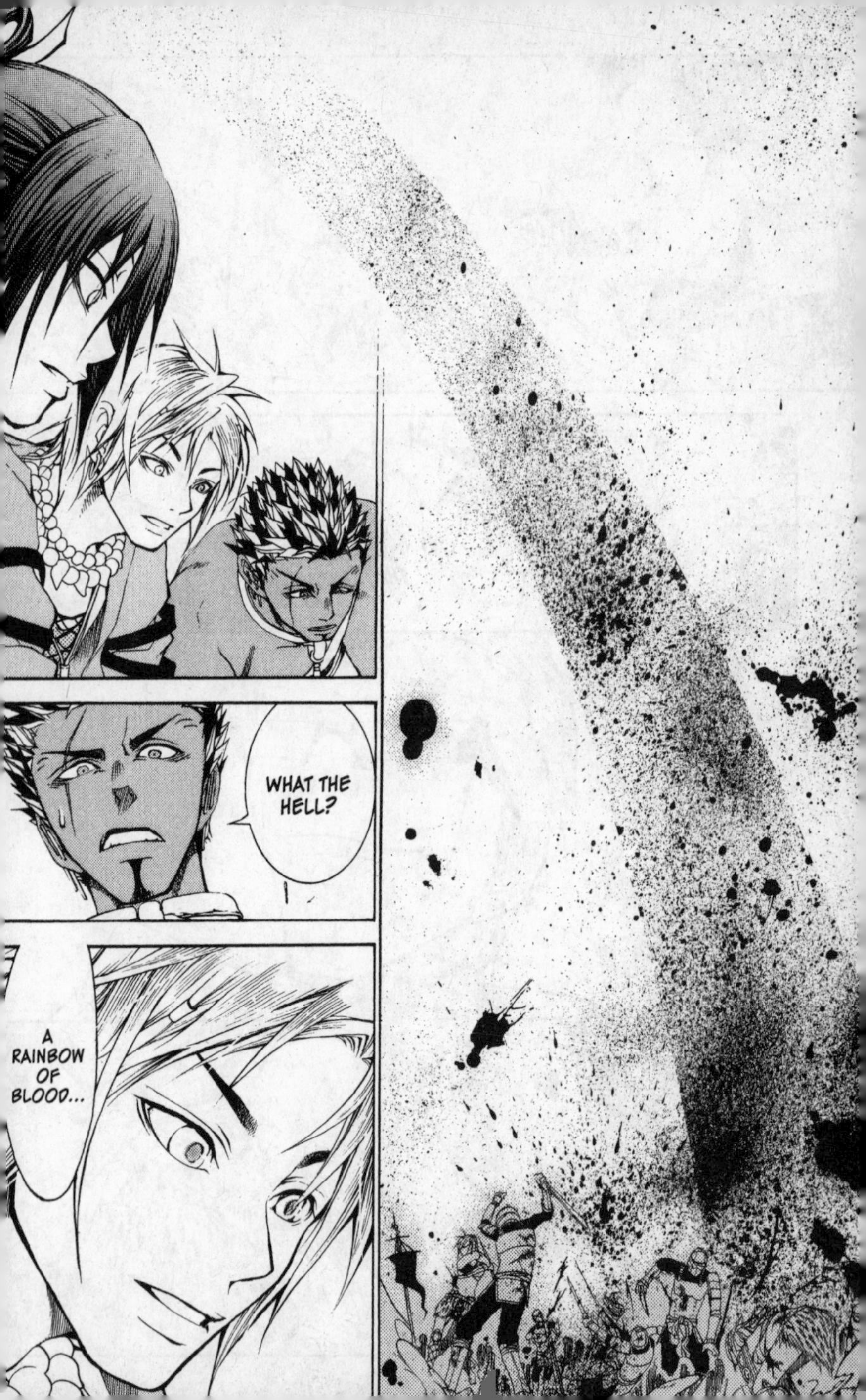
WHAT THE HELL?
A RAINBOW OF BLOOD...

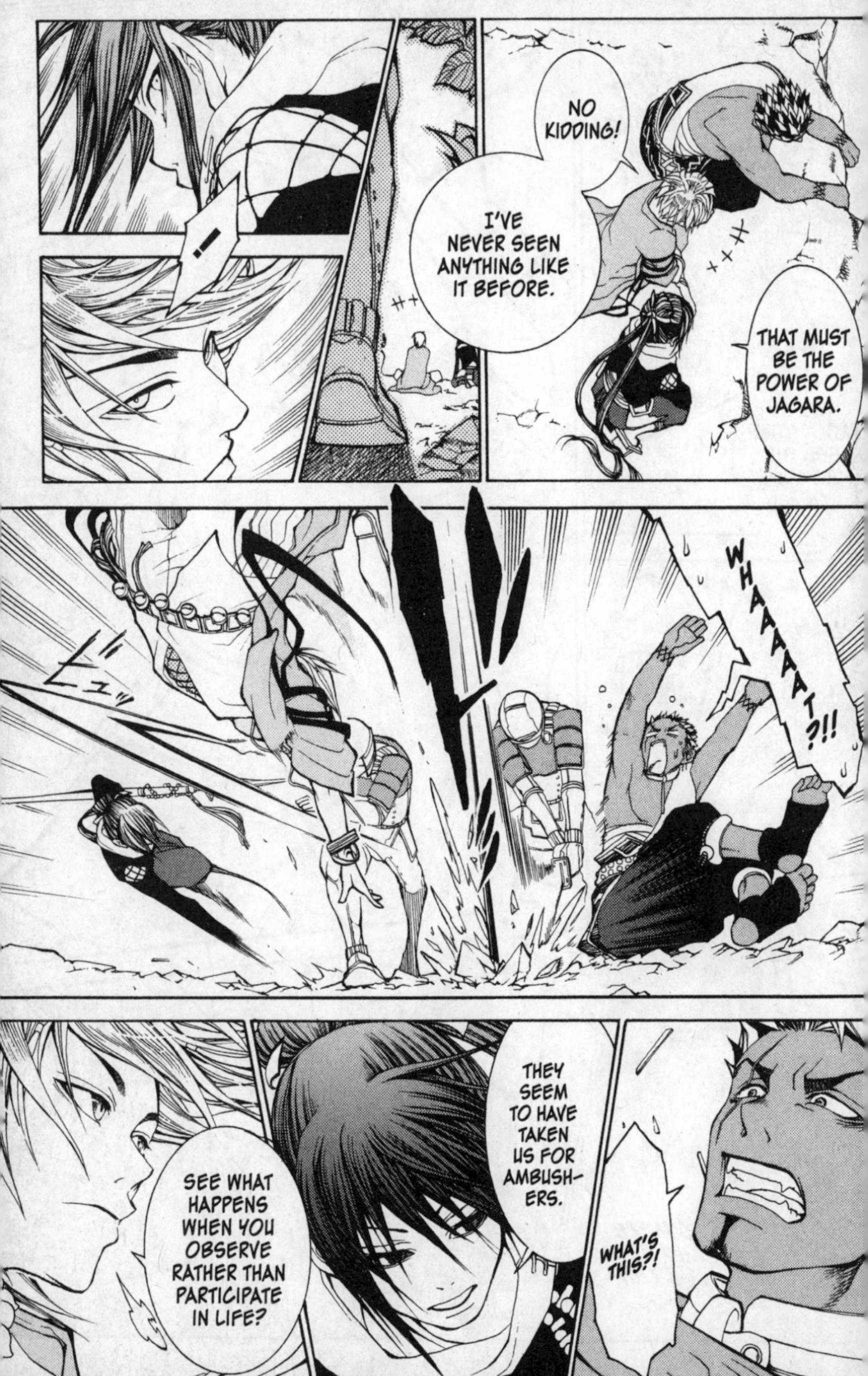
THAT MUST BE THE POWER OF JAGARA.
NO KIDDING!
I'VE NEVER SEEN ANYTHING LIKE IT BEFORE.
!
WHAAAAAT?!!
ビュッ
WHAT'S THIS?!
THEY SEEM TO HAVE TAKEN US FOR AMBUSH-ERS.
SEE WHAT HAPPENS WHEN YOU OBSERVE RATHER THAN PARTICIPATE IN LIFE?

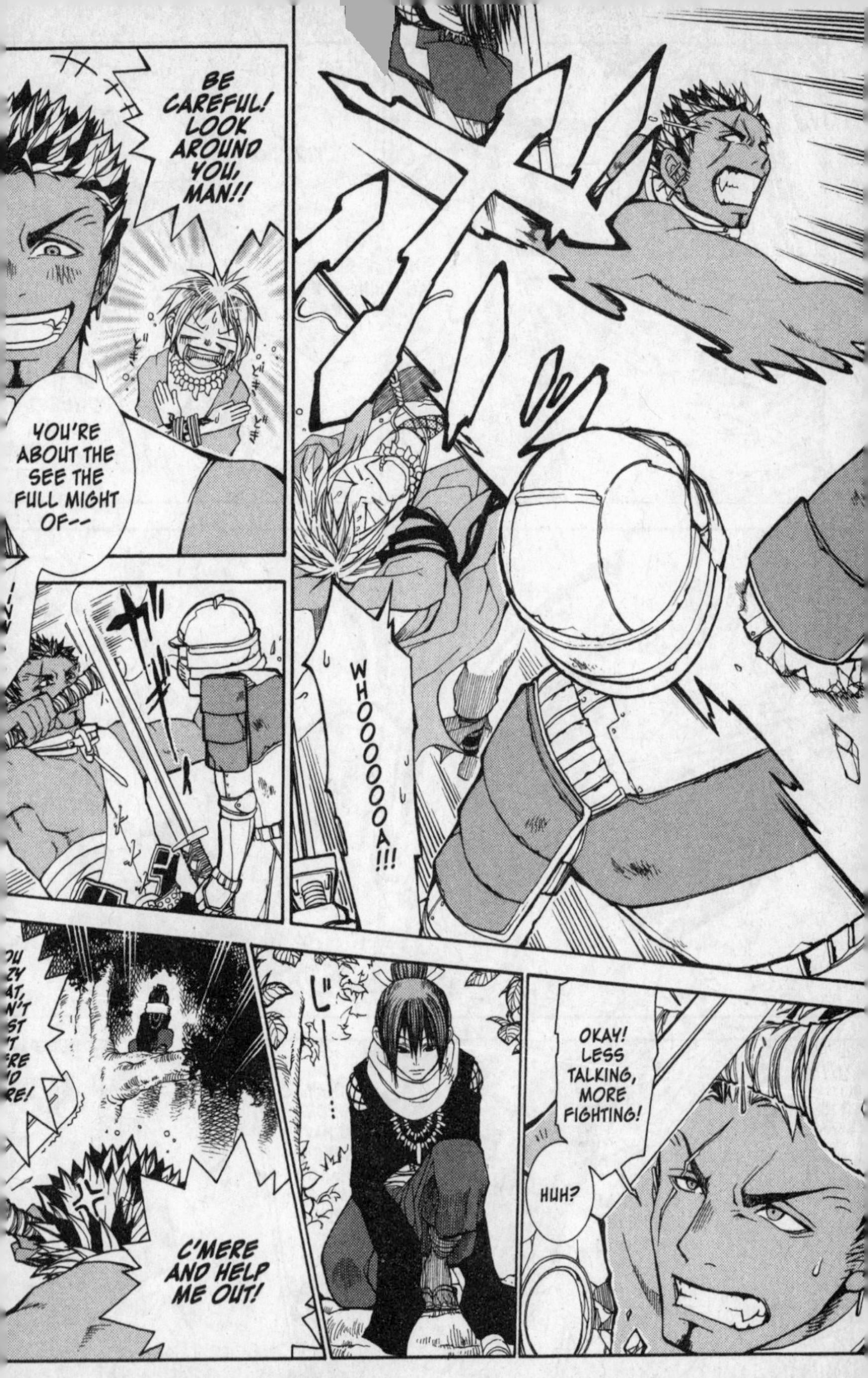
WHOOOOOOOA!!!
BE CAREFUL! LOOK AROUND YOU, MAN!!
YOU'RE ABOUT THE SEE THE FULL MIGHT OF--
OKAY! LESS TALKING, MORE FIGHTING!
HUH?
C'MERE AND HELP ME OUT!

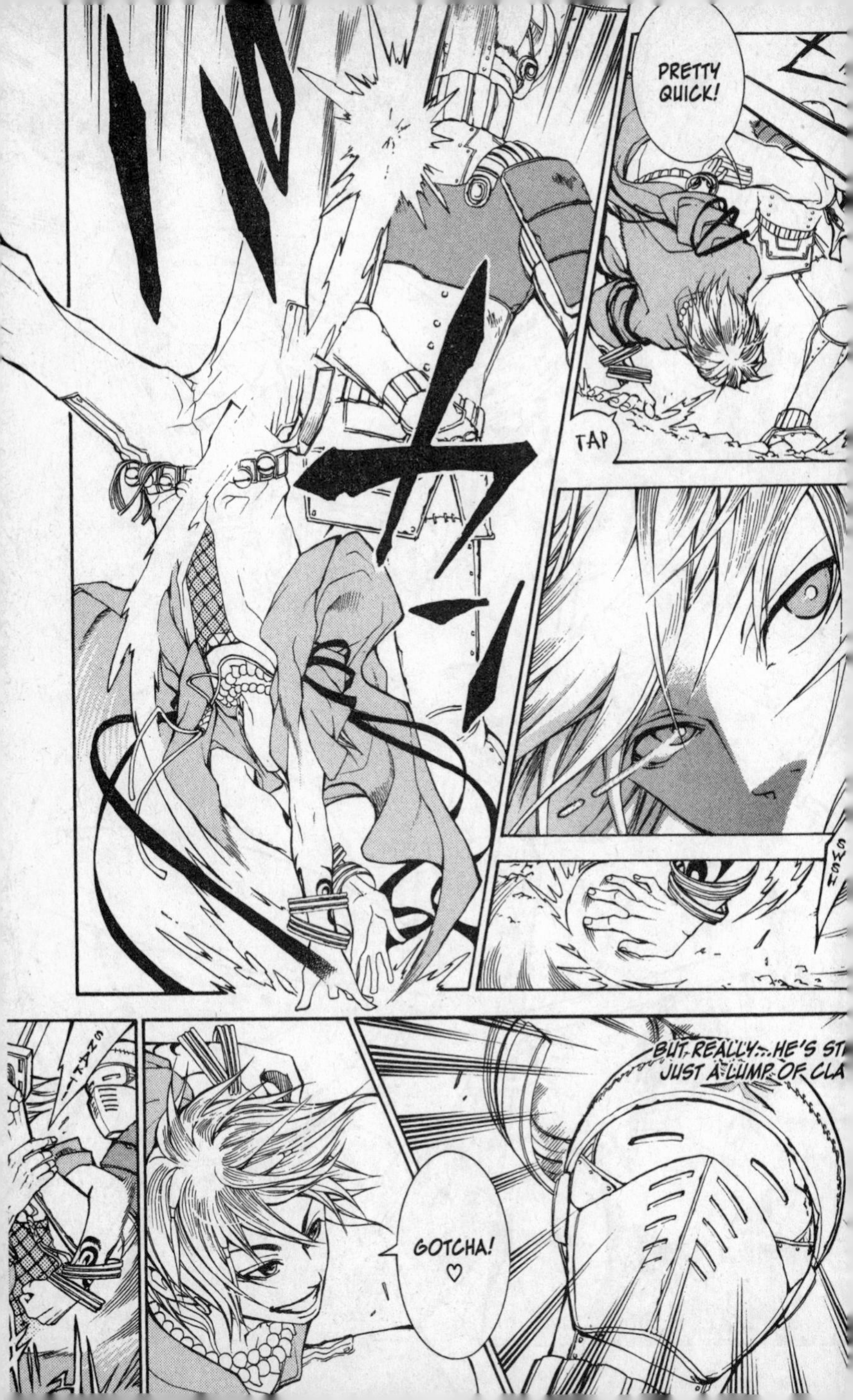
PRETTY QUICK!
TAP
SWSH
BUT REALLY... HE'S STI
JUST A LUMP OF CLA
GOTCHA! ♡

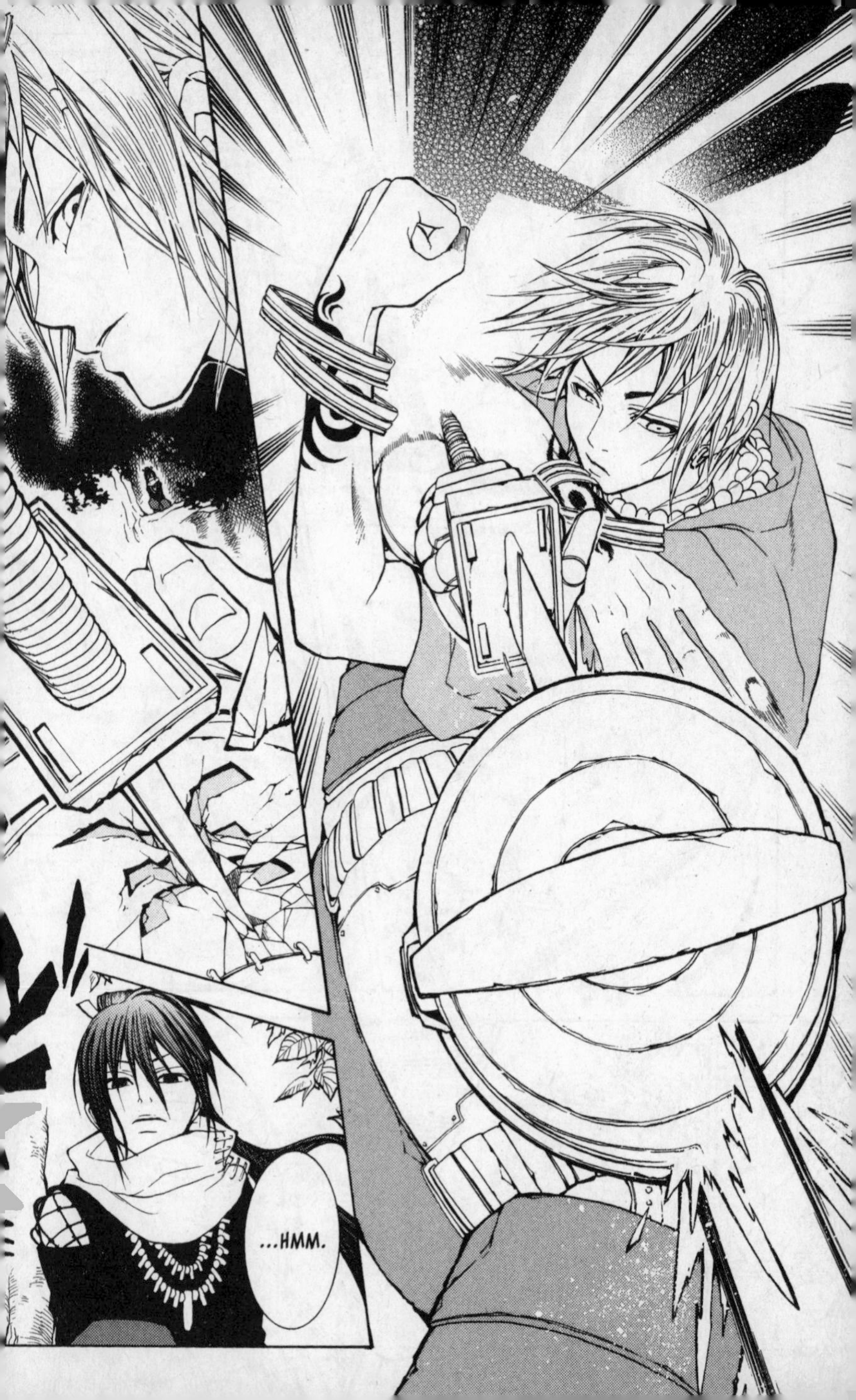
...HMM.

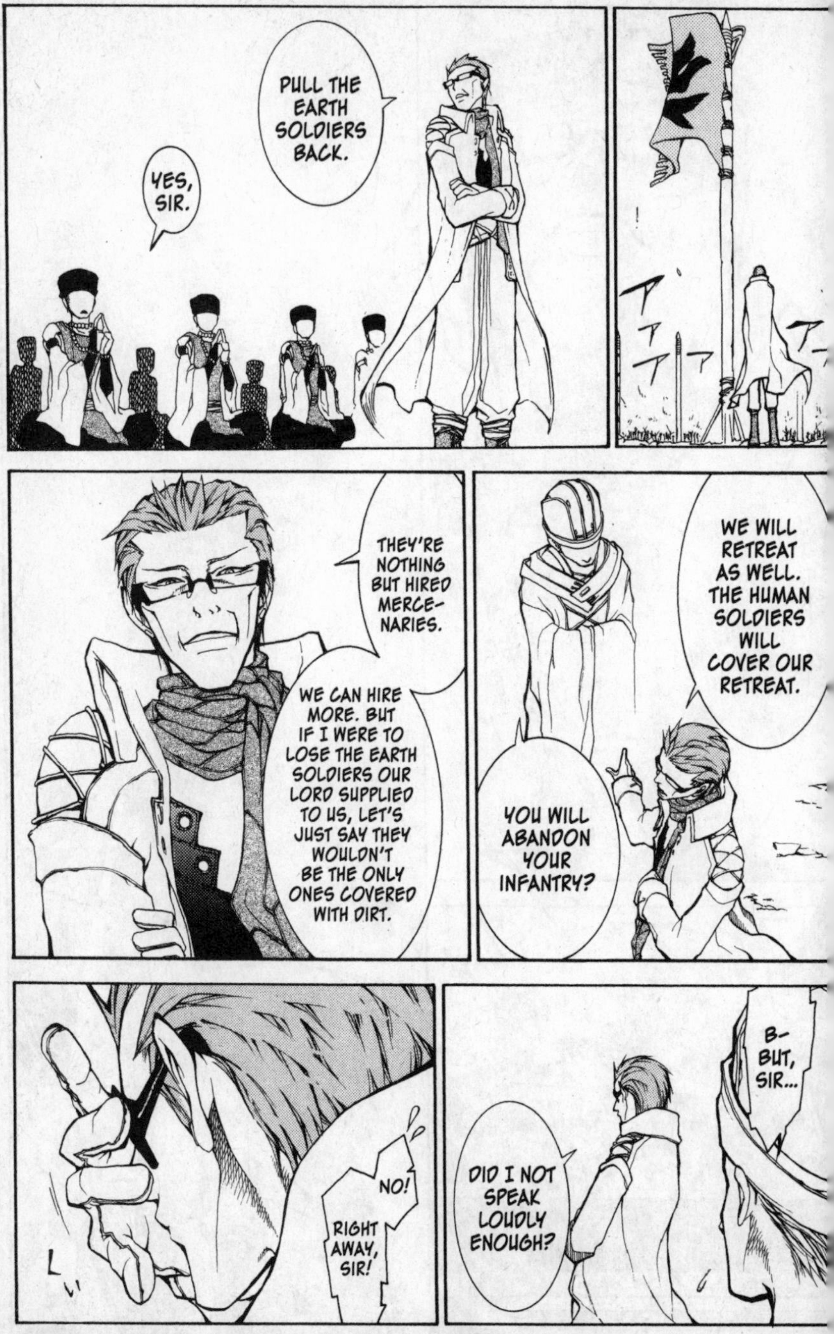
PULL THE EARTH SOLDIERS BACK.
YES, SIR.
WE WILL RETREAT AS WELL. THE HUMAN SOLDIERS WILL COVER OUR RETREAT.
YOU WILL ABANDON YOUR INFANTRY?
THEY'RE NOTHING BUT HIRED MERCE-NARIES.
WE CAN HIRE MORE. BUT IF I WERE TO LOSE THE EARTH SOLDIERS OUR LORD SUPPLIED TO US, LET'S JUST SAY THEY WOULDN'T BE THE ONLY ONES COVERED WITH DIRT.
B-BUT, SIR...
DID I NOT SPEAK LOUDLY ENOUGH?
NO!
RIGHT AWAY, SIR!

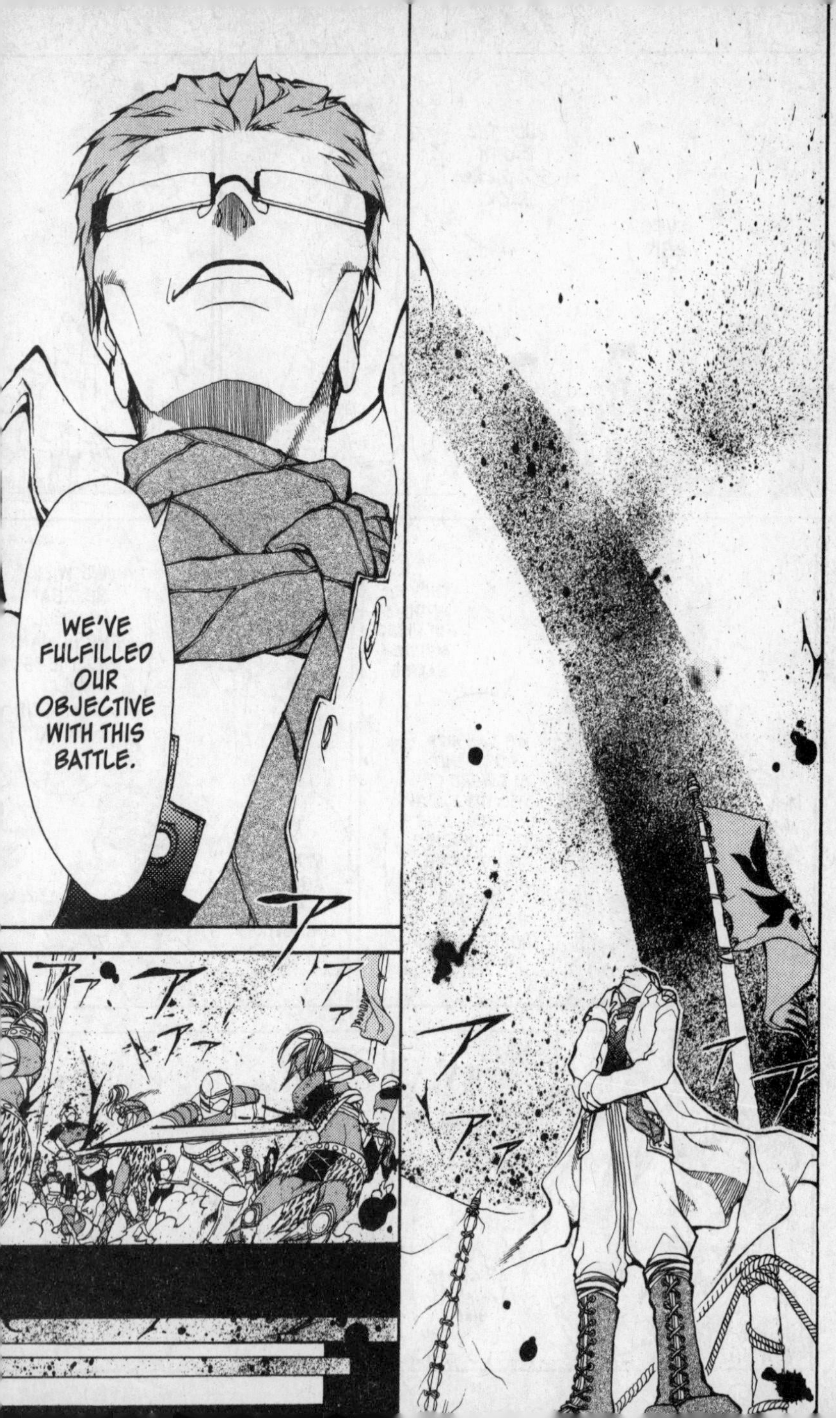
WE'VE FULFILLED OUR OBJECTIVE WITH THIS BATTLE.

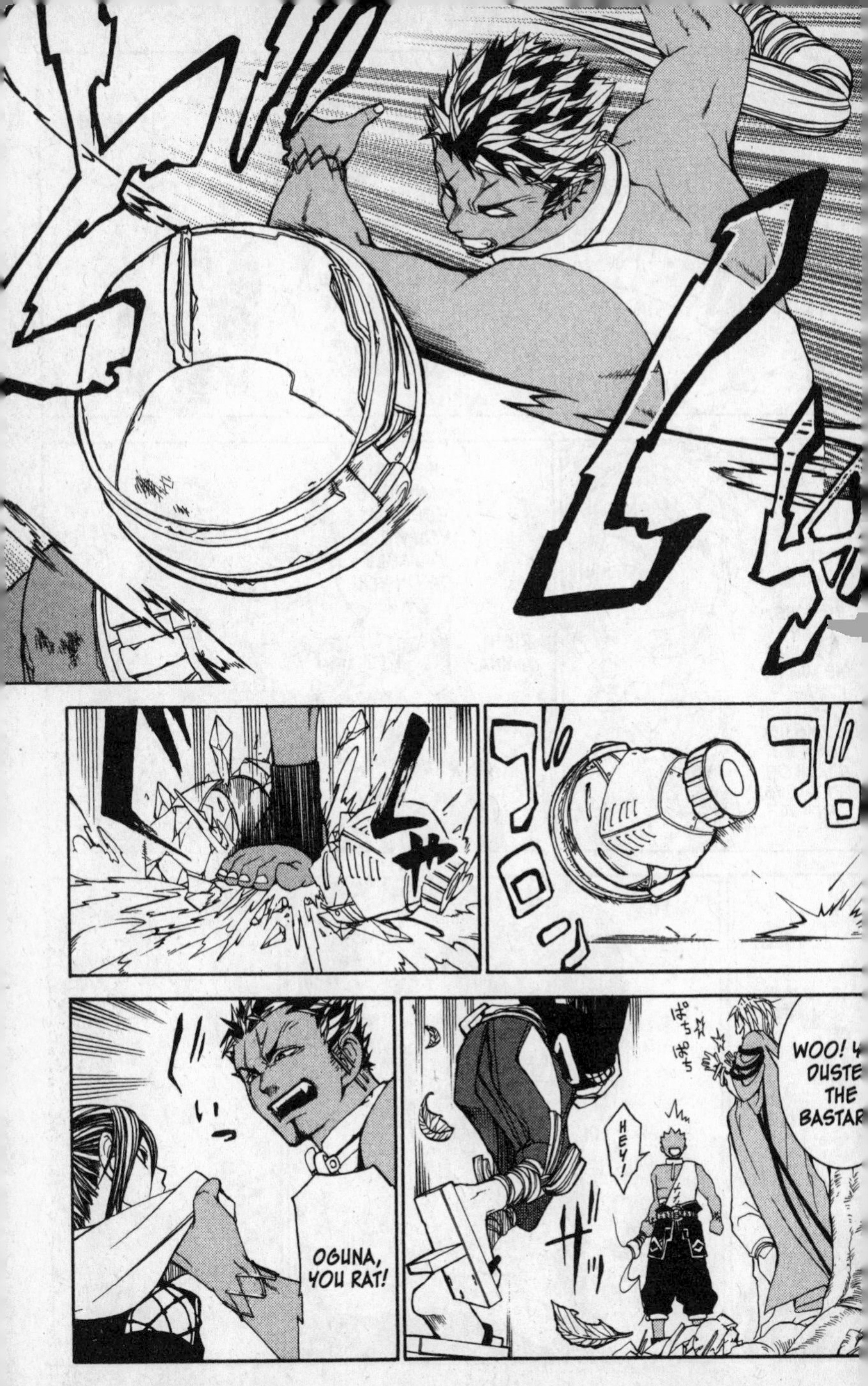
WOO! Y
DUSTE
THE
BASTAR
ぱち
ぱち
HEY!
OGUNA, YOU RAT!

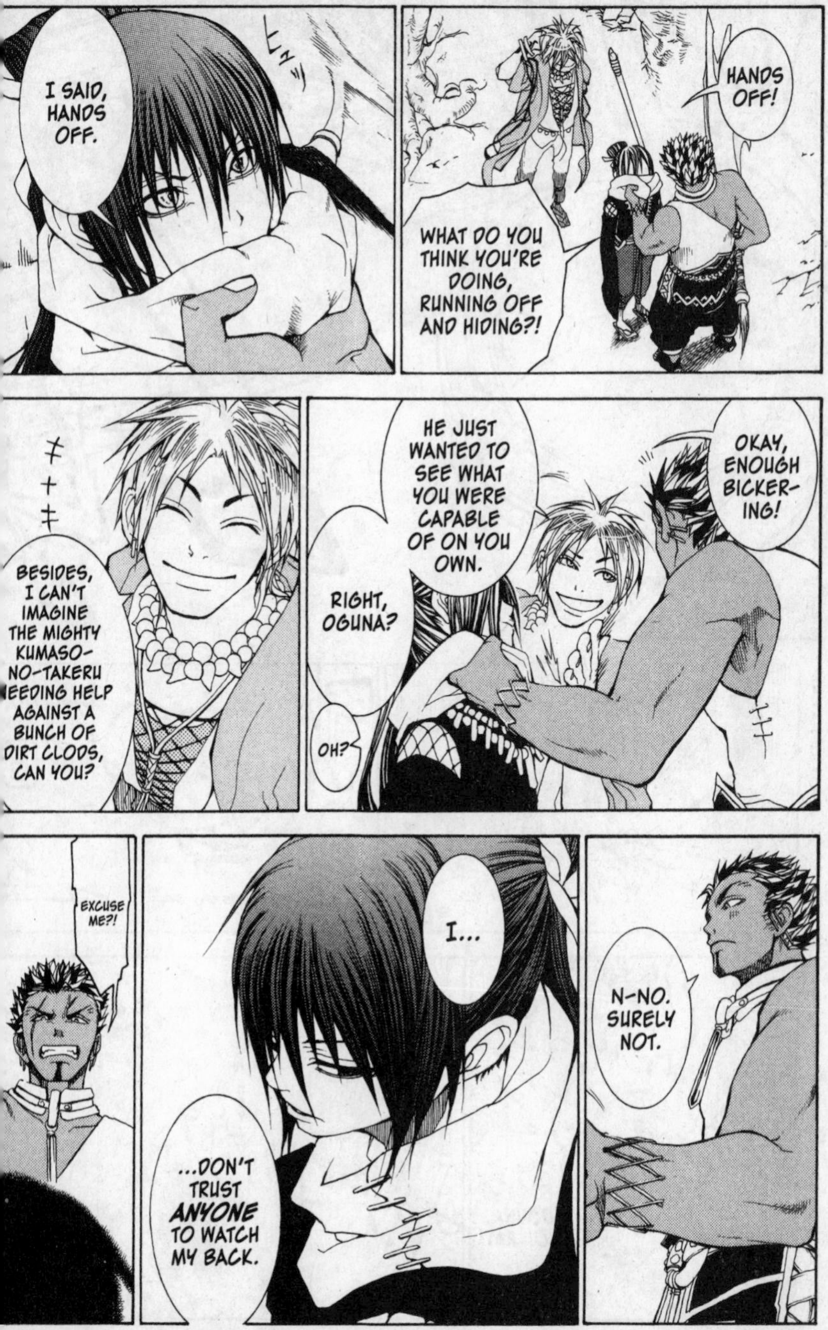
HANDS OFF!
WHAT DO YOU THINK YOU'RE DOING, RUNNING OFF AND HIDING?!
I SAID, HANDS OFF.
OKAY, ENOUGH BICKER-ING!
HE JUST WANTED TO SEE WHAT YOU WERE CAPABLE OF ON YOU OWN.
RIGHT, OGUNA?
OH?
BESIDES, I CAN'T IMAGINE THE MIGHTY KUMASO-NO-TAKERU EEDING HELP AGAINST A BUNCH OF DIRT CLODS, CAN YOU?
N-NO. SURELY NOT.
I...
...DON'T TRUST ANYONE TO WATCH MY BACK.
EXCUSE ME?!

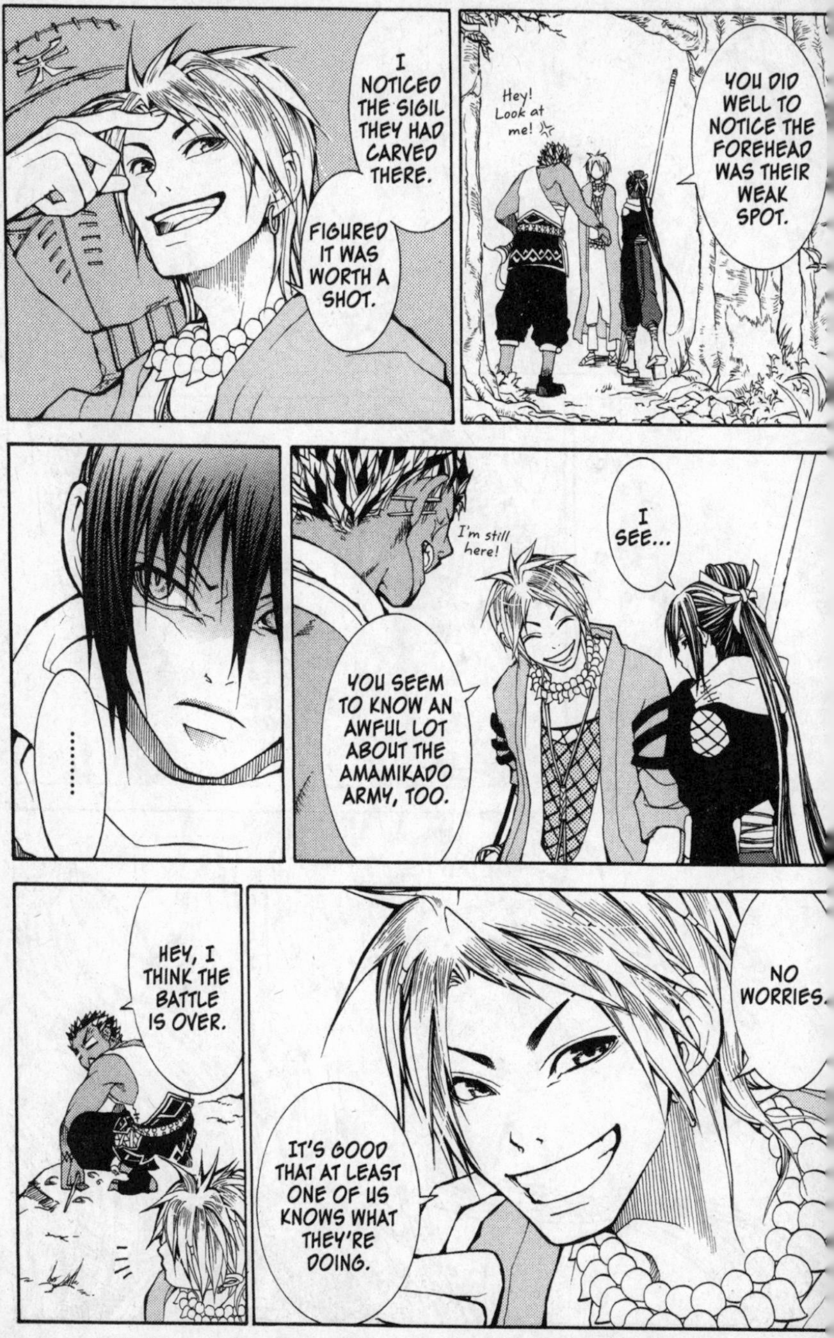
YOU DID WELL TO NOTICE THE FOREHEAD WAS THEIR WEAK SPOT.
Hey! Look at me!
I NOTICED THE SIGIL THEY HAD CARVED THERE.
FIGURED IT WAS WORTH A SHOT.
I SEE...
I'm still here!
YOU SEEM TO KNOW AN AWFUL LOT ABOUT THE AMAMIKADO ARMY, TOO.
......
NO WORRIES.
IT'S GOOD THAT AT LEAST ONE OF US KNOWS WHAT THEY'RE DOING.
HEY, I THINK THE BATTLE IS OVER.

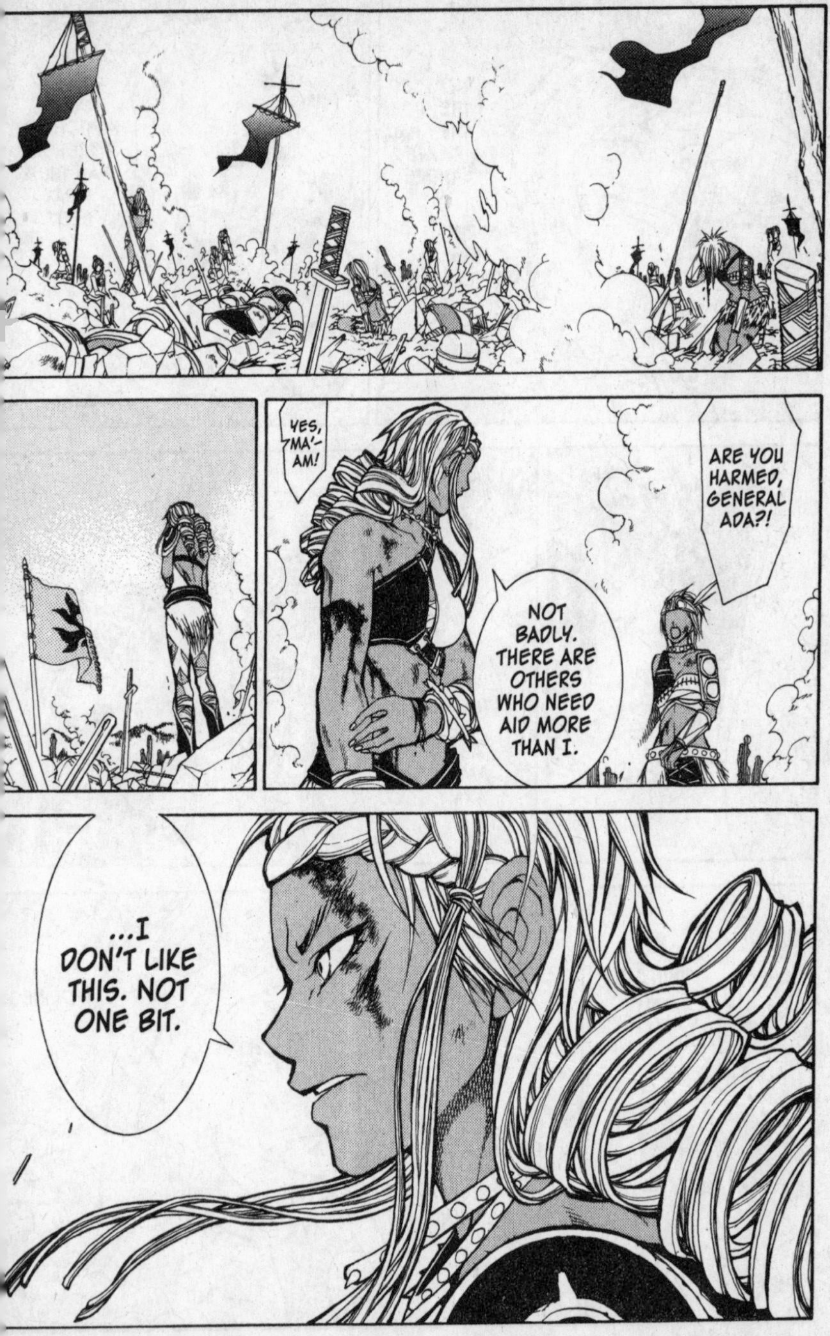
ARE YOU HARMED, GENERAL ADA?!
NOT BADLY. THERE ARE OTHERS WHO NEED AID MORE THAN I.
YES, MA'-AM!
...I DON'T LIKE THIS. NOT ONE BIT.

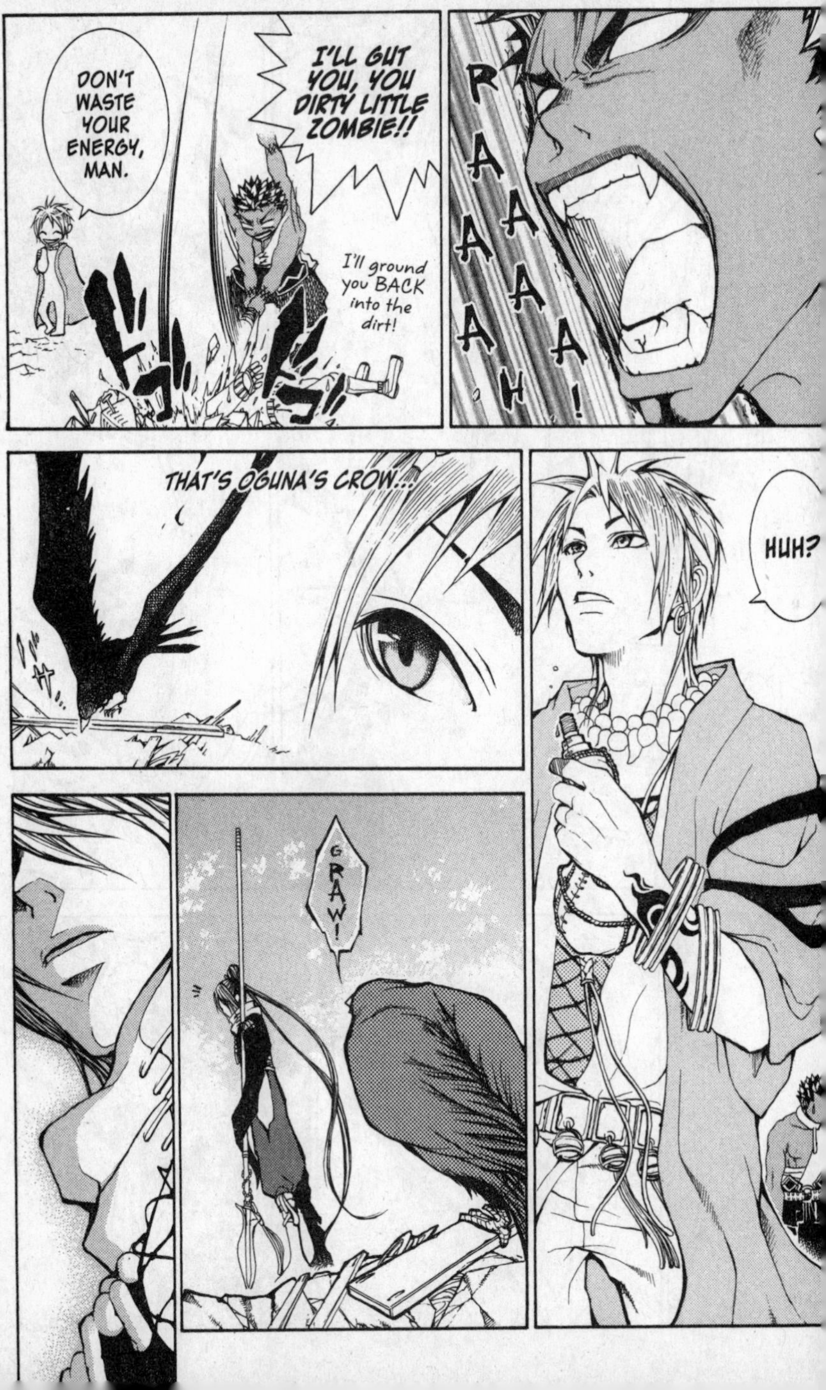
RAAAAAAH!
I'LL GUT YOU, YOU DIRTY LITTLE ZOMBIE!!
I'll ground you BACK into the dirt!
DON'T WASTE YOUR ENERGY, MAN.
HUH?
THAT'S OGUNA'S CROW...
GRAW!

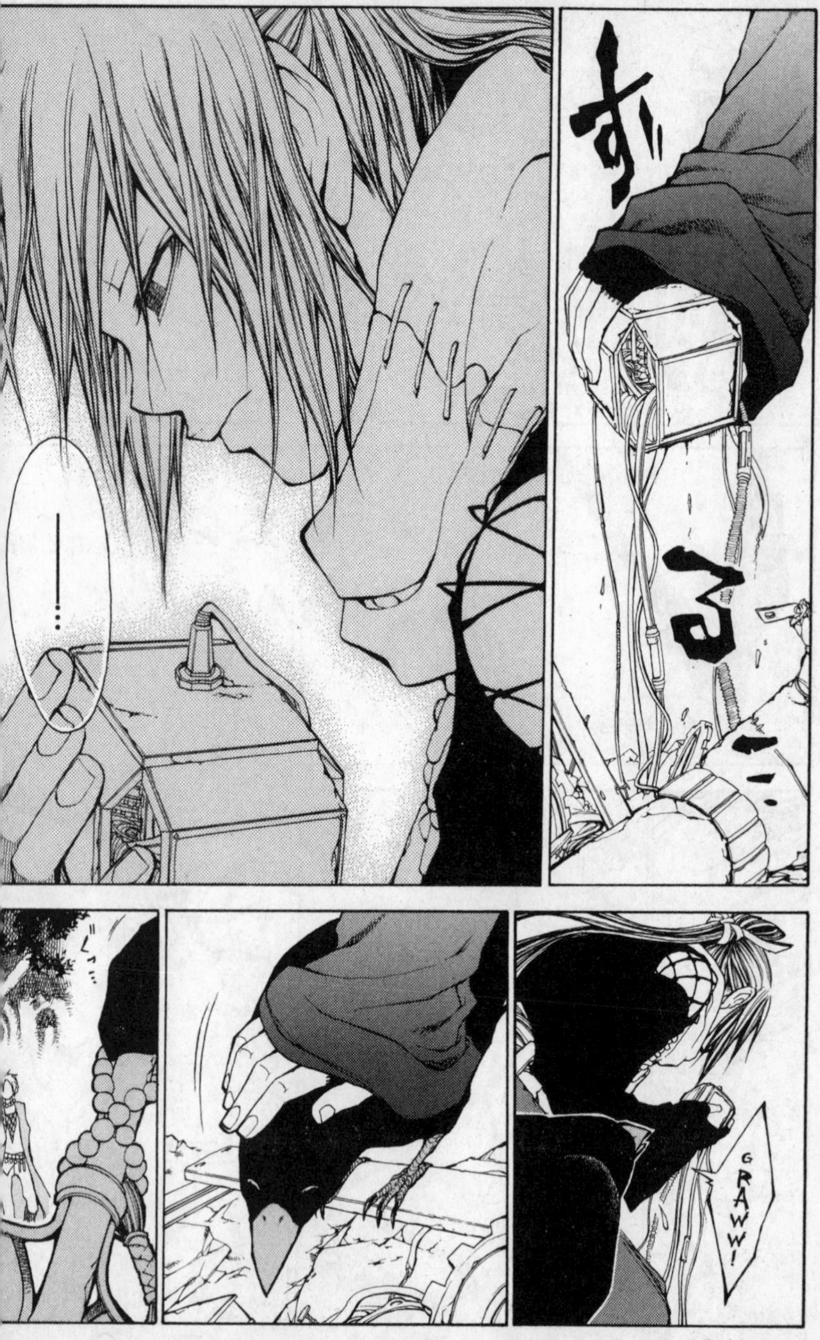

する
――!…
GRAWW!

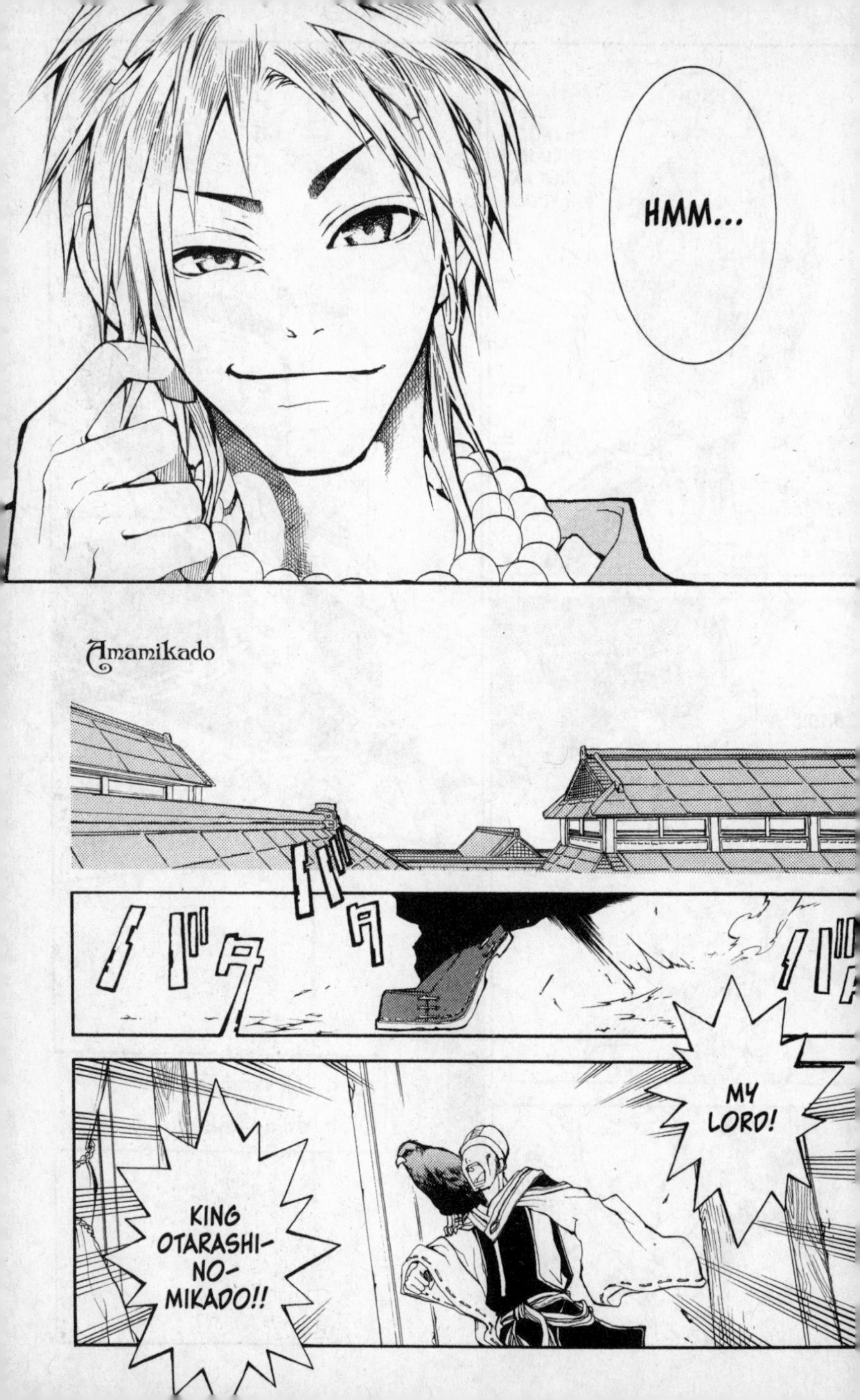
HMM...
バタ
バタ
バタ
MY LORD!
KING OTARASHI-NO-MIKADO!!

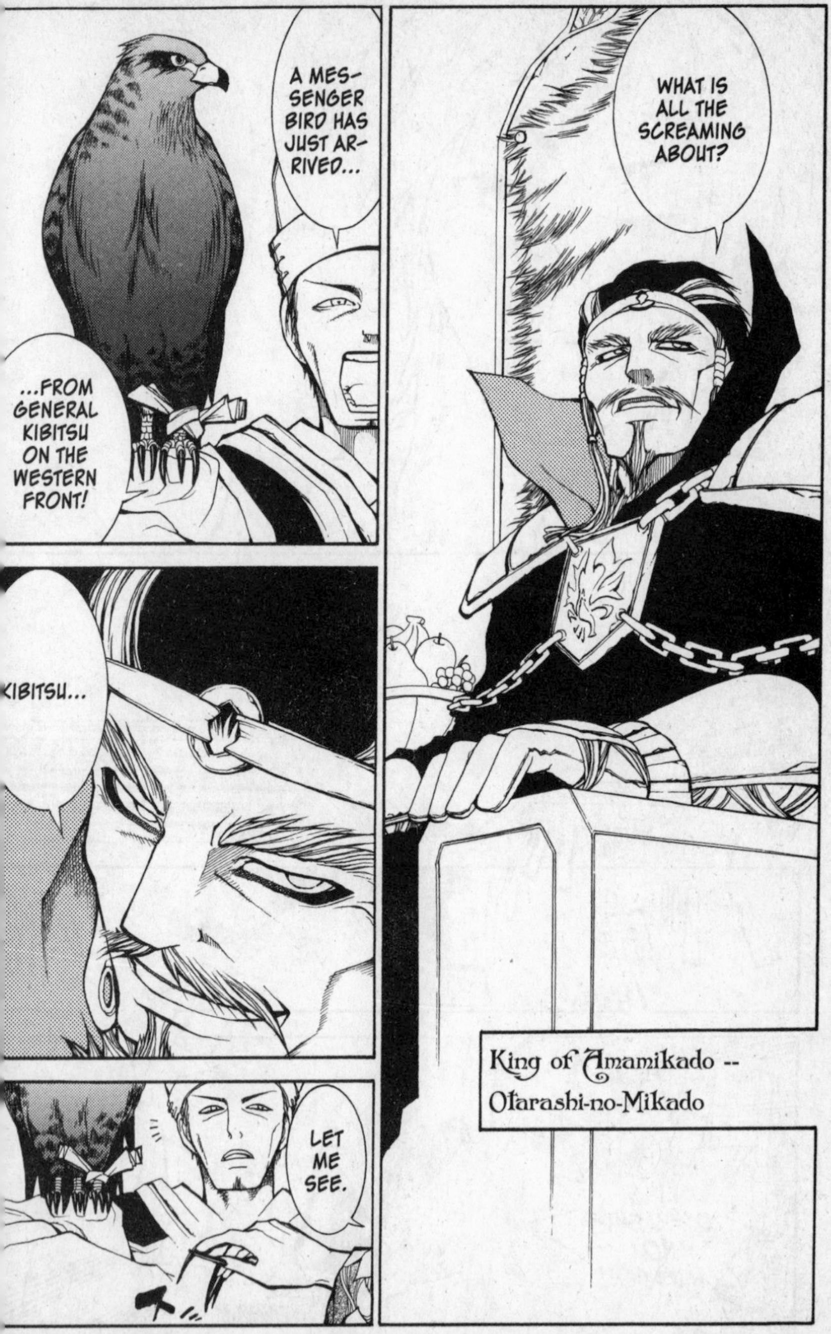
WHAT IS ALL THE SCREAMING ABOUT?
King of Amamikado -- Otarashi-no-Mikado
A MES-SENGER BIRD HAS JUST AR-RIVED...
...FROM GENERAL KIBITSU ON THE WESTERN FRONT!
KIBITSU...
LET ME SEE.

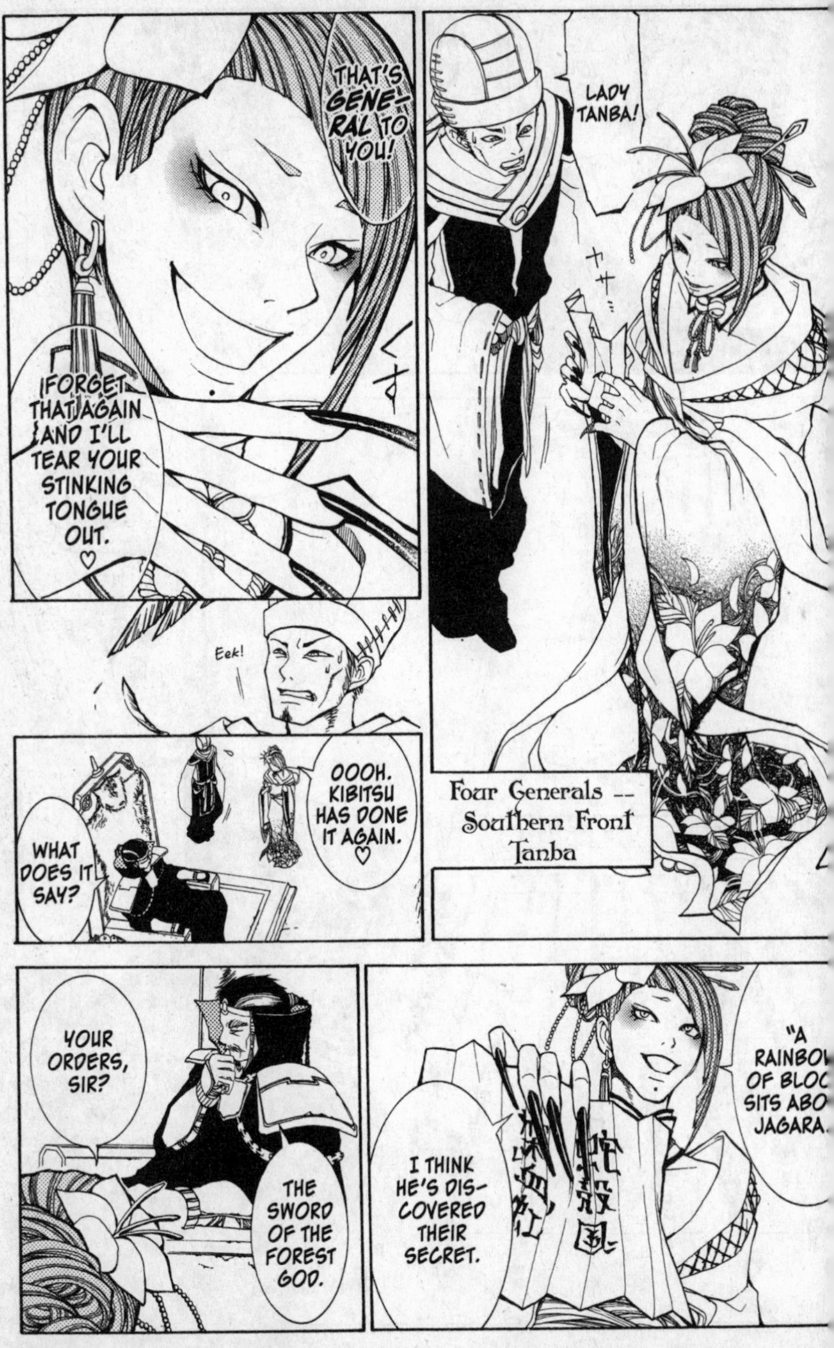
LADY TANBA!
Four Generals -- Southern Front Tanba
THAT'S GENERAL TO YOU!
FORGET THAT AGAIN AND I'LL TEAR YOUR STINKING TONGUE OUT. ♡
Eek!
OOOH. KIBITSU HAS DONE IT AGAIN. ♡
WHAT DOES IT SAY?
"A RAINBOW OF BLOO SITS ABO JAGARA.
I THINK HE'S DISCOVERED THEIR SECRET.
YOUR ORDERS, SIR?
THE SWORD OF THE FOREST GOD.

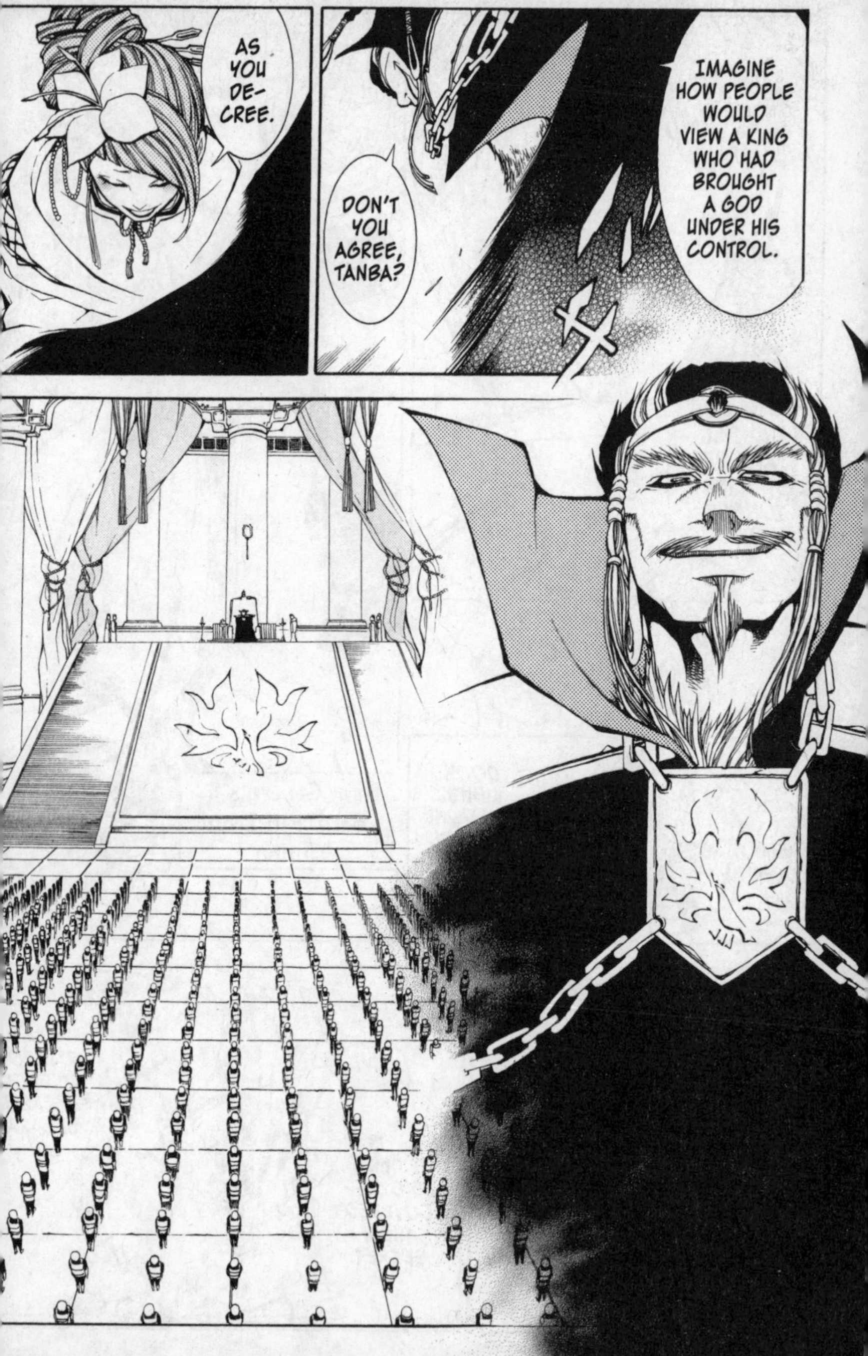
IMAGINE HOW PEOPLE WOULD VIEW A KING WHO HAD BROUGHT A GOD UNDER HIS CONTROL.
DON'T YOU AGREE, TANBA?
AS YOU DE-CREE.

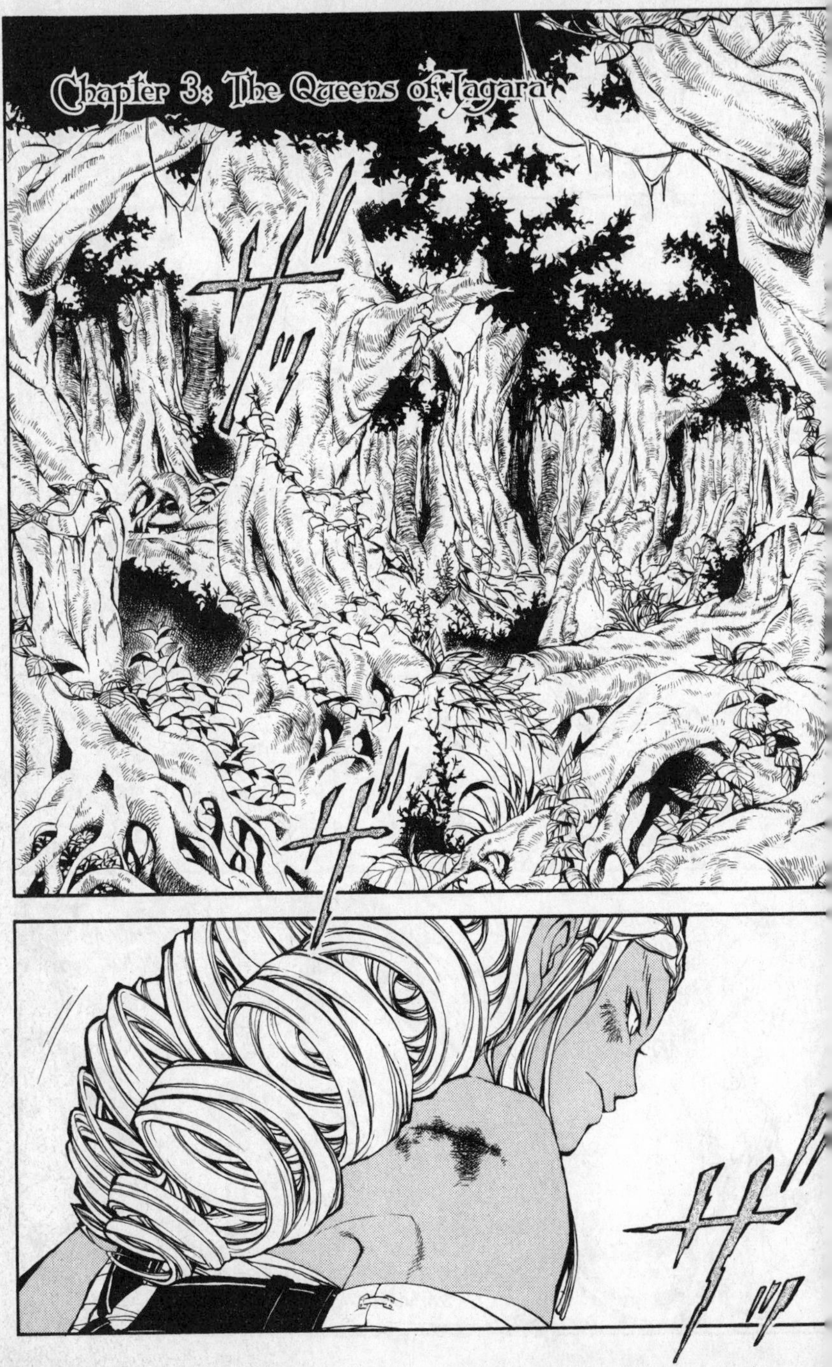
Chapter 3: The Queens of Jagara

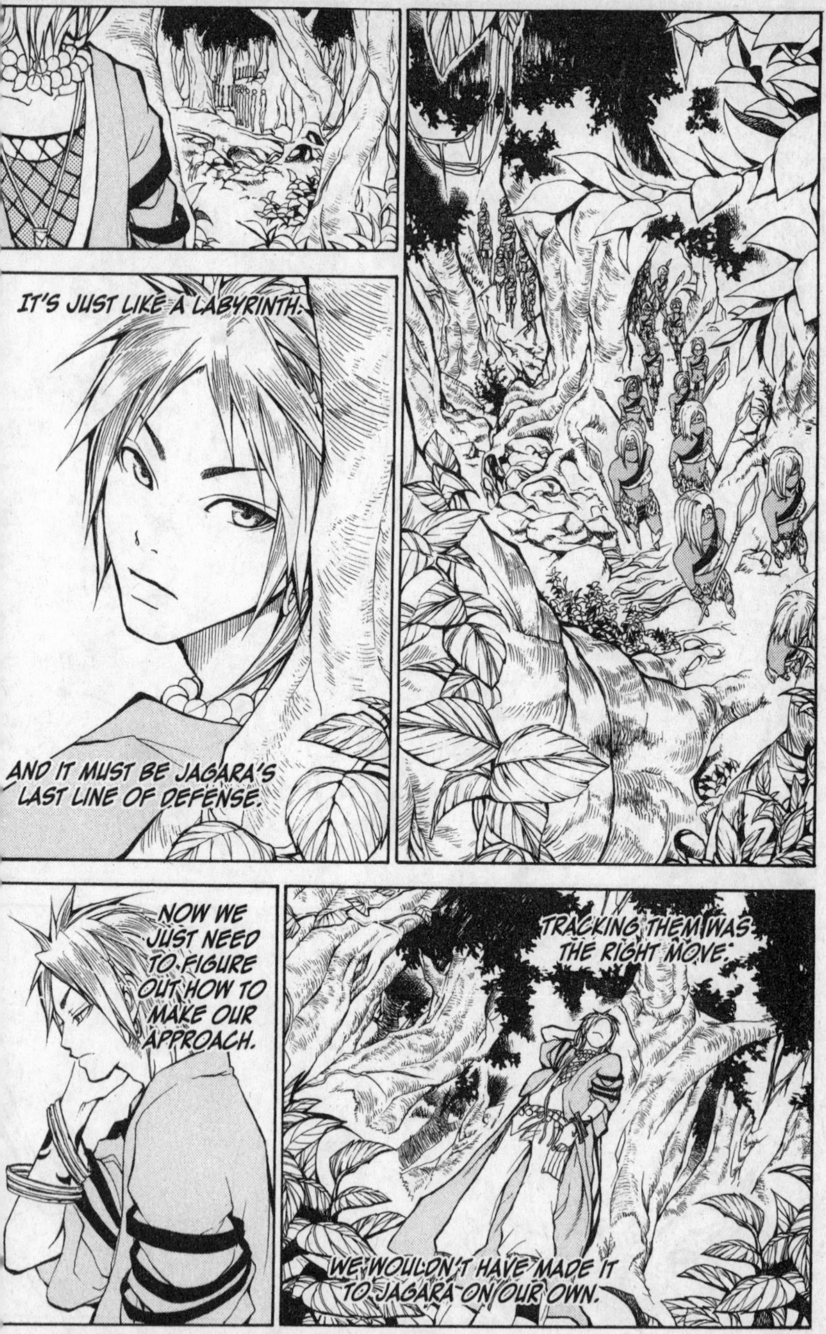
IT'S JUST LIKE A LABYRINTH.
AND IT MUST BE JAGARA'S LAST LINE OF DEFENSE.
TRACKING THEM WAS THE RIGHT MOVE.
WE WOULDN'T HAVE MADE IT TO JAGARA ON OUR OWN.
NOW WE JUST NEED TO FIGURE OUT HOW TO MAKE OUR APPROACH.

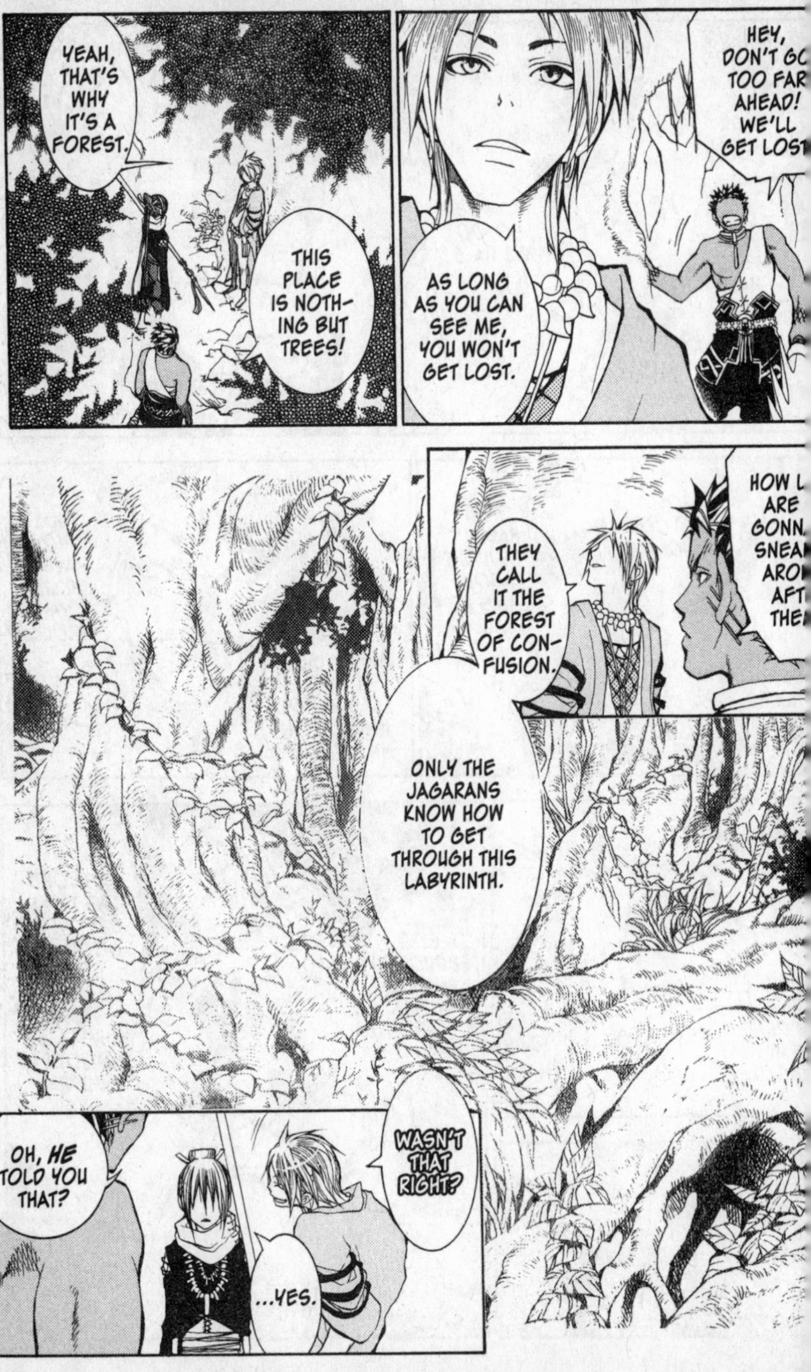
HEY, DON'T GO TOO FAR AHEAD! WE'LL GET LOST
AS LONG AS YOU CAN SEE ME, YOU WON'T GET LOST.
THIS PLACE IS NOTHING BUT TREES!
YEAH, THAT'S WHY IT'S A FOREST.
HOW L ARE GONN SNEA ARO AFT THE
THEY CALL IT THE FOREST OF CONFUSION.
ONLY THE JAGARANS KNOW HOW TO GET THROUGH THIS LABYRINTH.
WASN'T THAT RIGHT?
...YES.
OH, *HE* TOLD YOU THAT?

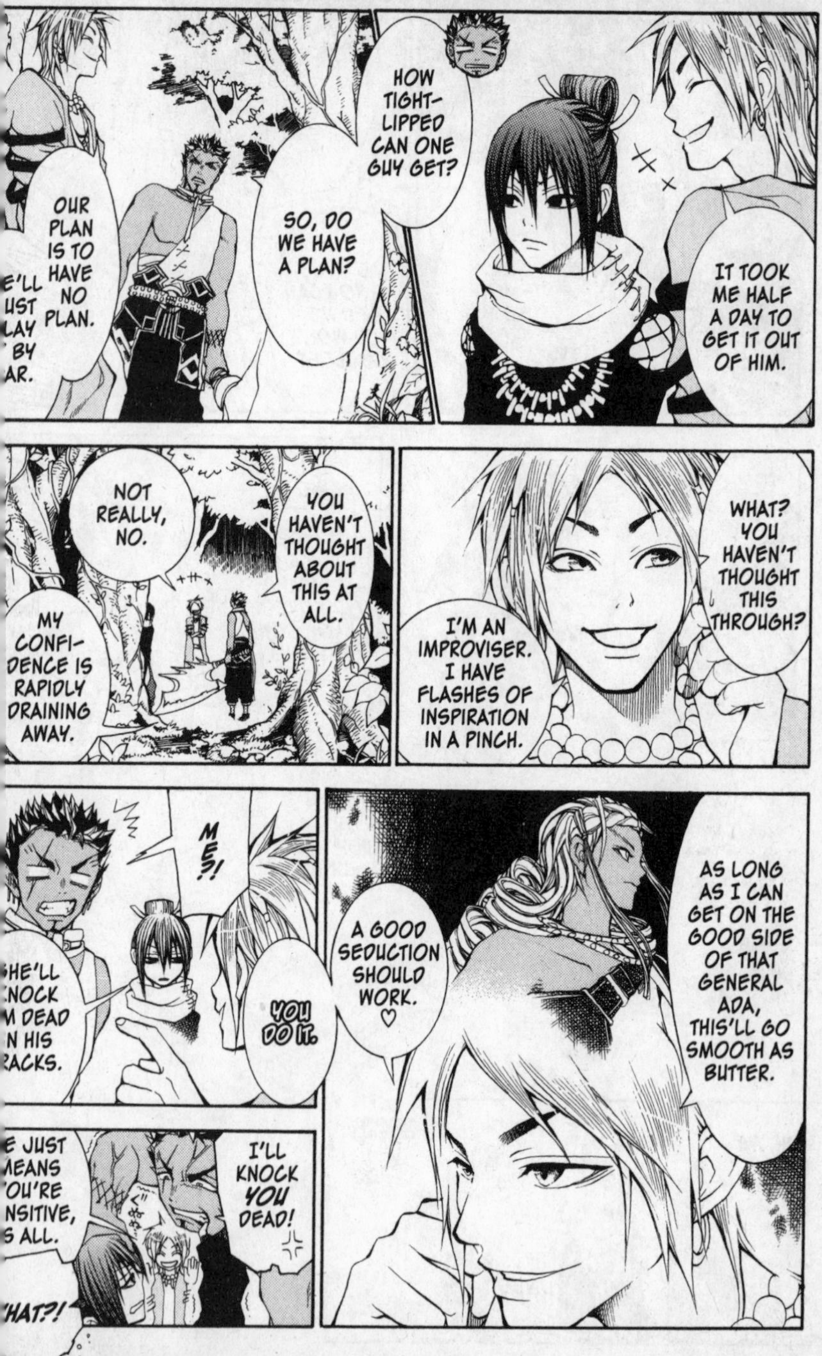
IT TOOK ME HALF A DAY TO GET IT OUT OF HIM.
HOW TIGHT-LIPPED CAN ONE GUY GET?
SO, DO WE HAVE A PLAN?
OUR PLAN IS TO HAVE NO PLAN.
E'LL UST LAY BY AR.
WHAT? YOU HAVEN'T THOUGHT THIS THROUGH?
I'M AN IMPROVISER. I HAVE FLASHES OF INSPIRATION IN A PINCH.
YOU HAVEN'T THOUGHT ABOUT THIS AT ALL.
NOT REALLY, NO.
MY CONFIDENCE IS RAPIDLY DRAINING AWAY.
AS LONG AS I CAN GET ON THE GOOD SIDE OF THAT GENERAL ADA, THIS'LL GO SMOOTH AS BUTTER.
A GOOD SEDUCTION SHOULD WORK. ♡
YOU DO IT.
ME?!
HE'LL NOCK M DEAD N HIS RACKS.
I'LL KNOCK YOU DEAD!
E JUST MEANS OU'RE NSITIVE, S ALL.
HAT?!

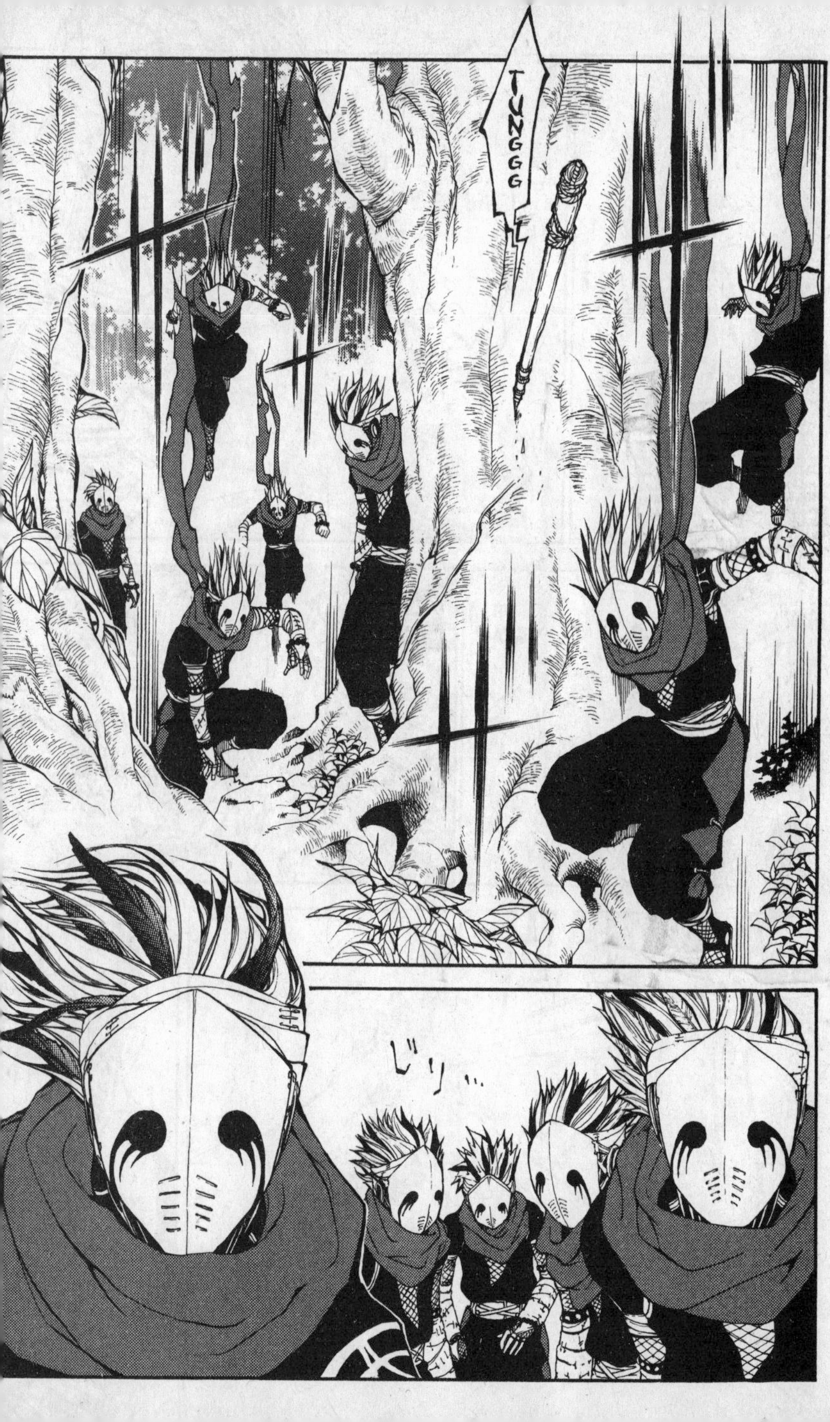
TUNGGG
じり‥

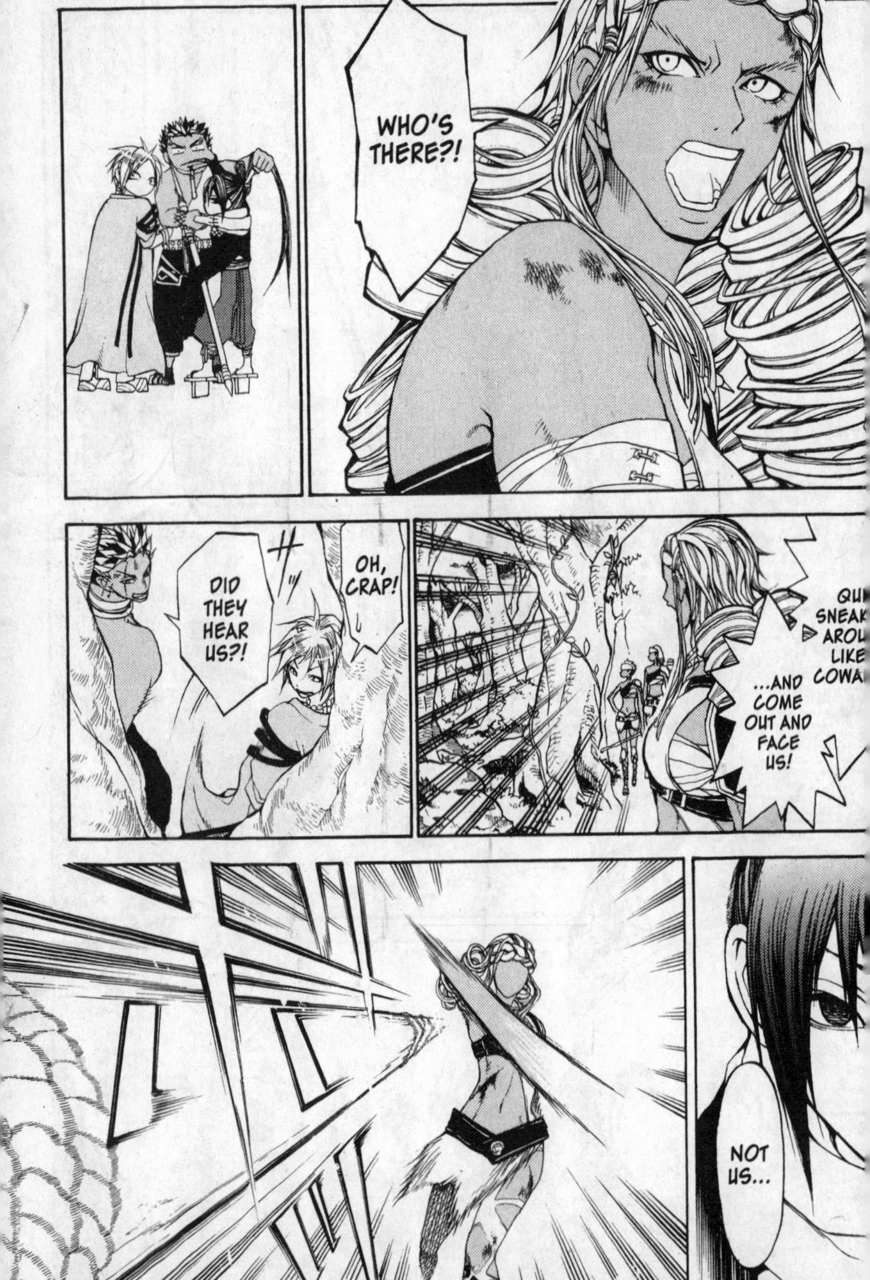
WHO'S THERE?!
...AND COME OUT AND FACE US!
OH, CRAP!
DID THEY HEAR US?!
NOT US...

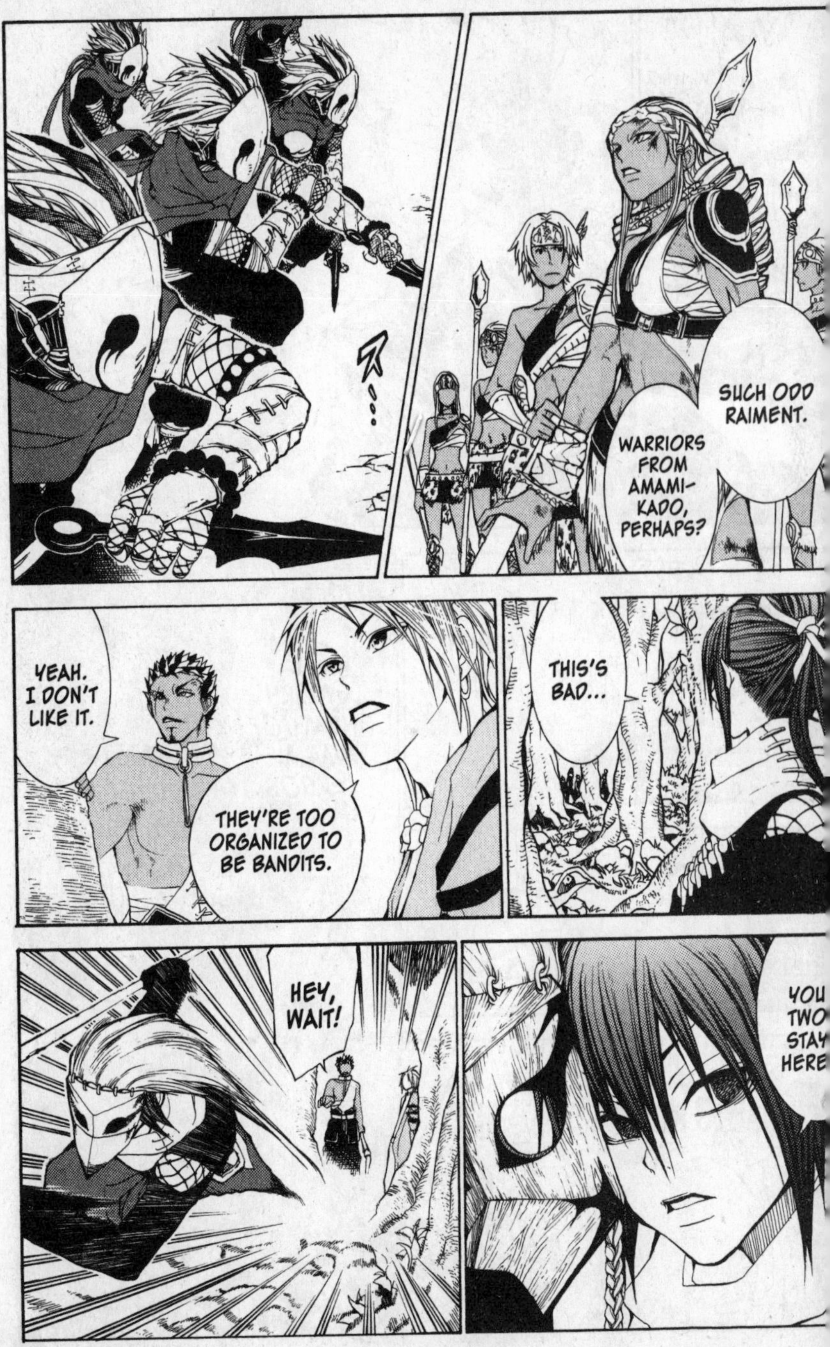
SUCH ODD RAIMENT.
WARRIORS FROM AMAMI-KADO, PERHAPS?
THIS'S BAD...
YEAH. I DON'T LIKE IT.
THEY'RE TOO ORGANIZED TO BE BANDITS.
YOU TWO STAY HERE
HEY, WAIT!

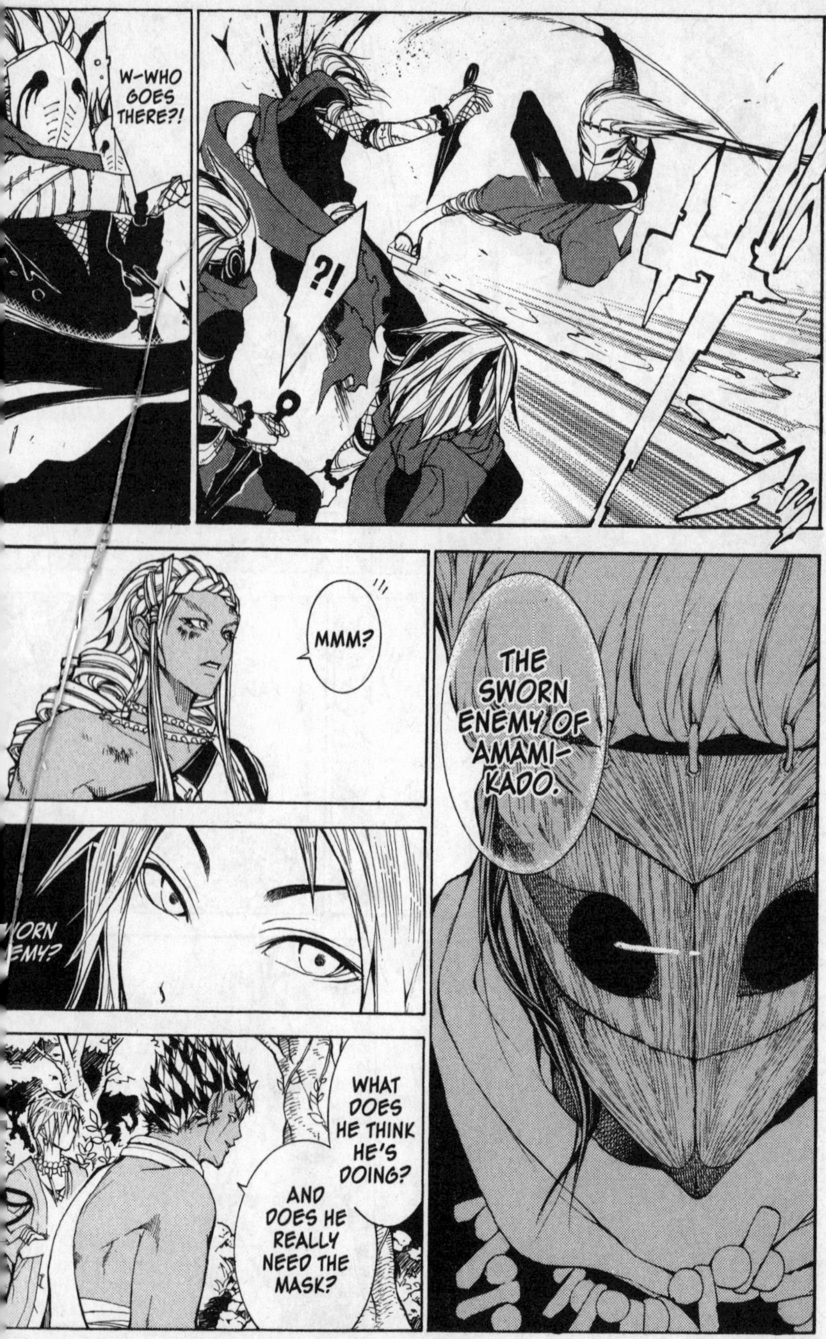
?!
W-WHO GOES THERE?!
THE SWORN ENEMY OF AMAMI-KADO.
MMM?
WORN EMY?
WHAT DOES HE THINK HE'S DOING?
AND DOES HE REALLY NEED THE MASK?

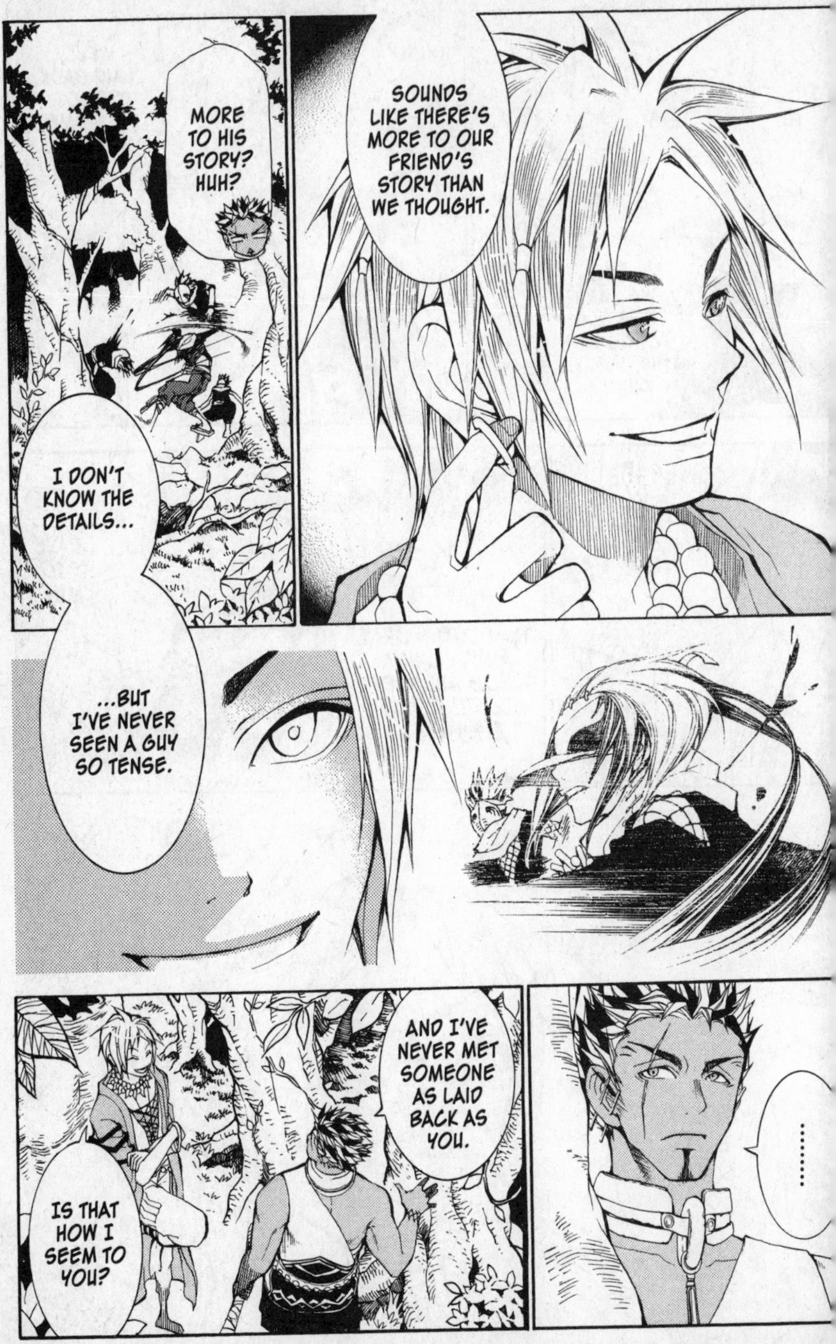
SOUNDS LIKE THERE'S MORE TO OUR FRIEND'S STORY THAN WE THOUGHT.
MORE TO HIS STORY? HUH?
I DON'T KNOW THE DETAILS...
...BUT I'VE NEVER SEEN A GUY SO TENSE.
......
AND I'VE NEVER MET SOMEONE AS LAID BACK AS YOU.
IS THAT HOW I SEEM TO YOU?

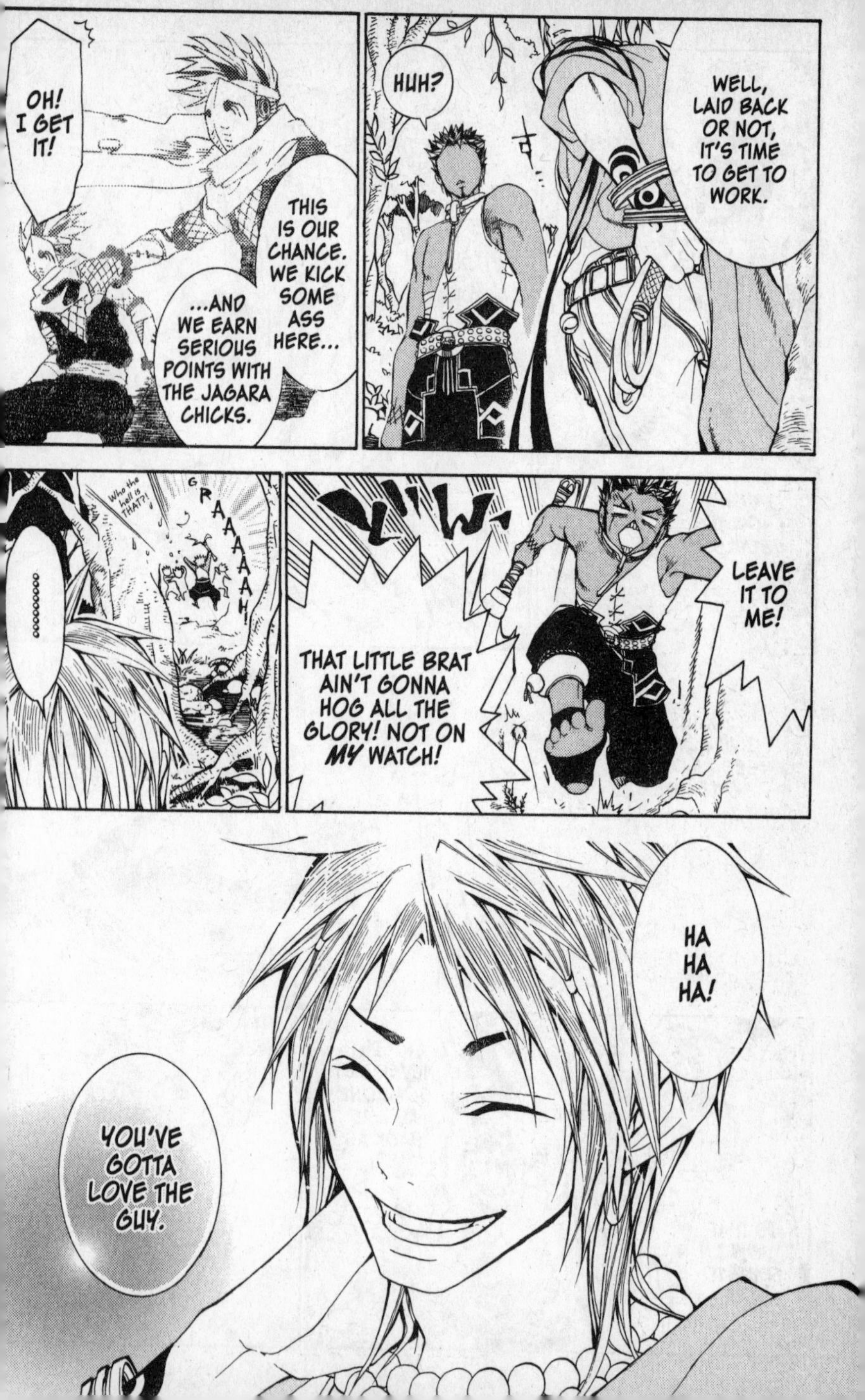
WELL, LAID BACK OR NOT, IT'S TIME TO GET TO WORK.
HUH?
OH! I GET IT!
THIS IS OUR CHANCE. WE KICK SOME ASS HERE...
...AND WE EARN SERIOUS POINTS WITH THE JAGARA CHICKS.
LEAVE IT TO ME!
THAT LITTLE BRAT AIN'T GONNA HOG ALL THE GLORY! NOT ON *MY* WATCH!
Who the hell is THAT?!
GRAAAAAAH!
....
HA HA HA!
YOU'VE GOTTA LOVE THE GUY.

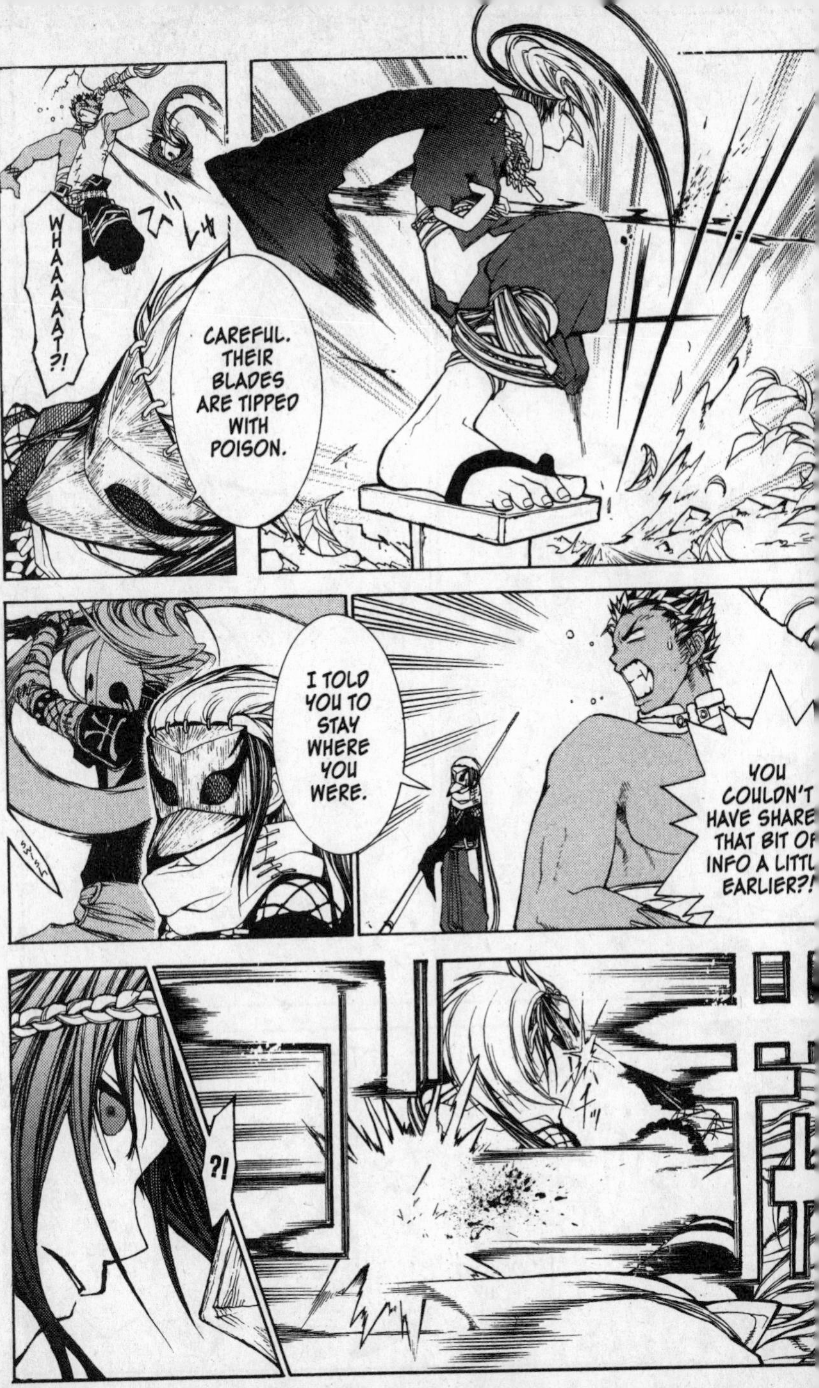
WHAAAAAT?!
CAREFUL. THEIR BLADES ARE TIPPED WITH POISON.
YOU COULDN'T HAVE SHARE THAT BIT OF INFO A LITTL EARLIER?!
I TOLD YOU TO STAY WHERE YOU WERE.
?!

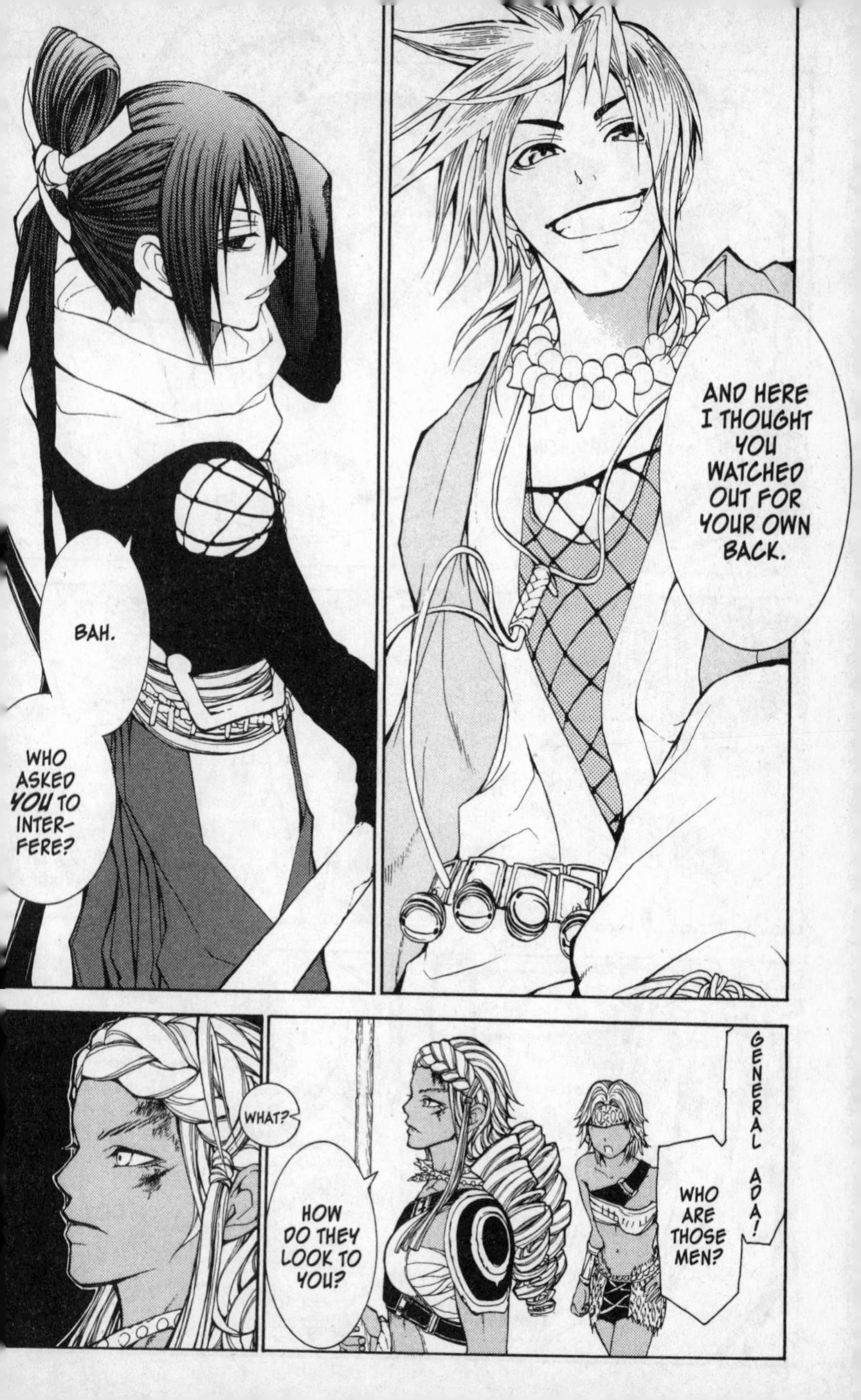
AND HERE I THOUGHT YOU WATCHED OUT FOR YOUR OWN BACK.
BAH.
WHO ASKED YOU TO INTERFERE?
GENERAL ADA!
WHO ARE THOSE MEN?
WHAT?
HOW DO THEY LOOK TO YOU?

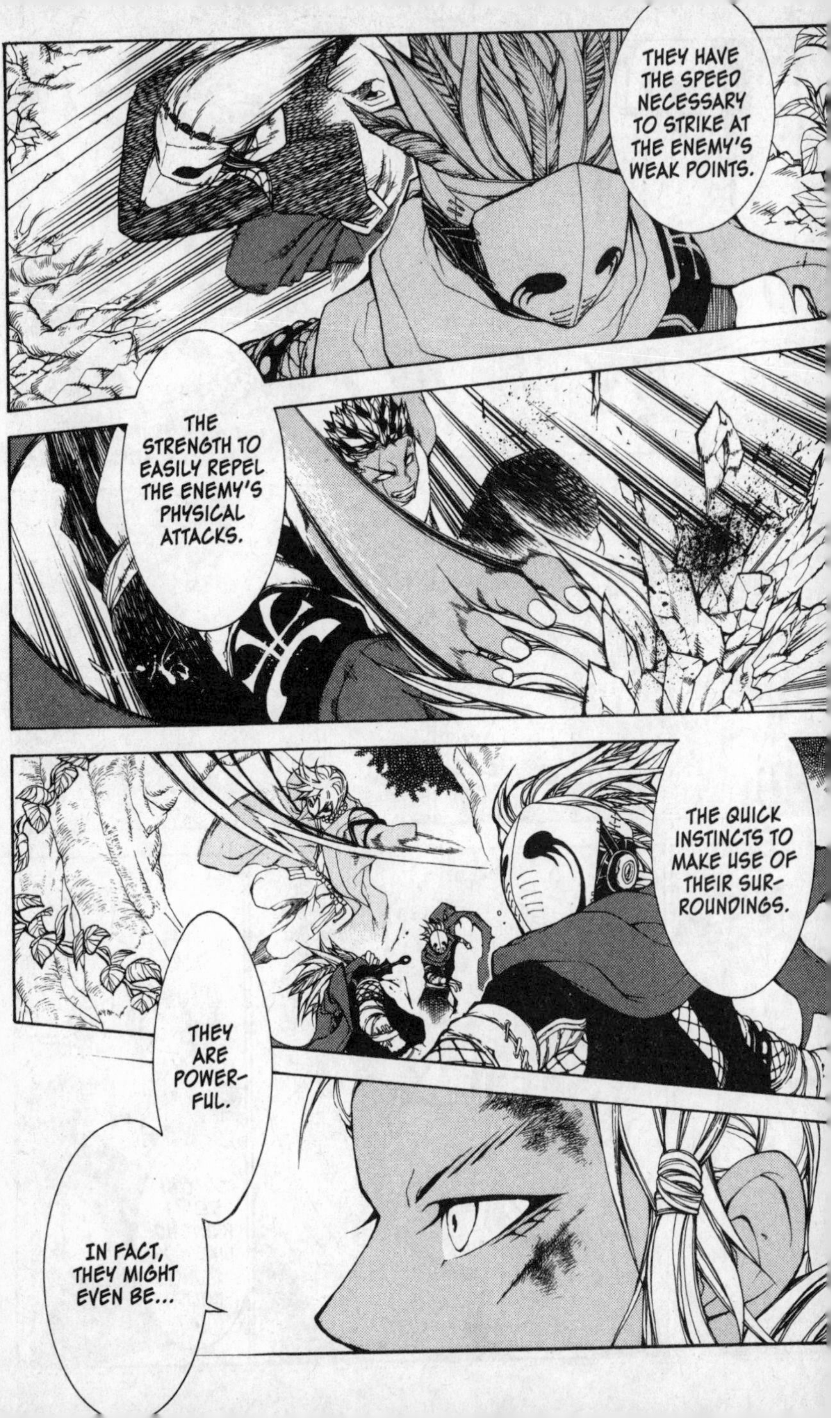
THEY HAVE THE SPEED NECESSARY TO STRIKE AT THE ENEMY'S WEAK POINTS.
THE STRENGTH TO EASILY REPEL THE ENEMY'S PHYSICAL ATTACKS.
THE QUICK INSTINCTS TO MAKE USE OF THEIR SUR-ROUNDINGS.
THEY ARE POWER-FUL.
IN FACT, THEY MIGHT EVEN BE...

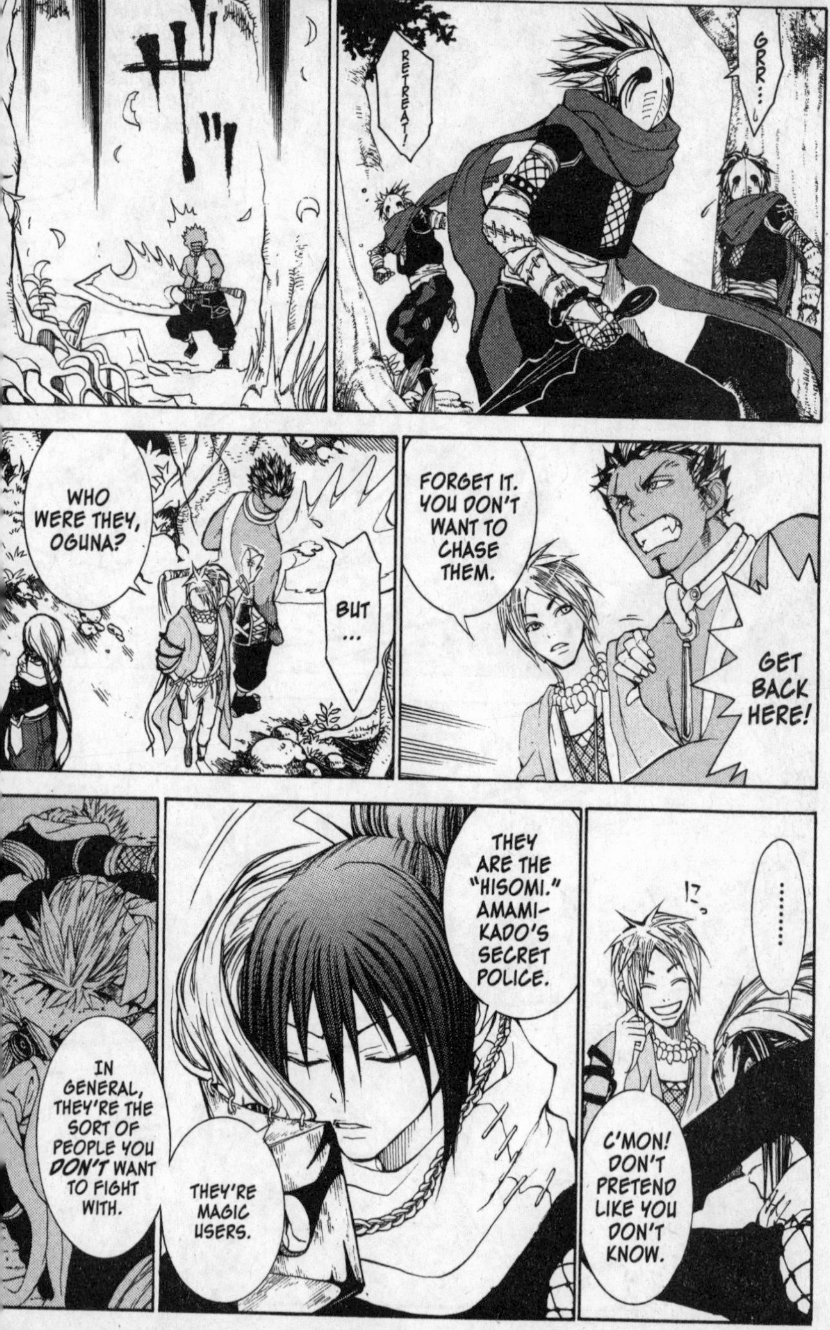
GRR...
RETREAT!
FORGET IT. YOU DON'T WANT TO CHASE THEM.
GET BACK HERE!
BUT ...
WHO WERE THEY, OGUNA?
......
!?
C'MON! DON'T PRETEND LIKE YOU DON'T KNOW.
THEY ARE THE "HISOMI." AMAMI-KADO'S SECRET POLICE.
THEY'RE MAGIC USERS.
IN GENERAL, THEY'RE THE SORT OF PEOPLE YOU *DON'T* WANT TO FIGHT WITH.

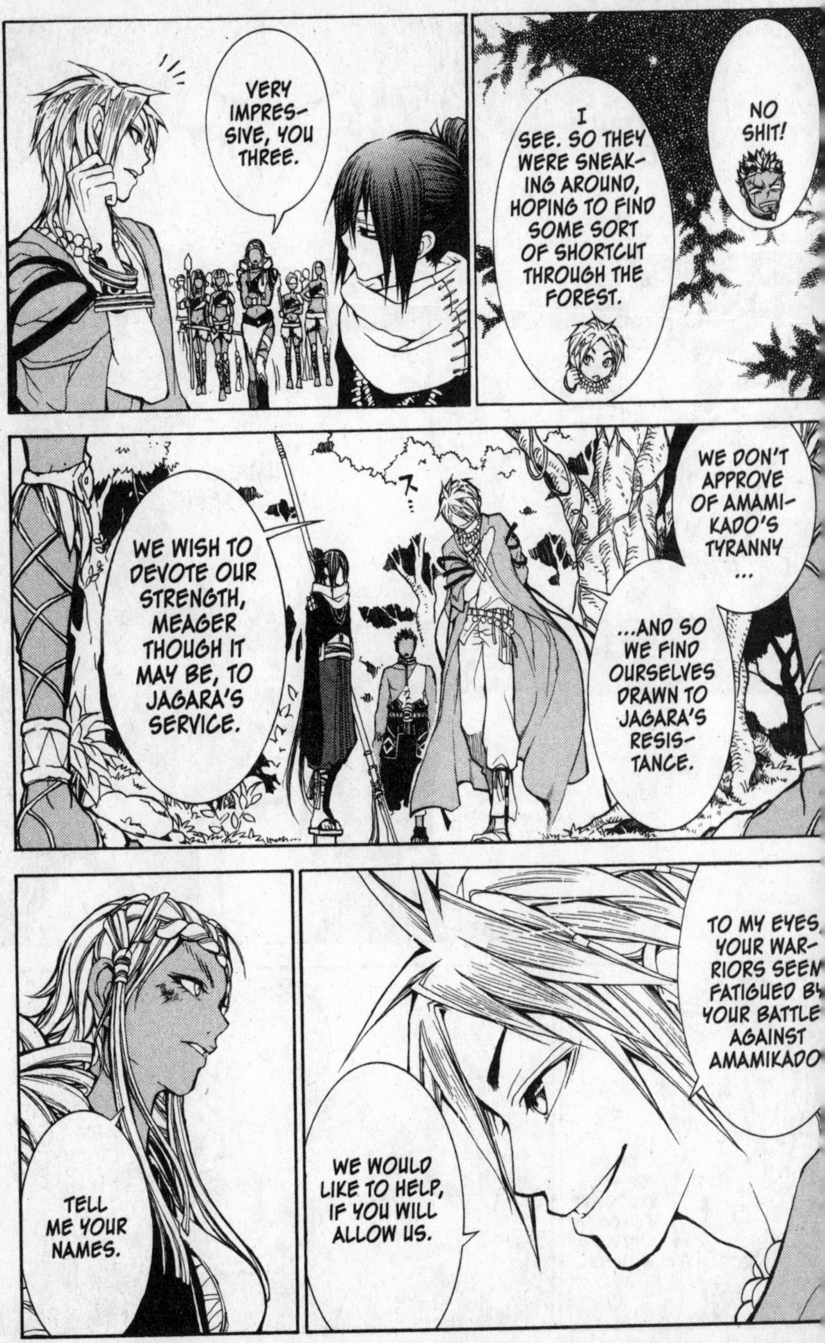
I SEE. SO THEY WERE SNEAKING AROUND, HOPING TO FIND SOME SORT OF SHORTCUT THROUGH THE FOREST.
NO SHIT!
VERY IMPRESSIVE, YOU THREE.
WE DON'T APPROVE OF AMAMIKADO'S TYRANNY ...
...AND SO WE FIND OURSELVES DRAWN TO JAGARA'S RESISTANCE.
WE WISH TO DEVOTE OUR STRENGTH, MEAGER THOUGH IT MAY BE, TO JAGARA'S SERVICE.
TO MY EYES, YOUR WARRIORS SEEM FATIGUED BY YOUR BATTLE AGAINST AMAMIKADO
WE WOULD LIKE TO HELP, IF YOU WILL ALLOW US.
TELL ME YOUR NAMES.

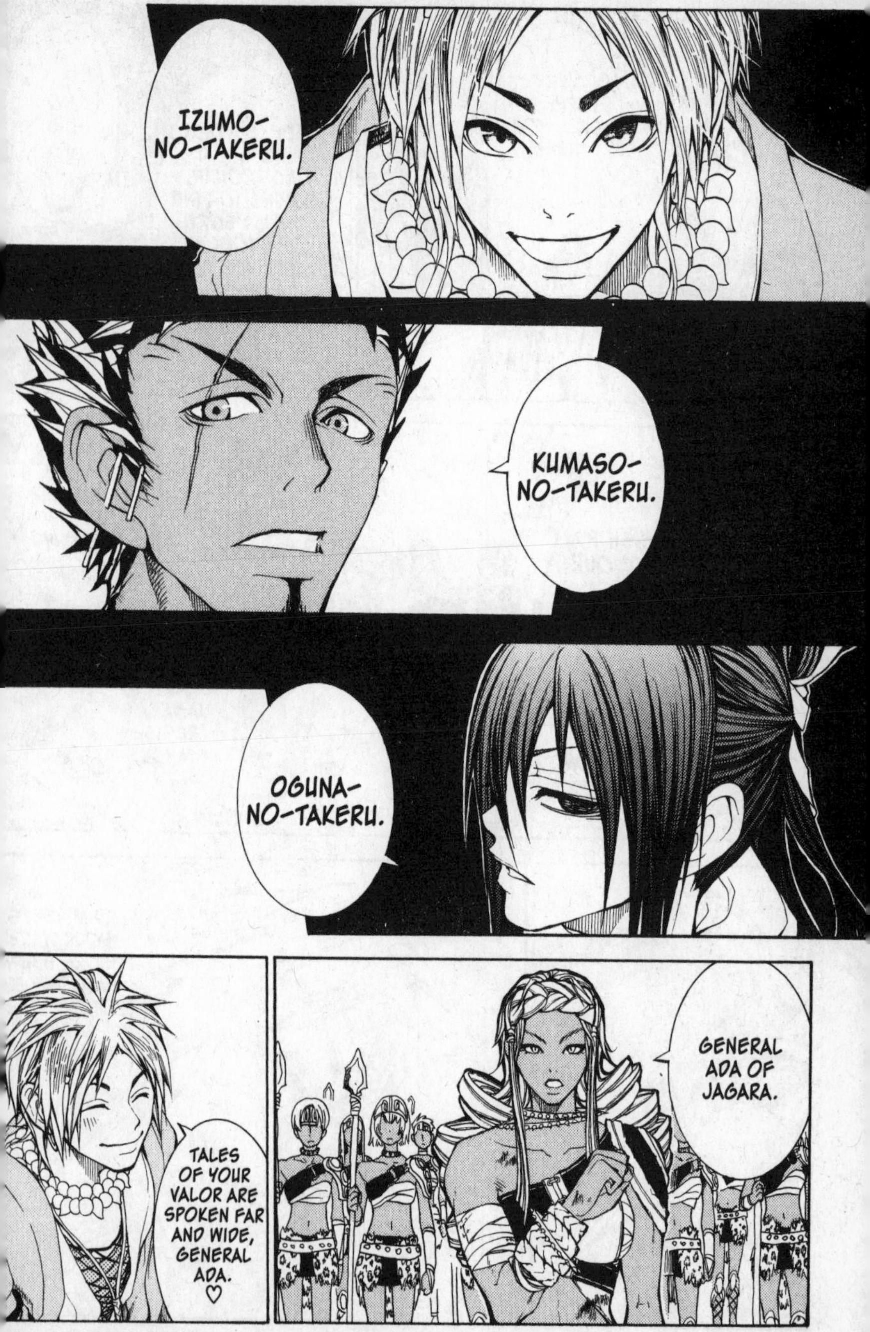
IZUMO-NO-TAKERU.
KUMASO-NO-TAKERU.
OGUNA-NO-TAKERU.
GENERAL ADA OF JAGARA.
TALES OF YOUR VALOR ARE SPOKEN FAR AND WIDE, GENERAL ADA. ♡

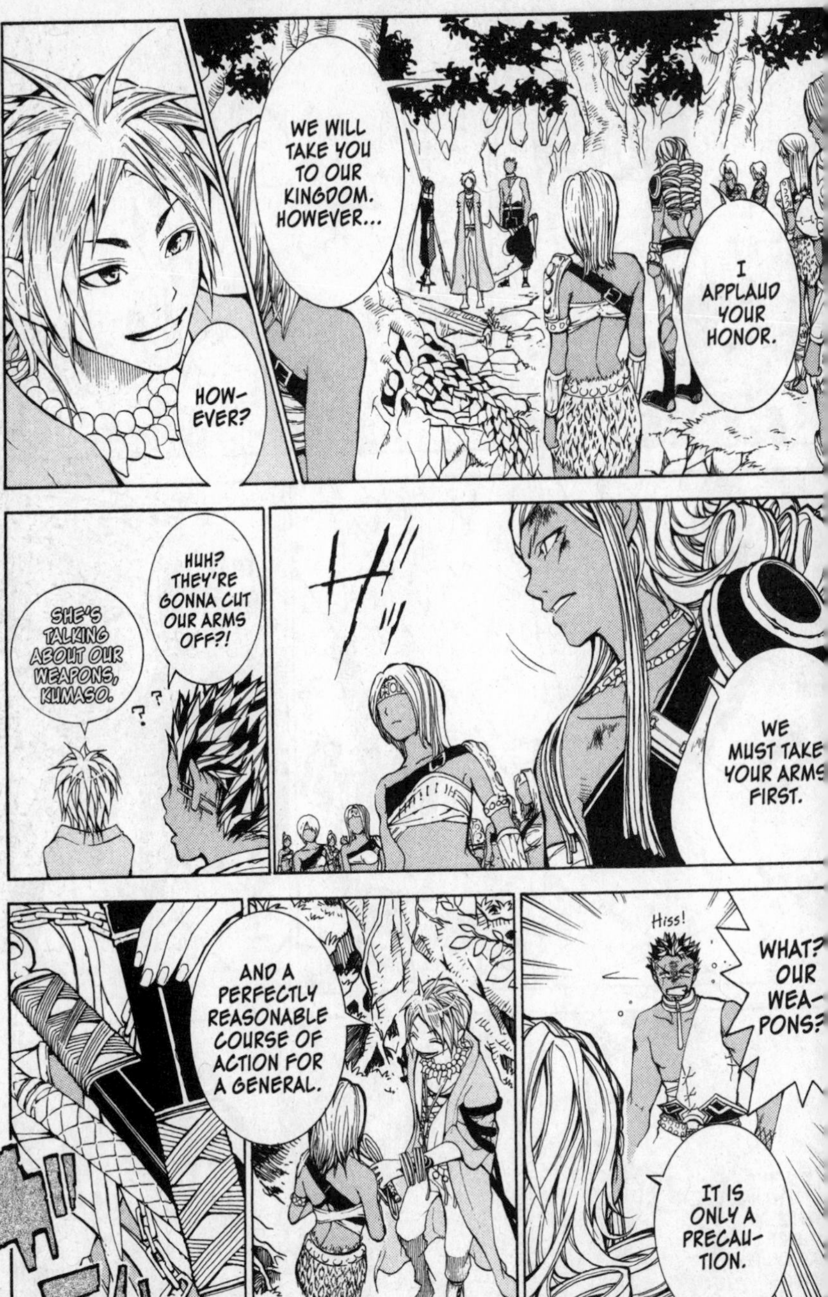
I APPLAUD YOUR HONOR.
WE WILL TAKE YOU TO OUR KINGDOM. HOWEVER...
HOW-EVER?
WE MUST TAKE YOUR ARMS FIRST.
HUH? THEY'RE GONNA CUT OUR ARMS OFF?!
SHE'S TALKING ABOUT OUR WEAPONS, KUMASO.
Hiss!
WHAT? OUR WEA-PONS?
IT IS ONLY A PRECAU-TION.
AND A PERFECTLY REASONABLE COURSE OF ACTION FOR A GENERAL.

・・・・・・・・

IF YOU
SAY SO.

GO
ON.

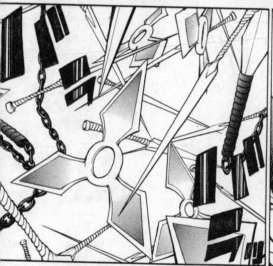

THAT
ALL?

・・・・・・・・

I DON'T
EVEN WANNA
GUESS
WHERE HE
WAS KEEPIN'
THOSE.

○○○○○○○

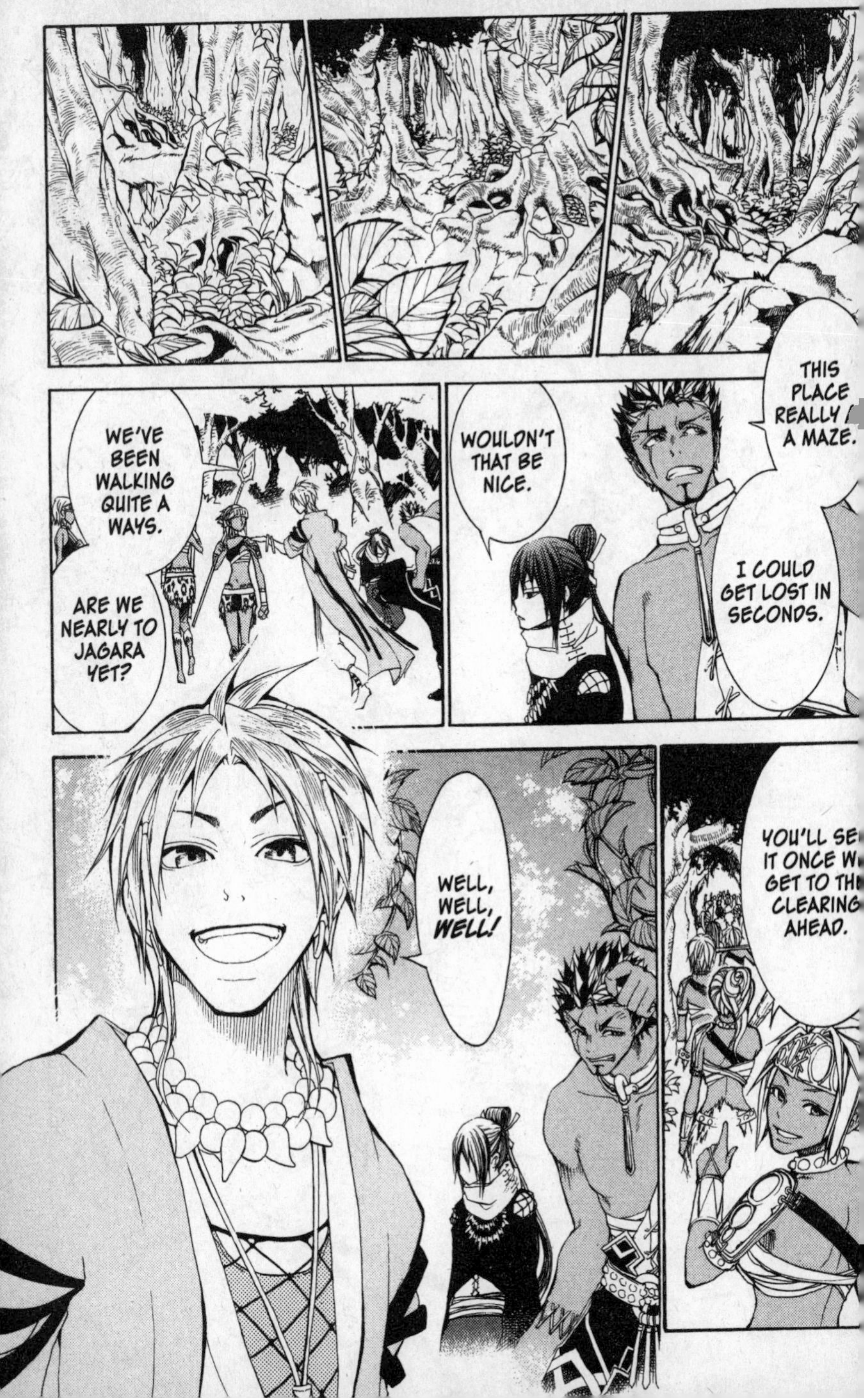
THIS PLACE REALLY A MAZE.
I COULD GET LOST IN SECONDS.
WOULDN'T THAT BE NICE.
WE'VE BEEN WALKING QUITE A WAYS.
ARE WE NEARLY TO JAGARA YET?
YOU'LL SE IT ONCE W GET TO TH CLEARING AHEAD.
WELL, WELL, *WELL!*

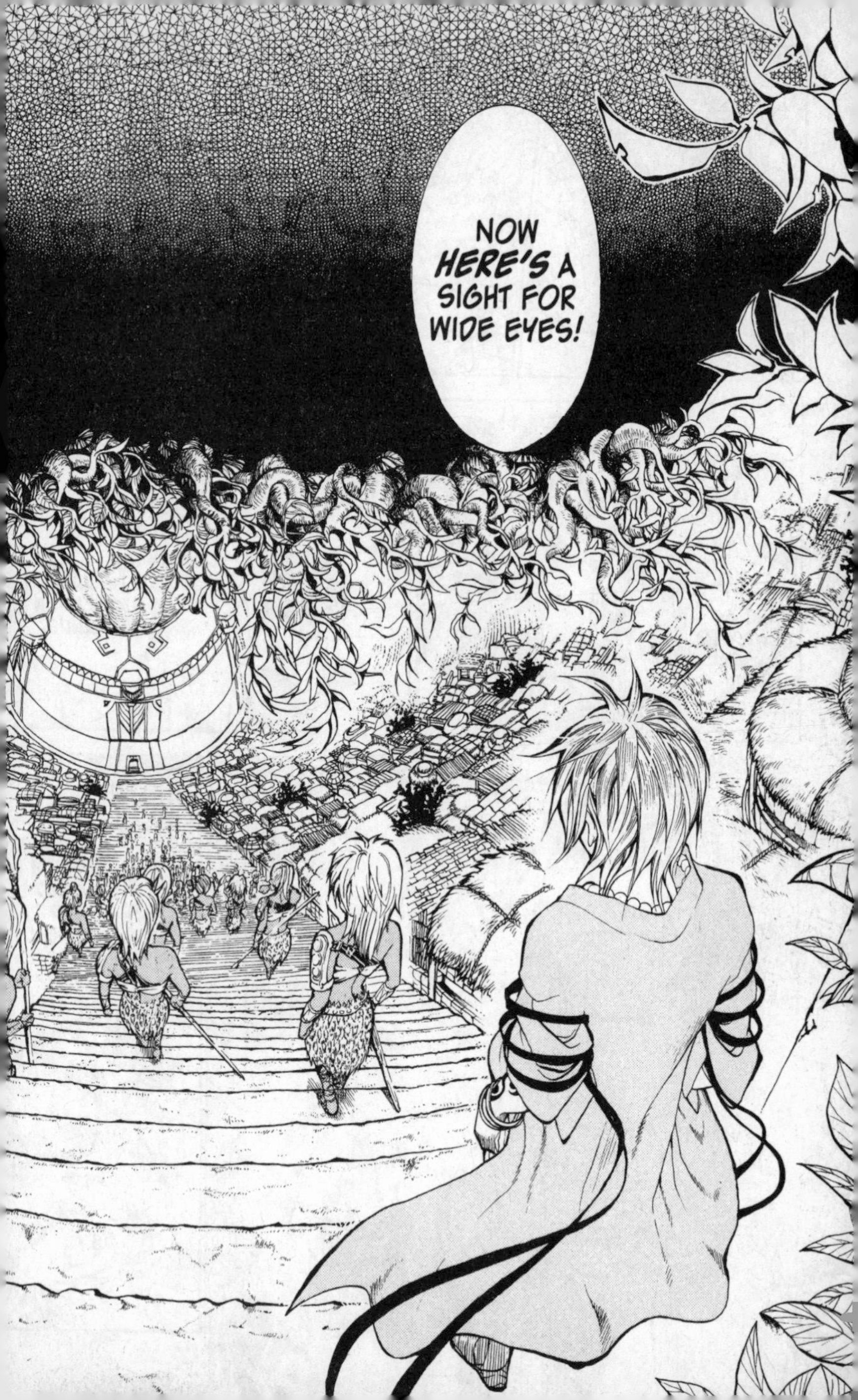
NOW HERE'S A SIGHT FOR WIDE EYES!

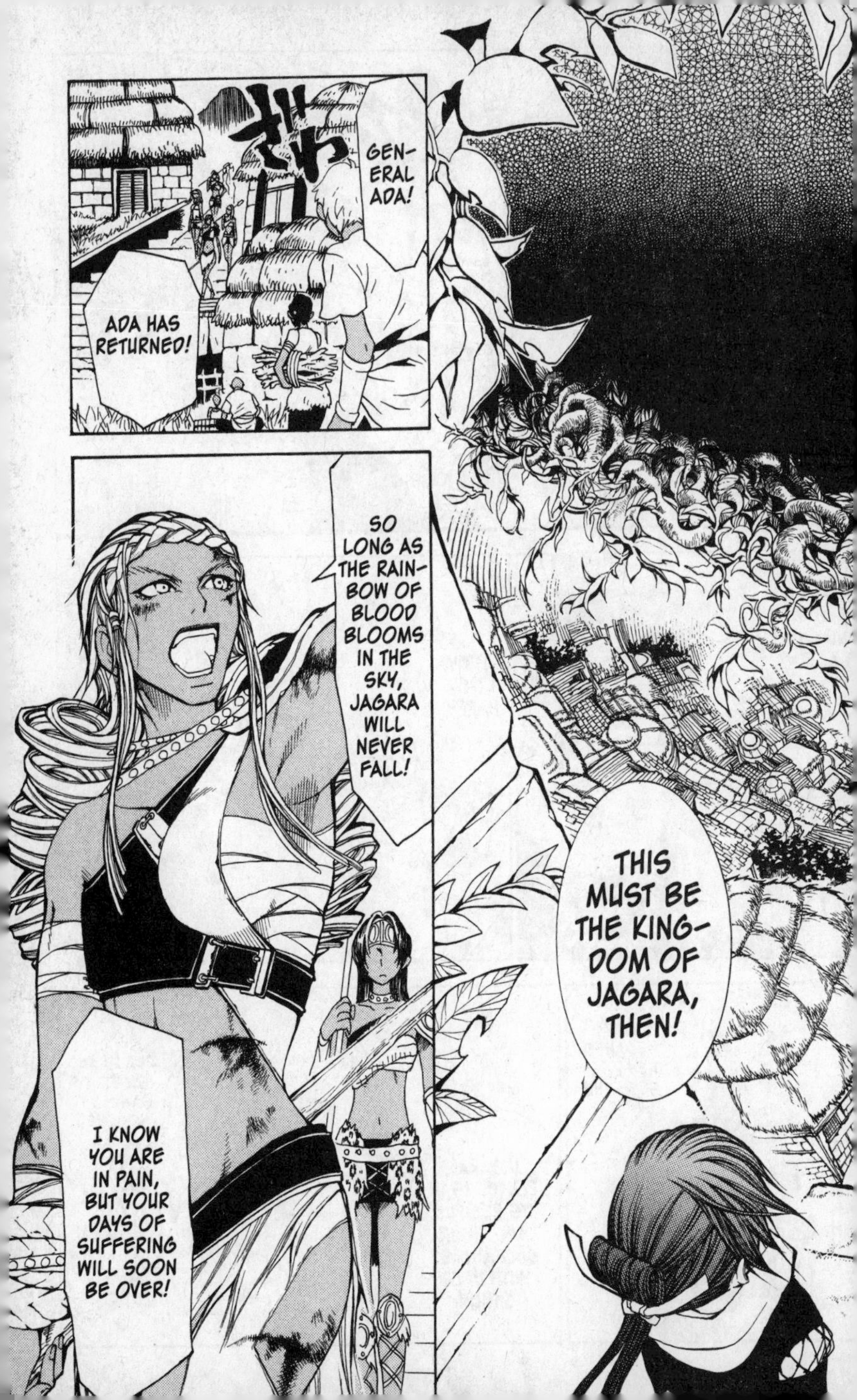
THIS MUST BE THE KING-DOM OF JAGARA, THEN!
GEN-ERAL ADA!
ADA HAS RETURNED!
SO LONG AS THE RAIN-BOW OF BLOOD BLOOMS IN THE SKY, JAGARA WILL NEVER FALL!
I KNOW YOU ARE IN PAIN, BUT YOUR DAYS OF SUFFERING WILL SOON BE OVER!

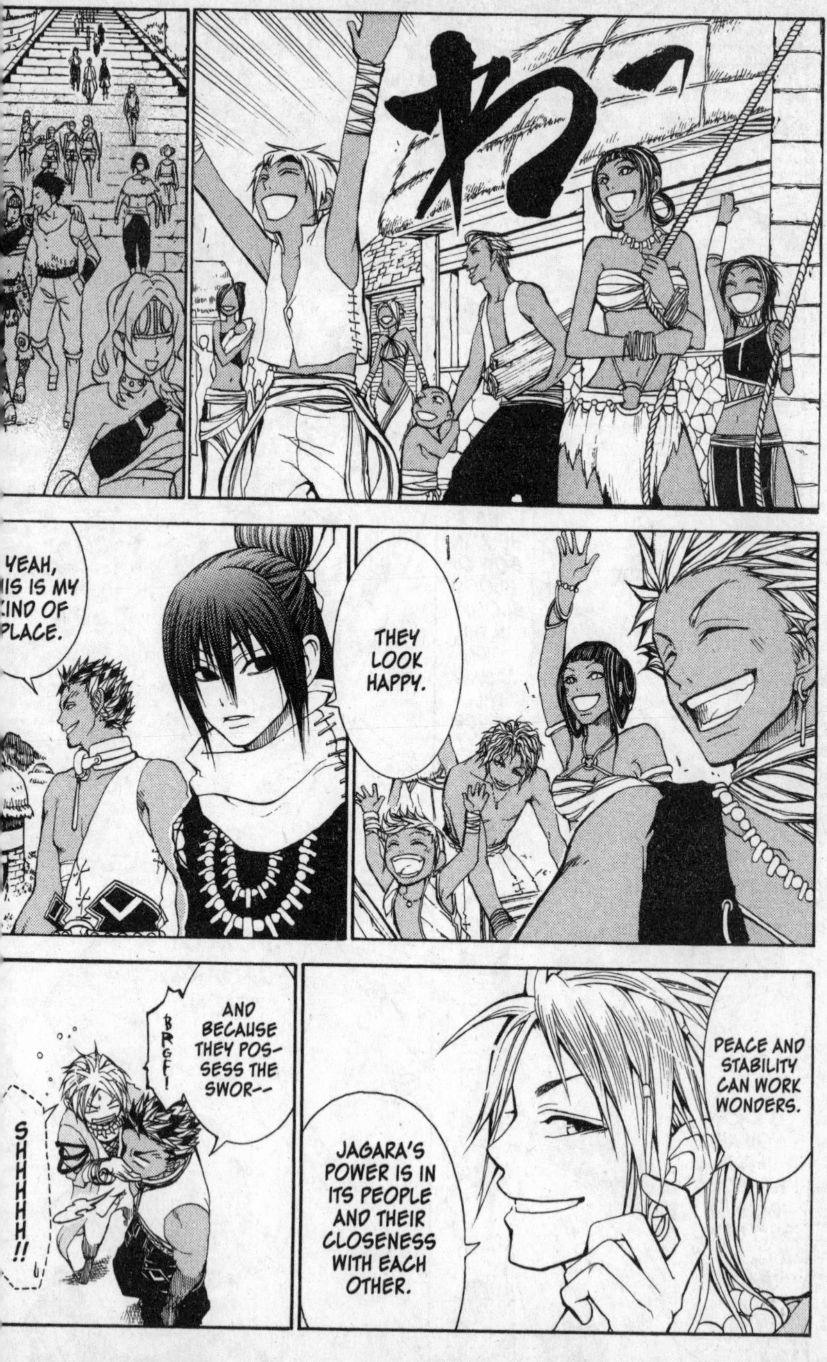
わっ
THEY LOOK HAPPY.
YEAH, IS IS MY IND OF PLACE.
PEACE AND STABILITY CAN WORK WONDERS.
JAGARA'S POWER IS IN ITS PEOPLE AND THEIR CLOSENESS WITH EACH OTHER.
AND BECAUSE THEY POS-SESS THE SWOR--
BRGF!
SHHHHH!!

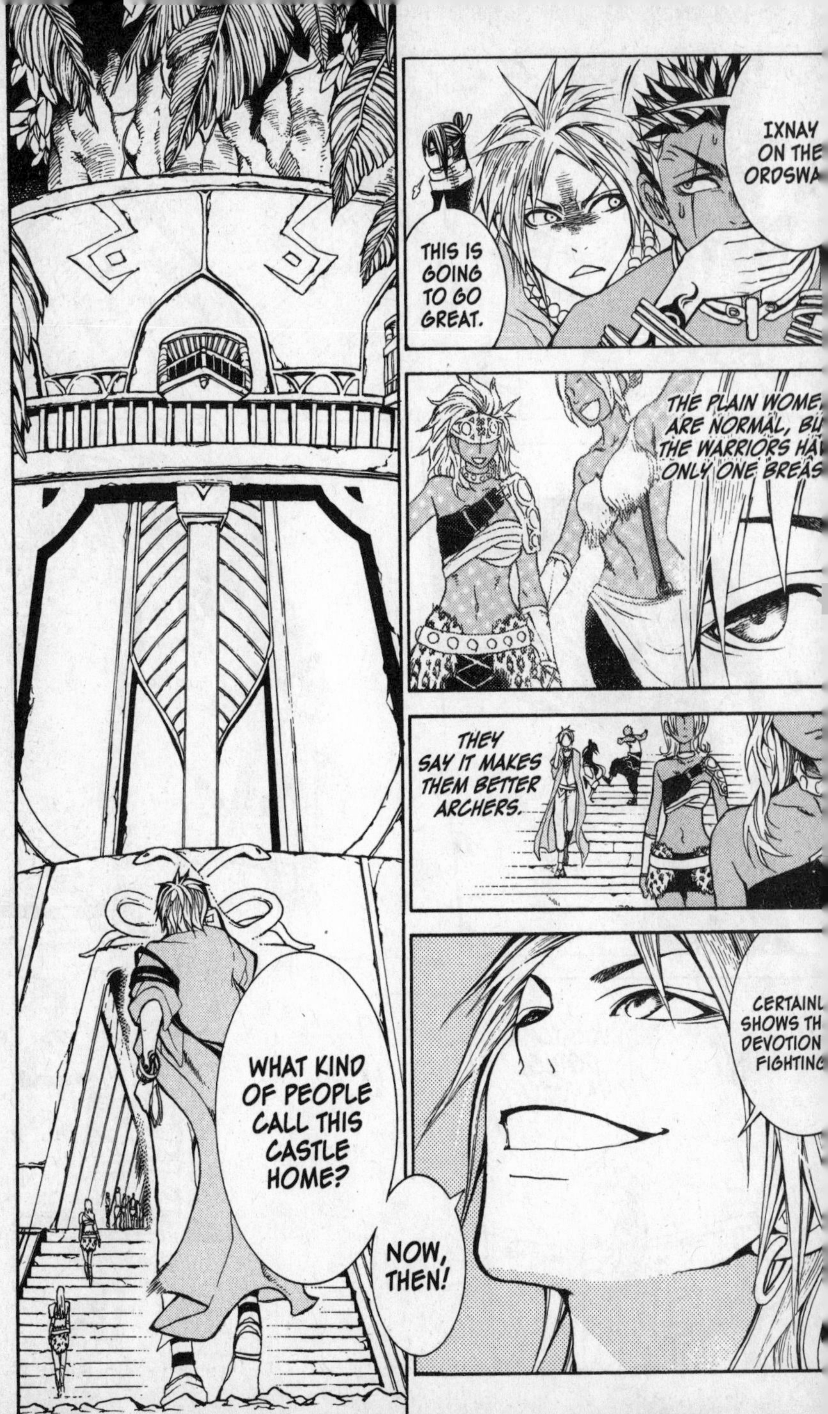
IXNAY ON THE ORDSWA
THIS IS GOING TO GO GREAT.
THE PLAIN WOME, ARE NORMAL, BU THE WARRIORS HA ONLY ONE BREAS
THEY SAY IT MAKES THEM BETTER ARCHERS.
CERTAINL SHOWS TH DEVOTION FIGHTING
WHAT KIND OF PEOPLE CALL THIS CASTLE HOME?
NOW, THEN!

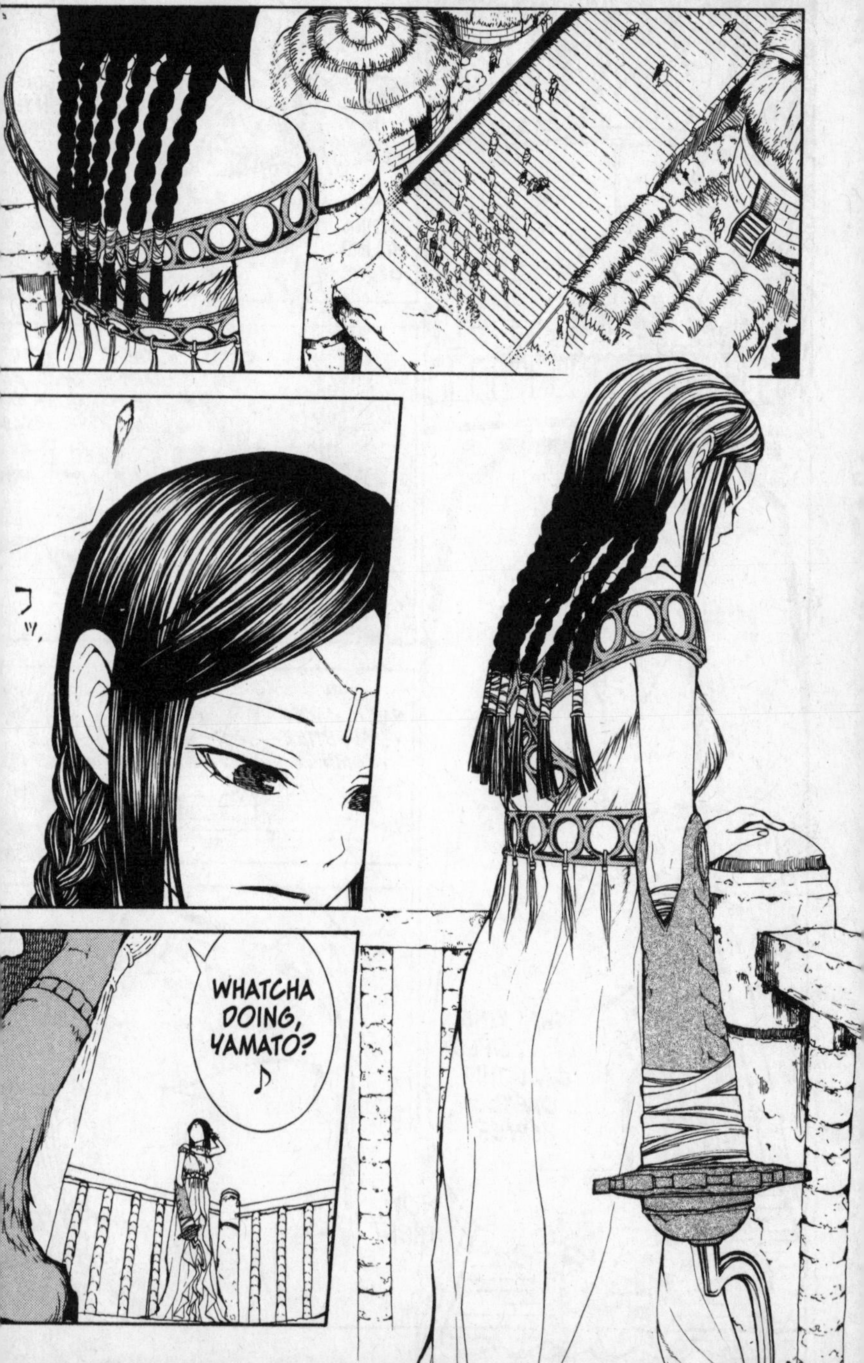
WHATCHA DOING, YAMATO? ♪

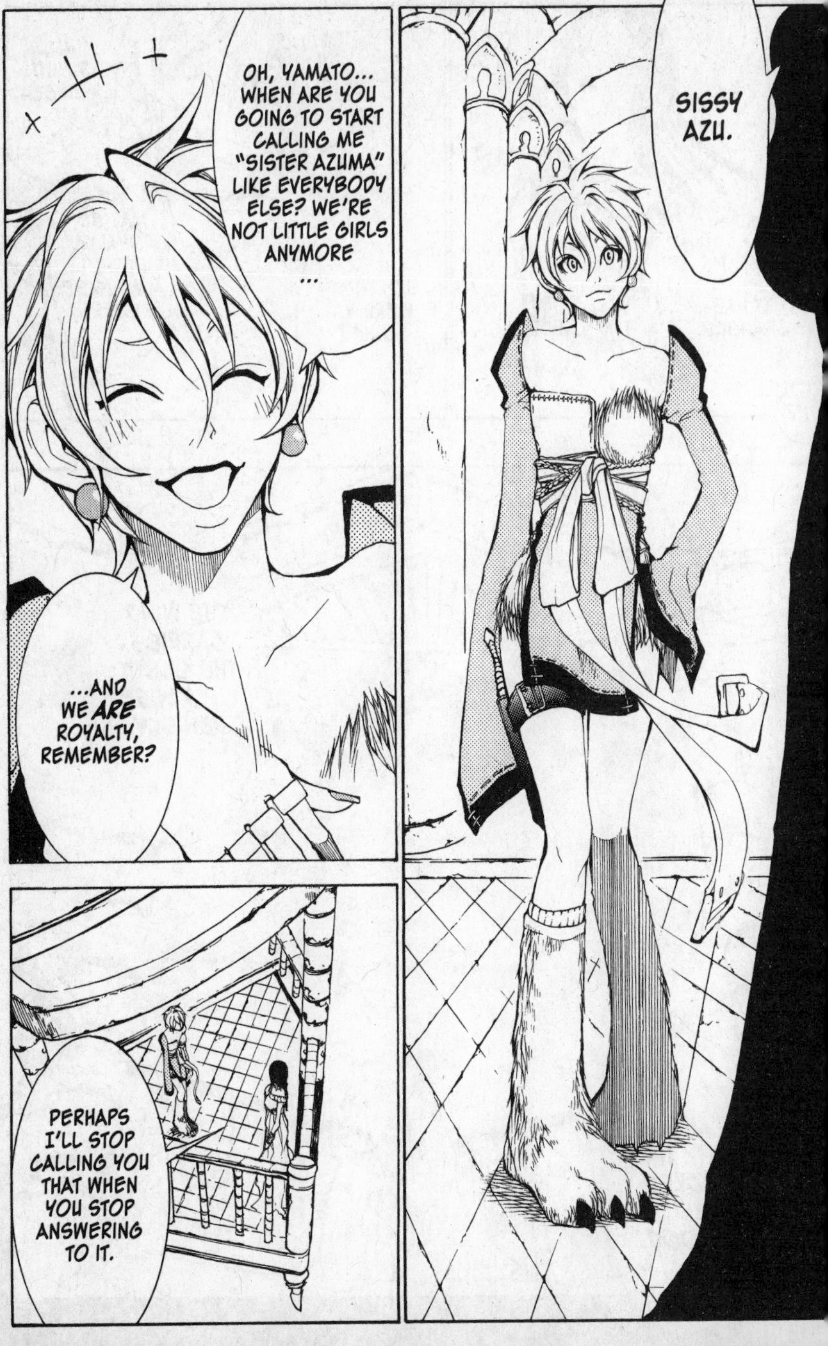
SISSY AZU.
OH, YAMATO... WHEN ARE YOU GOING TO START CALLING ME "SISTER AZUMA" LIKE EVERYBODY ELSE? WE'RE NOT LITTLE GIRLS ANYMORE ...
...AND WE *ARE* ROYALTY, REMEMBER?
PERHAPS I'LL STOP CALLING YOU THAT WHEN YOU STOP ANSWERING TO IT.

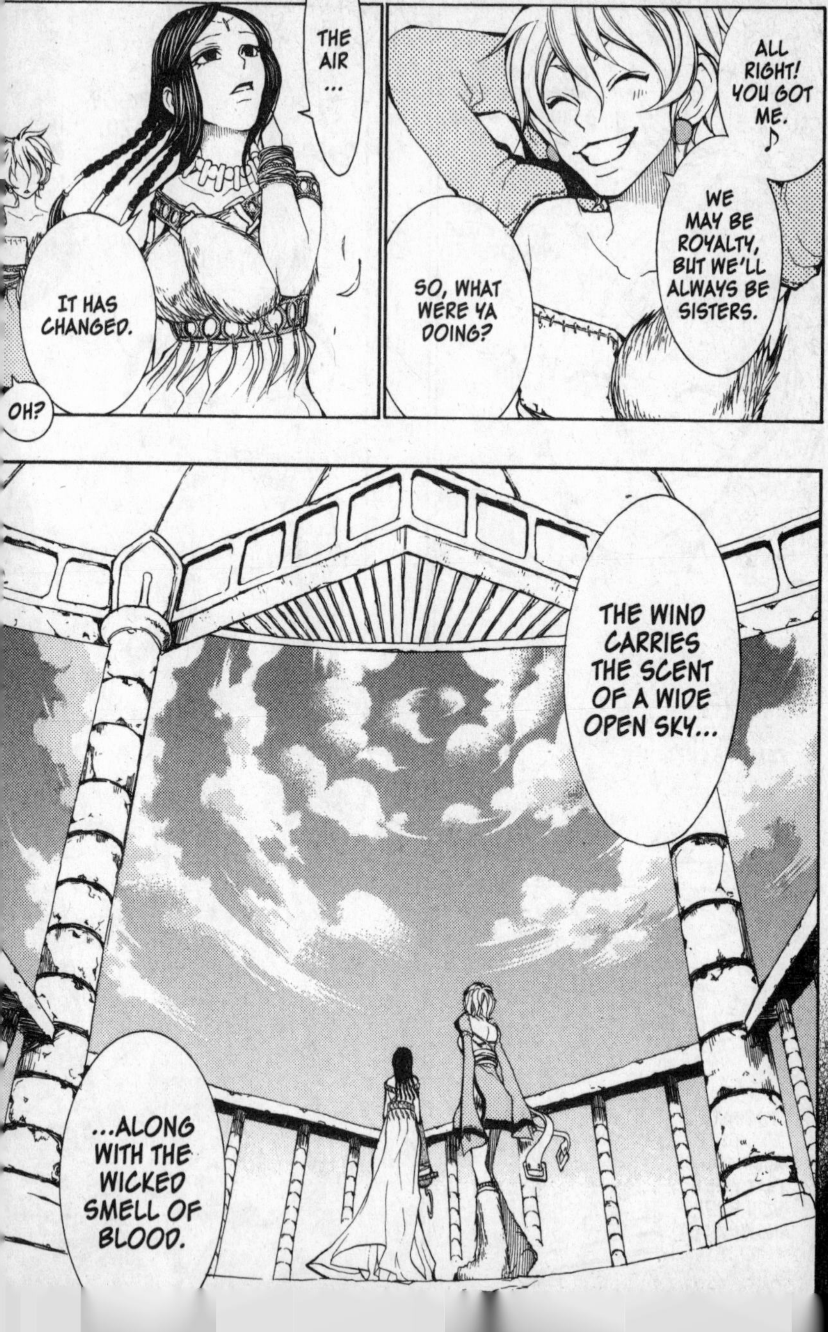
ALL RIGHT! YOU GOT ME. ♪
WE MAY BE ROYALTY, BUT WE'LL ALWAYS BE SISTERS.
SO, WHAT WERE YA DOING?
THE AIR ...
IT HAS CHANGED.
OH?
THE WIND CARRIES THE SCENT OF A WIDE OPEN SKY...
...ALONG WITH THE WICKED SMELL OF BLOOD.

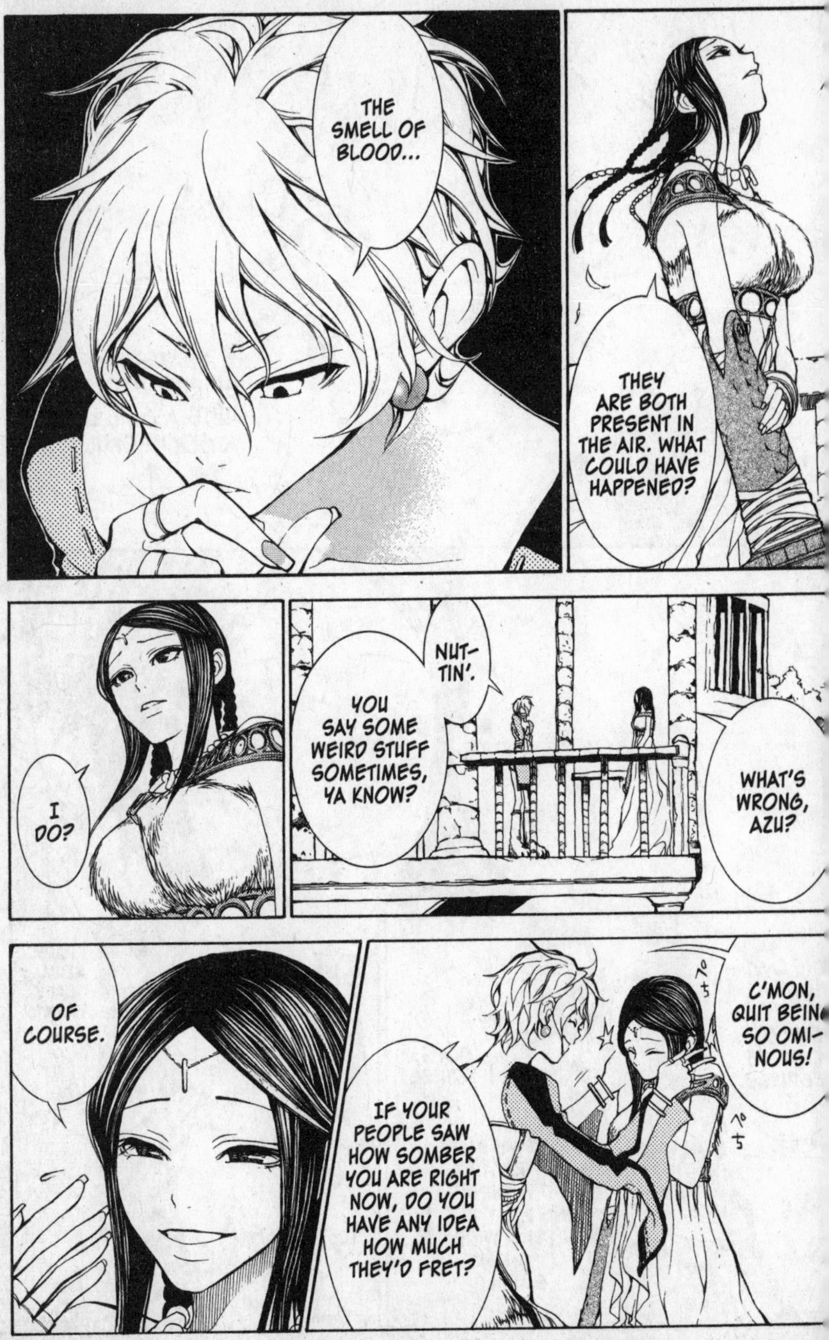
THEY ARE BOTH PRESENT IN THE AIR. WHAT COULD HAVE HAPPENED?
THE SMELL OF BLOOD...
WHAT'S WRONG, AZU?
NUT-TIN'.
YOU SAY SOME WEIRD STUFF SOMETIMES, YA KNOW?
I DO?
C'MON, QUIT BEIN SO OMI-NOUS!
ぺち
ぺち
IF YOUR PEOPLE SAW HOW SOMBER YOU ARE RIGHT NOW, DO YOU HAVE ANY IDEA HOW MUCH THEY'D FRET?
OF COURSE.

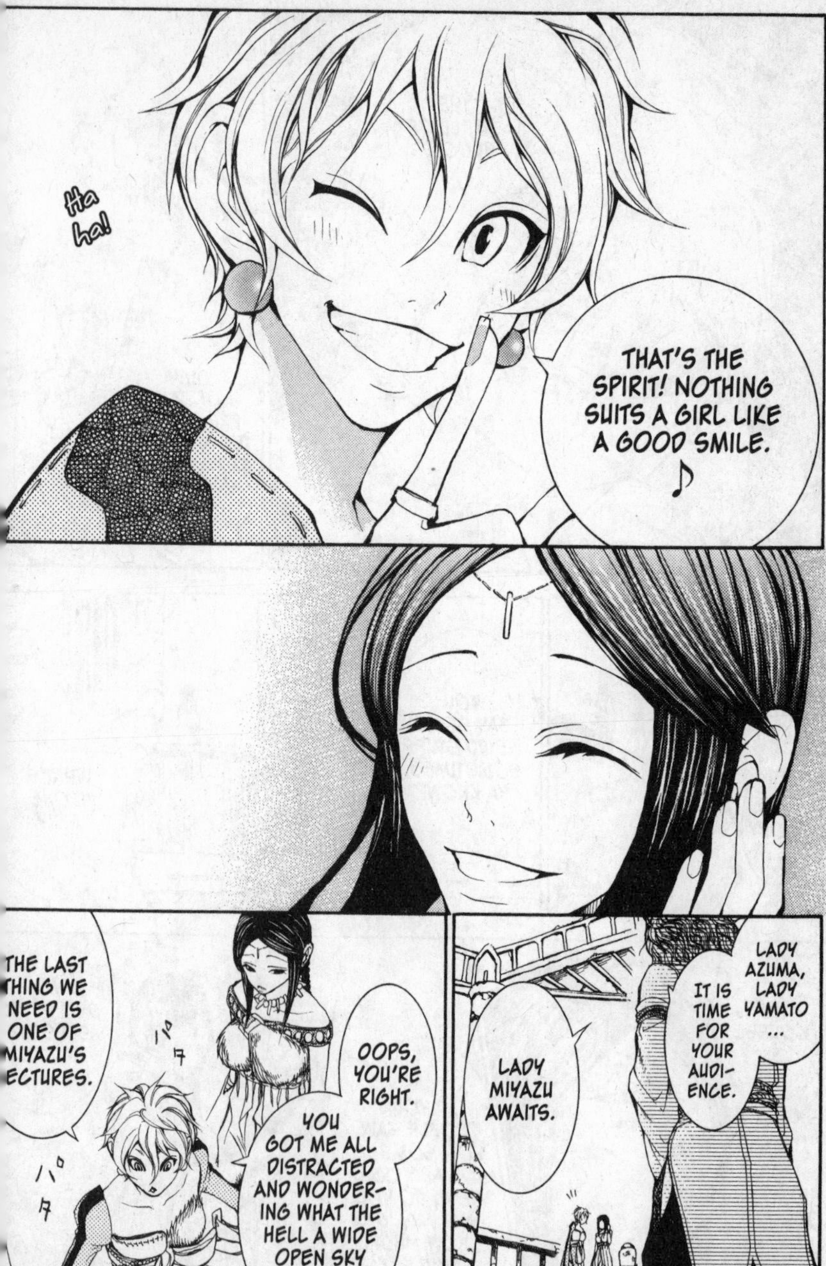
THAT'S THE SPIRIT! NOTHING SUITS A GIRL LIKE A GOOD SMILE. ♪
Ha ha!
LADY AZUMA, LADY YAMATO ...
IT IS TIME FOR YOUR AUDIENCE.
LADY MIYAZU AWAITS.
THE LAST THING WE NEED IS ONE OF MIYAZU'S LECTURES.
OOPS, YOU'RE RIGHT.
YOU GOT ME ALL DISTRACTED AND WONDERING WHAT THE HELL A WIDE OPEN SKY SMELLS LIKE.

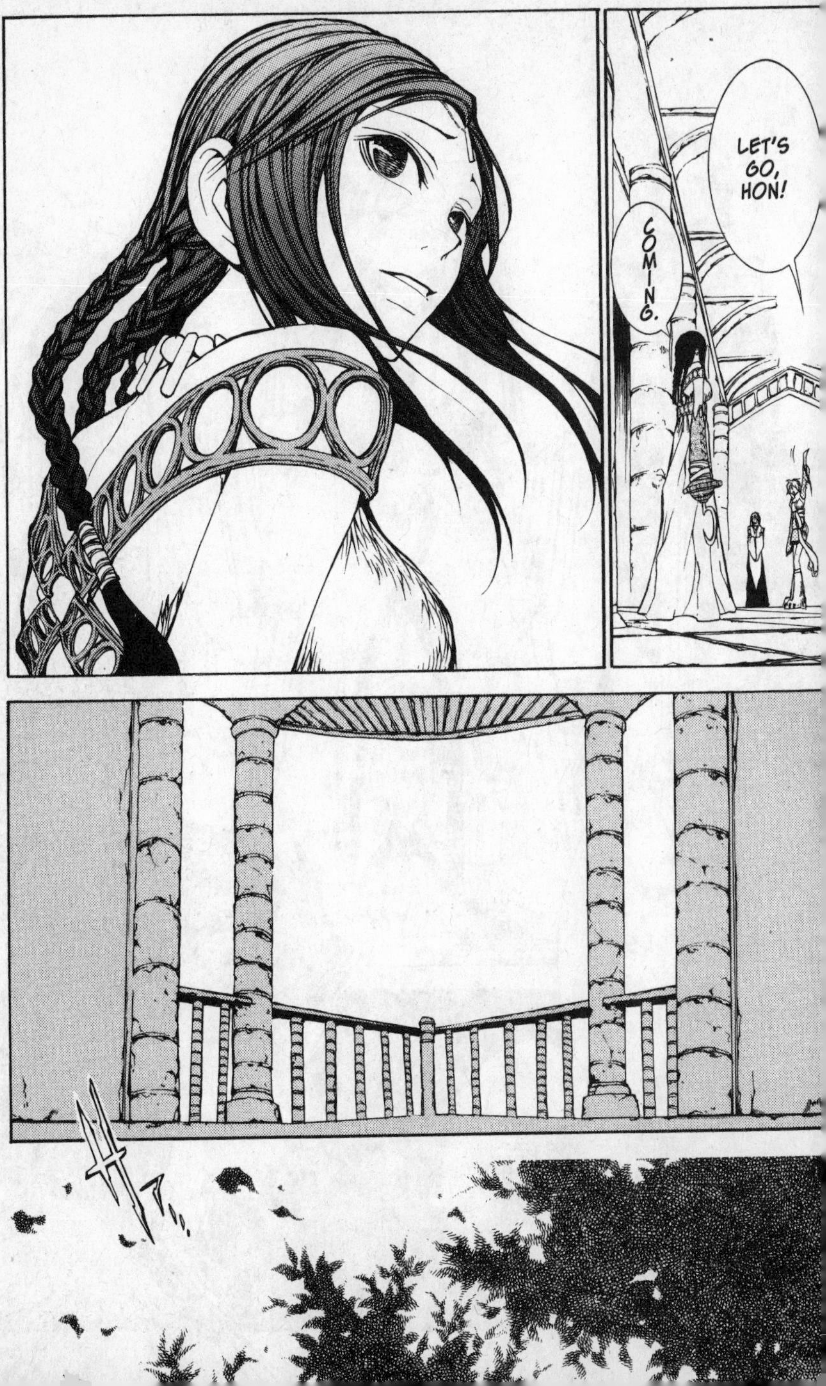
LET'S GO, HON!
COMING.

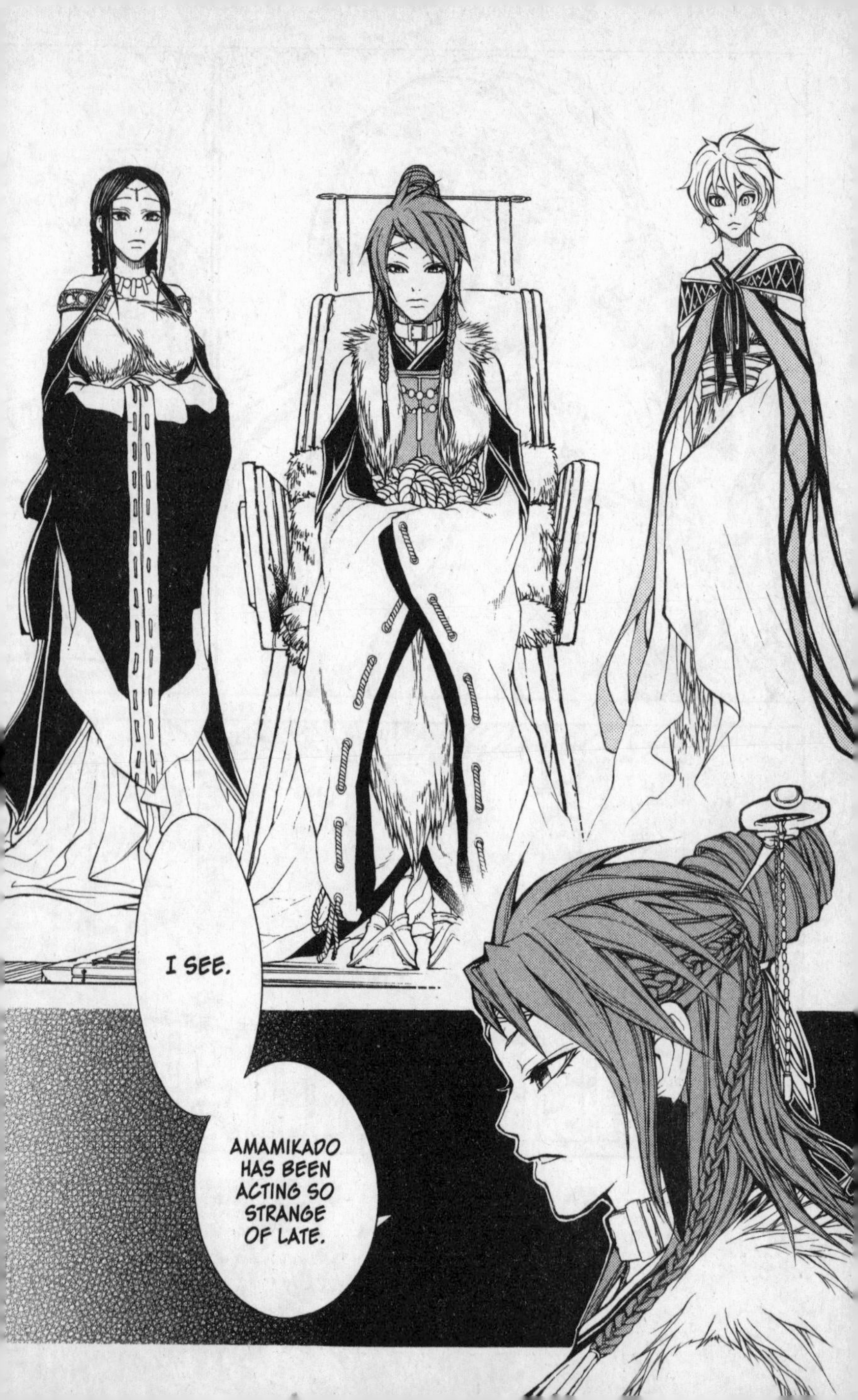
I SEE.
AMAMIKADO HAS BEEN ACTING SO STRANGE OF LATE.

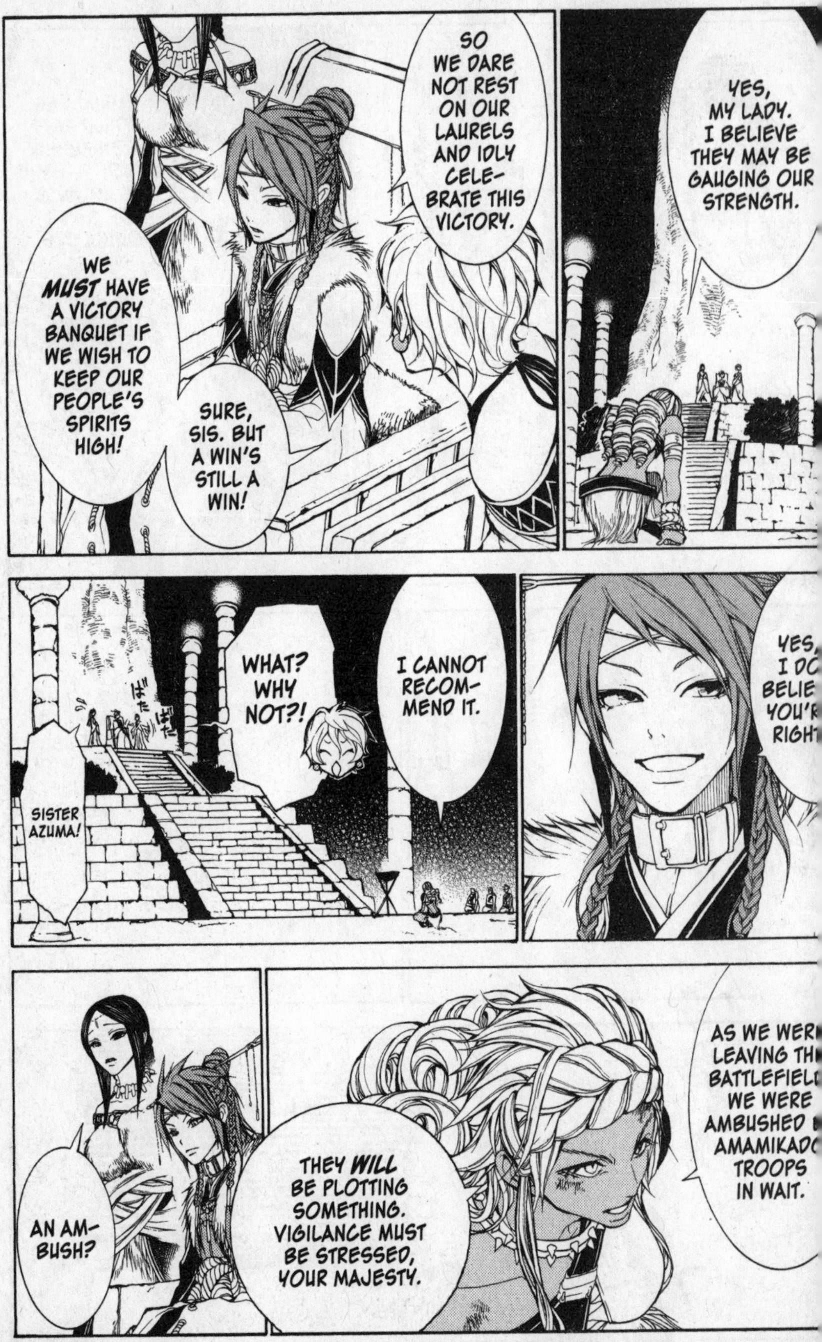
YES, MY LADY. I BELIEVE THEY MAY BE GAUGING OUR STRENGTH.
SO WE DARE NOT REST ON OUR LAURELS AND IDLY CELE- BRATE THIS VICTORY.
WE MUST HAVE A VICTORY BANQUET IF WE WISH TO KEEP OUR PEOPLE'S SPIRITS HIGH!
SURE, SIS. BUT A WIN'S STILL A WIN!
YES, I DC BELIE YOU'R RIGHT
I CANNOT RECOM- MEND IT.
WHAT? WHY NOT?!
ばた ばた
SISTER AZUMA!
AS WE WER LEAVING TH BATTLEFIEL WE WERE AMBUSHED AMAMIKAD TROOPS IN WAIT.
THEY WILL BE PLOTTING SOMETHING. VIGILANCE MUST BE STRESSED, YOUR MAJESTY.
AN AM- BUSH?

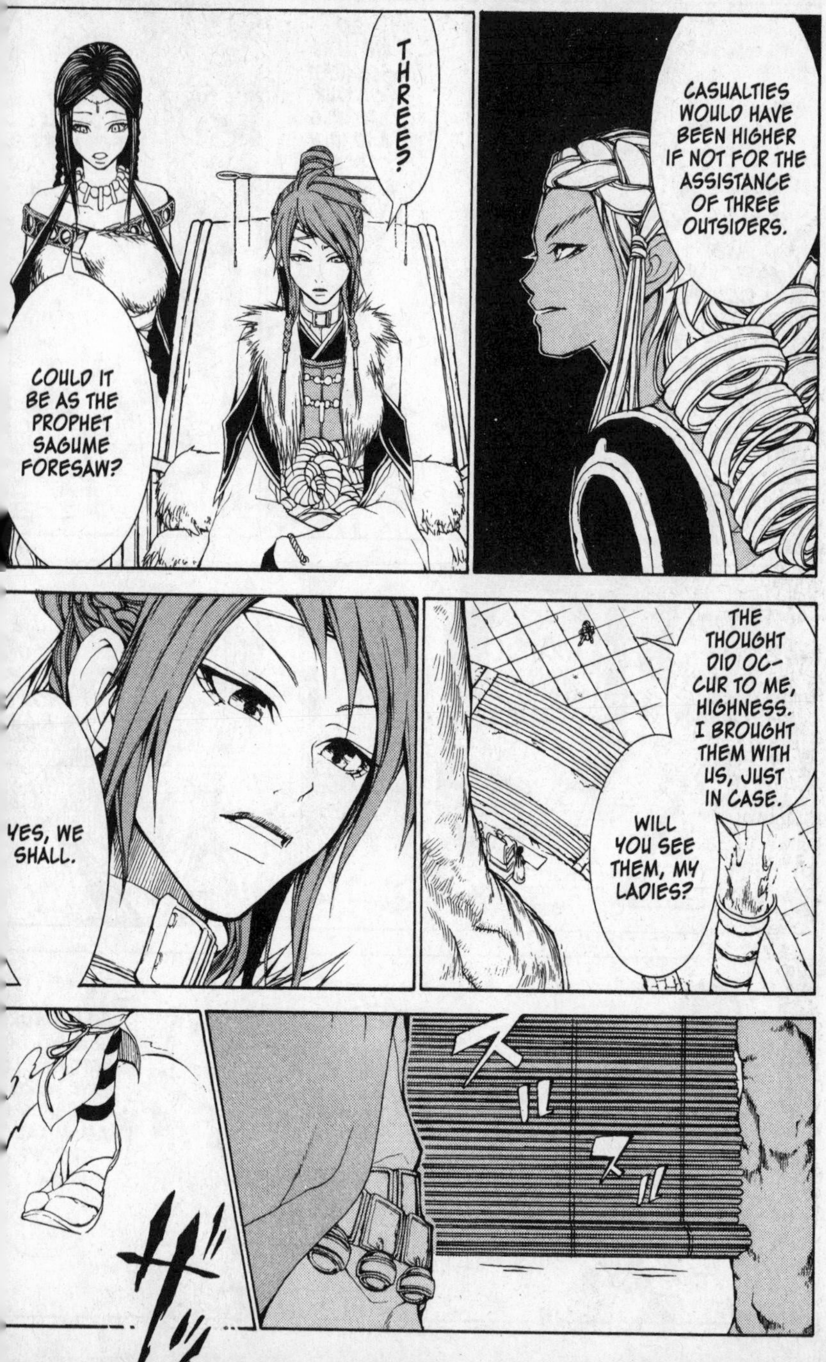
CASUALTIES WOULD HAVE BEEN HIGHER IF NOT FOR THE ASSISTANCE OF THREE OUTSIDERS.
THREE?
COULD IT BE AS THE PROPHET SAGUME FORESAW?
THE THOUGHT DID OC-CUR TO ME, HIGHNESS. I BROUGHT THEM WITH US, JUST IN CASE.
WILL YOU SEE THEM, MY LADIES?
YES, WE SHALL.

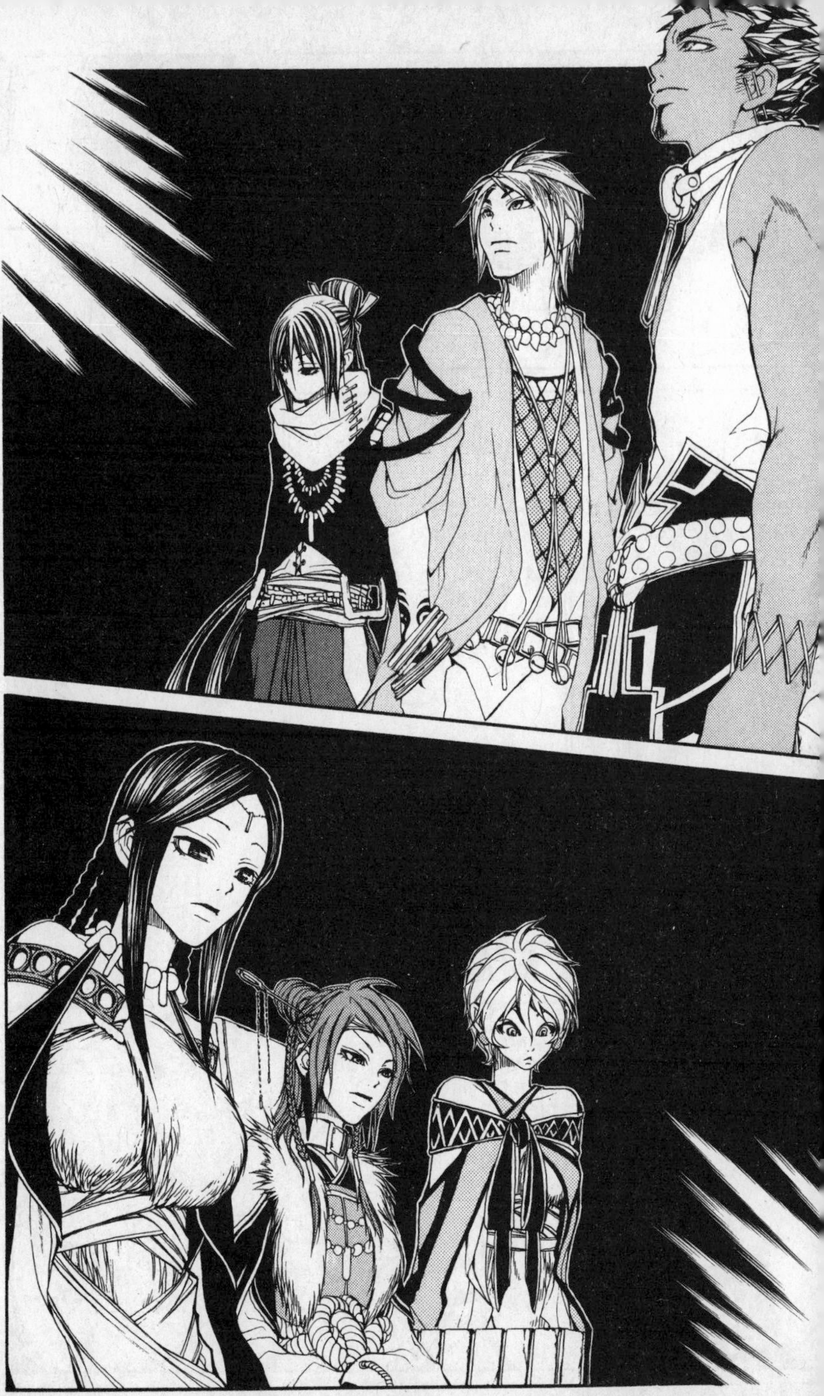

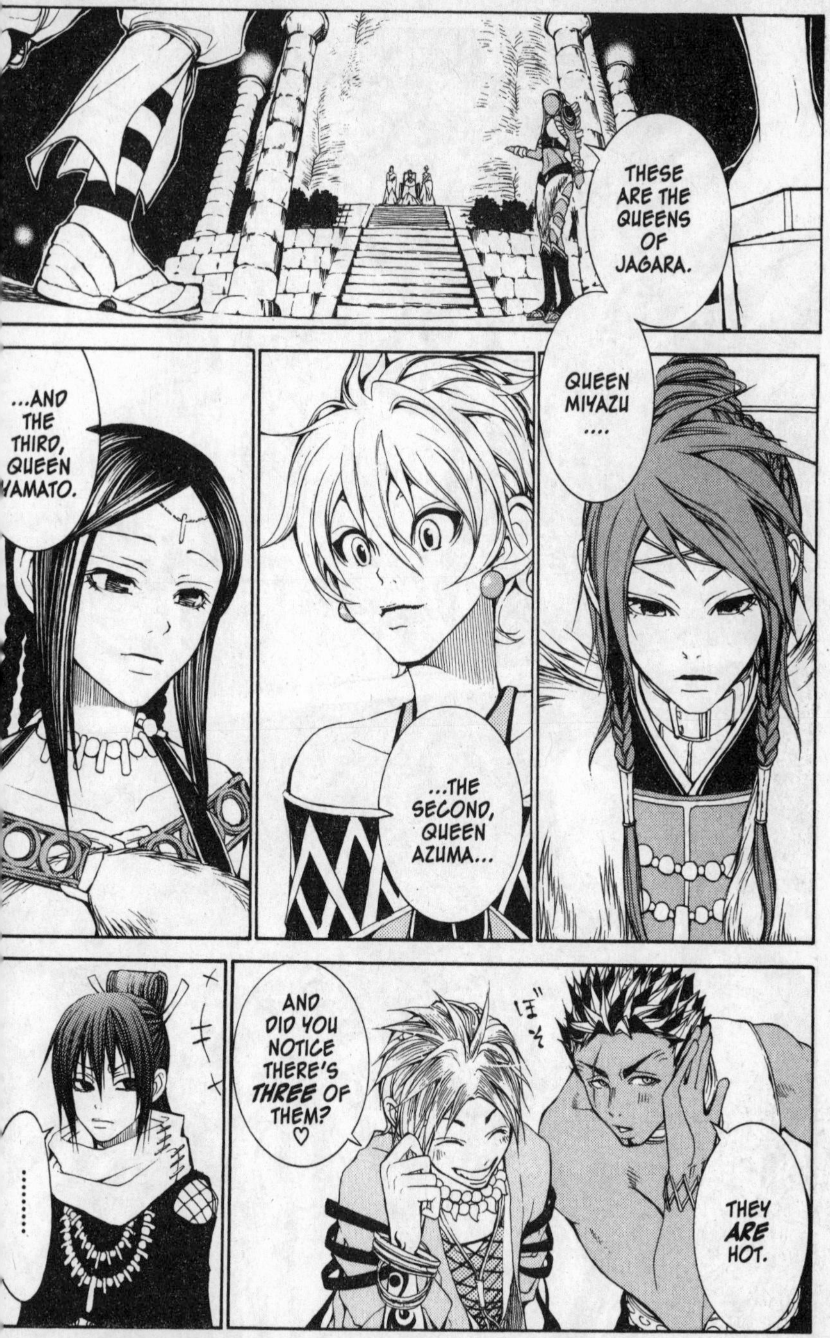
THESE ARE THE QUEENS OF JAGARA.
QUEEN MIYAZU ....
...THE SECOND, QUEEN AZUMA...
...AND THE THIRD, QUEEN YAMATO.
AND DID YOU NOTICE THERE'S *THREE* OF THEM? ♡
ぼそ
THEY *ARE* HOT.
....

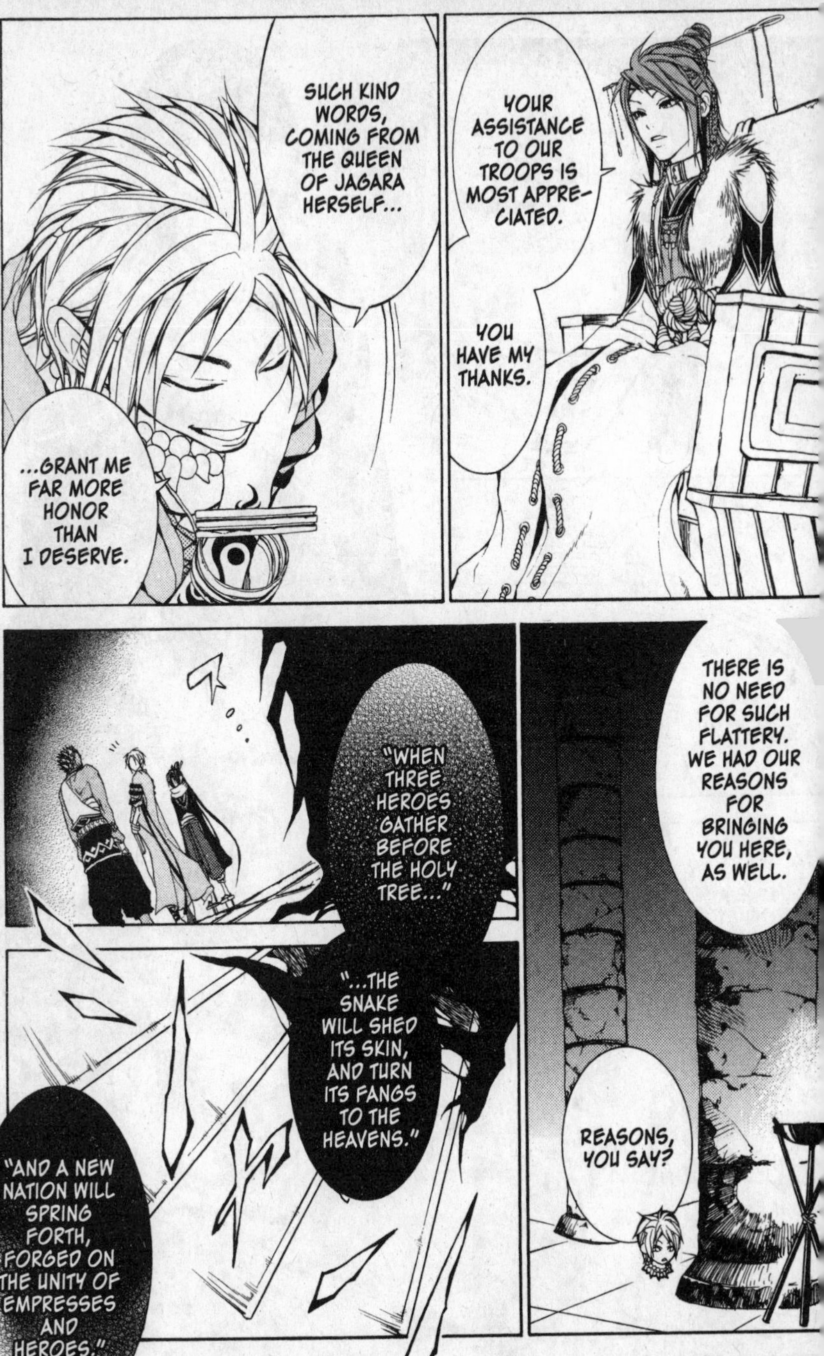
YOUR ASSISTANCE TO OUR TROOPS IS MOST APPRE-CIATED.
YOU HAVE MY THANKS.
SUCH KIND WORDS, COMING FROM THE QUEEN OF JAGARA HERSELF...
...GRANT ME FAR MORE HONOR THAN I DESERVE.
THERE IS NO NEED FOR SUCH FLATTERY. WE HAD OUR REASONS FOR BRINGING YOU HERE, AS WELL.
REASONS, YOU SAY?
"WHEN THREE HEROES GATHER BEFORE THE HOLY TREE..."
"...THE SNAKE WILL SHED ITS SKIN, AND TURN ITS FANGS TO THE HEAVENS."
"AND A NEW NATION WILL SPRING FORTH, FORGED ON THE UNITY OF EMPRESSES AND HEROES."

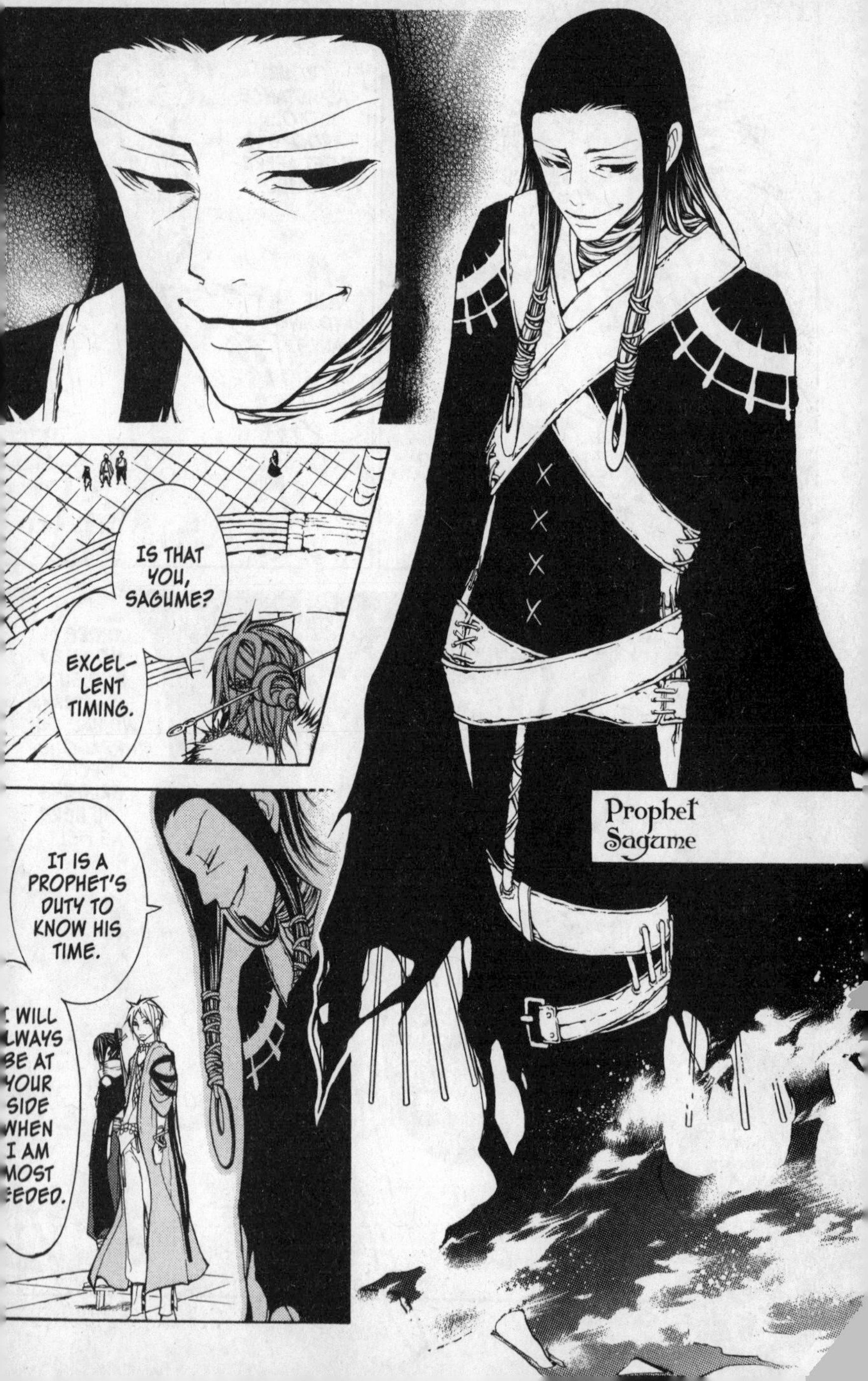
Prophet Sagume
IS THAT YOU, SAGUME?
EXCEL-LENT TIMING.
IT IS A PROPHET'S DUTY TO KNOW HIS TIME.
WILL LWAYS BE AT YOUR SIDE WHEN I AM MOST EEDED.

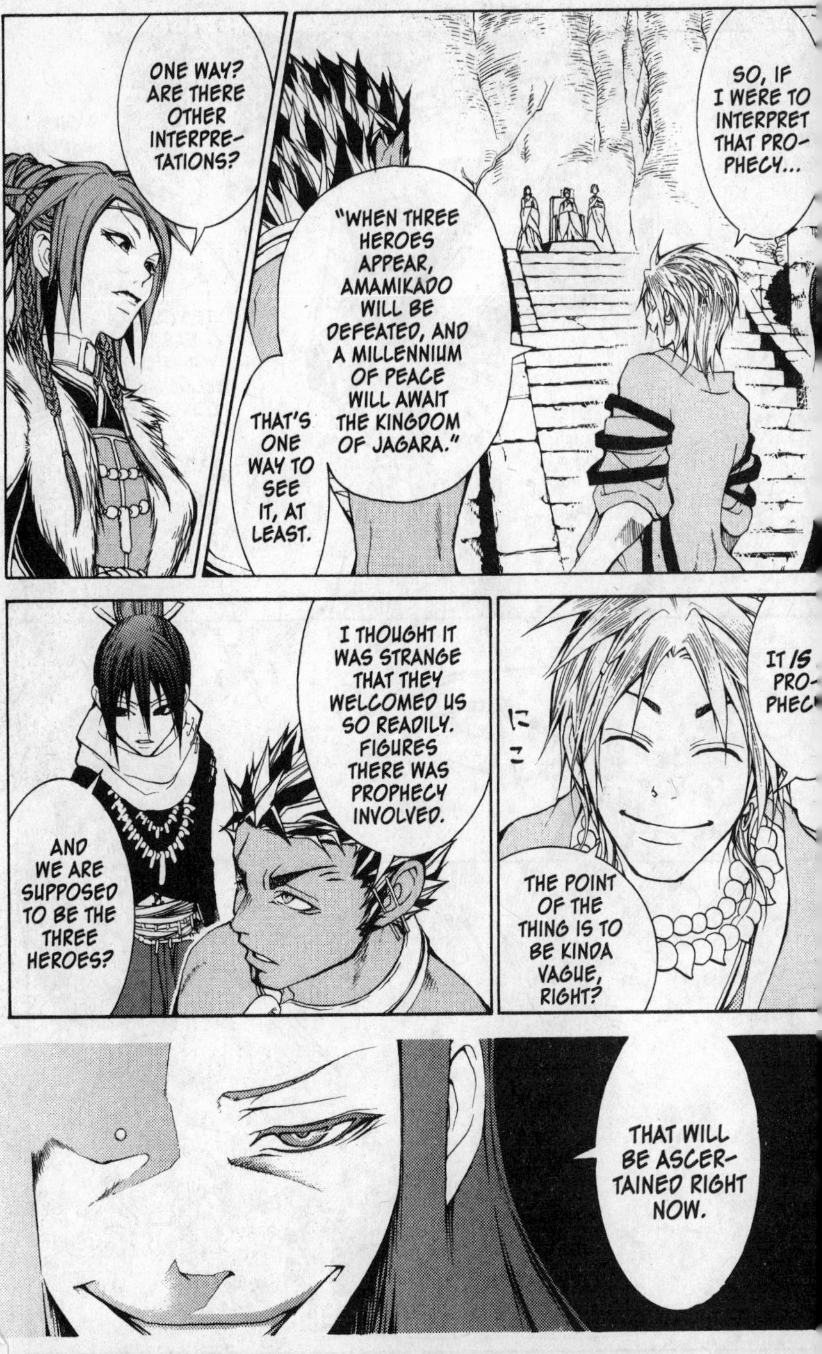
SO, IF I WERE TO INTERPRET THAT PROPHECY...
"WHEN THREE HEROES APPEAR, AMAMIKADO WILL BE DEFEATED, AND A MILLENNIUM OF PEACE WILL AWAIT THE KINGDOM OF JAGARA."
THAT'S ONE WAY TO SEE IT, AT LEAST.
ONE WAY? ARE THERE OTHER INTERPRETATIONS?
IT IS PRO- PHEC
にこ
THE POINT OF THE THING IS TO BE KINDA VAGUE, RIGHT?
I THOUGHT IT WAS STRANGE THAT THEY WELCOMED US SO READILY. FIGURES THERE WAS PROPHECY INVOLVED.
AND WE ARE SUPPOSED TO BE THE THREE HEROES?
THAT WILL BE ASCERTAINED RIGHT NOW.

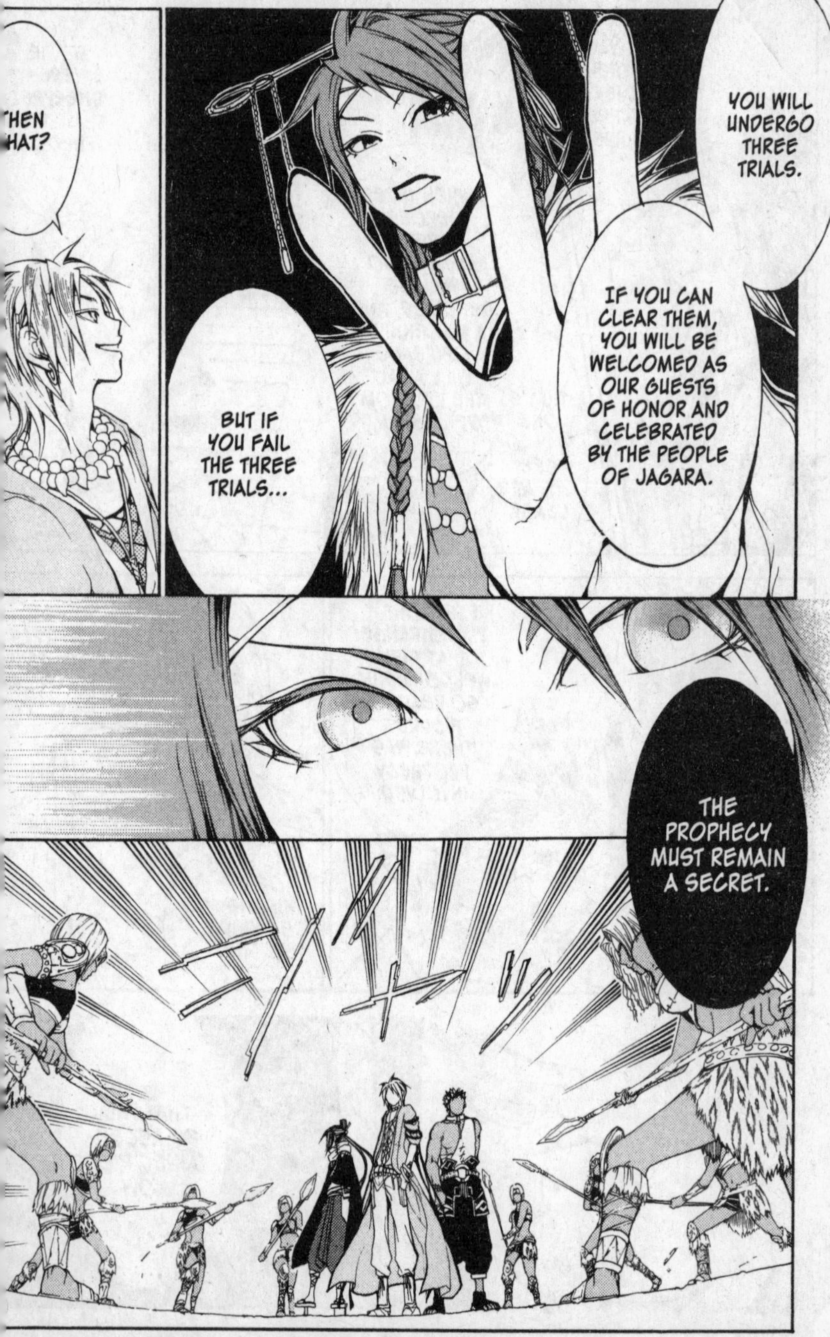
YOU WILL UNDERGO THREE TRIALS.
IF YOU CAN CLEAR THEM, YOU WILL BE WELCOMED AS OUR GUESTS OF HONOR AND CELEBRATED BY THE PEOPLE OF JAGARA.
BUT IF YOU FAIL THE THREE TRIALS...
THEN HAT?
THE PROPHECY MUST REMAIN A SECRET.

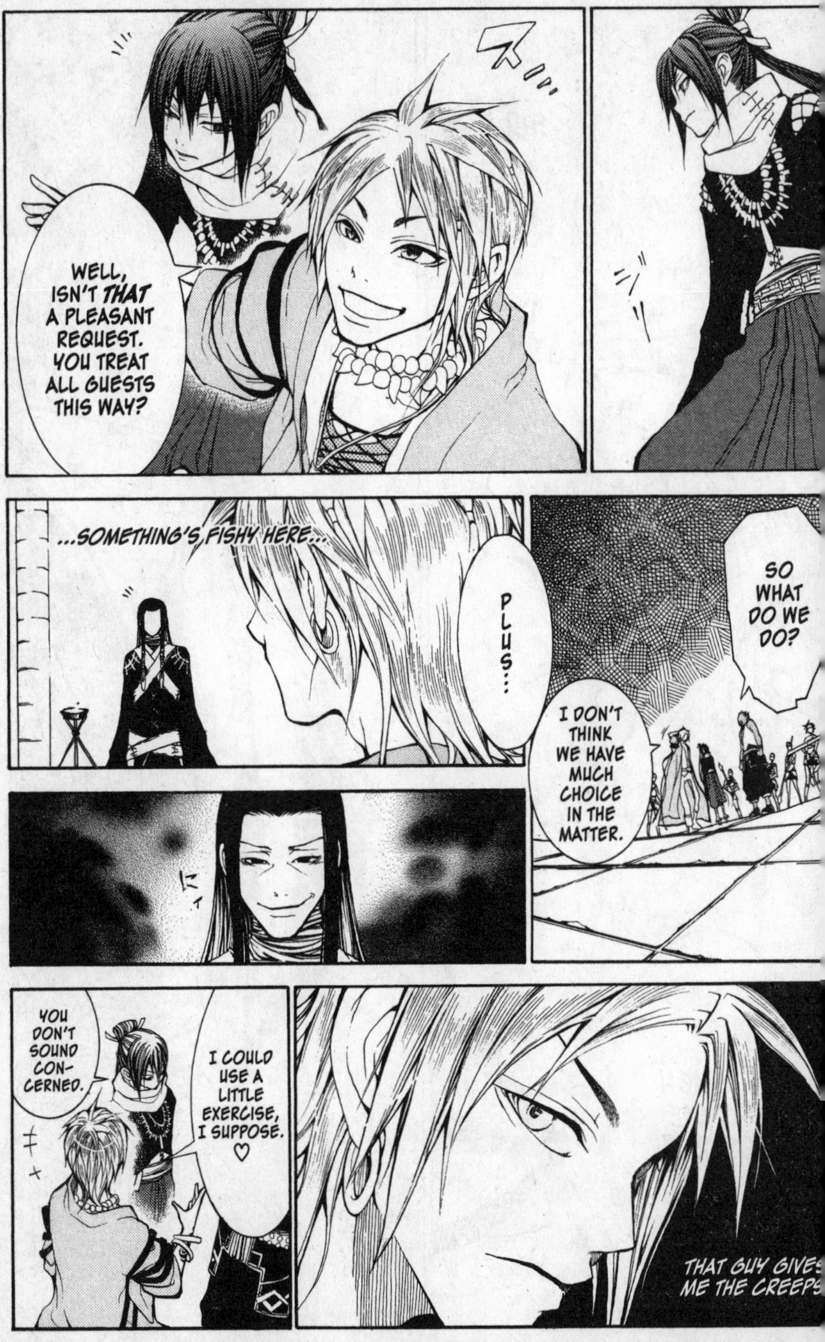
WELL, ISN'T THAT A PLEASANT REQUEST. YOU TREAT ALL GUESTS THIS WAY?
SO WHAT DO WE DO?
I DON'T THINK WE HAVE MUCH CHOICE IN THE MATTER.
...SOMETHING'S FISHY HERE...
PLUS...
THAT GUY GIVES ME THE CREEPS
I COULD USE A LITTLE EXERCISE, I SUPPOSE. ♡
YOU DON'T SOUND CON-CERNED.

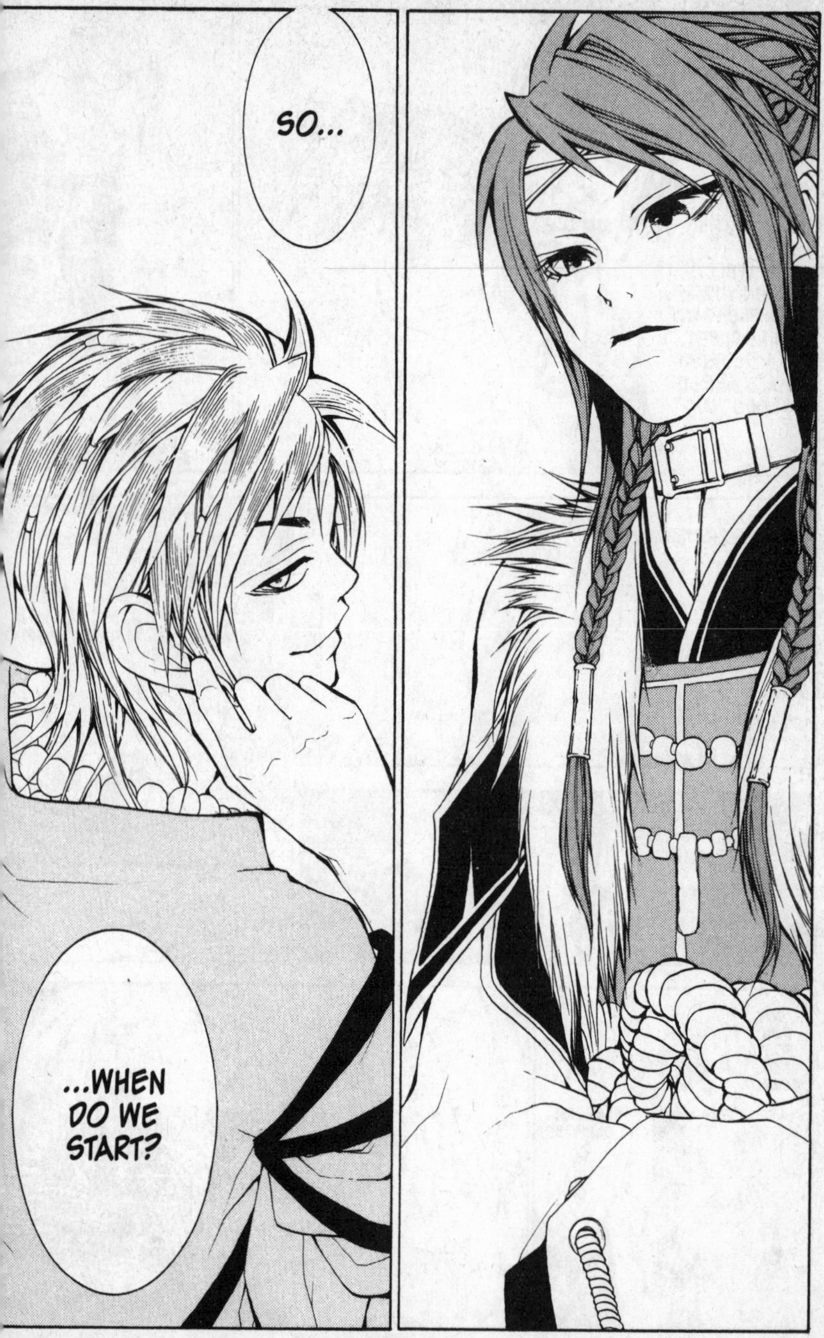
SO...
...WHEN DO WE START?

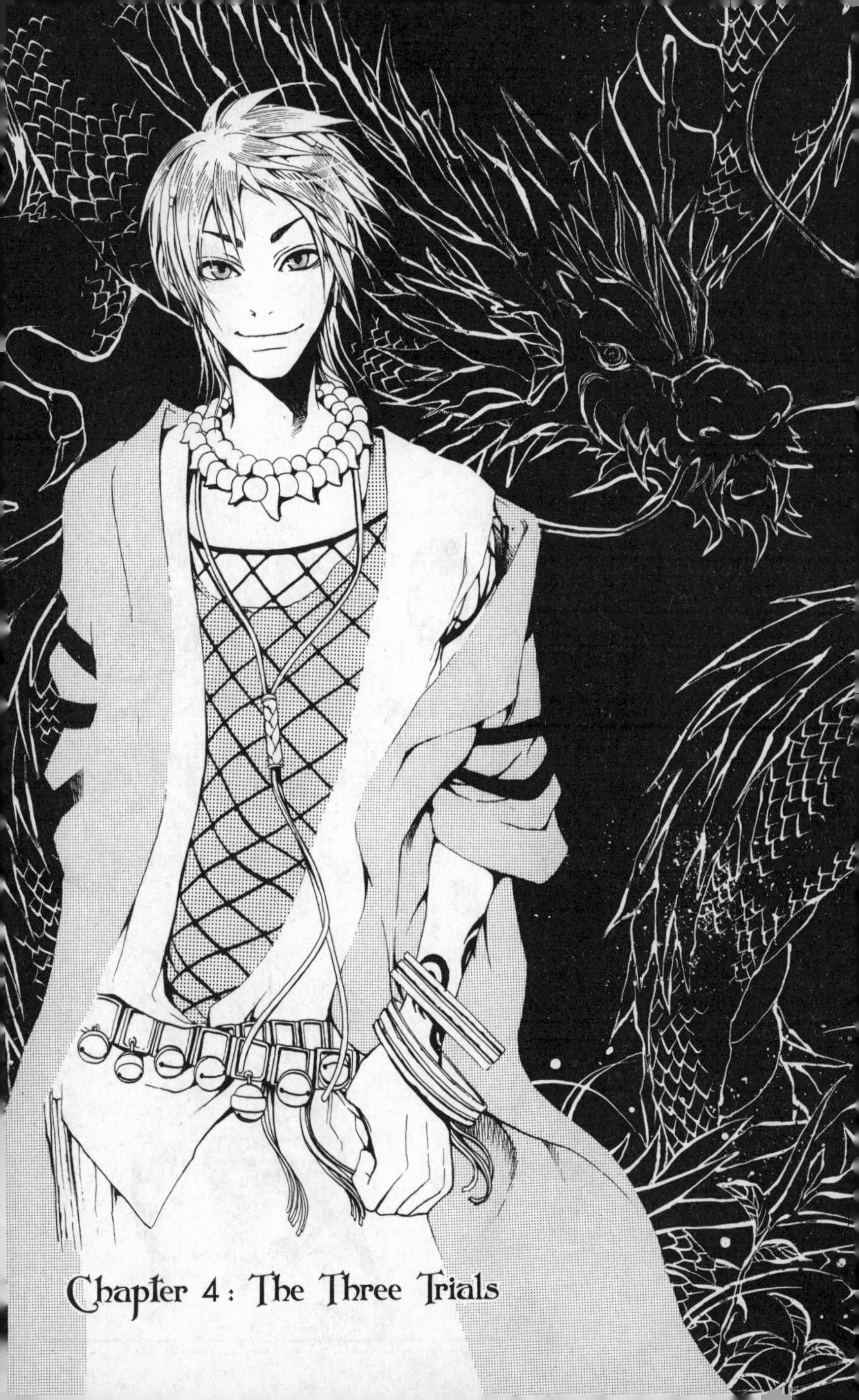

Chapter 4: The Three Trials

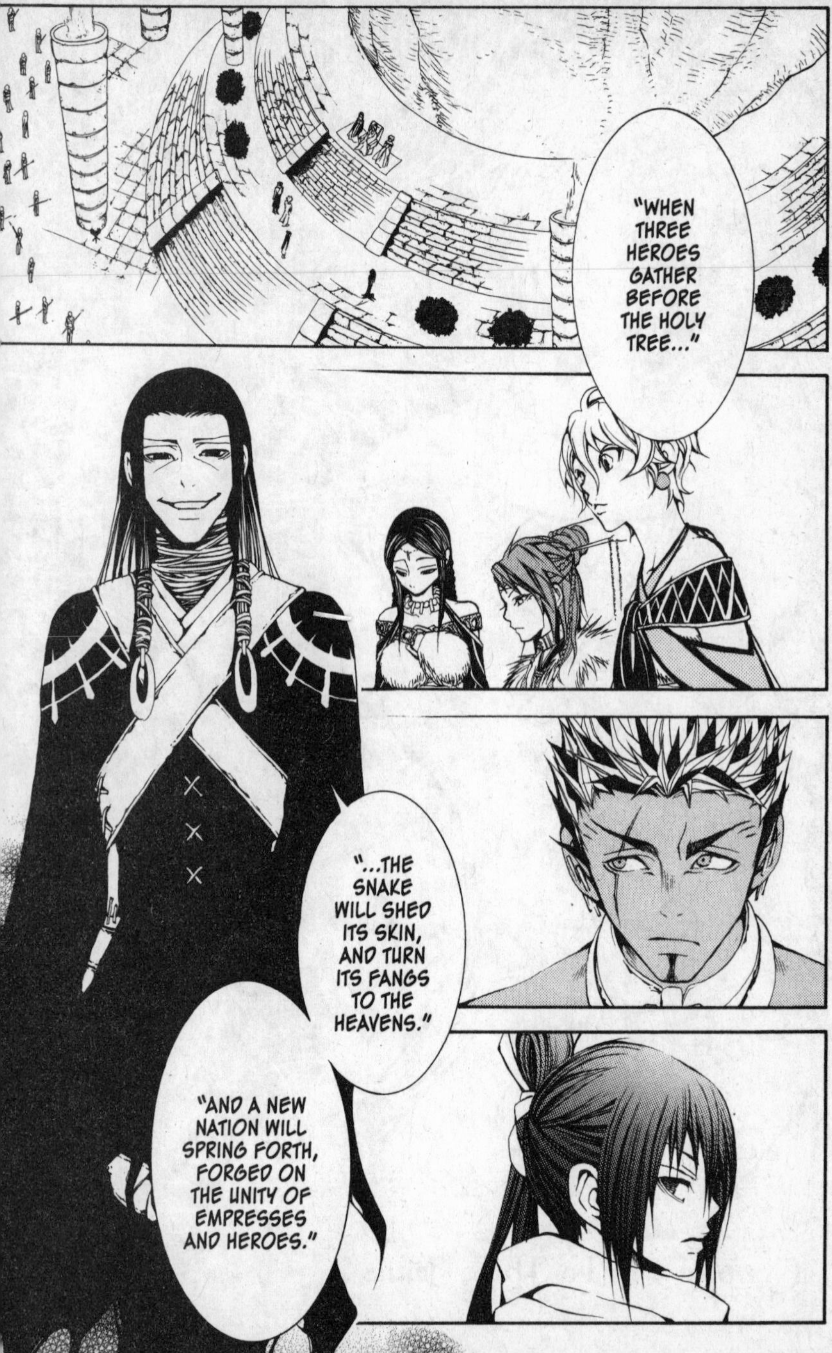
"WHEN THREE HEROES GATHER BEFORE THE HOLY TREE..."
"...THE SNAKE WILL SHED ITS SKIN, AND TURN ITS FANGS TO THE HEAVENS."
"AND A NEW NATION WILL SPRING FORTH, FORGED ON THE UNITY OF EMPRESSES AND HEROES."

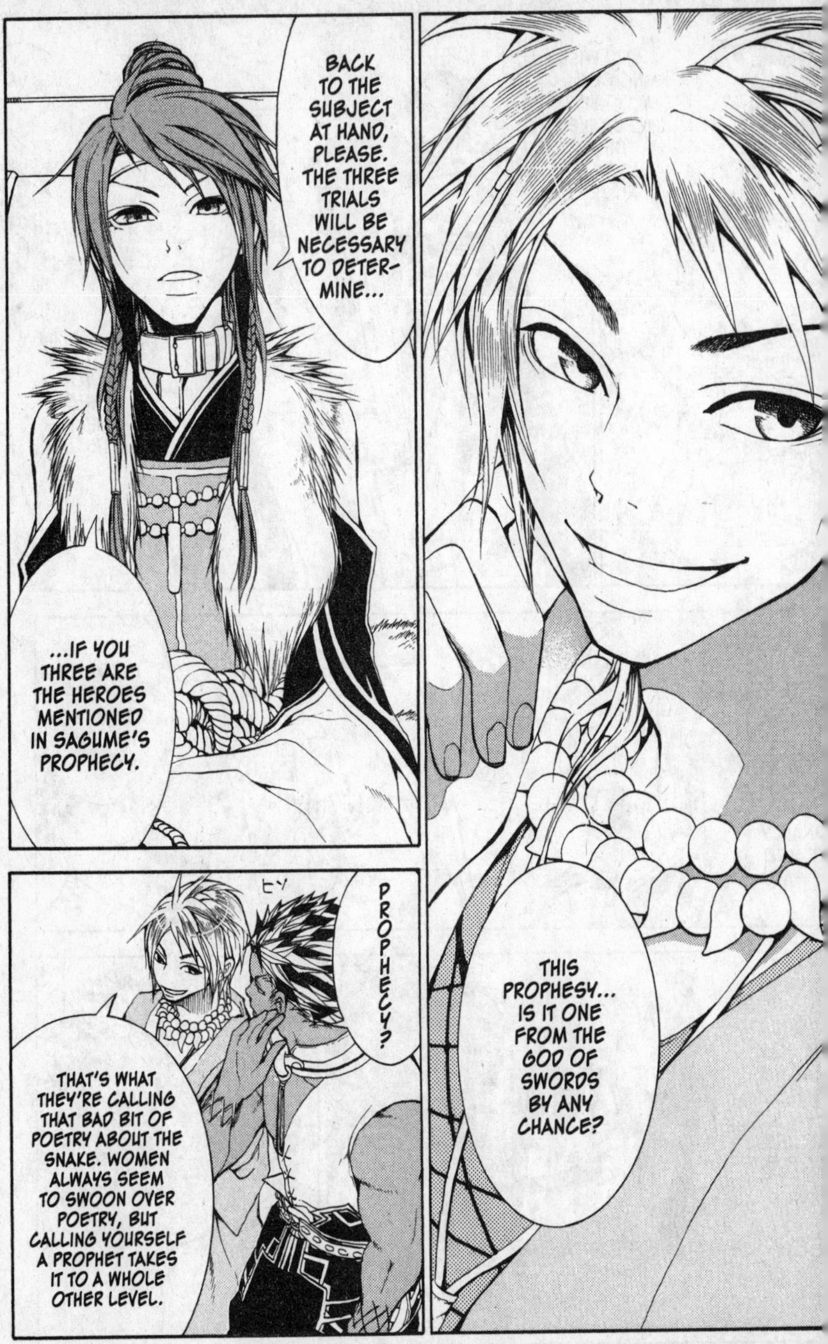
THIS PROPHESY... IS IT ONE FROM THE GOD OF SWORDS BY ANY CHANCE?
BACK TO THE SUBJECT AT HAND, PLEASE. THE THREE TRIALS WILL BE NECESSARY TO DETERMINE...
...IF YOU THREE ARE THE HEROES MENTIONED IN SAGUME'S PROPHECY.
PROPHECY?
ヒソ
THAT'S WHAT THEY'RE CALLING THAT BAD BIT OF POETRY ABOUT THE SNAKE. WOMEN ALWAYS SEEM TO SWOON OVER POETRY, BUT CALLING YOURSELF A PROPHET TAKES IT TO A WHOLE OTHER LEVEL.

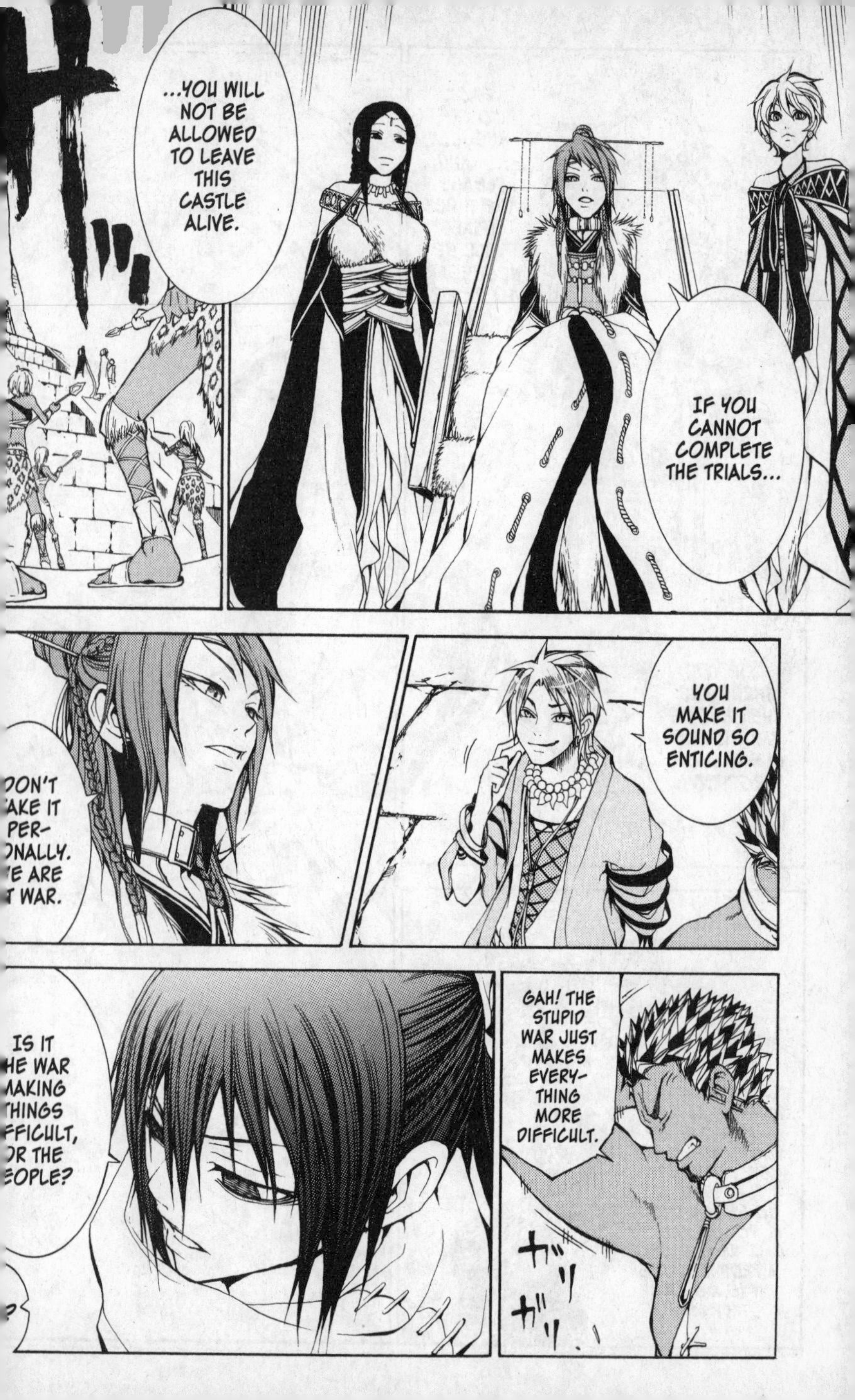
IF YOU CANNOT COMPLETE THE TRIALS...
...YOU WILL NOT BE ALLOWED TO LEAVE THIS CASTLE ALIVE.
YOU MAKE IT SOUND SO ENTICING.
DON'T AKE IT PER- ONALLY. E ARE WAR.
GAH! THE STUPID WAR JUST MAKES EVERY- THING MORE DIFFICULT.
IS IT HE WAR MAKING THINGS FFICULT, OR THE EOPLE?

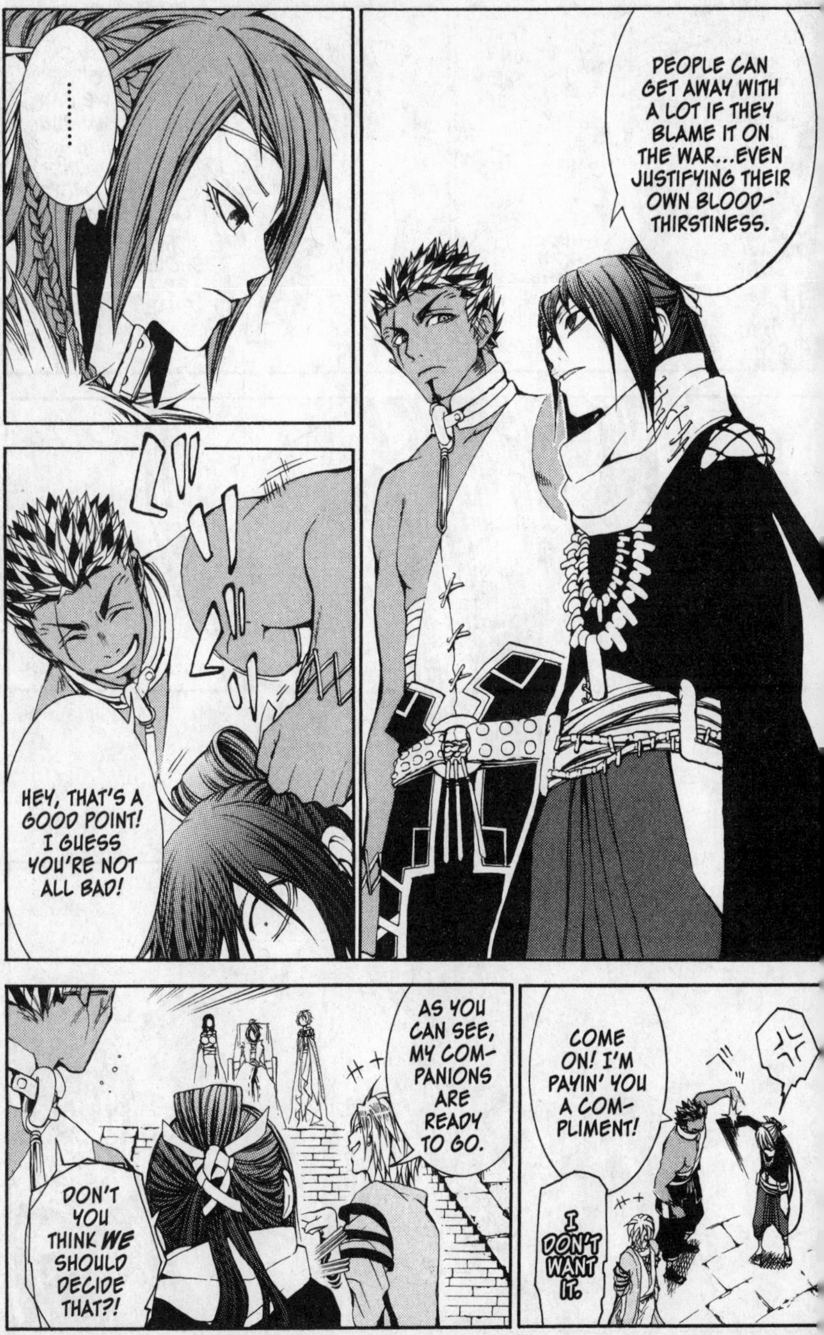
PEOPLE CAN GET AWAY WITH A LOT IF THEY BLAME IT ON THE WAR...EVEN JUSTIFYING THEIR OWN BLOOD-THIRSTINESS.
......
HEY, THAT'S A GOOD POINT! I GUESS YOU'RE NOT ALL BAD!
COME ON! I'M PAYIN' YOU A COM-PLIMENT!
I DON'T WANT IT.
AS YOU CAN SEE, MY COM-PANIONS ARE READY TO GO.
DON'T YOU THINK WE SHOULD DECIDE THAT?!

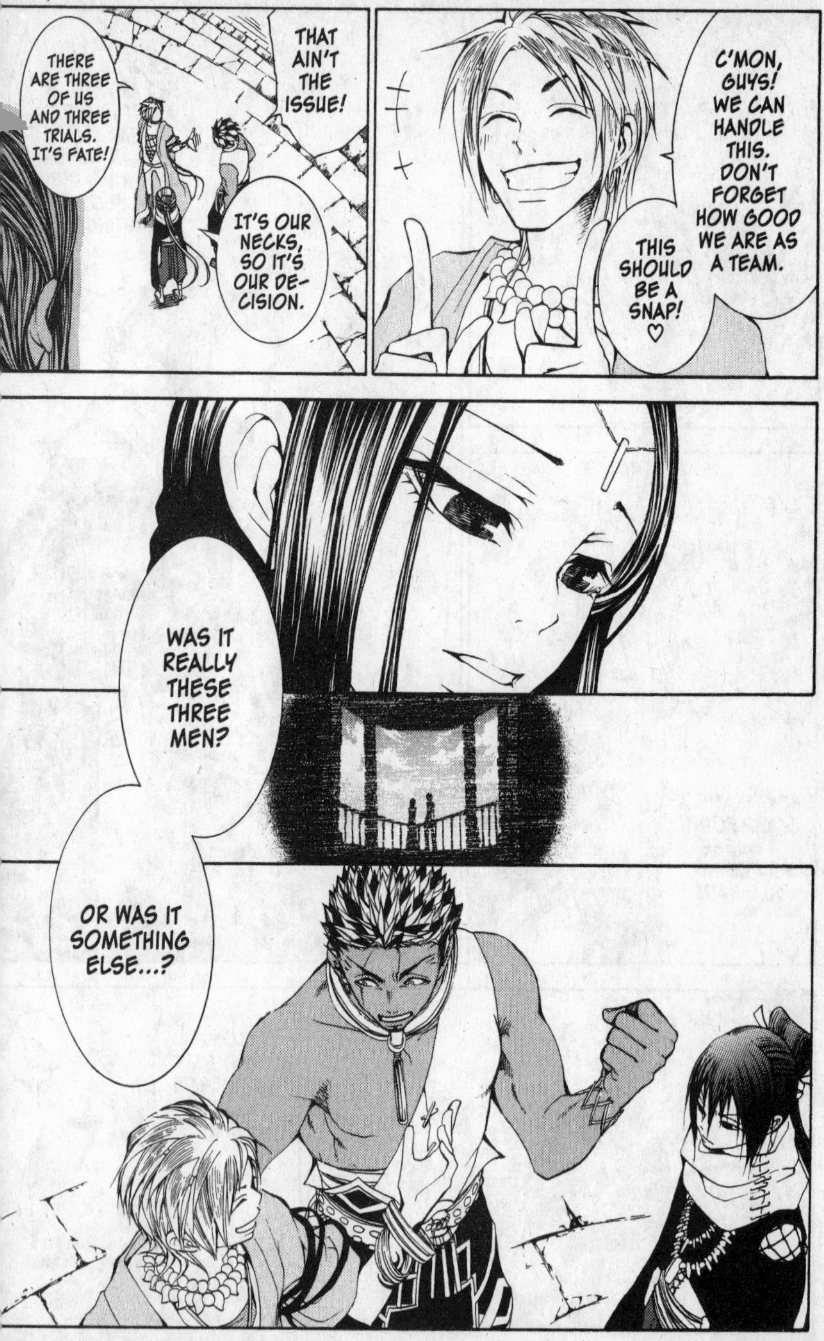
C'MON, GUYS! WE CAN HANDLE THIS. DON'T FORGET HOW GOOD WE ARE AS A TEAM.
THIS SHOULD BE A SNAP! ♡
THAT AIN'T THE ISSUE!
THERE ARE THREE OF US AND THREE TRIALS. IT'S FATE!
IT'S OUR NECKS, SO IT'S OUR DE-CISION.
WAS IT REALLY THESE THREE MEN?
OR WAS IT SOMETHING ELSE...?

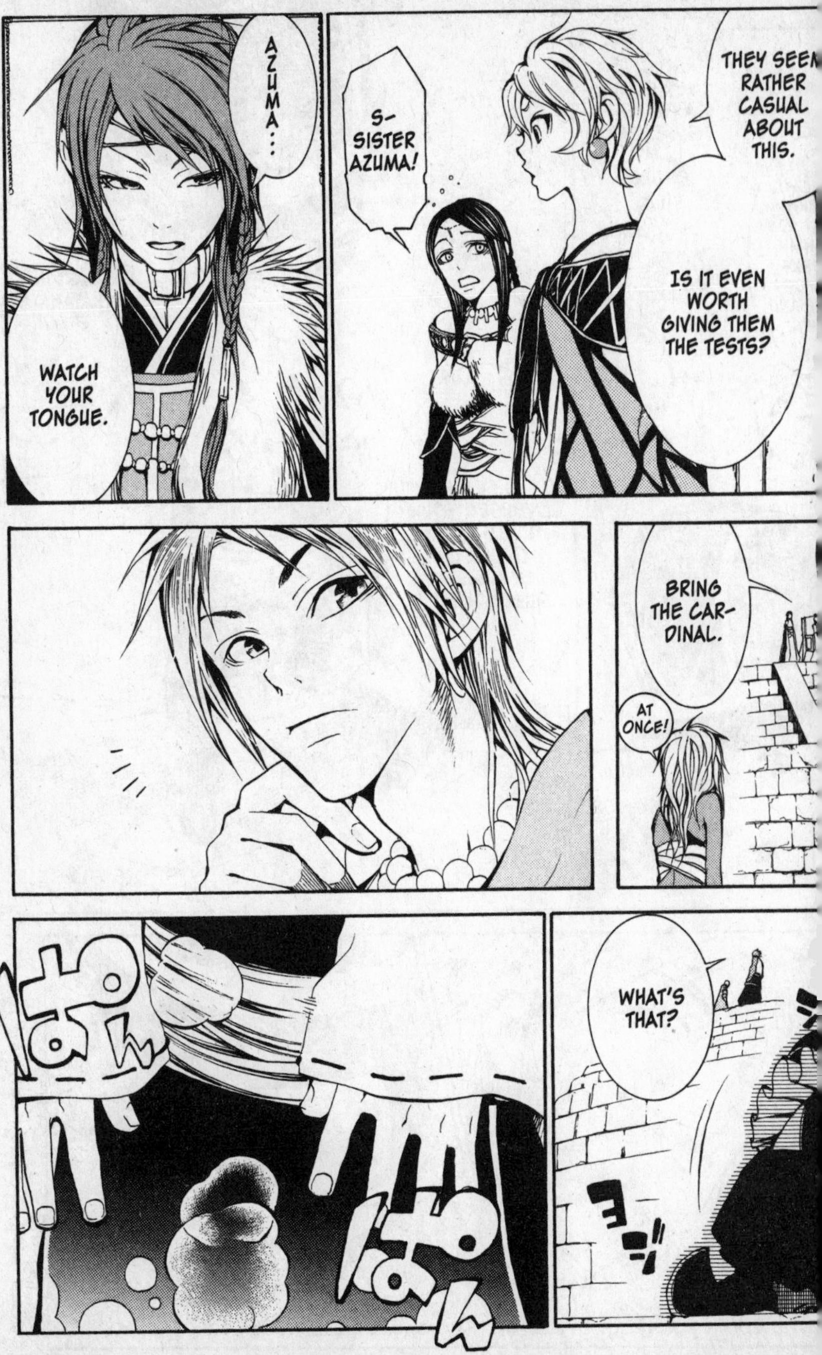
THEY SEEM RATHER CASUAL ABOUT THIS.
IS IT EVEN WORTH GIVING THEM THE TESTS?
S-SISTER AZUMA!
AZUMA...
WATCH YOUR TONGUE.
BRING THE CAR-DINAL.
AT ONCE!
WHAT'S THAT?

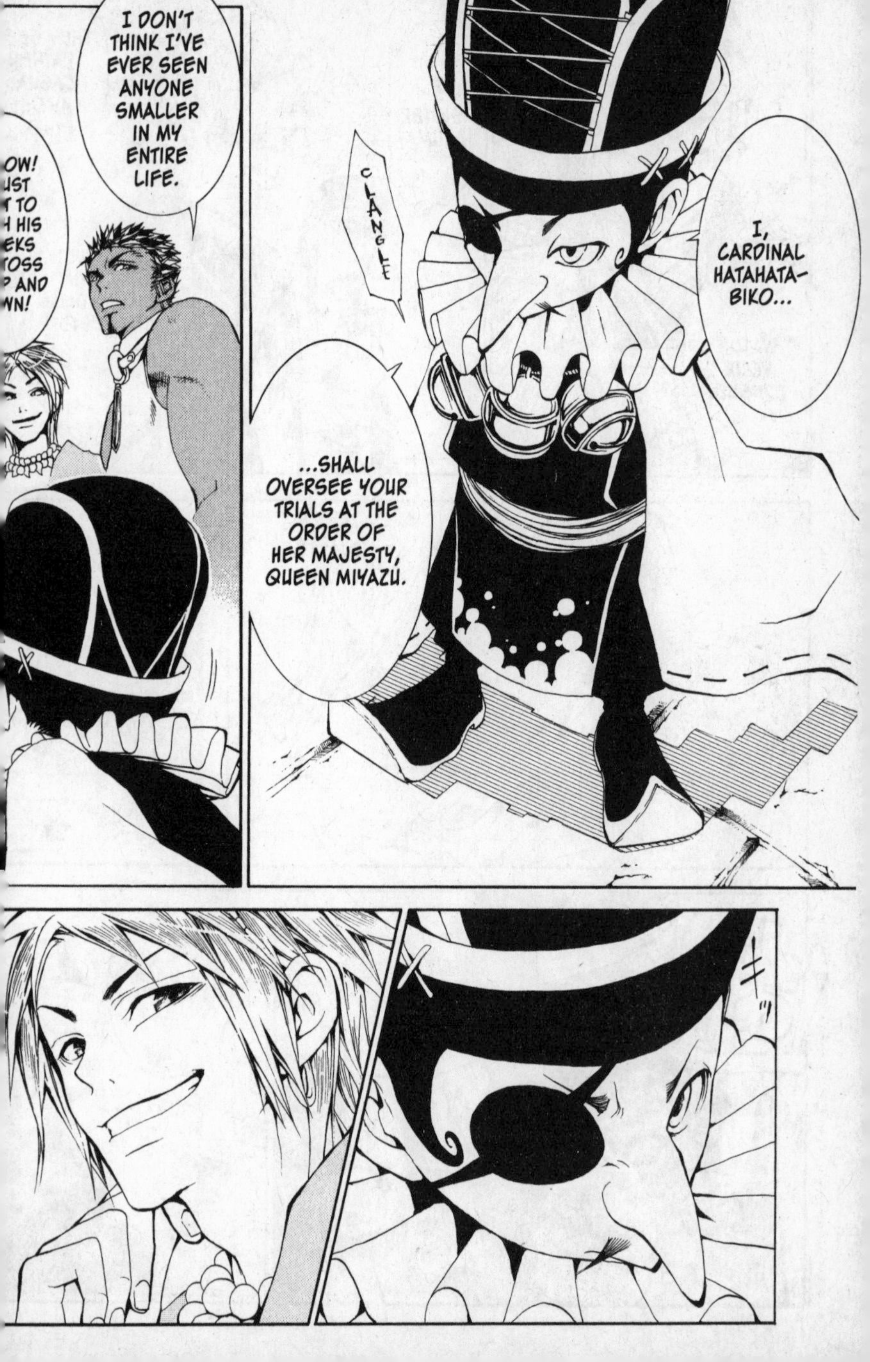

I, CARDINAL HATAHATA-BIKO...
CLANGLE
...SHALL OVERSEE YOUR TRIALS AT THE ORDER OF HER MAJESTY, QUEEN MIYAZU.
I DON'T THINK I'VE EVER SEEN ANYONE SMALLER IN MY ENTIRE LIFE.
OW! UST T TO H HIS EKS TOSS P AND NN!

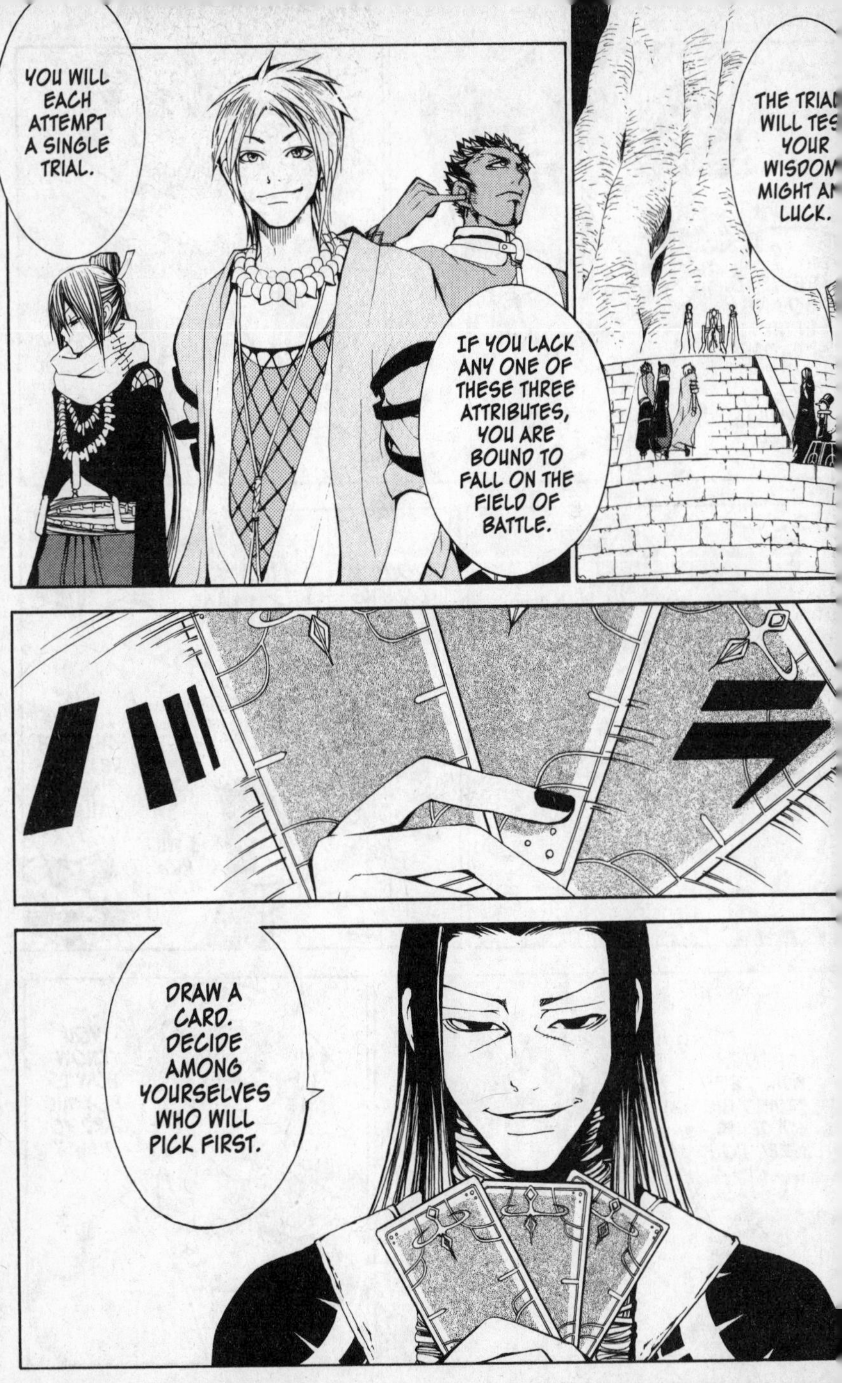
THE TRIA WILL TES YOUR WISDOM MIGHT A LUCK.
YOU WILL EACH ATTEMPT A SINGLE TRIAL.
IF YOU LACK ANY ONE OF THESE THREE ATTRIBUTES, YOU ARE BOUND TO FALL ON THE FIELD OF BATTLE.
DRAW A CARD. DECIDE AMONG YOURSELVES WHO WILL PICK FIRST.

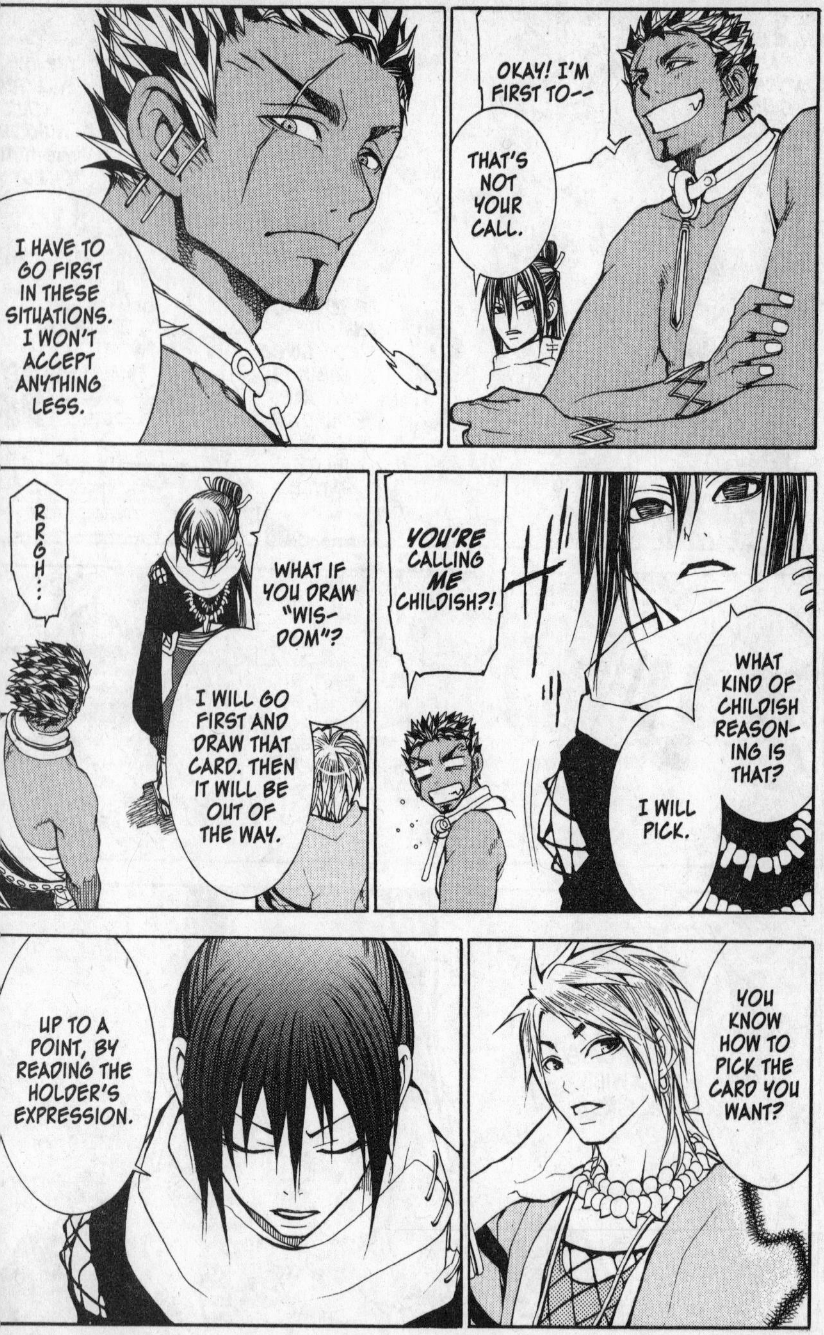
OKAY! I'M FIRST TO--
THAT'S NOT YOUR CALL.
I HAVE TO GO FIRST IN THESE SITUATIONS. I WON'T ACCEPT ANYTHING LESS.
WHAT KIND OF CHILDISH REASONING IS THAT?
I WILL PICK.
YOU'RE CALLING *ME* CHILDISH?!
WHAT IF YOU DRAW "WISDOM"?
I WILL GO FIRST AND DRAW THAT CARD. THEN IT WILL BE OUT OF THE WAY.
RRGH...
YOU KNOW HOW TO PICK THE CARD YOU WANT?
UP TO A POINT, BY READING THE HOLDER'S EXPRESSION.

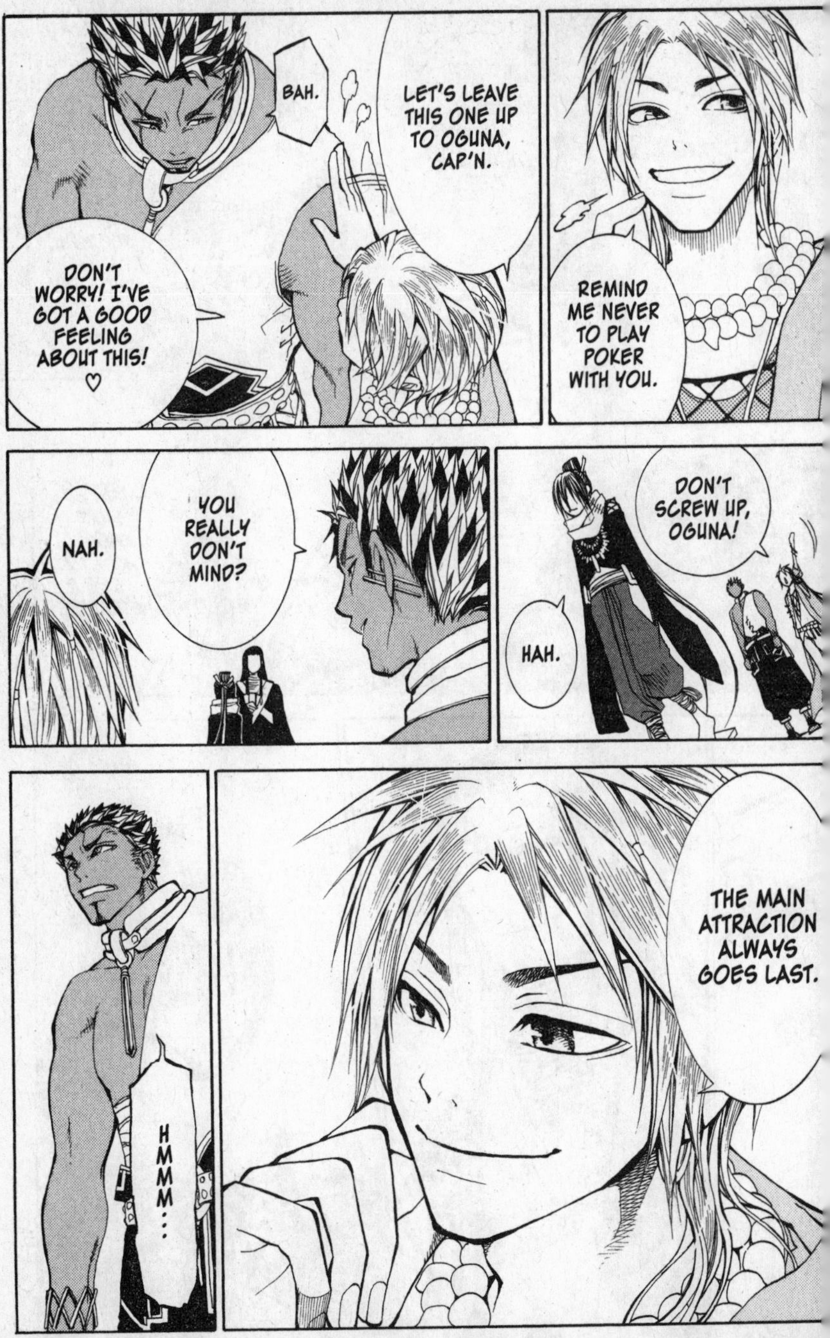
REMIND ME NEVER TO PLAY POKER WITH YOU.
LET'S LEAVE THIS ONE UP TO OGUNA, CAP'N.
BAH.
DON'T WORRY! I'VE GOT A GOOD FEELING ABOUT THIS! ♡
DON'T SCREW UP, OGUNA!
HAH.
YOU REALLY DON'T MIND?
NAH.
THE MAIN ATTRACTION ALWAYS GOES LAST.
HMMM...

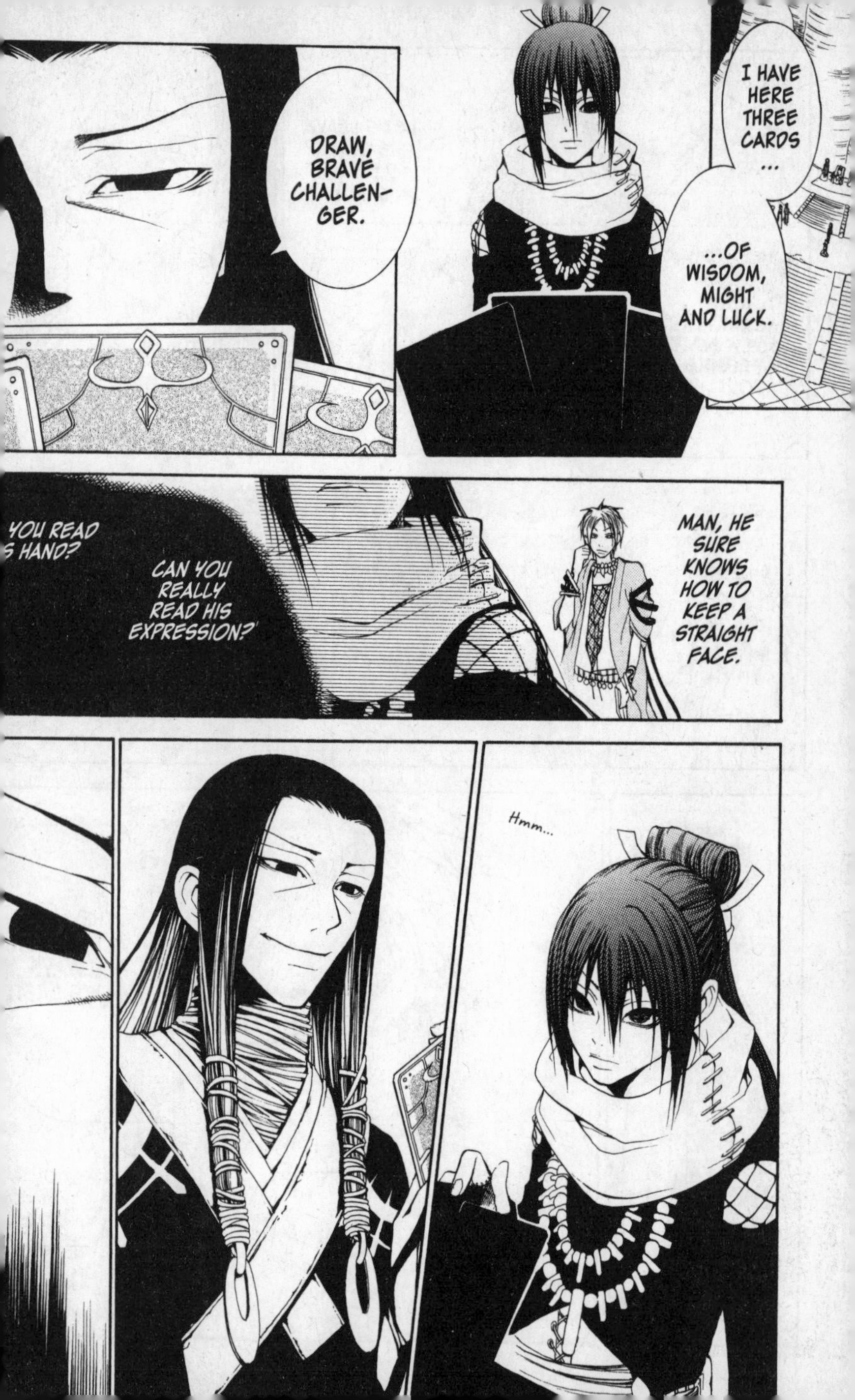

I HAVE HERE THREE CARDS ...
...OF WISDOM, MIGHT AND LUCK.
DRAW, BRAVE CHALLEN-GER.
MAN, HE SURE KNOWS HOW TO KEEP A STRAIGHT FACE.
YOU READ S HAND?
CAN YOU REALLY READ HIS EXPRESSION?'
Hmm...

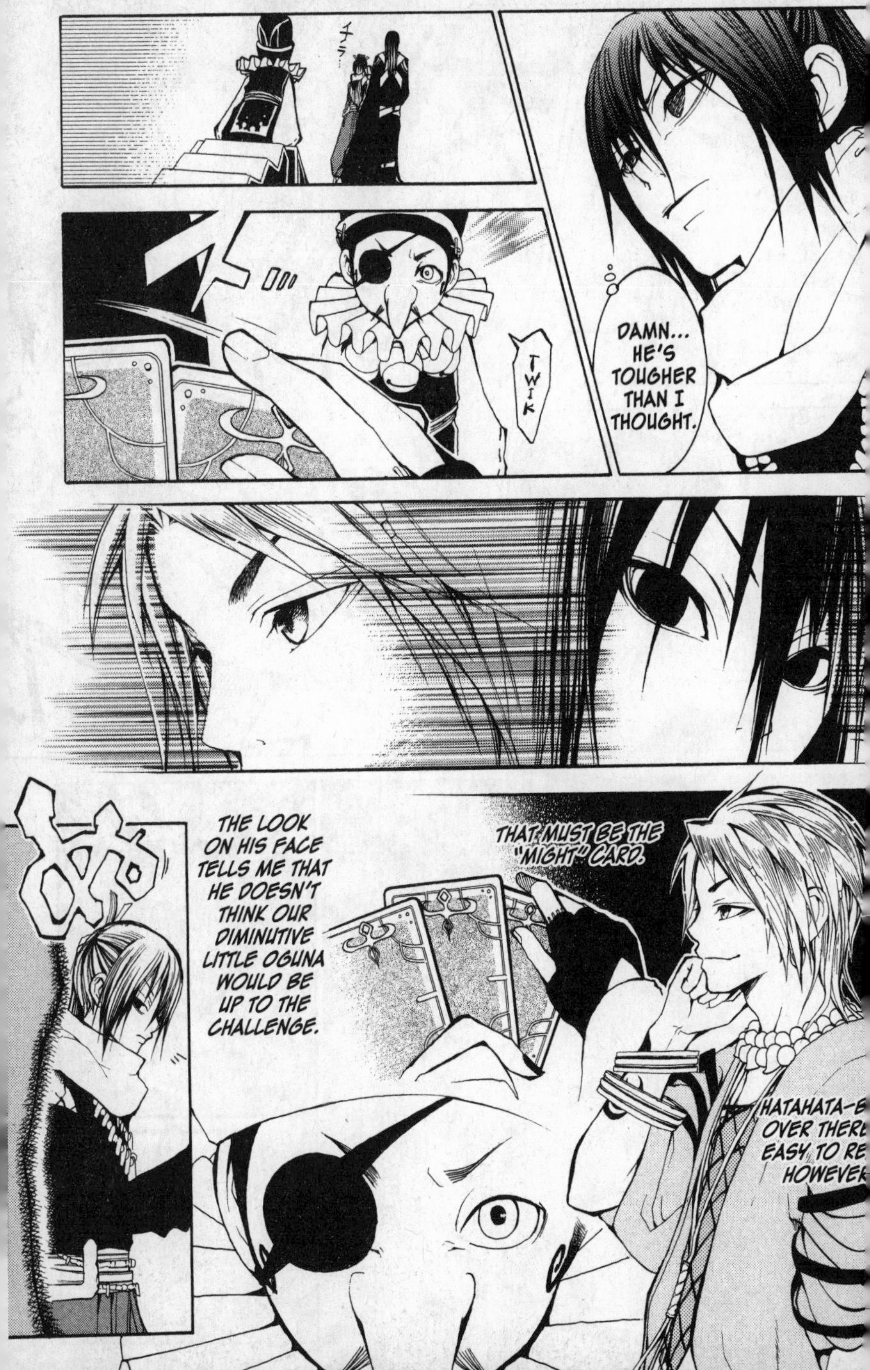
DAMN... HE'S TOUGHER THAN I THOUGHT.
イチラ…
TWIK
THAT MUST BE THE "MIGHT" CARD.
HATAHATA-B
OVER THERE
EASY TO RE
HOWEVER
THE LOOK ON HIS FACE TELLS ME THAT HE DOESN'T THINK OUR DIMINUTIVE LITTLE OGUNA WOULD BE UP TO THE CHALLENGE.

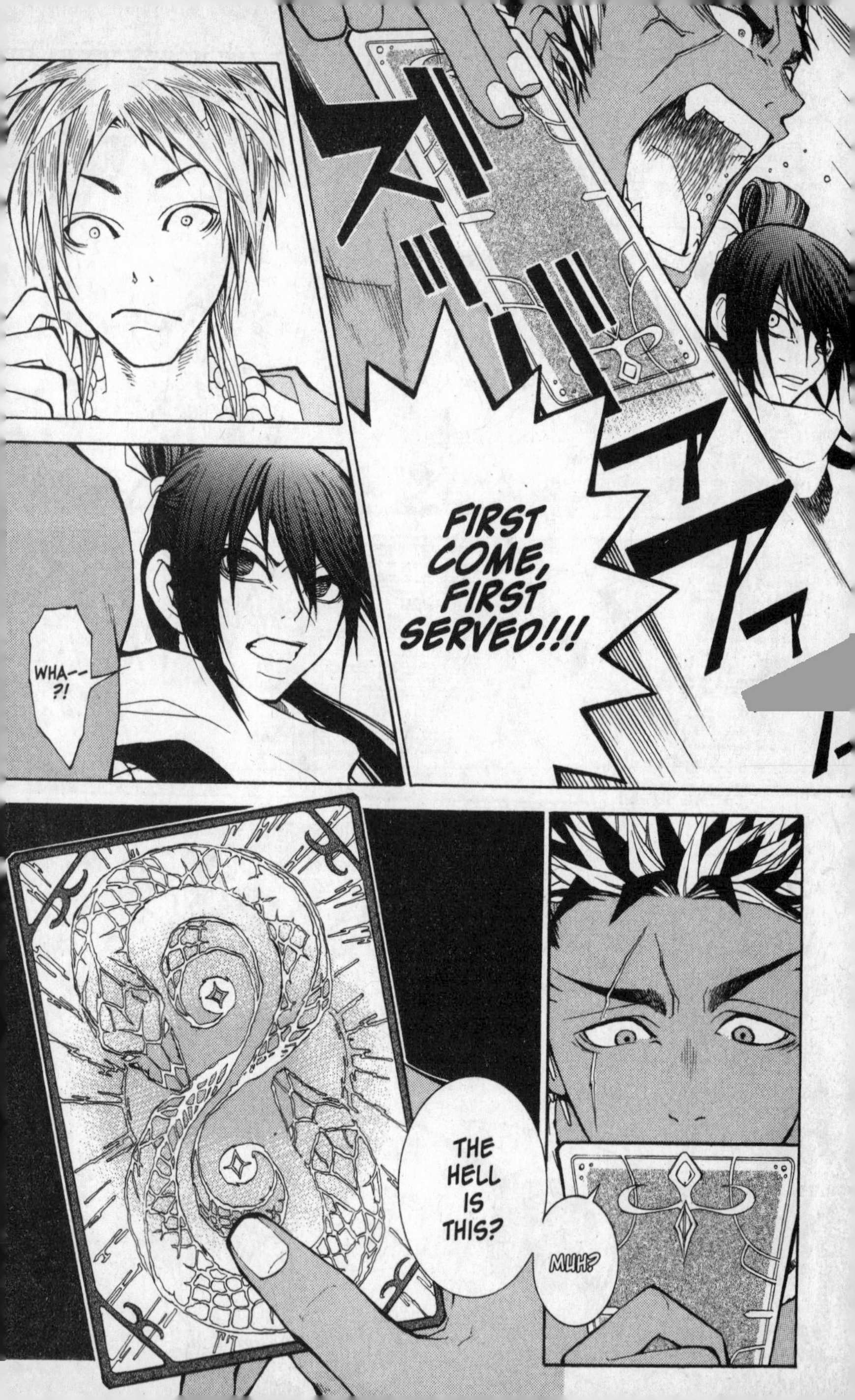
FIRST COME, FIRST SERVED!!!
WHA-- ?!
MUH?
THE HELL IS THIS?

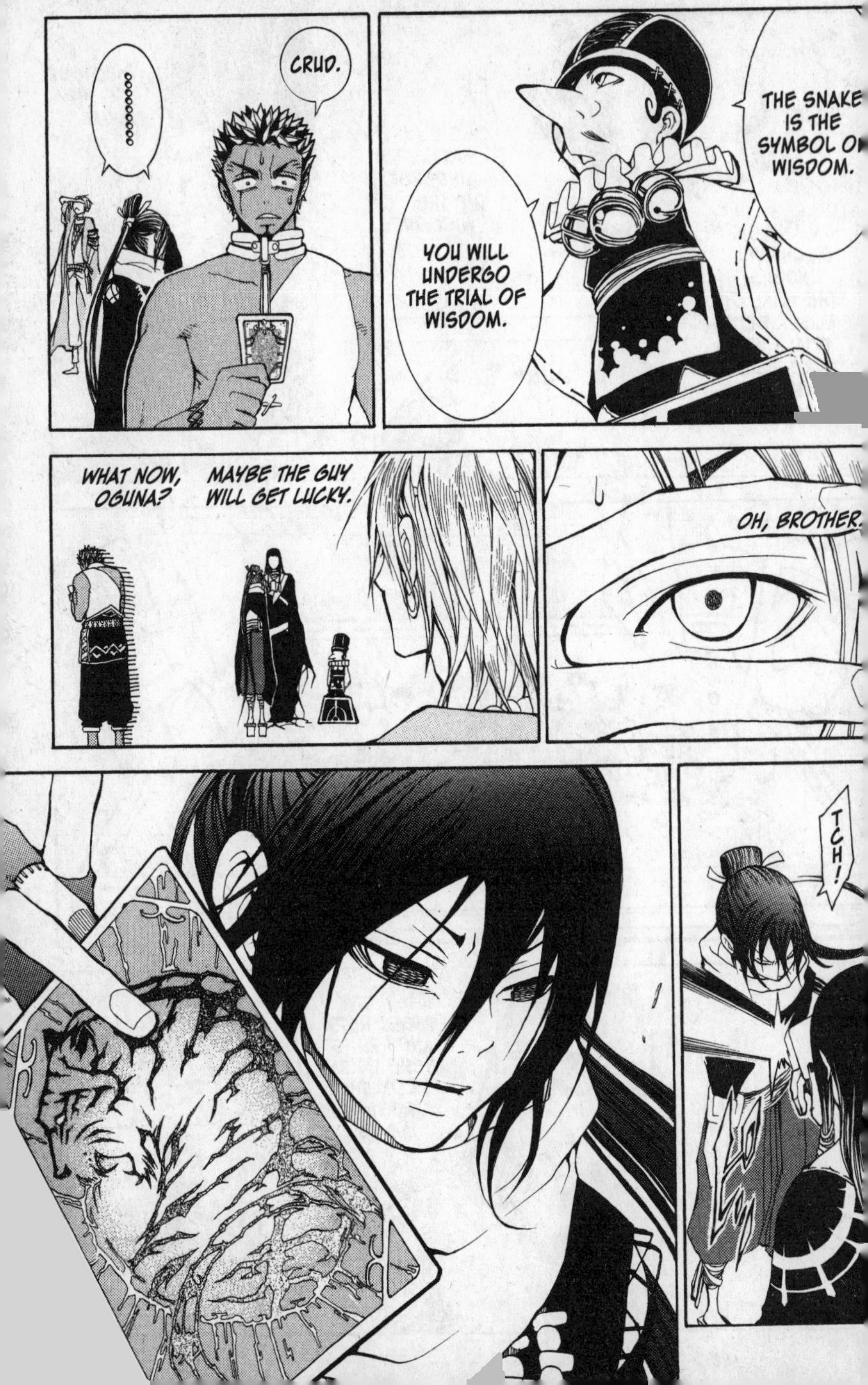
THE SNAKE IS THE SYMBOL OF WISDOM.
YOU WILL UNDERGO THE TRIAL OF WISDOM.
CRUD.
....
OH, BROTHER.
MAYBE THE GUY WILL GET LUCKY.
WHAT NOW, OGUNA?
TCH!

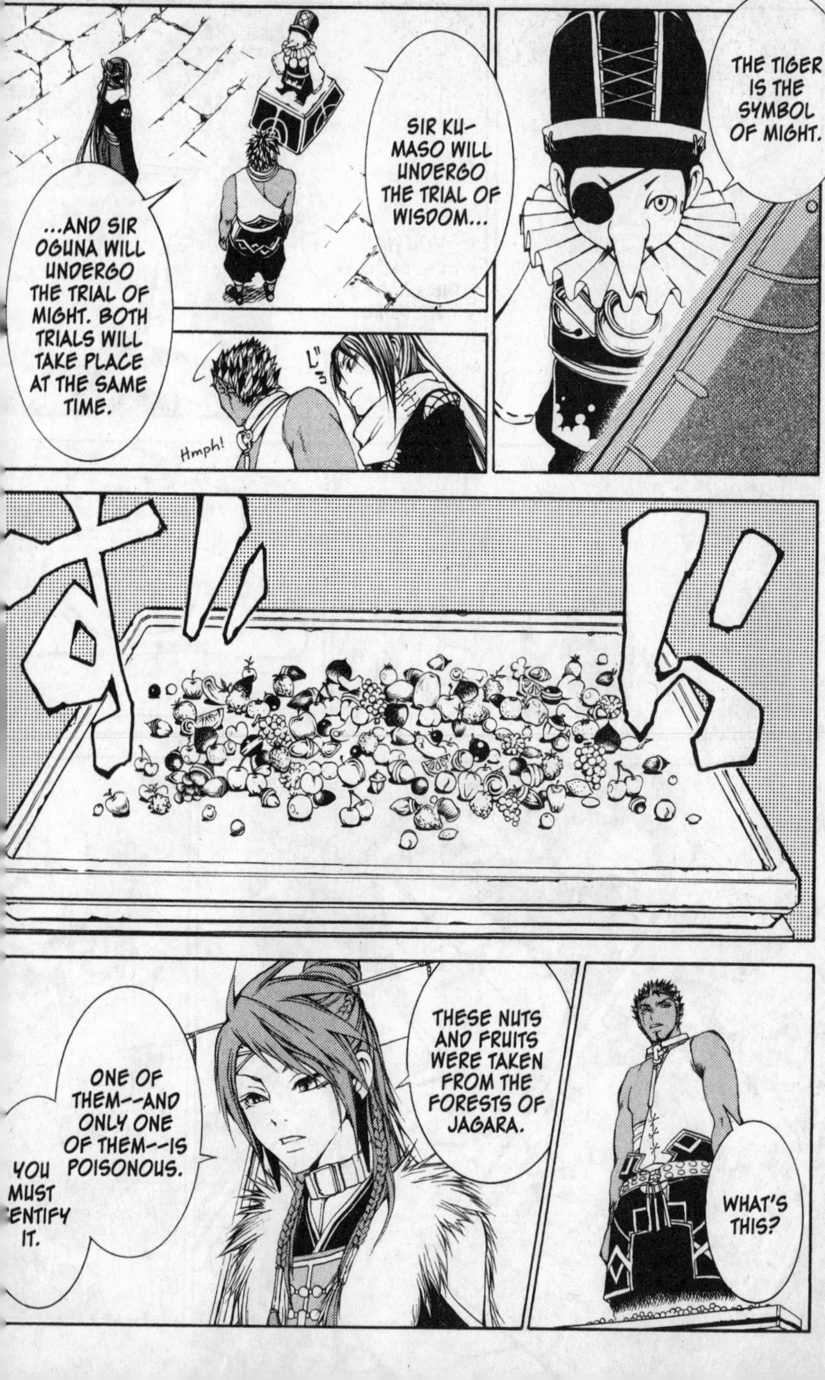
THE TIGER IS THE SYMBOL OF MIGHT.
SIR KU-MASO WILL UNDERGO THE TRIAL OF WISDOM...
...AND SIR OGUNA WILL UNDERGO THE TRIAL OF MIGHT. BOTH TRIALS WILL TAKE PLACE AT THE SAME TIME.
Hmph!
WHAT'S THIS?
THESE NUTS AND FRUITS WERE TAKEN FROM THE FORESTS OF JAGARA.
ONE OF THEM--AND ONLY ONE OF THEM--IS POISONOUS.
YOU MUST ENTIFY IT.

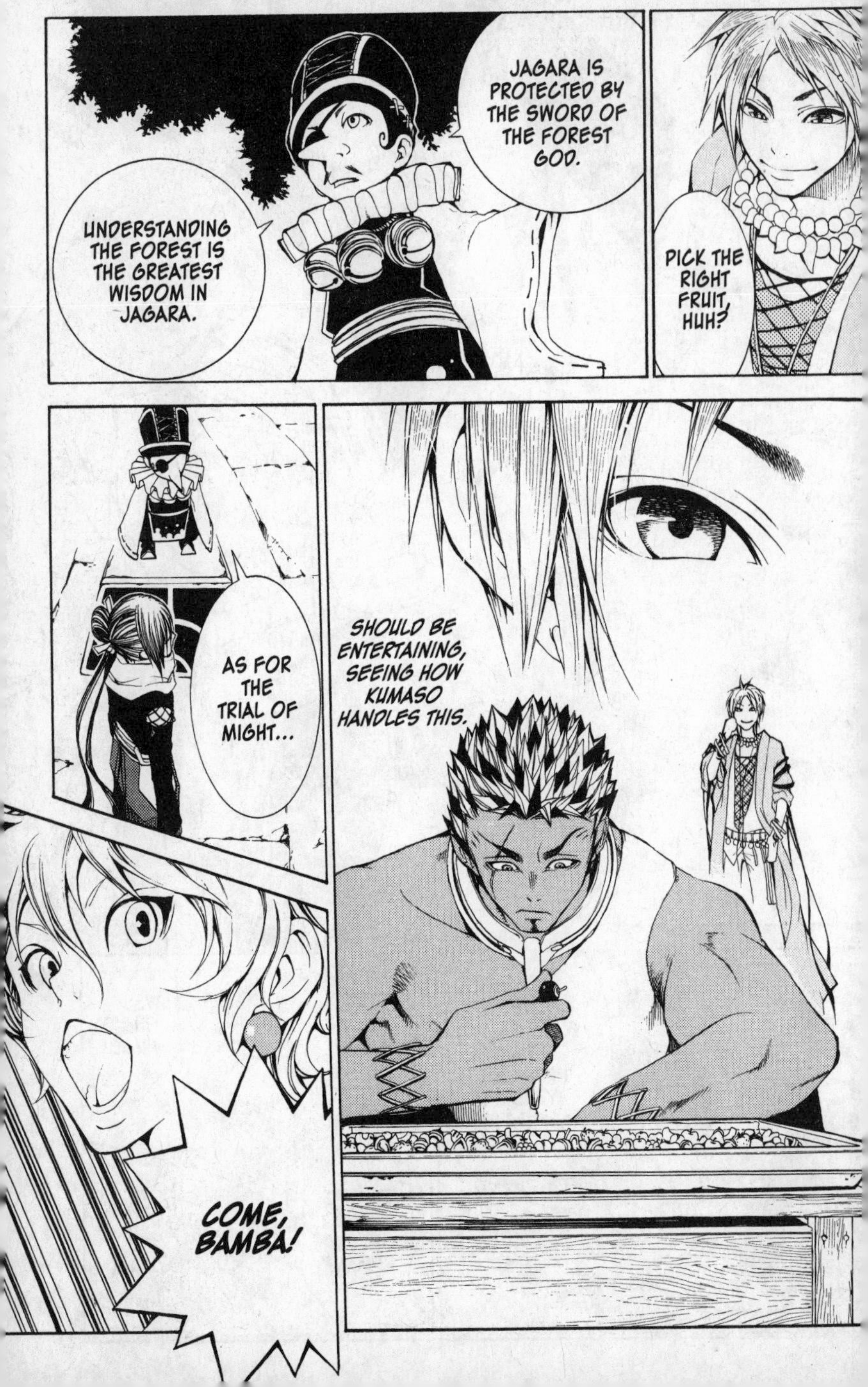
PICK THE RIGHT FRUIT, HUH?
JAGARA IS PROTECTED BY THE SWORD OF THE FOREST GOD.
UNDERSTANDING THE FOREST IS THE GREATEST WISDOM IN JAGARA.
SHOULD BE ENTERTAINING, SEEING HOW KUMASO HANDLES THIS.
AS FOR THE TRIAL OF MIGHT...
COME, BAMBA!

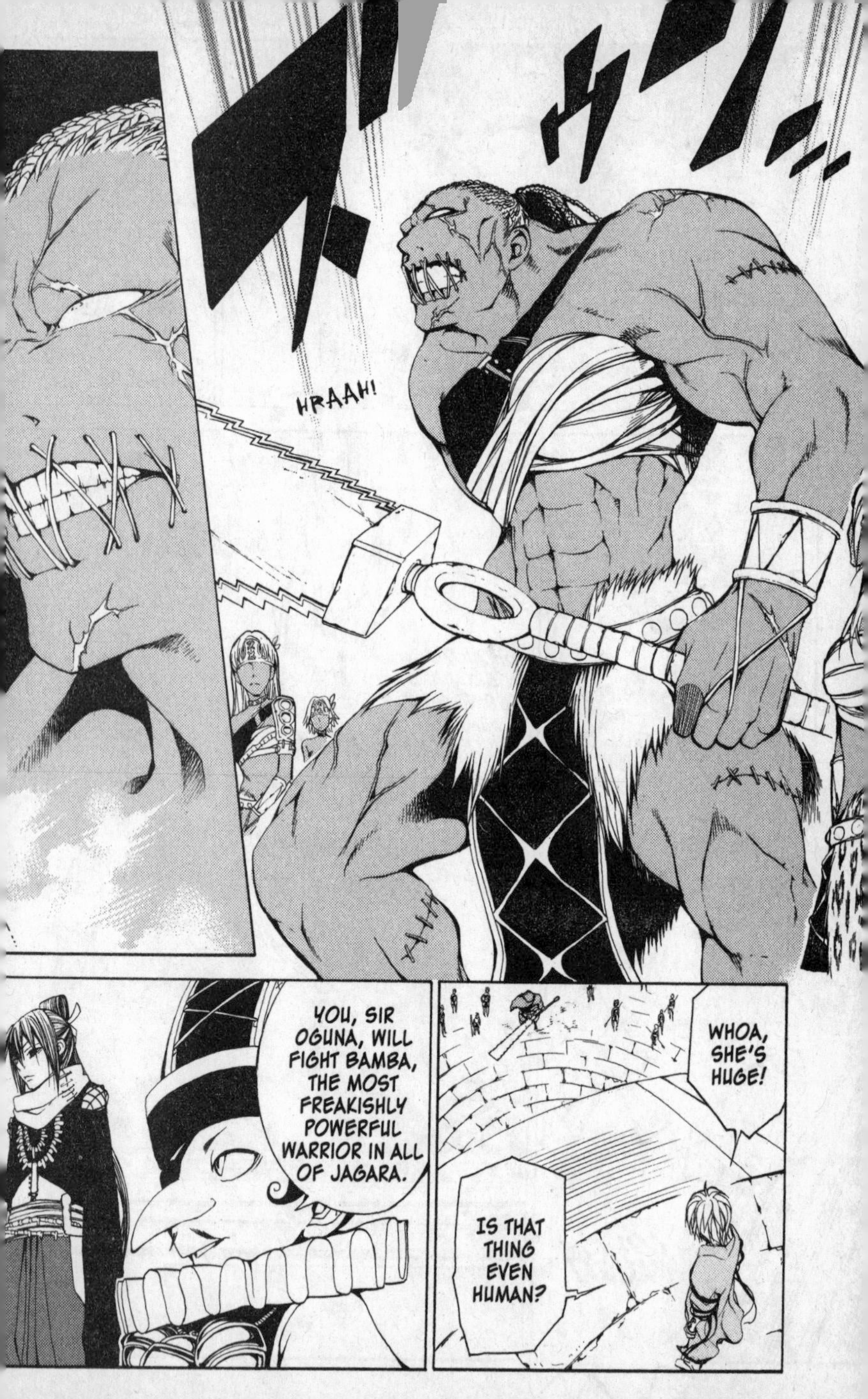
HRAAH!
WHOA, SHE'S HUGE!
IS THAT THING EVEN HUMAN?
YOU, SIR OGUNA, WILL FIGHT BAMBA, THE MOST FREAKISHLY POWERFUL WARRIOR IN ALL OF JAGARA.

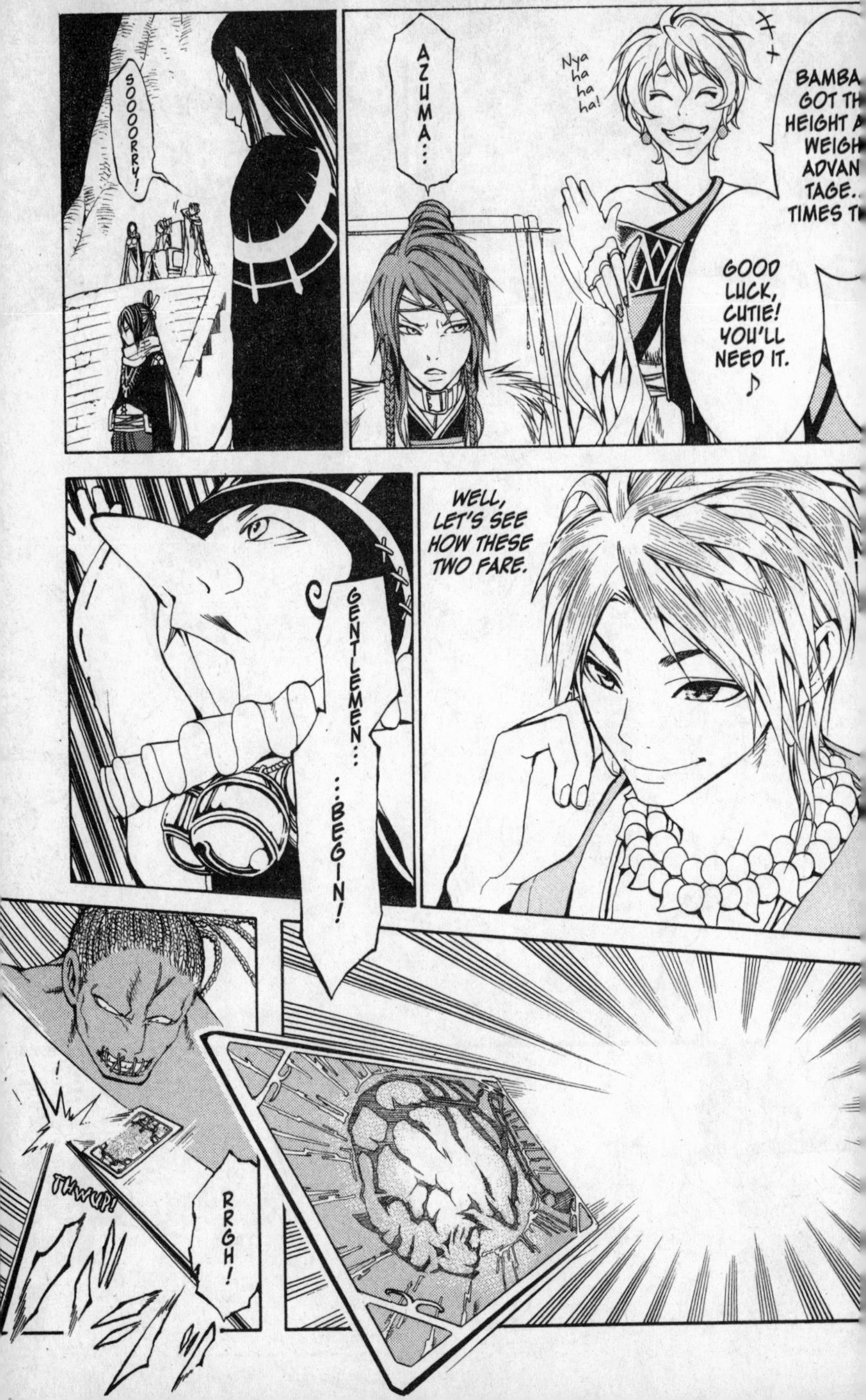

Nya ha ha ha!
BAMBA GOT TH HEIGHT A WEIGH ADVAN TAGE.. TIMES T
GOOD LUCK, CUTIE! YOU'LL NEED IT. ♪
AZUMA...
SOOOOORRY!
WELL, LET'S SEE HOW THESE TWO FARE.
GENTLEMEN...
...BEGIN!
RRGH!
THWUP!

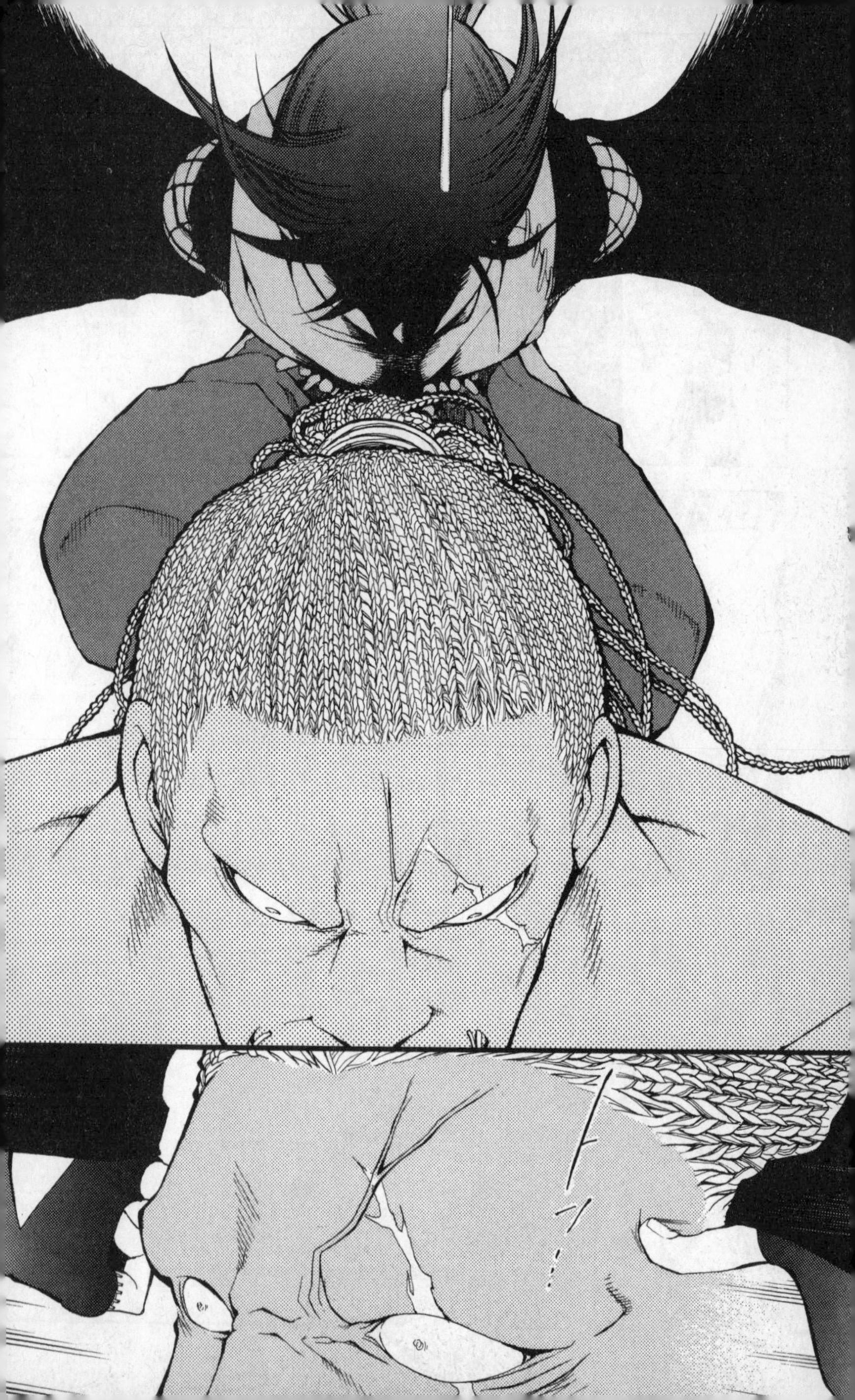
トン…

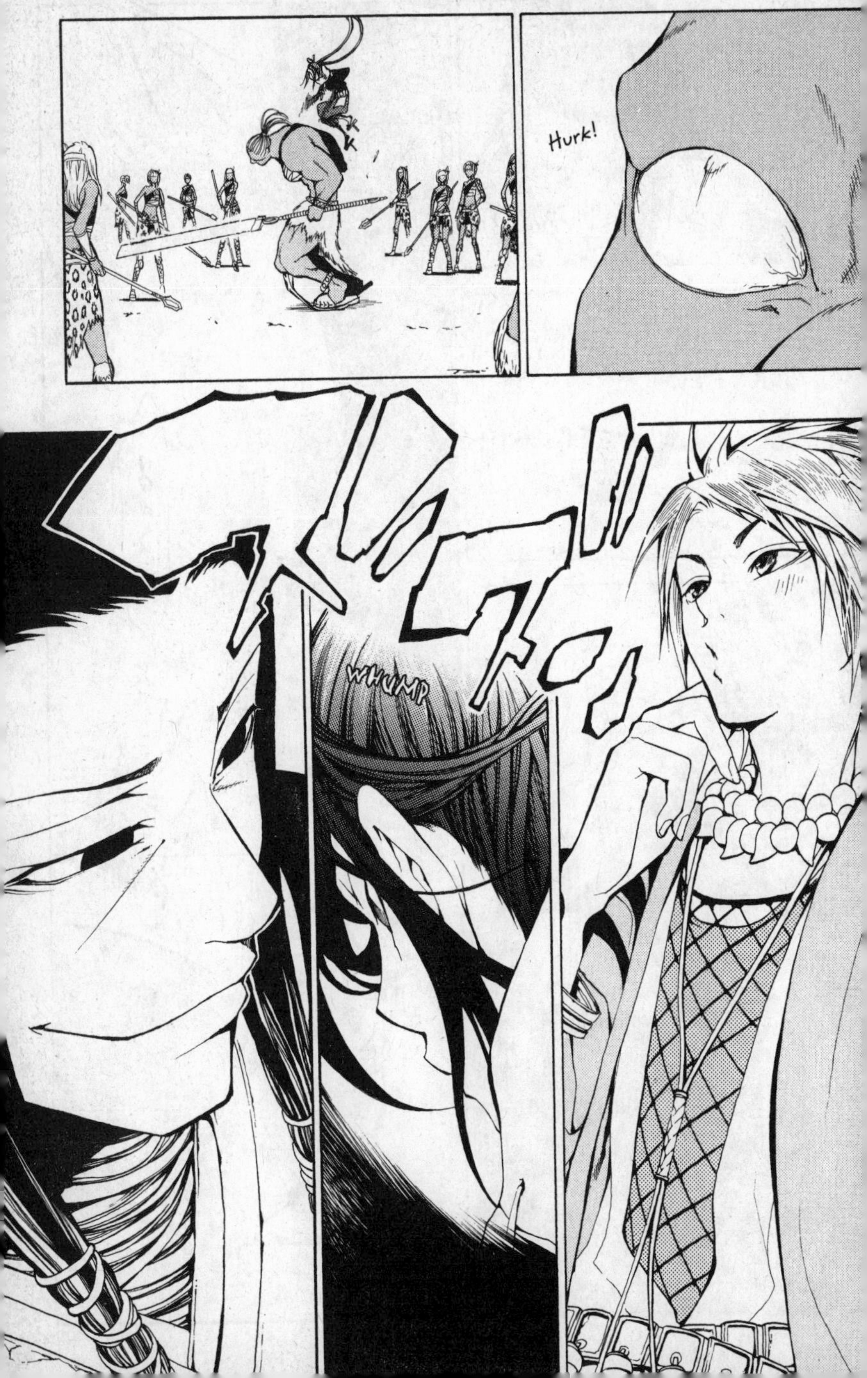
Hurk!
WHUMP

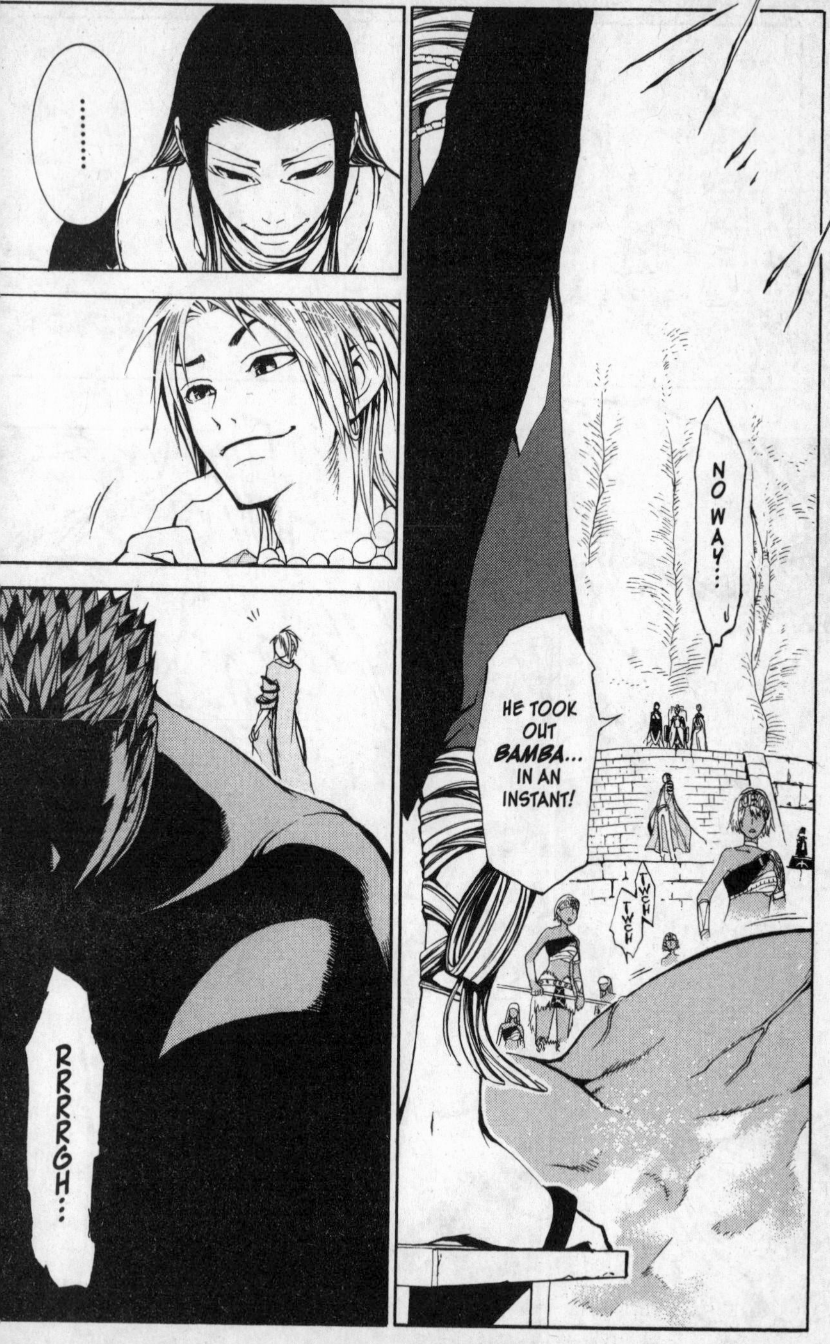
NO WAY...
HE TOOK OUT BAMBA... IN AN INSTANT!
TWCH TWCH
......
RRRRGH...

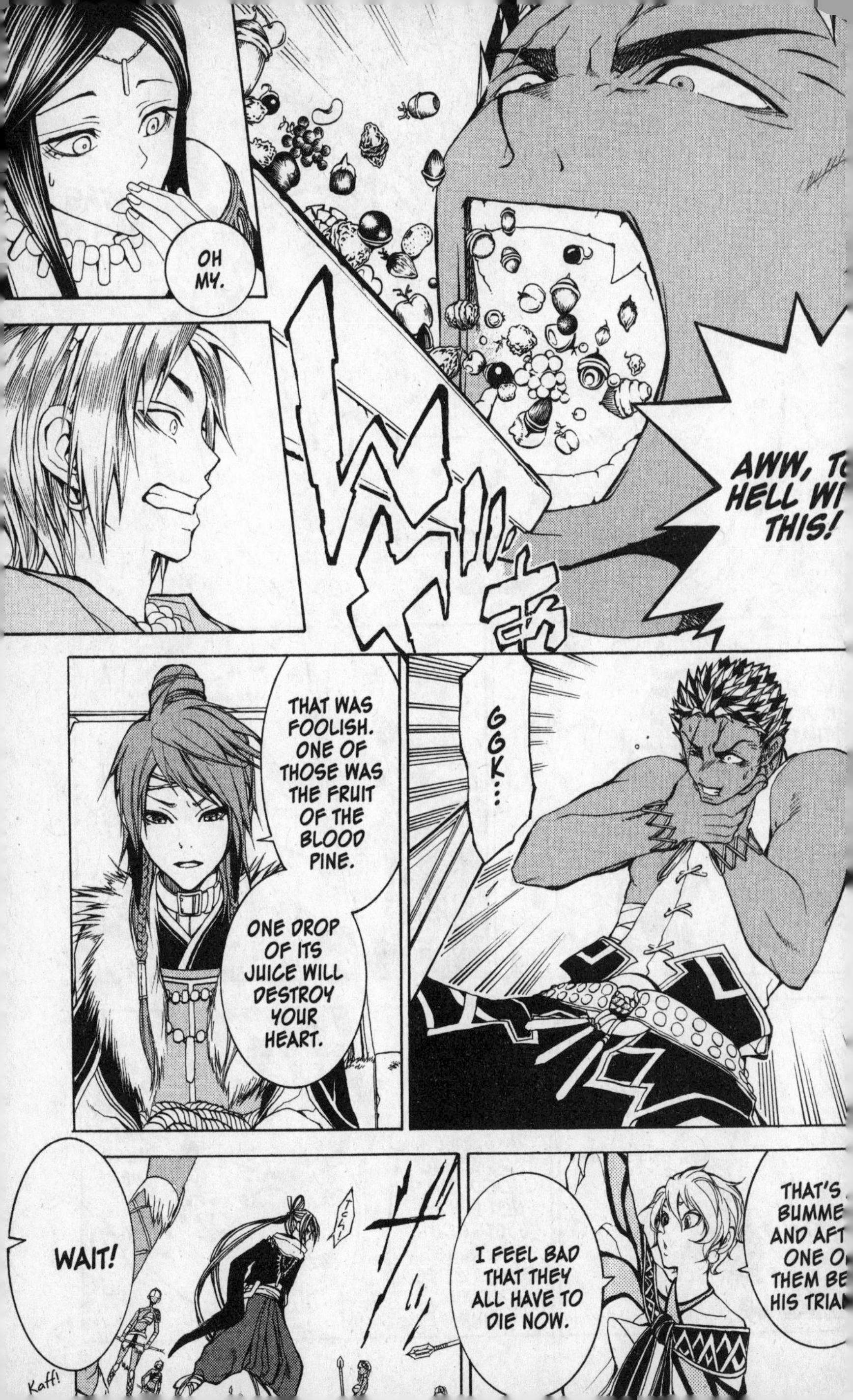
AWW, T
HELL WI
THIS!
OH MY.
GGK...
THAT WAS FOOLISH. ONE OF THOSE WAS THE FRUIT OF THE BLOOD PINE.
ONE DROP OF ITS JUICE WILL DESTROY YOUR HEART.
THAT'S
BUMME
AND AFT
ONE O
THEM BE
HIS TRIA
I FEEL BAD THAT THEY ALL HAVE TO DIE NOW.
WAIT!
Kaff!

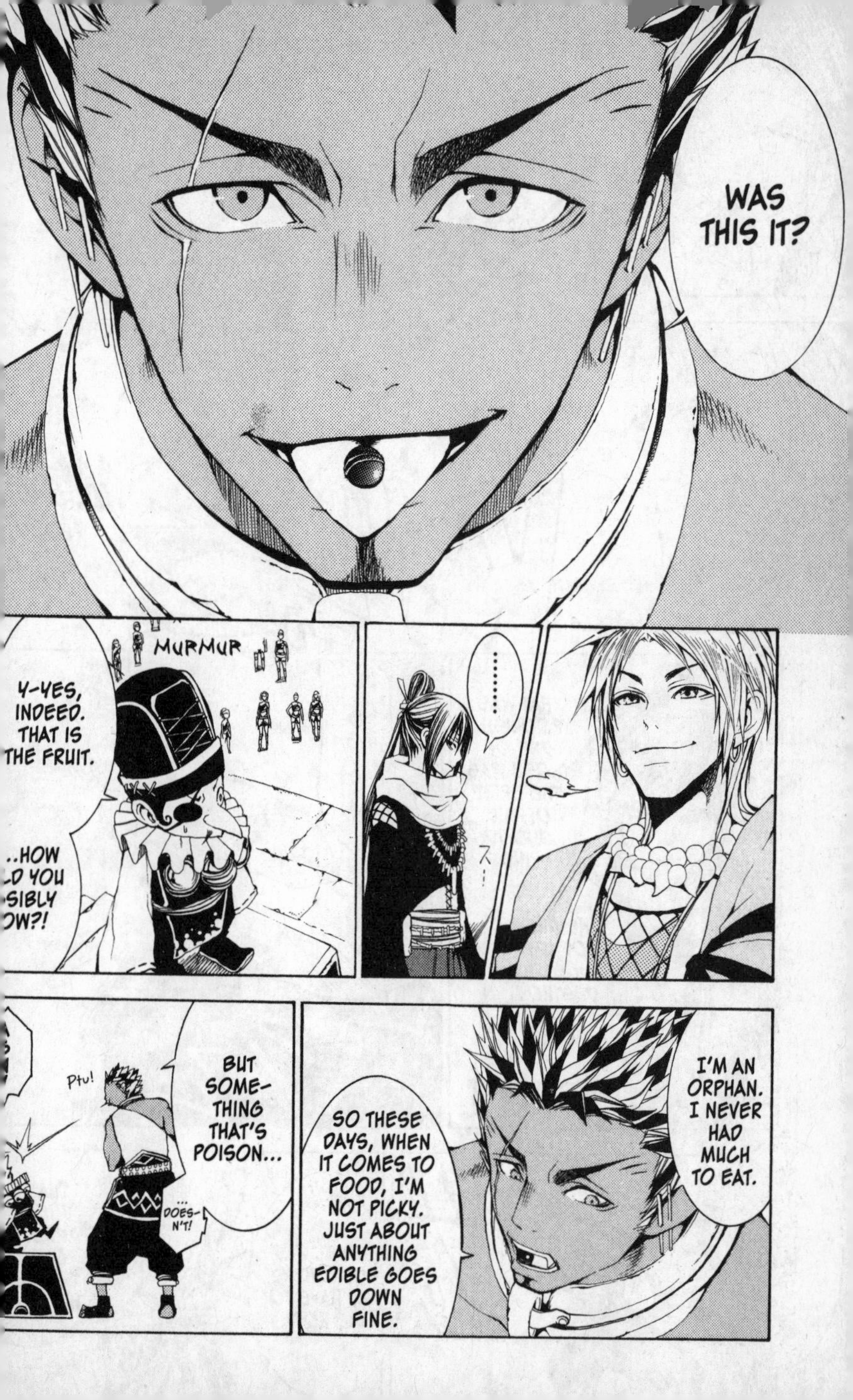
WAS THIS IT?
......
ス…
MURMUR
Y-YES, INDEED. THAT IS THE FRUIT.
..HOW
I'M AN ORPHAN. I NEVER HAD MUCH TO EAT.
SO THESE DAYS, WHEN IT COMES TO FOOD, I'M NOT PICKY. JUST ABOUT ANYTHING EDIBLE GOES DOWN FINE.
BUT SOME-THING THAT'S POISON...
Ptu!
...DOES-N'T!

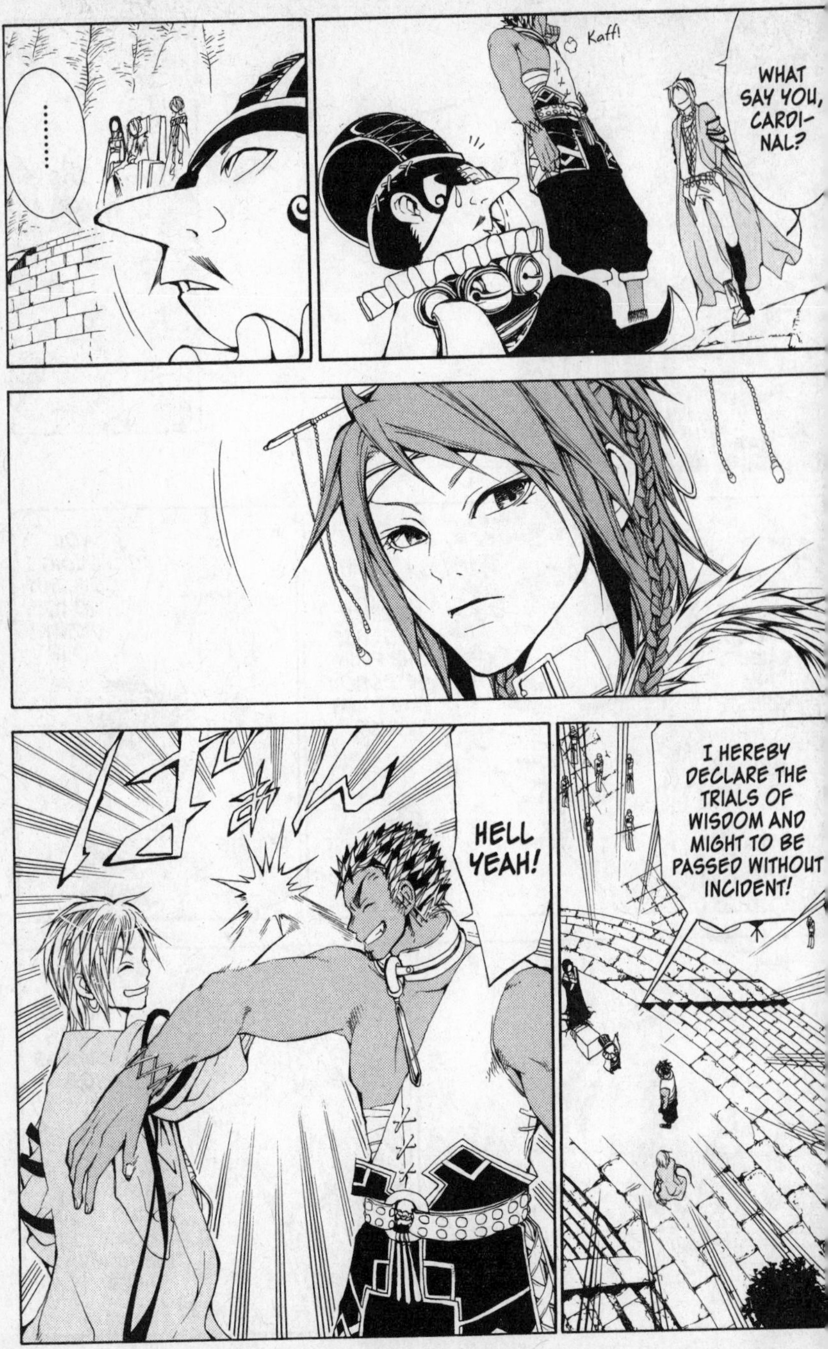
Kaff!
WHAT SAY YOU, CARDINAL?
......
I HEREBY DECLARE THE TRIALS OF WISDOM AND MIGHT TO BE PASSED WITHOUT INCIDENT!
HELL YEAH!

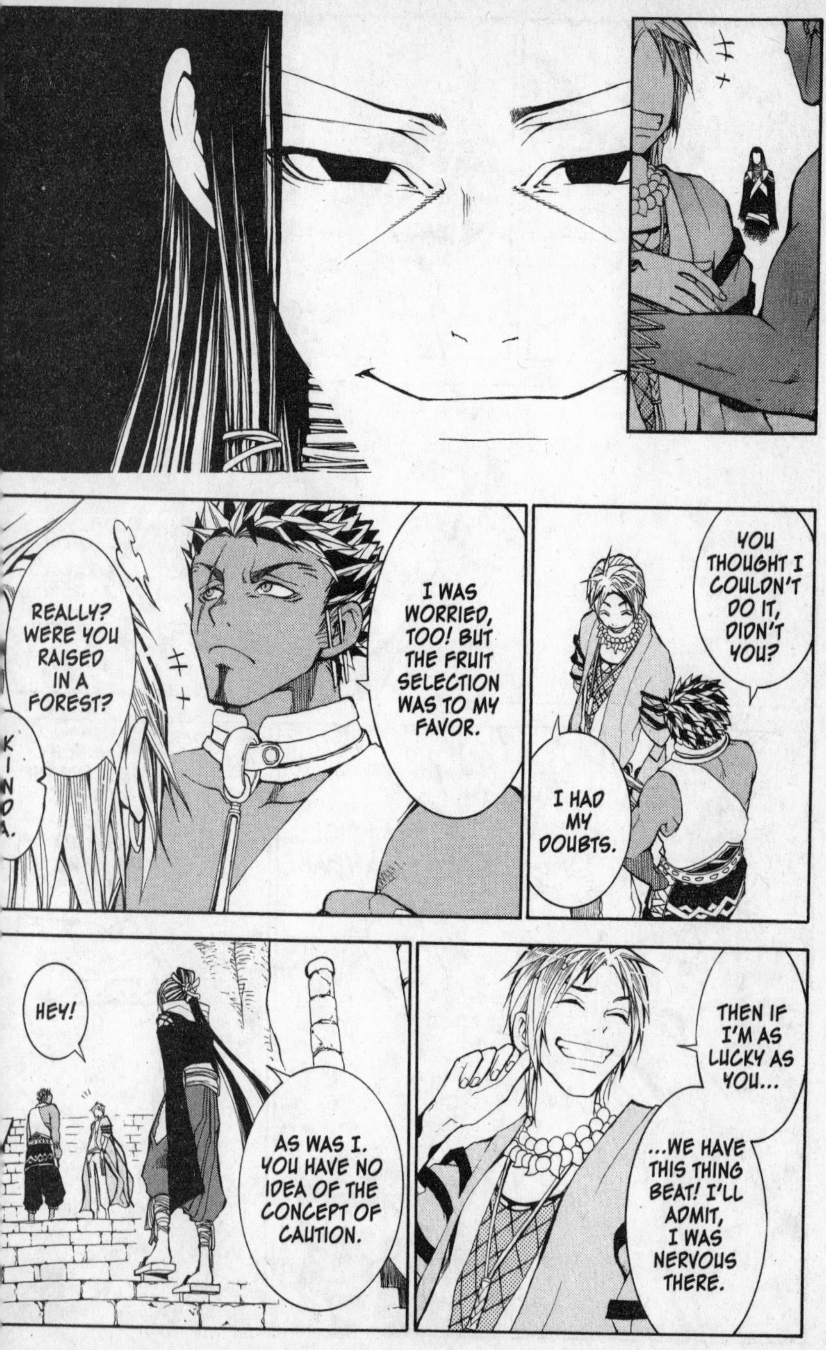
YOU THOUGHT I COULDN'T DO IT, DIDN'T YOU?
I HAD MY DOUBTS.
I WAS WORRIED, TOO! BUT THE FRUIT SELECTION WAS TO MY FAVOR.
REALLY? WERE YOU RAISED IN A FOREST?
KINDA.
THEN IF I'M AS LUCKY AS YOU...
...WE HAVE THIS THING BEAT! I'LL ADMIT, I WAS NERVOUS THERE.
AS WAS I. YOU HAVE NO IDEA OF THE CONCEPT OF CAUTION.
HEY!

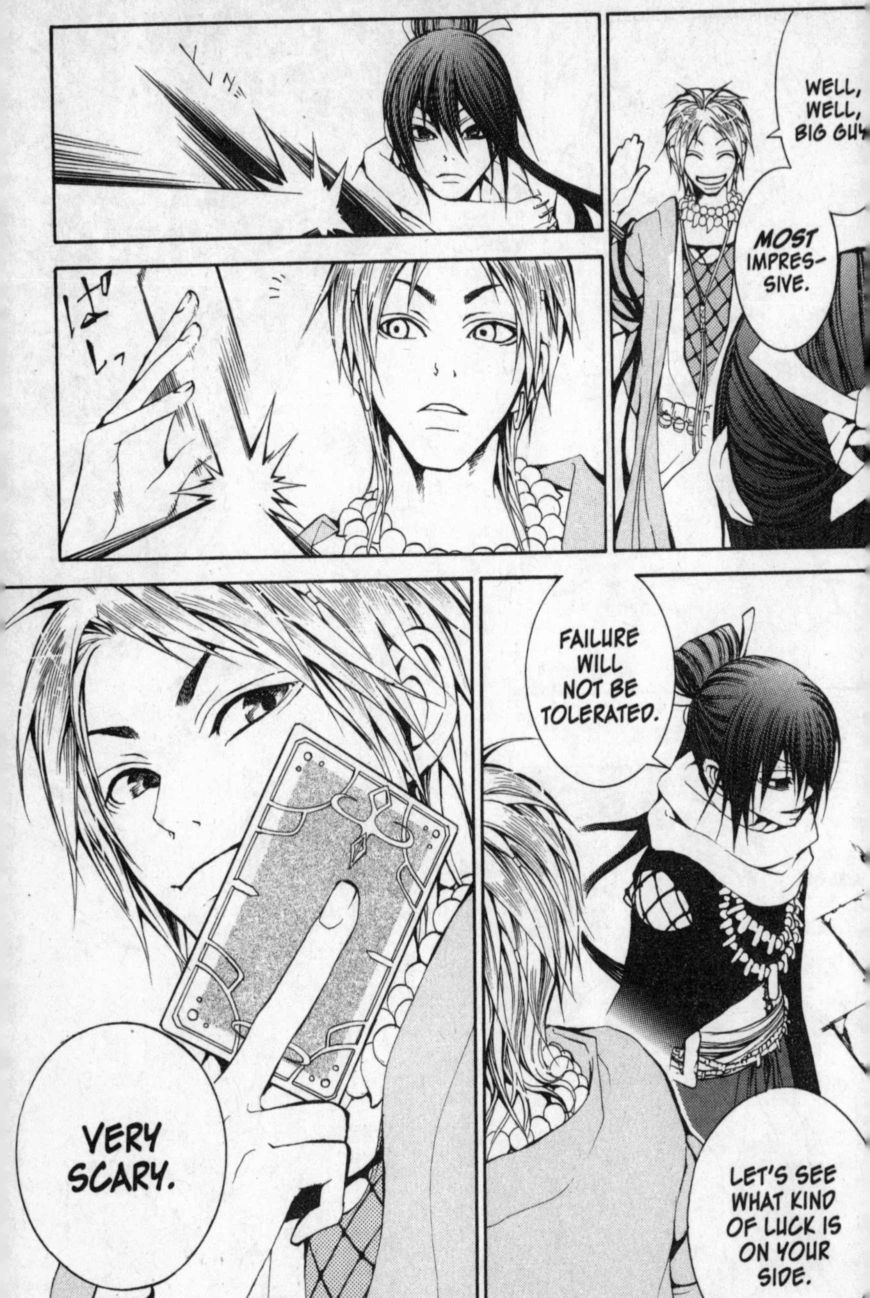
WELL, WELL, BIG GUY
MOST IMPRESSIVE.
ぱしっ
FAILURE WILL NOT BE TOLERATED.
LET'S SEE WHAT KIND OF LUCK IS ON YOUR SIDE.
VERY SCARY.

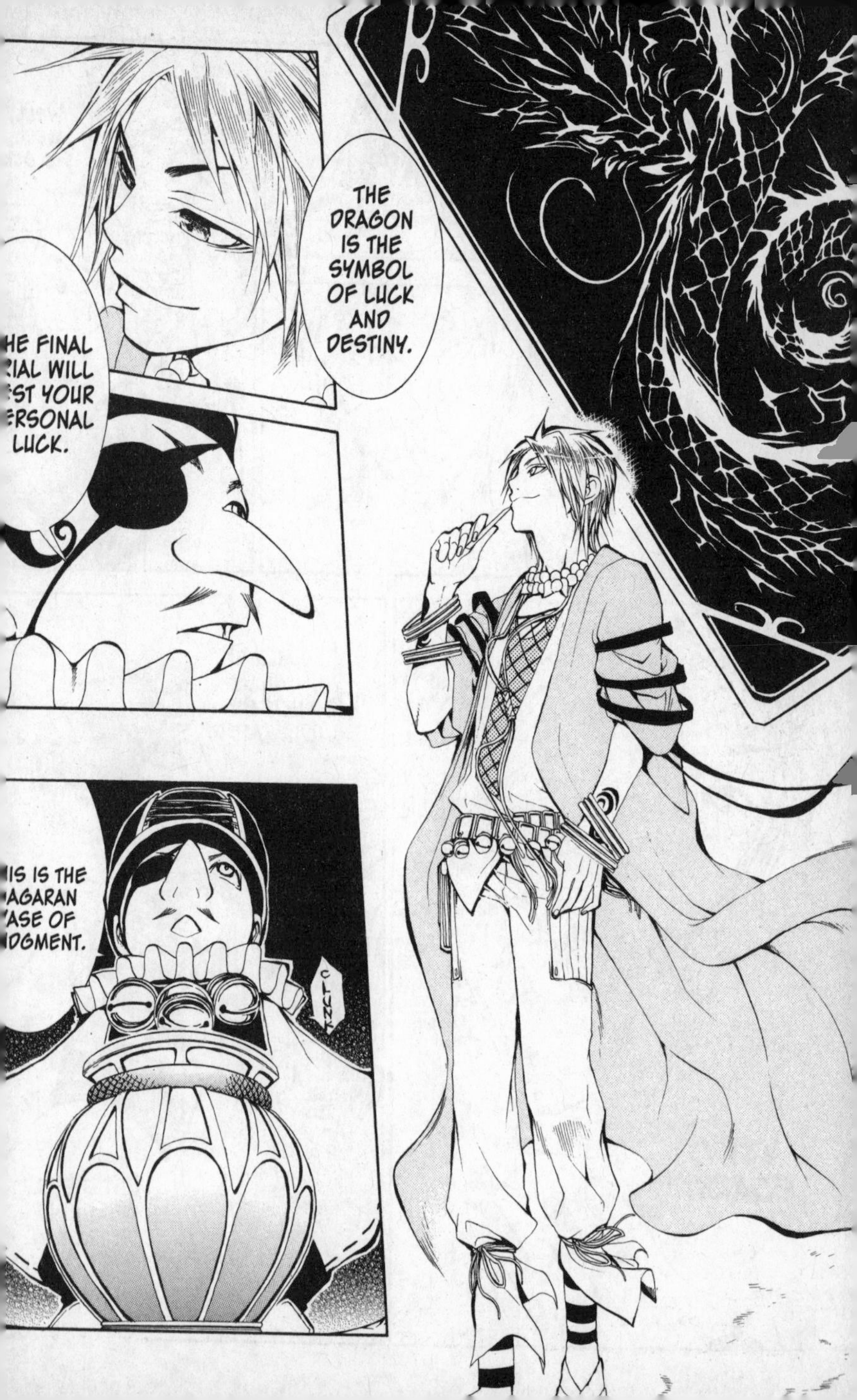
THE DRAGON IS THE SYMBOL OF LUCK AND DESTINY.
HE FINAL RIAL WILL EST YOUR ERSONAL LUCK.
IS IS THE AGARAN ASE OF DGMENT.
CLUNK

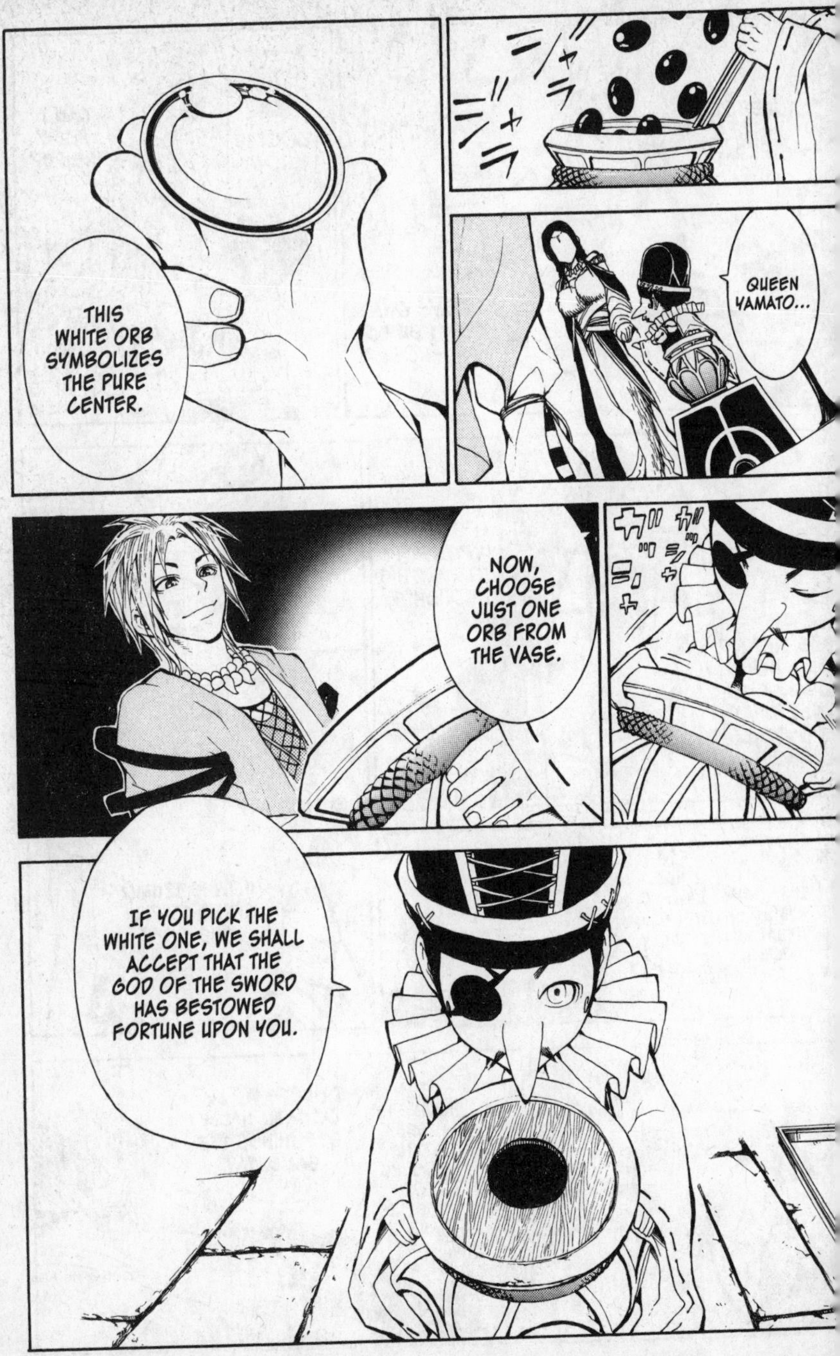
ジャラ
ジャラ
QUEEN YAMATO...
THIS WHITE ORB SYMBOLIZES THE PURE CENTER.
NOW, CHOOSE JUST ONE ORB FROM THE VASE.
IF YOU PICK THE WHITE ONE, WE SHALL ACCEPT THAT THE GOD OF THE SWORD HAS BESTOWED FORTUNE UPON YOU.

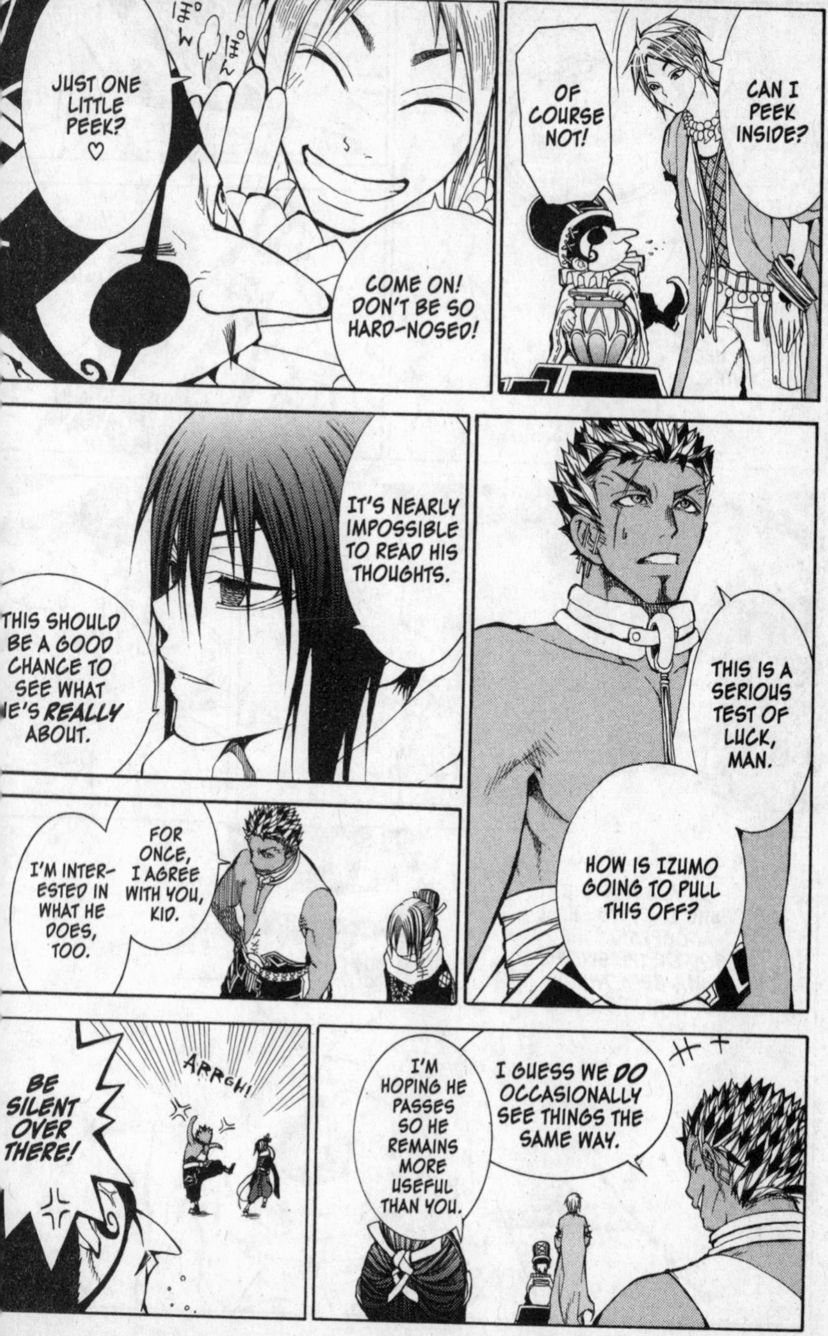
CAN I PEEK INSIDE?
OF COURSE NOT!
ぽん ぽん
COME ON! DON'T BE SO HARD-NOSED!
JUST ONE LITTLE PEEK? ♡
THIS IS A SERIOUS TEST OF LUCK, MAN.
HOW IS IZUMO GOING TO PULL THIS OFF?
IT'S NEARLY IMPOSSIBLE TO READ HIS THOUGHTS.
THIS SHOULD BE A GOOD CHANCE TO SEE WHAT E'S *REALLY* ABOUT.
FOR ONCE, I AGREE WITH YOU, KID.
I'M INTER-ESTED IN WHAT HE DOES, TOO.
I GUESS WE *DO* OCCASIONALLY SEE THINGS THE SAME WAY.
I'M HOPING HE PASSES SO HE REMAINS MORE USEFUL THAN YOU.
ARRGH!
BE SILENT OVER THERE!

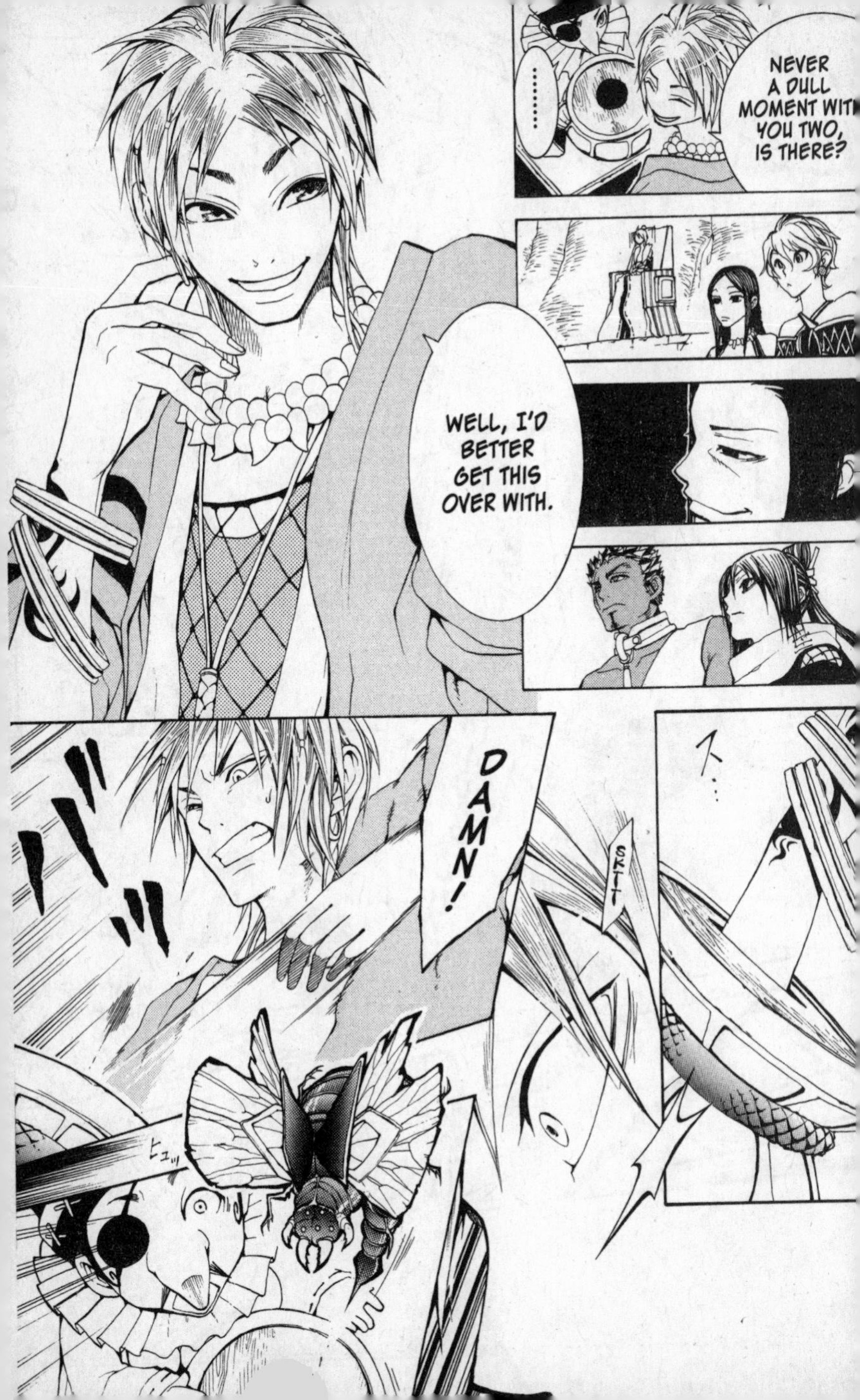
NEVER A DULL MOMENT WIT YOU TWO, IS THERE?
......
WELL, I'D BETTER GET THIS OVER WITH.
SKITT
DAMN!
ヒュッ

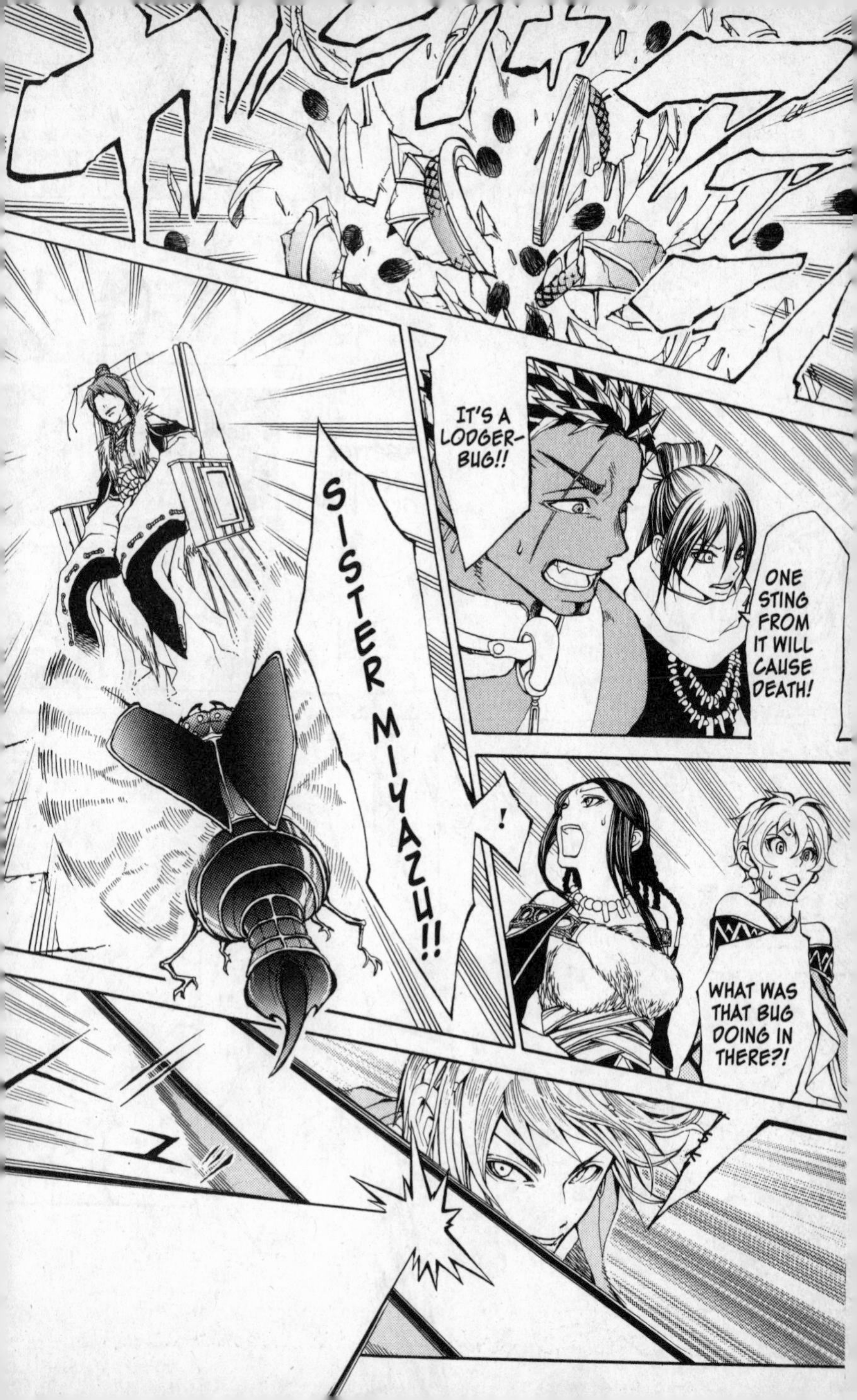
IT'S A LODGER-BUG!!
ONE STING FROM IT WILL CAUSE DEATH!
!
WHAT WAS THAT BUG DOING IN THERE?!
SISTER MIYAZU!!

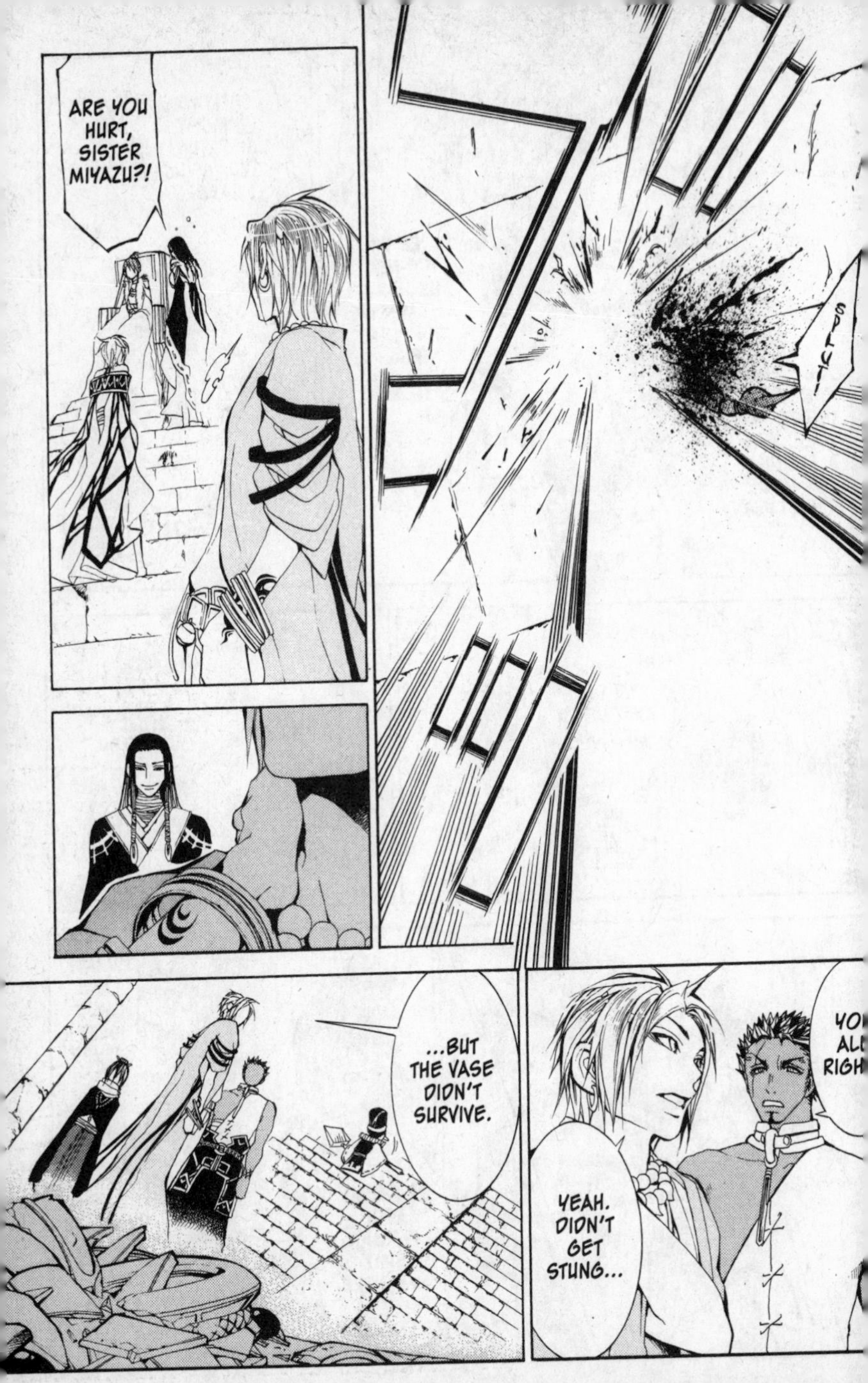
SPLUT!
ARE YOU HURT, SISTER MIYAZU?!
YO ALL RIGH
YEAH. DIDN'T GET STUNG...
...BUT THE VASE DIDN'T SURVIVE.

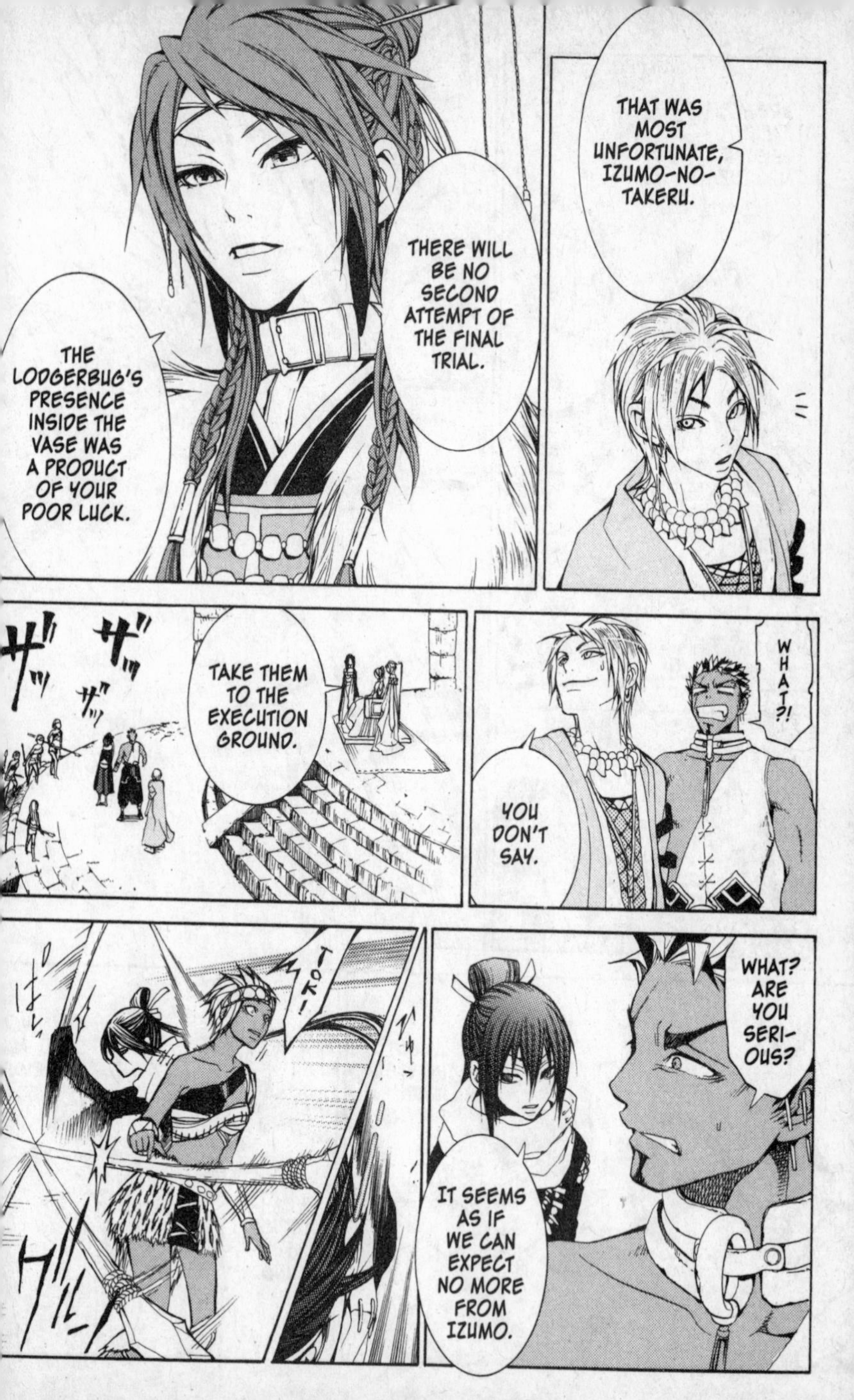
THAT WAS MOST UNFORTUNATE, IZUMO-NO-TAKERU.
THERE WILL BE NO SECOND ATTEMPT OF THE FINAL TRIAL.
THE LODGERBUG'S PRESENCE INSIDE THE VASE WAS A PRODUCT OF YOUR POOR LUCK.
WHAT?!
YOU DON'T SAY.
TAKE THEM TO THE EXECUTION GROUND.
WHAT? ARE YOU SERI-OUS?
IT SEEMS AS IF WE CAN EXPECT NO MORE FROM IZUMO.
TOK!

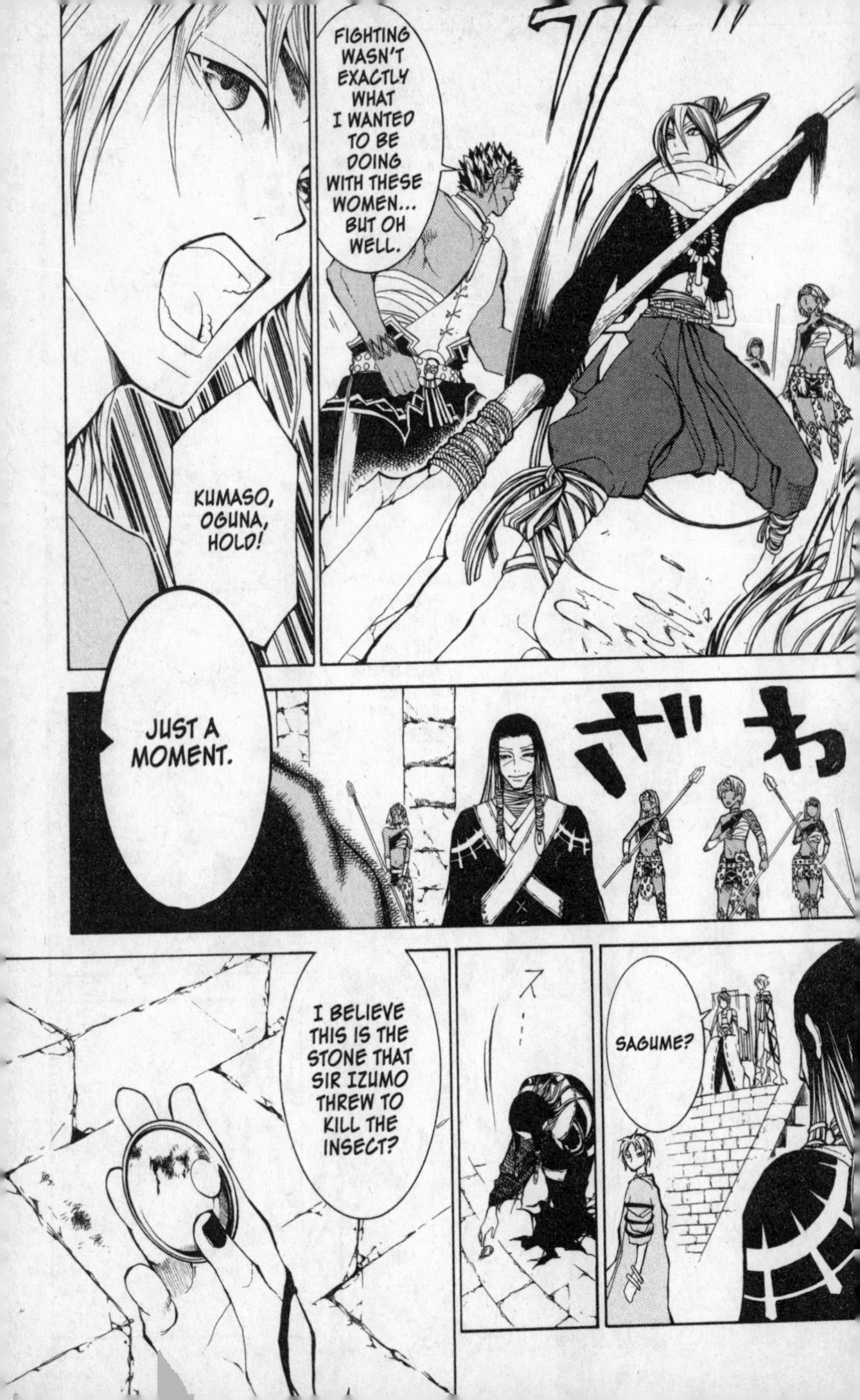
FIGHTING WASN'T EXACTLY WHAT I WANTED TO BE DOING WITH THESE WOMEN... BUT OH WELL.
KUMASO, OGUNA, HOLD!
JUST A MOMENT.
ざわ
SAGUME?
ス
I BELIEVE THIS IS THE STONE THAT SIR IZUMO THREW TO KILL THE INSECT?

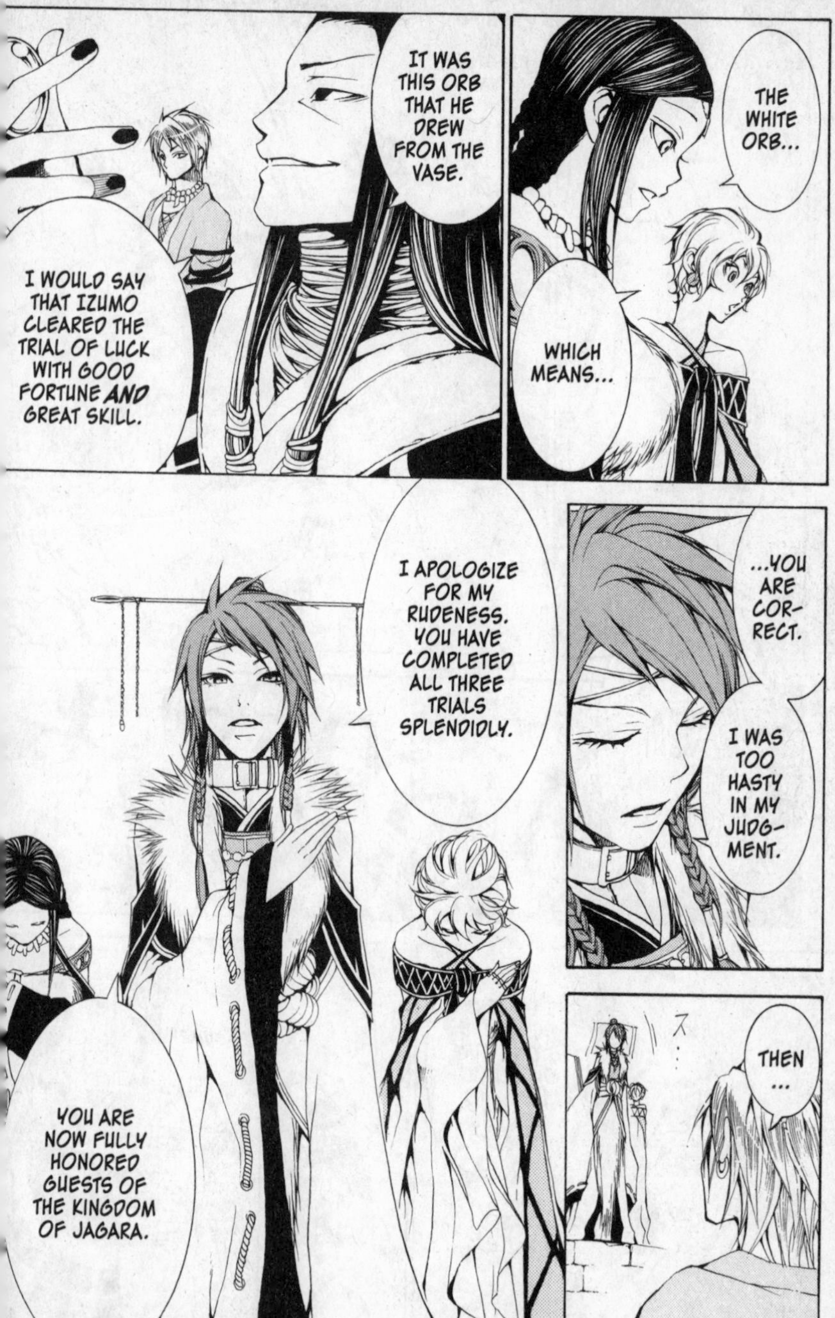
THE WHITE ORB...
WHICH MEANS...
IT WAS THIS ORB THAT HE DREW FROM THE VASE.
I WOULD SAY THAT IZUMO CLEARED THE TRIAL OF LUCK WITH GOOD FORTUNE AND GREAT SKILL.
...YOU ARE COR- RECT.
I WAS TOO HASTY IN MY JUDG- MENT.
ス...
THEN ...
I APOLOGIZE FOR MY RUDENESS. YOU HAVE COMPLETED ALL THREE TRIALS SPLENDIDLY.
YOU ARE NOW FULLY HONORED GUESTS OF THE KINGDOM OF JAGARA.

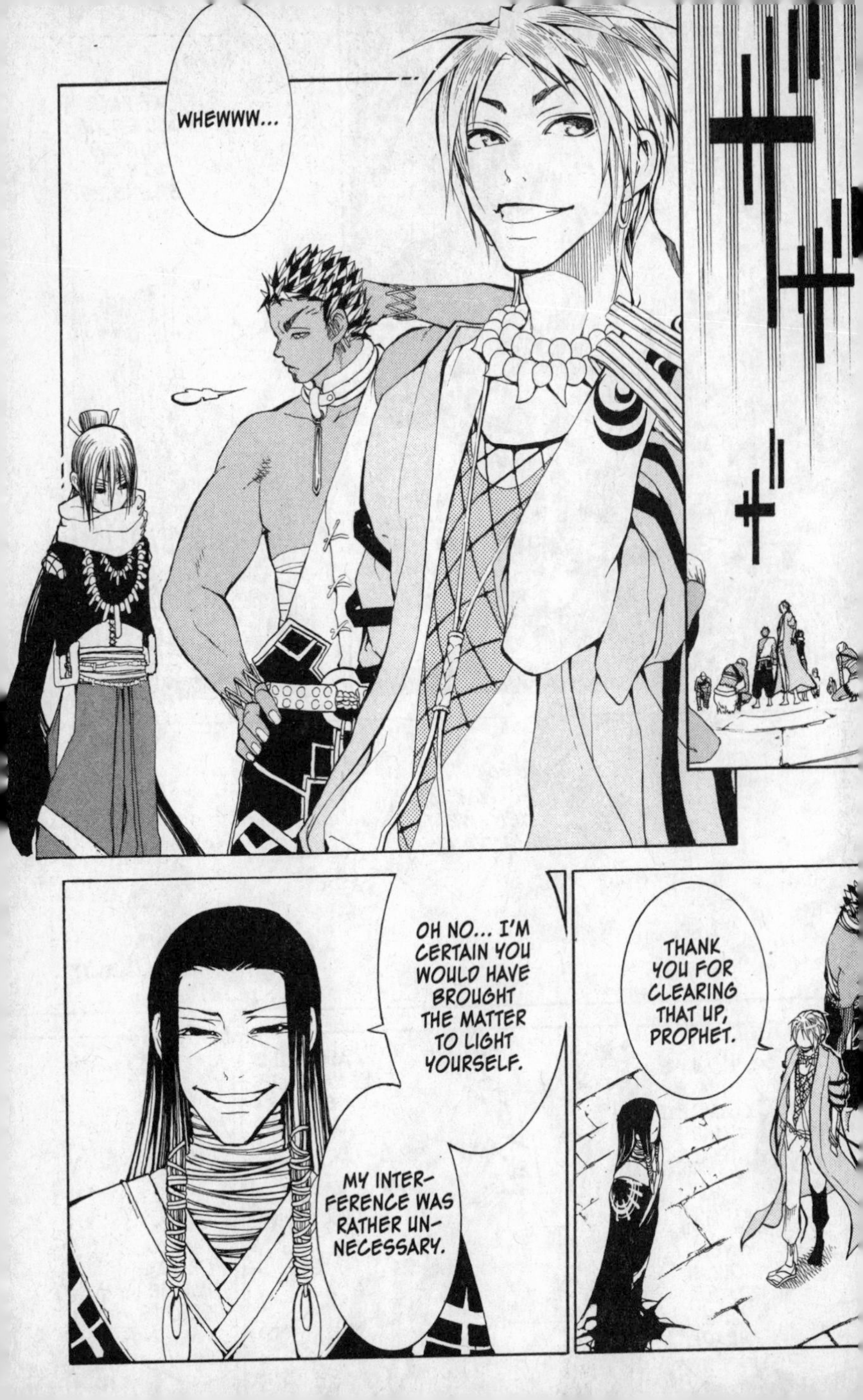
WHEWWW...
THANK YOU FOR CLEARING THAT UP, PROPHET.
OH NO... I'M CERTAIN YOU WOULD HAVE BROUGHT THE MATTER TO LIGHT YOURSELF.
MY INTERFERENCE WAS RATHER UNNECESSARY.

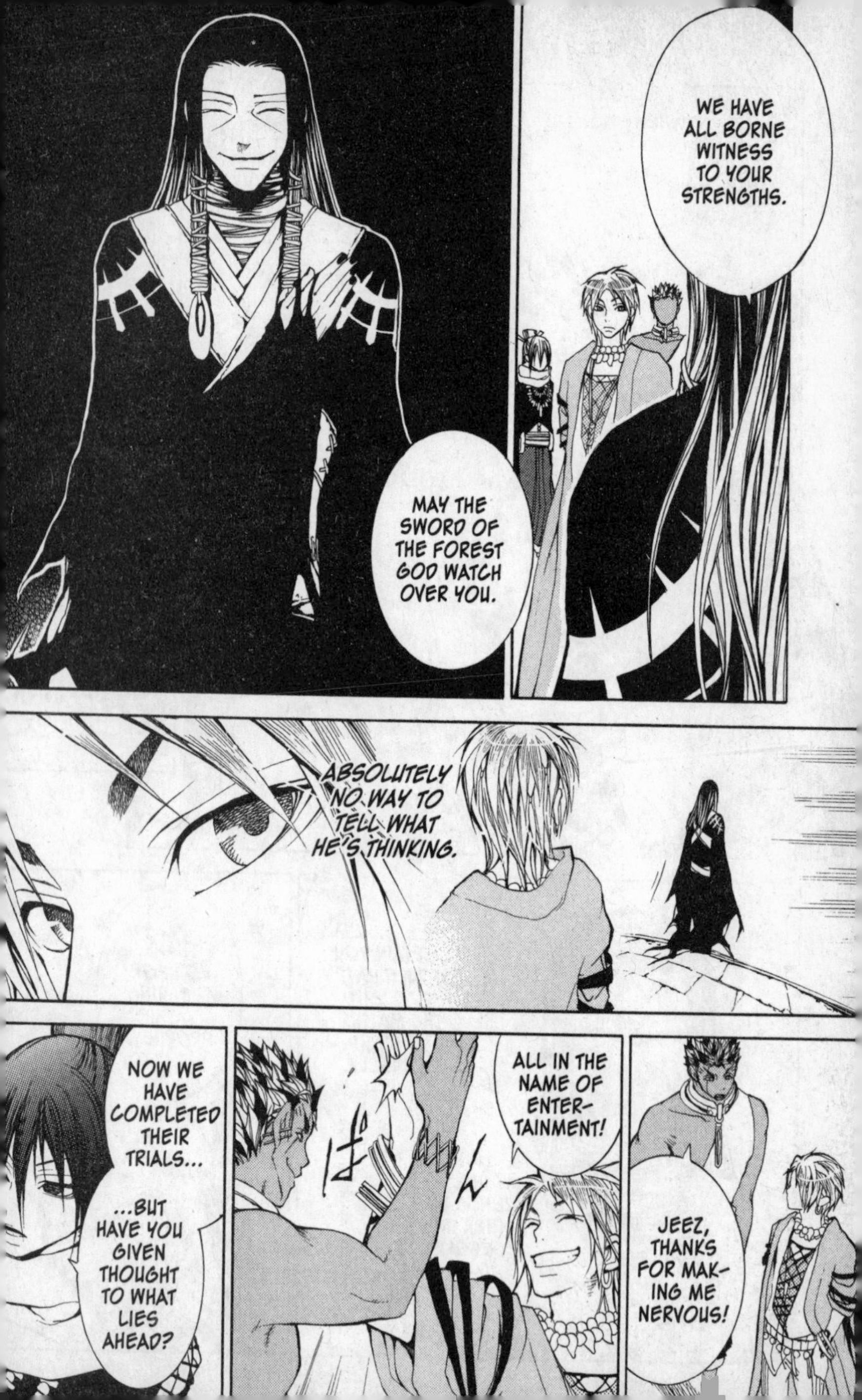
WE HAVE ALL BORNE WITNESS TO YOUR STRENGTHS.
MAY THE SWORD OF THE FOREST GOD WATCH OVER YOU.
ABSOLUTELY NO WAY TO TELL WHAT HE'S THINKING.
JEEZ, THANKS FOR MAKING ME NERVOUS!
ALL IN THE NAME OF ENTERTAINMENT!
ぱん
NOW WE HAVE COMPLETED THEIR TRIALS...
...BUT HAVE YOU GIVEN THOUGHT TO WHAT LIES AHEAD?

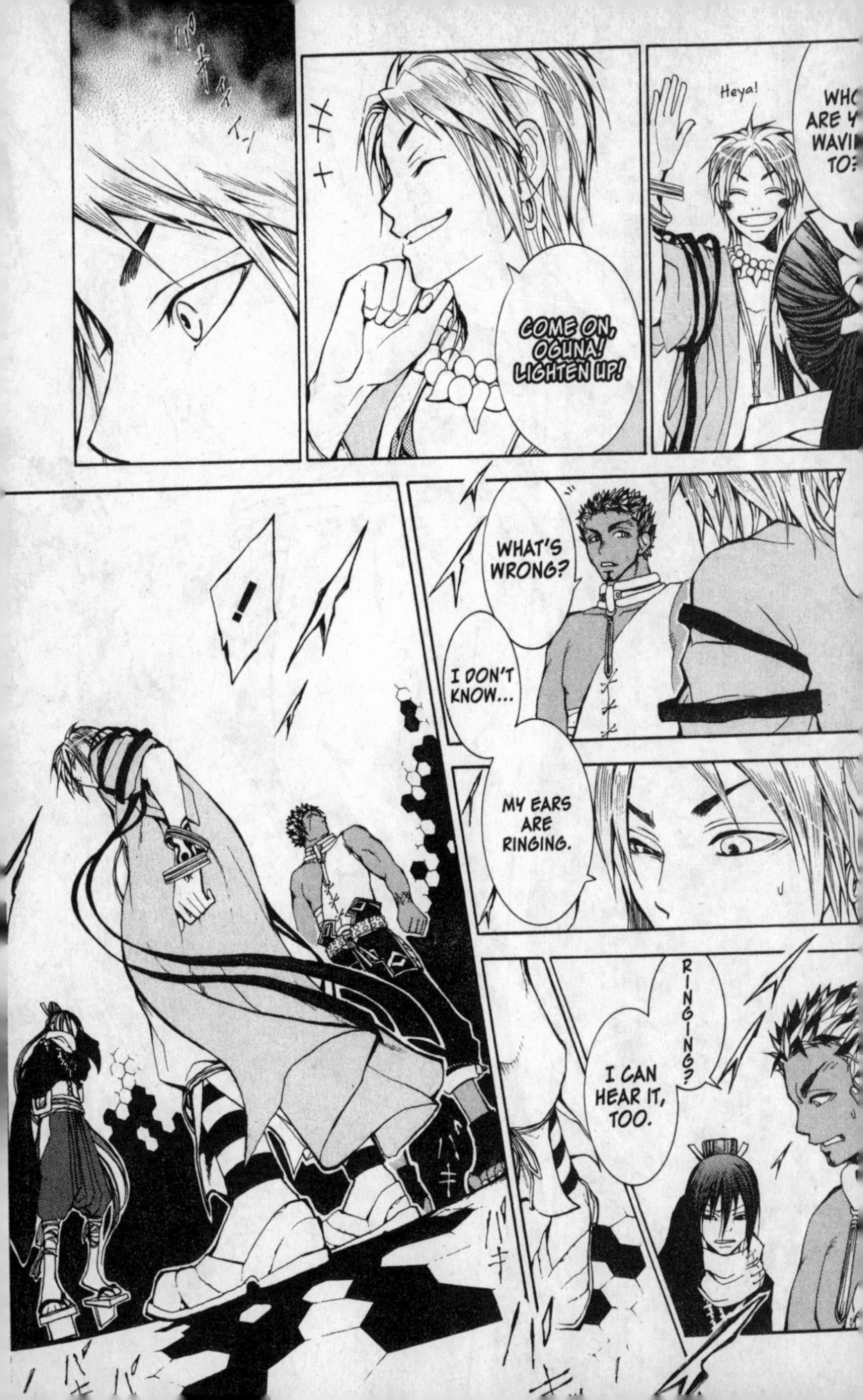

Heya!
WHO ARE Y WAVI TO?
COME ON, OGUNA! LIGHTEN UP!
WHAT'S WRONG?
I DON'T KNOW...
MY EARS ARE RINGING.
!
RINGING?
I CAN HEAR IT, TOO.

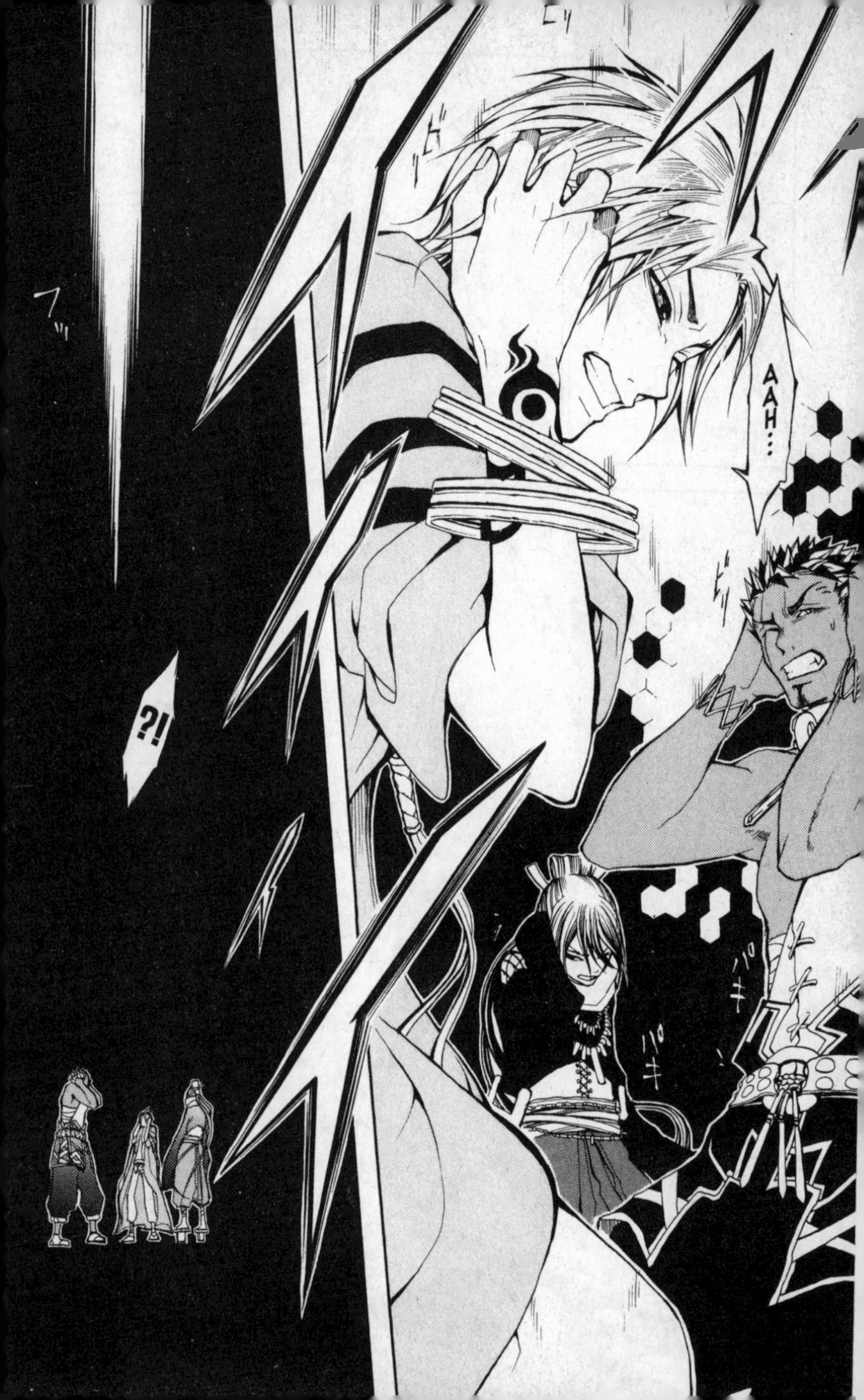
AAH...
?!

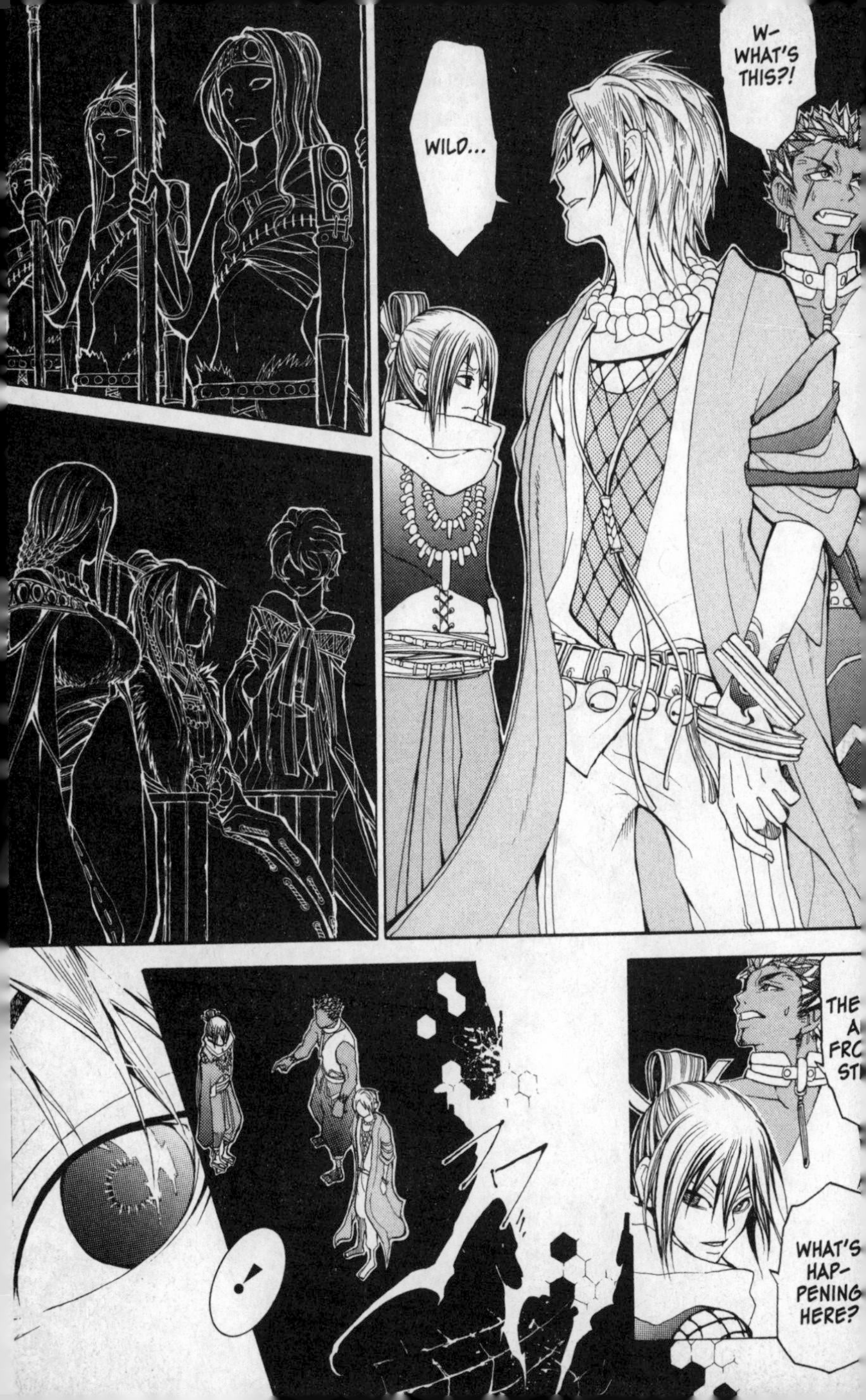
W-WHAT'S THIS?!
WILD...
THE
WHAT'S HAP-PENING HERE?
!

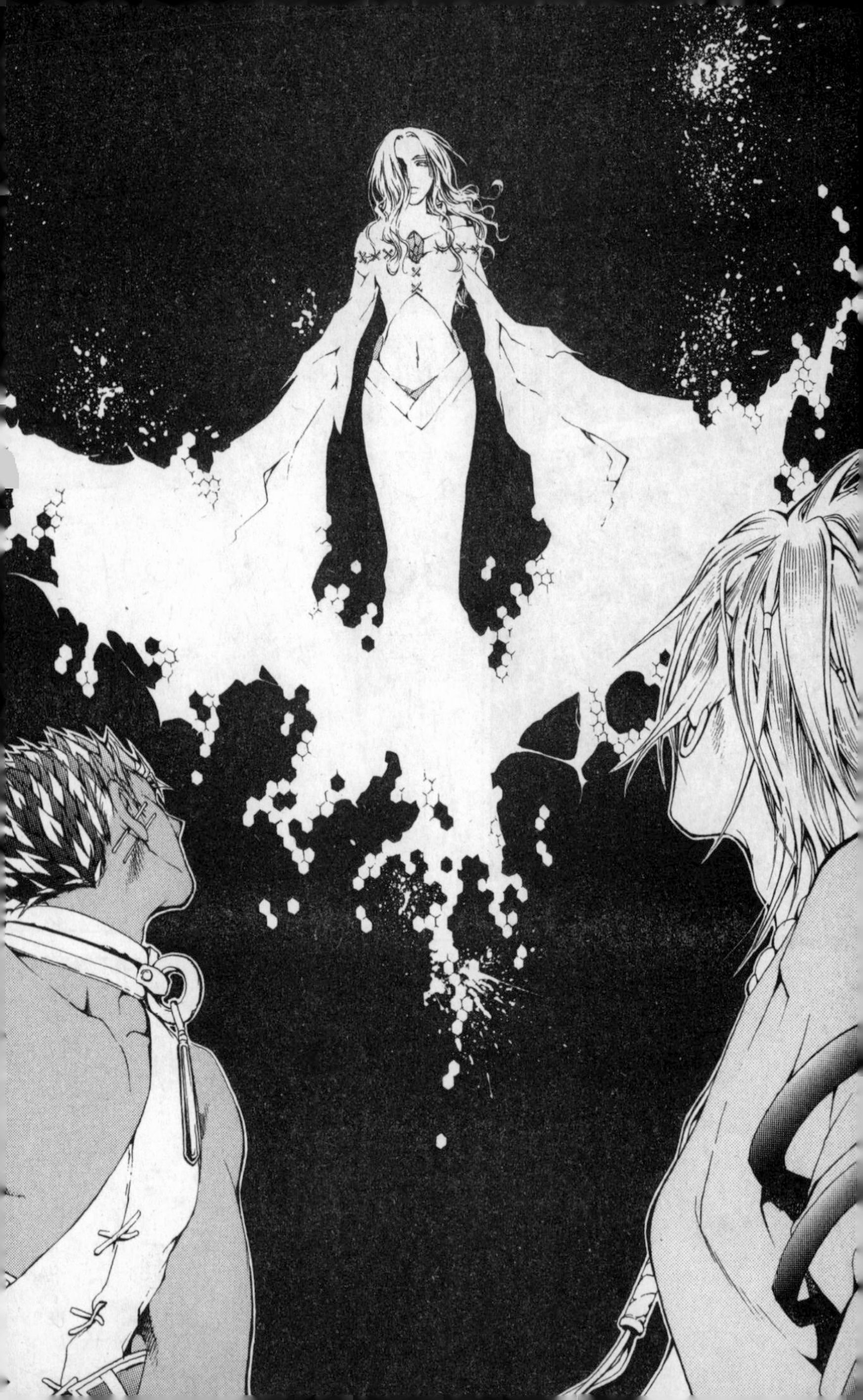

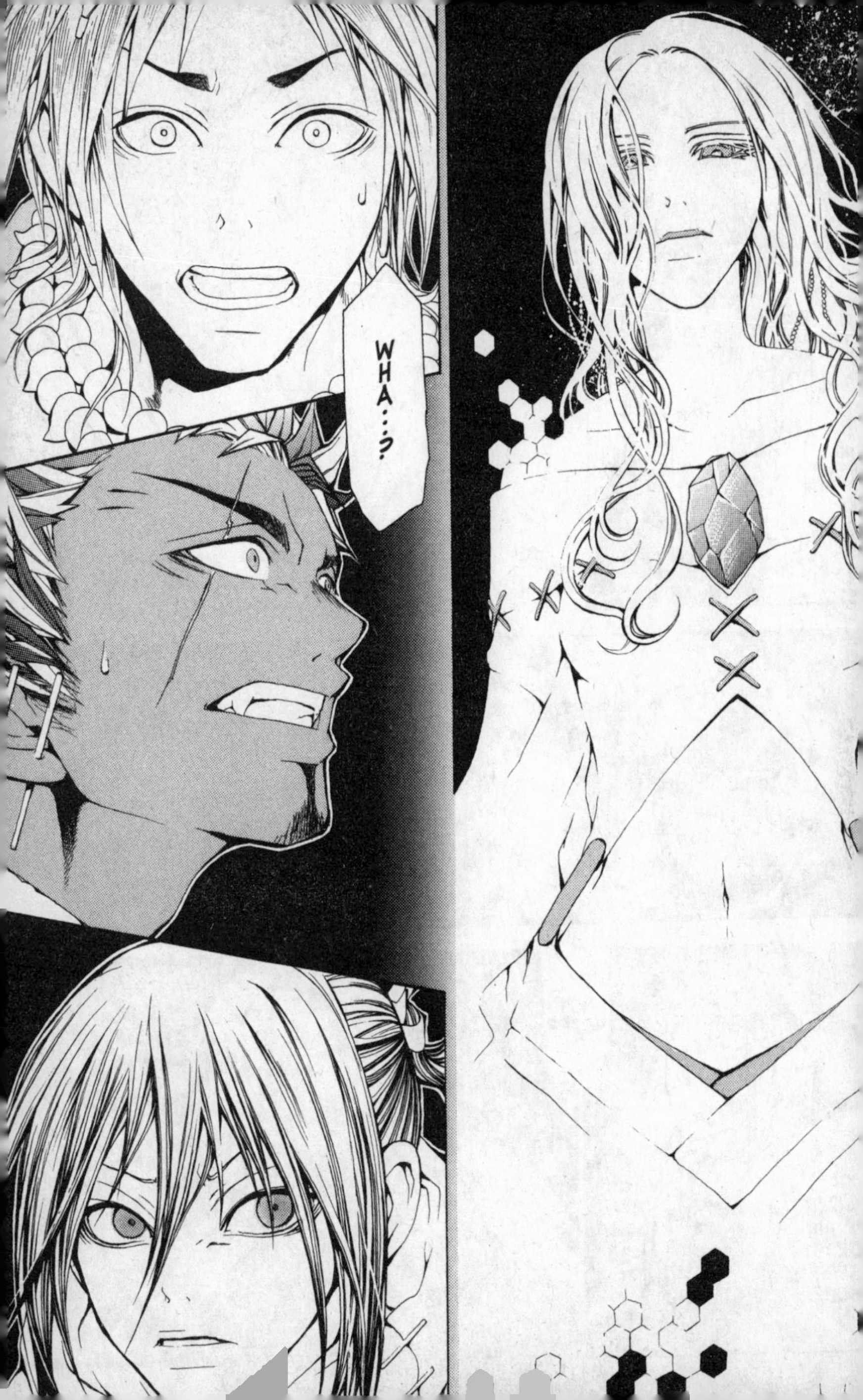
WHA...?

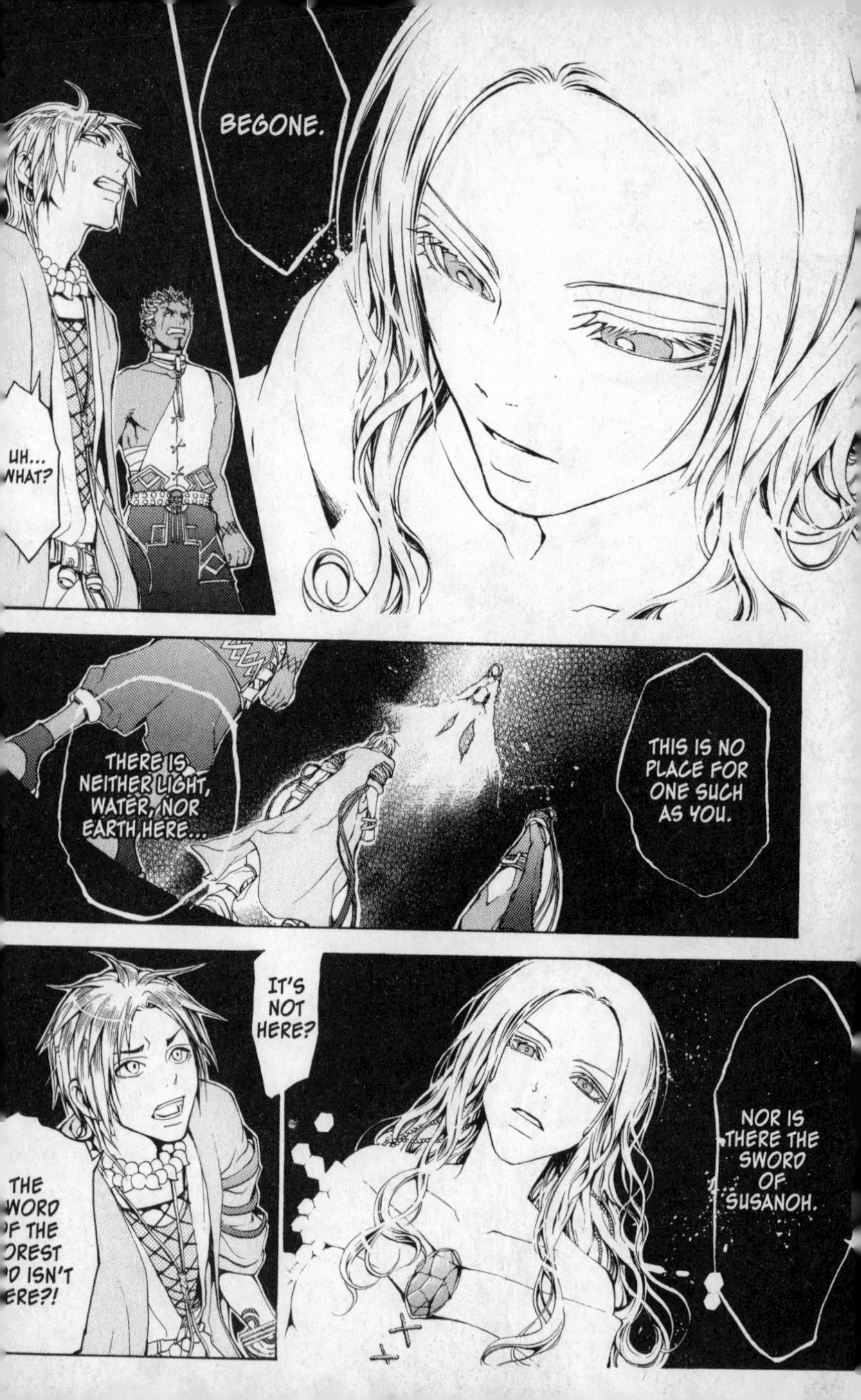
BEGONE.
UH... WHAT?
THIS IS NO PLACE FOR ONE SUCH AS YOU.
THERE IS NEITHER LIGHT, WATER, NOR EARTH HERE...
NOR IS THERE THE SWORD OF SUSANOH.
IT'S NOT HERE?
THE WORD F THE OREST D ISN'T ERE?!

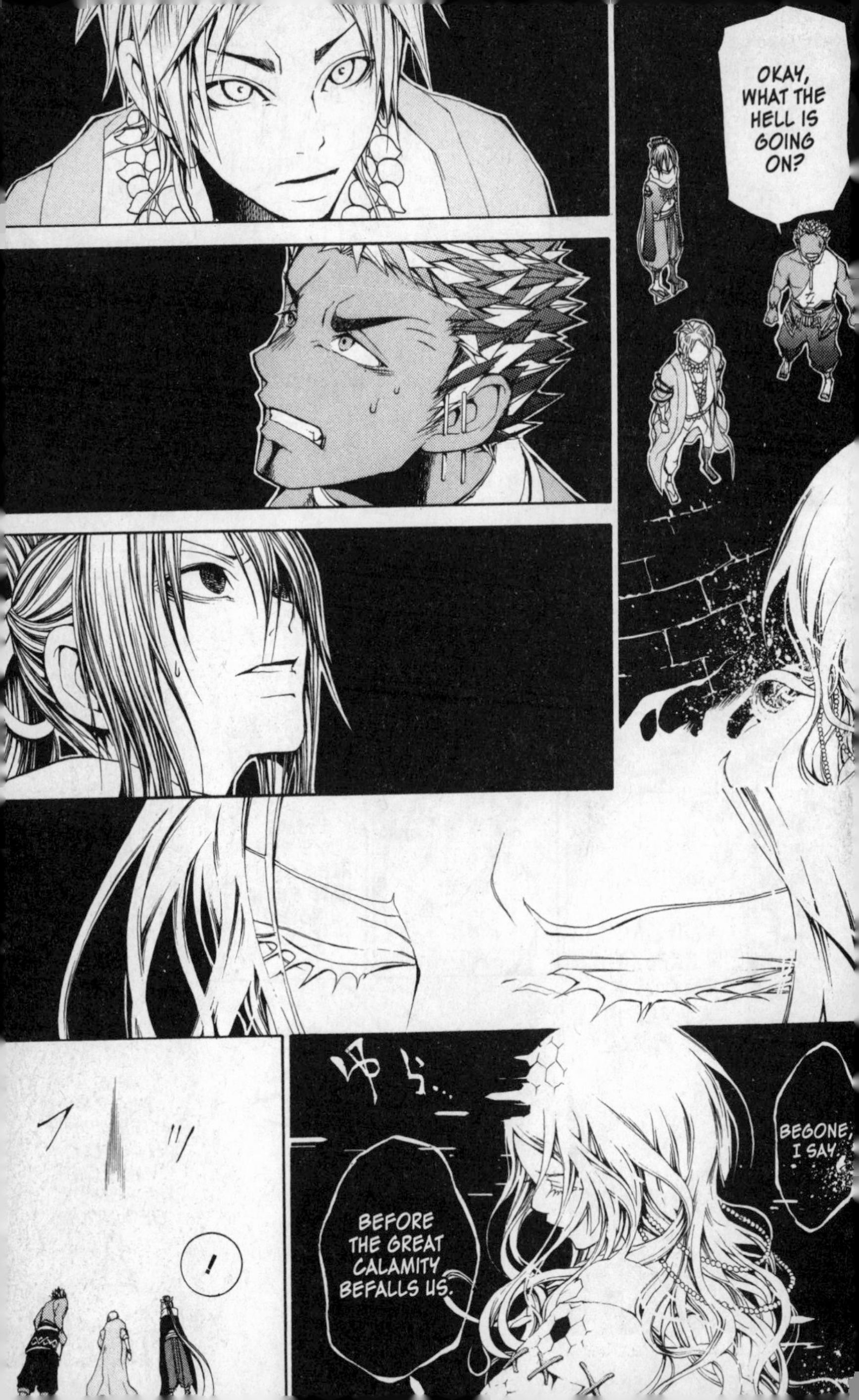
OKAY, WHAT THE HELL IS GOING ON?
BEGONE, I SAY.
BEFORE THE GREAT CALAMITY BEFALLS US.
!

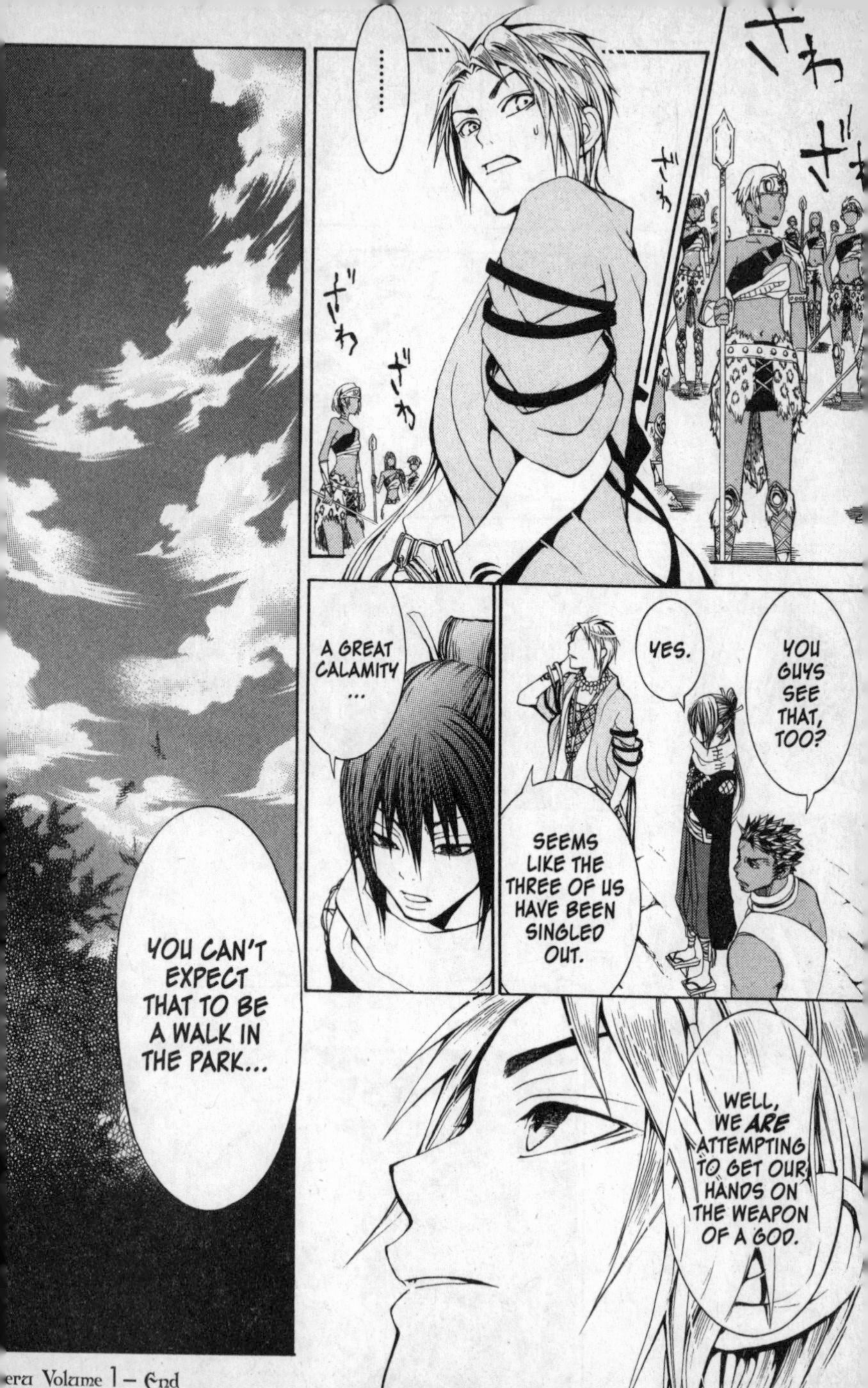
さわ
ざわ
……
ざわ
ざわ
ざわ
YOU GUYS SEE THAT, TOO?
YES.
SEEMS LIKE THE THREE OF US HAVE BEEN SINGLED OUT.
A GREAT CALAMITY...
WELL, WE *ARE* ATTEMPTING TO GET OUR HANDS ON THE WEAPON OF A GOD.
YOU CAN'T EXPECT THAT TO BE A WALK IN THE PARK...

eru Volume 1 – End

VOLUME 1 AFTERWORD

Gosh, how many years ago was it that my editor suggested doing a manga adaptation of a Shinkansen play?

The theater troupe Shinkansen often adapts manga and movies for the stage, so we thought it would be fun to reverse the concept and make one of their plays into a manga, instead. Due to circumstances beyond our control, the manga met with a few delays, but we've finally managed to get this volume into your hands so you can read it. This would not have been possible without the persistence of my editor, Mr. H, and the enthusiasm of Ms. Y, the newly-appointed series editor, and of course, the talented young artist, KarakaraKemuri.

It's already been six or seven years since the original play was written and performed. In the process of turning it into a manga, I've been altering and refining the story with each new chapter. Seeing Kemuri-san improve her already fabulous art throughout the process has been a fascinating and heartening experience. It's easy to see, through the complex relations and interactions of Izumo, Oguna and Kumaso, that she really understands and loves our three heroes. I'm nearly twice as old as Kemuri-san, but working with her has been a good incentive to keep my energy up, if for no other reason than to show the young whippersnapper that I've still got it!

As we enter our second volume, the battle over the Sword of the Forest God becomes fierce and cruel. I hope you stick with us and remain intrigued as to how this little tale will end.

Kazuki Nakashim

ARTIST'S AFTERWORD

Hello, I'm KarakaraKemuri, and I'd like to thank you for buying this book. Unless, of course, you're reading this in the store, or borrowing it from a friend. In that case, I'd like to suggest you quit being such a moocher and buy your own dang copy!

Now, this being my very first manga volume, there is just one word to describe my emotions... Yahoo! It's hard to be a manga-ka. Ever since starting on a story, my life's been a whirlwind of activity. However, I feel like I've been spending my time very wisely and learning a lot.

Some of you might be thinking, "Why did SHE have to do the art for this?" I am telling you right now to go and toss that opinion out with the trash. Yes, I was shocked when I first got the offer. Having never had much interest in theater, I am ashamed to admit that I had no idea what the Shinkansen Troupe was at the time. However, the more I learn about them, the more I am intimidated by the greatness and importance of Nakashima-san. Sometimes I wonder if this responsibility is too big for a newbie like me, but after all the agonizing I've done over this, I prefer to just ignore those thoughts. If you think there's some merit to them, though, blame my editor!

As for me, I've decided simply to enjoy my good luck. I know there are plenty of places where my lack of skill is evident, but I hope to work hard enough so that one day I am a totally boring person who causes no stress for her fellow professionals! Hopefully, you'll still be around to see it.

I'm sorry incoherent to everyone and everyone together. upon

about all the rude and ramblings. Thanks who read the book who helped put it May fortune shine you! Bye!

KarakaraKemuri

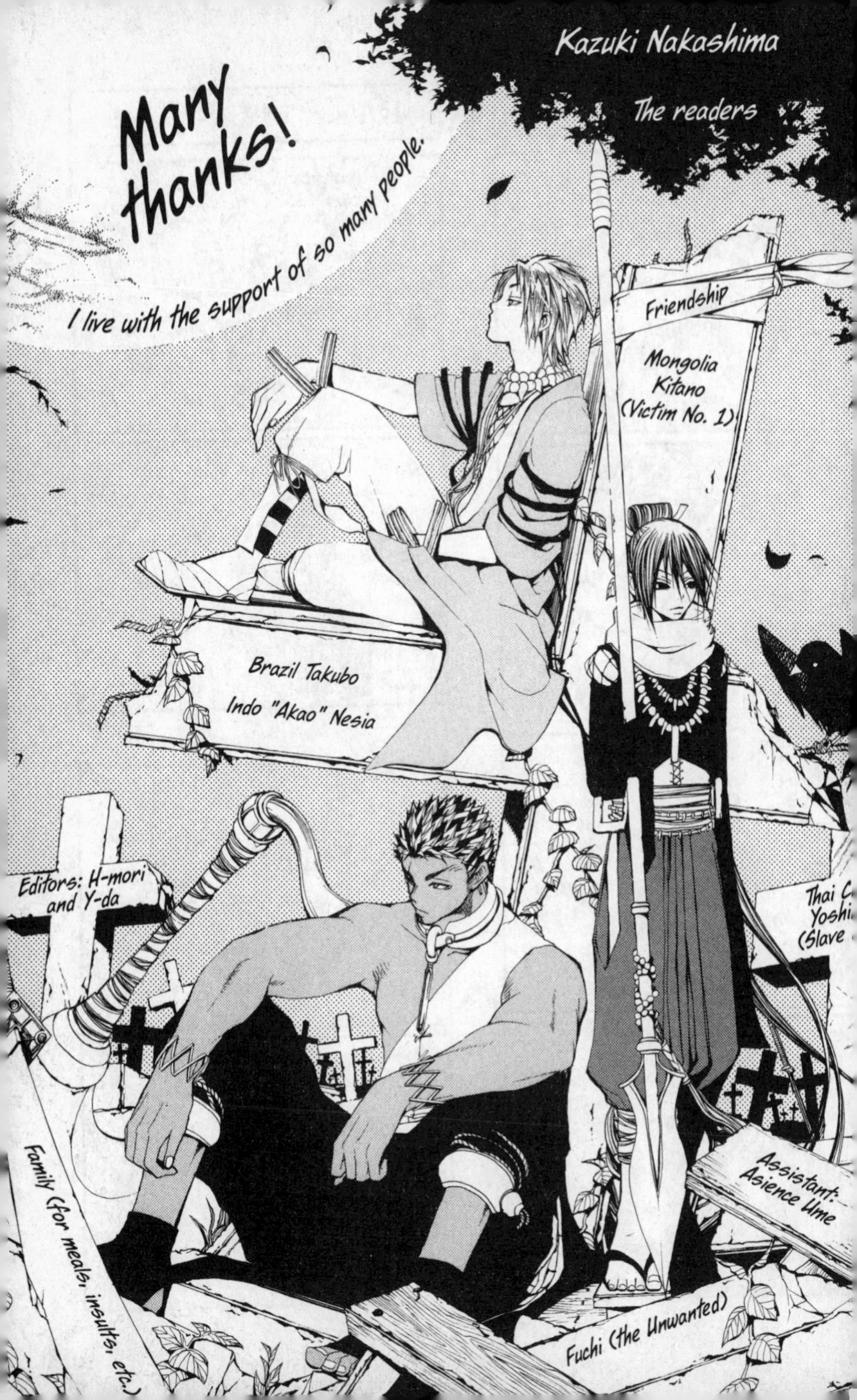
Many thanks!
I live with the support of so many people.
Kazuki Nakashima
The readers
Friendship
Mongolia Kitano (Victim No. 1)
Brazil Takubo
Indo "Akao" Nesia
Editors: H-mori and Y-da
Thai C
Yoshi
(Slave
Assistant: Asience Ume
Fuchi (the Unwanted)
Family (for meals, insults, etc.)

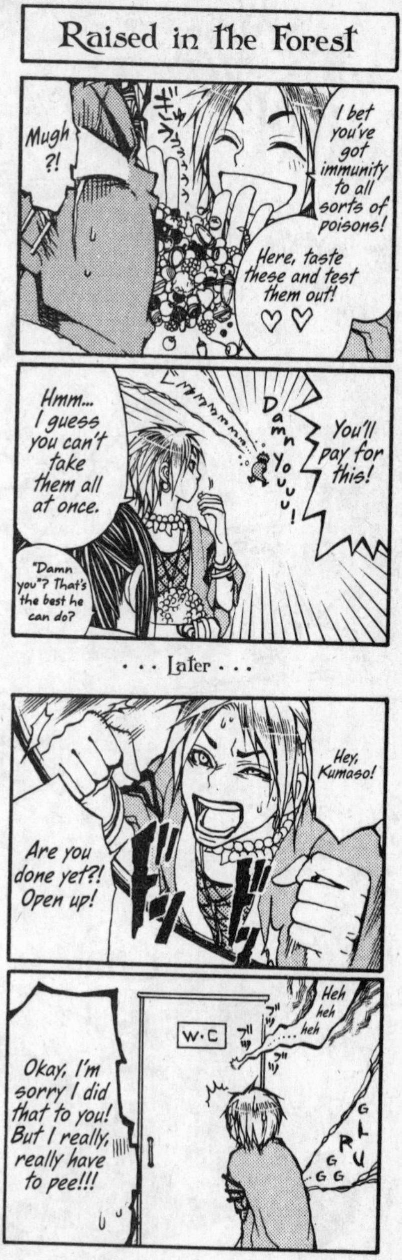
Raised in the Forest
I bet you've got immunity to all sorts of poisons!
Here, taste these and test them out! ♡ ♡
Mugh ?!
You'll pay for this!
Damn Youuuu!
Hmm... I guess you can't take them all at once.
"Damn you"? That's the best he can do?
. . . Later . . .
Hey, Kumaso!
Are you done yet?! Open up!
Heh heh heh
W·C
Okay, I'm sorry I did that to you! But I really, really have to pee!!!

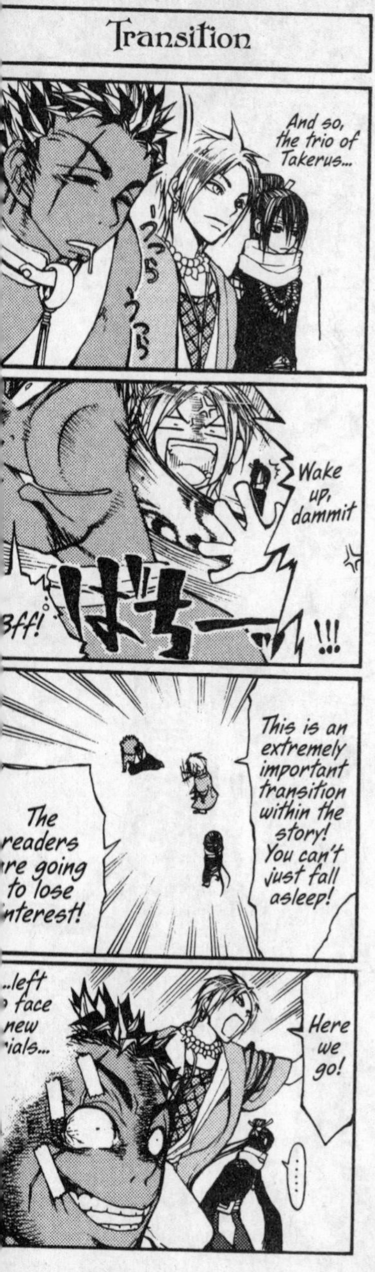
Transition
And so, the trio of Takerus...
Wake up, dammit
!!!
This is an extremely important transition within the story! You can't just fall asleep!
The readers re going to lose nterest!
Here we go!
..left face new rials...
......

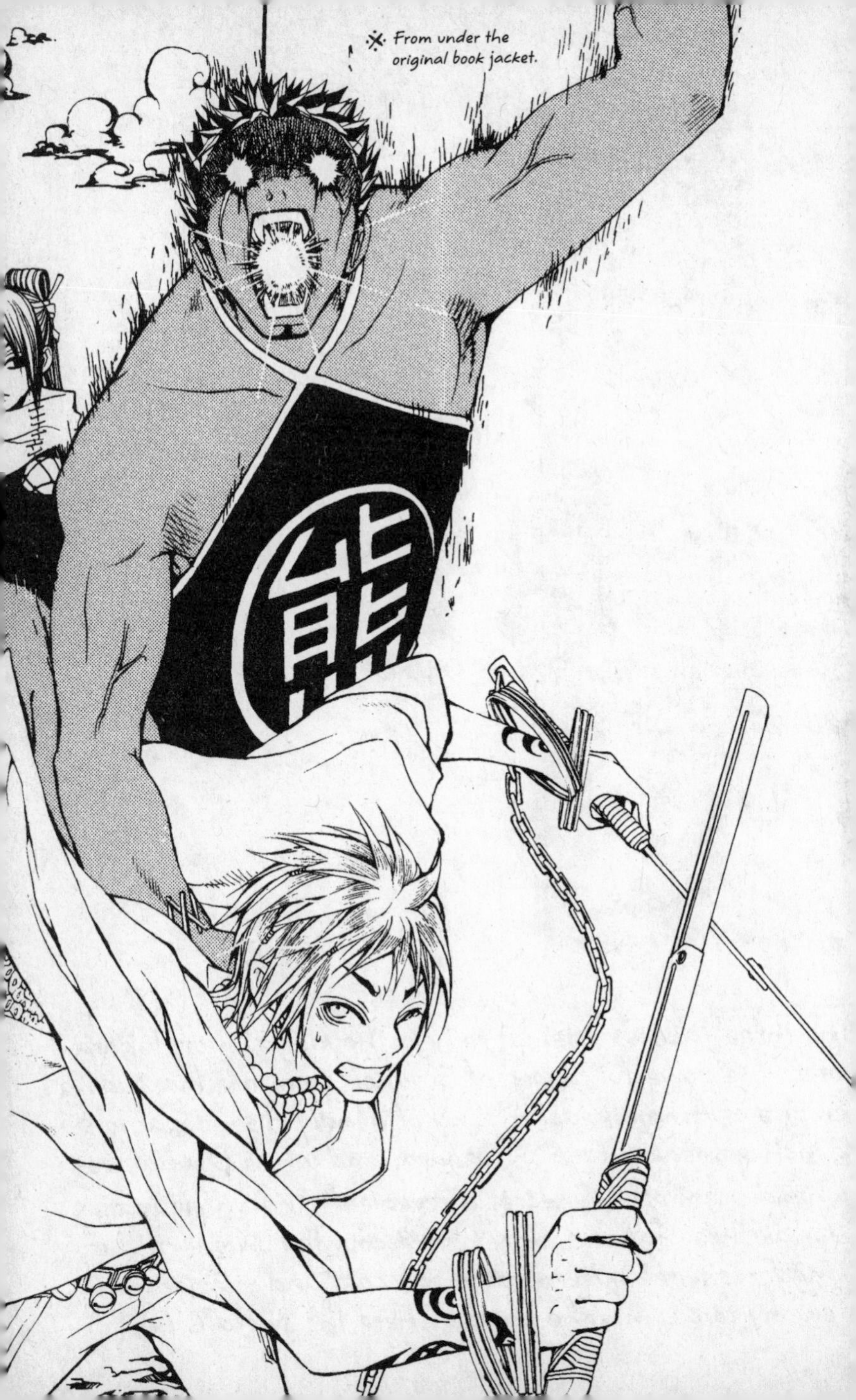
※ From under the original book jacket.

Once there is a legend of a sword.
It says that the sword of a rude god was
sealed up in "JAGARA-MOGARA".
When spilit of these tree,Light,Water and Earth,
meet together,the seal will break then the sword
was immortalize.
That is the sword of SUSANOH.
This is a tale who was fascinated by the
sword of SUSANOH.

中島かずき×唐々煙
kazuki nakashima×karakarakemuri presents

タケル —SUSANOH~魔性の剣(劇団☆新感線)より—

takeru
OPERA SUSANOH SWORD OF THE DEVIL

The three Takerus attempt to help the kingdom of Jagara
protect the powerful Sword of Susanoh from the marauding
empire of Amamikado. A band of deadly Hisomi warriors
launch a sneak attack on Jagara, and when Oguna goes
to head them off, his secret is revealed! And unfortunately
for all three Takerus, they hadn't counted on one of the
kingdom's three queens going turncoat and sneaking the
enemy forces into the palace where the sword is kept...

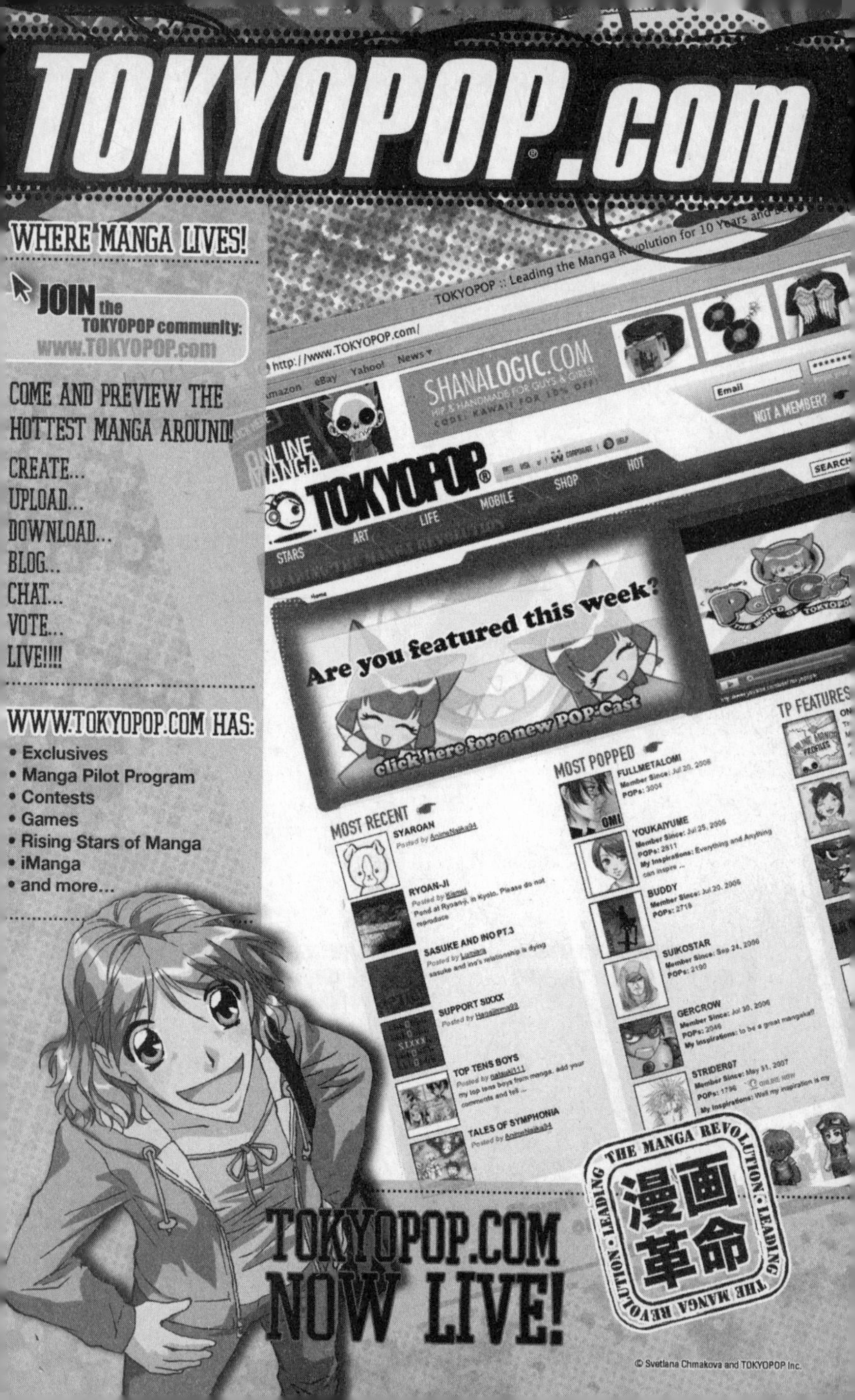
TOKYOPOP.com
WHERE MANGA LIVES!
JOIN the TOKYOPOP community: www.TOKYOPOP.com
COME AND PREVIEW THE HOTTEST MANGA AROUND!
CREATE...
UPLOAD...
DOWNLOAD...
BLOG...
CHAT...
VOTE...
LIVE!!!!
WWW.TOKYOPOP.COM HAS:
• Exclusives
• Manga Pilot Program
• Contests
• Games
• Rising Stars of Manga
• iManga
• and more...
TOKYOPOP :: Leading the Manga Revolution for 10 Years and Be
http://www.TOKYOPOP.com/
SHANALOGIC.COM
TOKYOPOP
STARS
ART
LIFE
MOBILE
SHOP
HOT
Are you featured this week?
click here for a new POP-Cast
MOST RECENT
MOST POPPED
TP FEATURES
TOKYOPOP.COM NOW LIVE!
THE MANGA REVOLUTION · LEADING
漫画革命
© Svetlana Chmakova and TOKYOPOP Inc.

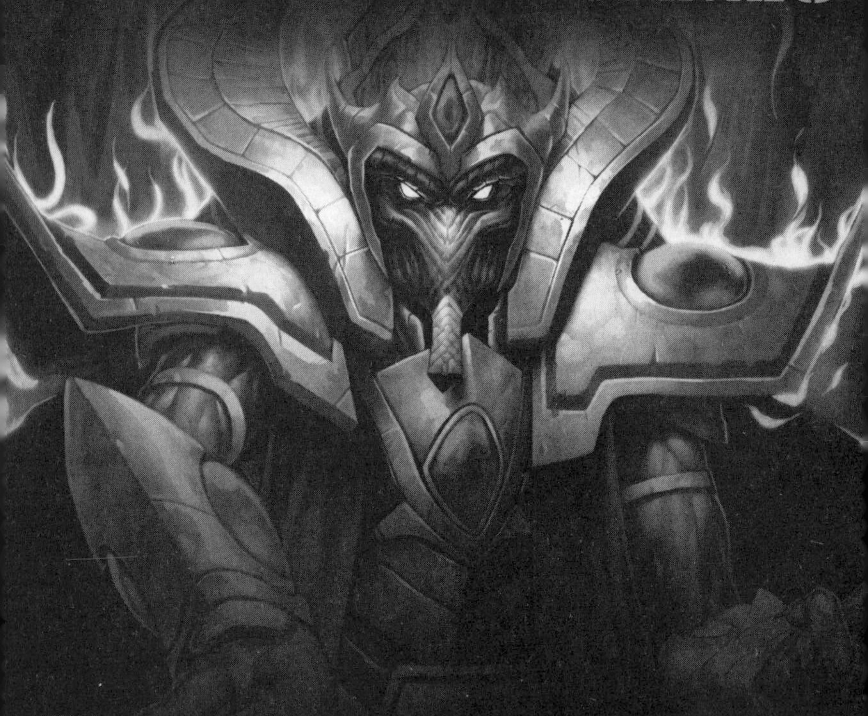

STOP!

This is the back of the book.
You wouldn't want to spoil a great ending!

This book is printed "manga-style," in the authentic Japanese right-to-left format. Since none of the artwork has been flipped or altered, readers get to experience the story just as the creator intended. You've been asking for it, so TOKYOPOP® delivered: authentic, hot-off-the-press, and far more fun!

1
2
3
4
5
6
7
8
9
10

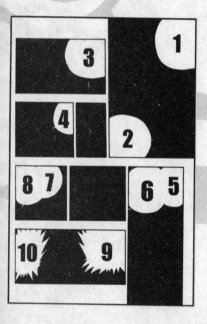

DIRECTIONS

If this is your first time reading manga-style, here's a quick guide to help you understand how it works.

It's easy... just start in the top right panel and follow the numbers. Have fun, and look for more 100% authentic manga from TOKYOPOP®!

THE MANGA REVOLUTION · LEADING THE MANGA REVOLUTION · LEADING

漫画革命

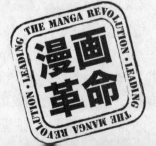